Chronicle
of
JEWISH HISTORY

from the Patriarchs to the 21st century

Sol Scharfstein

design & graphics by
Dorcas Gelabert

KTAV Publishing House, Inc.
Hoboken, N. J.

This book
is lovingly dedicated
to my parents
Asher and Feiga
of
blessed memory

Copyright © 1997
KTAV Publishing House, Inc.

Chronicle of Jewish History
ISBN 0-88125-606-4

This book was previously published in two paperback volumes, *Understanding Jewish History: From the Patriarchs to the Expulsion from Spain* (ISBN 0-88125-545-9) and *Understanding Jewish History, Part II: From the Renaissance to the 21st Century* (ISBN 0-88125-560-2).

The Library of Congress has cataloged volume 1 as follows:

Scharfstein, Sol. 1921–
    Understanding Jewish History / Sol Scharfstein ; design & graphics by Dorcas Gelabert.
      p.   cm.
    Includes index.
    Contents: 1. From the Patriarchs to the expulsion from Spain.
    ISBN 0-88125-545-9 (paper)
    1. Jews—History—Juvenile literature. I. Gelabert, Dorcas. II. Title.
DS118.S3176   1996
909'.04924—dc20
                                  96-11250
                                  CIP

Manufactured in Hong Kong

Contents

Contents

Contents

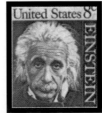

Introduction and Acknowledgments

It all began about 4,000 years ago in the ancient city of Ur, in what is now Iraq. Divinely inspired, Abraham and his wife Sarah, the first patriarch and matriarch, began a saga that produced the best of times and the worst of times for their descendants–the Jews.

Chronicle of Jewish History records the many stories of the journey of the Jewish people through the annals of history. It is a story filled with triumphs and defeats, joys and tragedies, destruction and rebuilding, and lastly, Holocaust and rebirth. The countless struggles conferred a historic immortality on some individuals and places scattered through a myriad of kingdoms and countries.

From the beginning, the Jewish homeland, Israel, was at the crossroads of many civilizations and was dominated by powerful nations. Yet, despite the overpowering foreign influences, the Jewish people managed to survive as a national entity. Even in exile, they miraculously retained their cohesiveness and their peoplehood.

There never was any doubt about what they were fighting for or whether their obstinancy was worth the price. They fought to retain the right to worship as they pleased and to maintain their own unique way of life.

Unfortunately, for thousands of years Jews were not masters of their own history. Defeats, dispersions, and expulsions scattered them throughout the world. More than any other people they have been actors in historical theaters other than their own. As Jews and as foreigners they were dependent on the events, politics, poverty, prosperity, and personalities of the dominant power.

Mostly, and especially during the Middle Ages, Jews were the pawns on the chessboard of power politics. When their usefulness ended, they became as scapegoats to divert the masses from their misery and powerlessness.

History and the calendar are witnesses. Five thousand years of destructions, exiles, inquisitions, forced conversions, assimilation, gulags, and the holocaust have not succeeded. Jewish survival is a miraculous achievement unequaled by any other ethnic or religious group.

Introduction and Acknowledgments

In every generation, from the Patriarchs to the 21st century Jews have been on the move, to lands not their own. Wherever they sat down and planted roots, they "wept when reminded of Zion."

After five thousand years, in 1948, that dream expressed in prayers, tears, heroes, and sacrifices became a reality. The rebirth of the State of Israel.

The historic task of the Jew, wherever he found himself, was to continue message of the prophets and labor for the welfare of mankind. This is the chronicle of their history. This is the chronicle of their survival. May this chronicle continue to grow, till the coming of the Messiah and world peace.

Acknowledgments

Numerous talented people have worked hard to bring *Chronicle of Jewish History* to life. They believed in the project and labored long and arduously, critiquing, editing, updating, and researching.

I wish to thank the following for their expert assistance. It is their sense, sensibility, sensitivity, and scholarship that have shaped the text.

Howard Adelman
Yaakov Elman
Robert Milch
Richard White

The final responsibility for any omissions, errors, and mistakes is my own.

The First Hebrews / ca. 2000–1700 B.C.E.

Abraham and Sarah

The first great figure to appear on the stage of Jewish history was Abraham. Many centuries ago (about 1900 B.C.E.), according to the Bible, God told Abraham and his family to leave their native city of Ur and settle in a place that would become their new homeland. Because they crossed the river Euphrates on their journey to the Promised Land, people called them Hebrews (Ivrim, "those who came from the other side"), a name which has stayed with the Jews to the present day.

In the fertile land of Mesopotamia where Abraham and his wife, Sarah, grew up, a great civilization had developed. Its chief city, Ur, was a short distance from the Euphrates. Modern archaeologists, excavating on the site of this ancient city, have unearthed many of its wonders. It was a thriving market center, visited by merchants from near and far.

The people who lived there worshipped many different gods. Abraham believed that there could be only one God.

The Fertile Crescent

As we trace Abraham's journey on the map, we see that he first went to Haran, a flourishing city in the kingdom of Mari. His father and brothers settled there, but Abraham moved on. We are told how Abraham worshipped the one true God, and how God promised Abraham the land

THE FERTILE CRESCENT

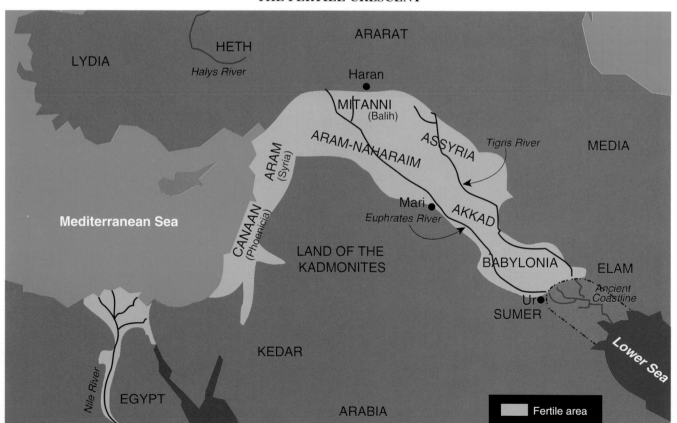

The Near East is the region between the Mediterranean, Caspian, and Red Seas and the Persian Gulf. It is in general a barren, arid area. However, in the midst of this uninviting expanse lies a crescent-shaped region of fertile, watered land called the Fertile Crescent. It is in the Fertile Crescent that the first great civilization appeared and man made the transition from a hunter of food to an organized, systematic food producer.

of Canaan as a homeland for him and for all his descendants. With Sarah, his servants, his household goods, and his cattle, Abraham pressed on to the Promised Land. His journey covered 600 miles, through the rich lands that bordered the great Arabian desert; from Ur near the Persian Gulf, up to Haran and on to Canaan. Following this route carefully on the map, we can clearly see that it forms a crescent, whence comes the name "Fertile Crescent," by which this area is often called, to contrast it with the barren desert on which it borders.

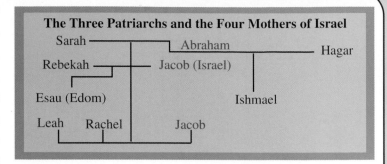

The Three Patriarchs and the Four Mothers of Israel

The inhabitants of Canaan cultivated barley fields, fig trees, and date palms, and tended cattle and sheep. Some of their towns were strongly fortified with walls and towers, so that people could take refuge from the frequent attacks of the desert nomads who stormed across the river Jordan to steal cattle and raid storehouses.

Excavation site of a temple in the ancient city of Ur.

Abraham in Canaan

Abraham settled in the hills of Canaan, where he was less exposed to attack and where the land seemed less desirable to the Canaanites. At Mamre, near Hebron, he pitched his black goatskin tents. Here Abraham raised his son and heir, Isaac; and here, eventually, he bought a piece of land from Ephron the Hittite, to bury his beloved wife, Sarah, in the cave of Machpelah.

The Bible relates that before Abraham died, he arranged for Isaac's marriage. He sent his servant Eliezer to Haran to seek a wife for Isaac from the family of Laban, his kinsman. Jacob, the son of Isaac, also sought a wife from among his distant kinsmen. After spending many years in the service of his uncle Laban, Jacob married

King Ur-Nammu, the Sumerian king of Ur is standing in front of a plant, bringing an offering to an idol. The third dynasty of Ur was founded by Ur-Nammu. This carving was found on a stela.

Laban's two daughters, Rachel and Leah, who, together with their handmaids, bore him twelve sons.

Abraham, Isaac, and Jacob

Thus did the patriarchs, Abraham, Isaac, and Jacob, establish themselves in the land of Canaan. One of Jacob's contributions to his people was a new name for them. We are told that on his return to Canaan after serving his uncle Laban, Jacob met a man while crossing the river Jabbok. After wrestling with Jacob, the man revealed himself as an angel, a messenger of God. He gave Jacob the name of Israel, which means "he who struggled with God." Henceforth, Jacob's descendants were called the Children of Israel.

THE WORLD OF THE PATRIARCHS AND MATRIARCHS

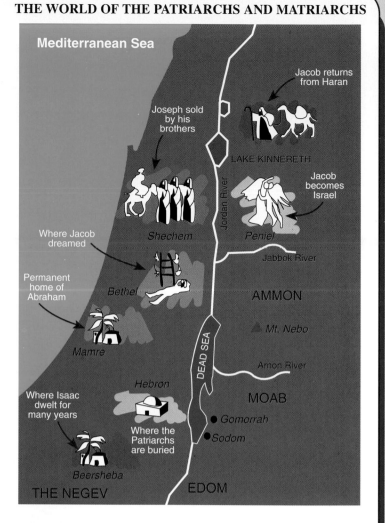

The Cave of Machpelah, where the patriarchs are buried, is behind the ancient walls of Hebron.

Hebron was David's capital until his conquest of Jerusalem. There was a Jewish community in Hebron during the Middle Ages and through the Turkish period. Hebron was ruled by Jordan from 1948 to 1967. It came under Israeli control during the Six-Day War, when the West Bank territories were conquered. In 1968 a new Jewish settlement called Kiryat Arba was established just outside of Hebron.

In 1995 as part of the peace agreement, the city of Hebron became a part of the Palestinian Authority.

The Children of Israel

The Hyksos in Egypt / ca. 1720–1600 B.C.E.

A time of famine came to Canaan, and the thoughts of Jacob-Israel turned longingly to the fertile land of the Nile, where food was plentiful even when other countries experienced famine. Joseph, one of Jacob's sons, was now living in Egypt, where he had risen from servitude to a position of great power, second in command only to the Pharaoh. At Joseph's invitation, Jacob brought his family and flocks into Egypt.

The Pharaoh assigned the territory of Goshen to the Israelites. It was good grazing land, and for many years the Israelites lived there in peace.

Modern historians believe that these events occurred about 1700 B.C.E., during the time when the Hyksos, a warlike tribe from Syria, swept into Egypt. The Hyksos ruled Egypt for about 120 years. Joseph was probably a high-ranking official under one of these powerful foreign rulers.

Slaves of Pharaoh / ca. 1290 B.C.E.

Eventually the Hyksos were defeated, and Egyptian kings once more ruled over the land. The new Pharaohs, as the Bible tells us, "did not know Joseph." No longer were the Israelites respected as the privileged descendants of a noble ancestor. Instead they were enslaved. Some historians believe that this took place during the reign of Rameses II (ca. 1290–1224 B.C.E.). Egypt

An Egyptian brick with the imprint of the seal of Rameses

was a growing empire and the new Pharaohs had great need for slaves to build their new cities and magnificent palaces.

Rameses feared an uprising among the slaves and took cruel precautions to prevent it. He issued a decree that all male children born to the Israelites must be killed. In this merciless way, Rameses hoped to keep the Israelites from growing in numbers.

Baby Moses

Soon after this decree was issued, a male child was born to Jochebed, an Israelite woman, and her husband Amram, of the tribe of Levi. Little did this couple dream that their son was destined to be known throughout the ages as one of the greatest leaders in history. Desperate to save the infant, they put him into a basket and set him afloat among the bulrushes of the Nile. He was found by an Egyptian princess while she and her handmaidens were bathing at the river.

A wall painting from about 1900 B.C.E. in an Egyptian tomb. This beautiful painting shows a group of Semites bringing gifts to the Egyptians.

Rameses II was most probably the Pharaoh who enslaved the Hebrews.

Earliest mention of Israel
The Egyptian text of two lines of Merneptah's stele, a transliteration, and a translation. After the word "Israel," note the figures of a man, a woman, and three straight lines.

The princess named him Moses, a name which means "drawn out of the water."

As a boy, Moses was given all the advantages enjoyed by members of Egypt's royal family. He may have learned to read and write on papyrus, a paperlike writing material which the Egyptians made from the leaves of the papyrus plant. Our word "paper" is derived from the name of this plant.

Fighting for Freedom

One day Moses was outraged to see an overseer beating an Israelite slave. Moses killed the overseer, and fled to the land of Midian in the Sinai desert. There he became a shepherd, living with a Kenite priest named Jethro. Moses married Jethro's daughter, Zipporah, who bore him two sons.

The Burning Bush

In the rugged mountains of Sinai, Moses had an inspiring experience. Through a vision of a Burning Bush that was not consumed, God told him to go down to Egypt, confront Pharaoh, and lead the Hebrew slaves to freedom. At first Moses refused, but eventually he accepted the responsibility. From that time forward, Moses was a man dedicated to the great task of leading his people to freedom. While the overseers lashed their weary bodies, Moses stirred their flagging spirits. The Israelites listened, and dared to dream of liberty and deliverance.

It was not an easy thing that Moses had chosen to do. Many obstacles were placed in his path by the Pharaoh, who according to some historians was Merneptah), the son of Rameses, who now sat on the throne of Egypt. Again and again Moses, with his brother Aaron, stood before him and pleaded for the Israelites' release. Pharaoh, full of confidence and power, turned a deaf ear to his pleas. But the burning sense of purpose that drove Moses on was more than a match for Pharaoh's stubbornness.

This scene of an overseer beating a slave was found in an Egyptian tomb.

The Exodus / ca. 1280 B.C.E.

Ten Plagues

Egypt had to be stricken by ten disastrous plagues before Pharaoh, fearing the wrath of the God whom Moses and his people worshipped, finally consented to release the Israelites and allow them to leave the land. A multitude of about 600,000 men together with women and children left Egypt on that memorable night of the Exodus. There was barely time to prepare the food they would need. The bread was so hurriedly baked that there was no time for the dough to rise. This was the origin of the custom of eating unleavened bread (matzot) on Passover (Pesach), the festival that commemorates the victory won for freedom so many centuries ago.

A group of wooden Nubian soldiers excavated from the tomb of an Egyptian prince. Such models were placed in tombs in the belief that they would serve the owner in the afterworld.

The Exodus: A March to Freedom / ca. 1280 B.C.E.

So the great march out of Egypt began, with families gathered together, each with its own tribe, twelve tribes in all. However, after begging the Israelites to leave, Pharaoh suddenly changed his mind and sent his charioteers to bring the slaves back. According to the Bible, Moses did not dare lead them by the established route, which was dangerously near Egypt's border forts, where soldiers might have attempted to prevent their escape. Instead, the great throng of people, young and old, carrying their meager belongings, marched slowly eastward to avoid the border posts.

Then their march was halted suddenly by an obstacle that seemed to be insurmountable. Silent and disheartened they stood, the light of hope slowly fading from their eyes as they gazed at the vast expanse of water before them. They had come to the end of dry land, to the shores of the Sea of Reeds (Yam Suf), the Suez arm of the Red Sea.

Bust of Merneptah (1235–1227 B.C.E.), son of Rameses II. Some historians believe that he was the Pharaoh of the Exodus.

Those who looked back in the direction of their former homes were greeted by a sight that chilled their already sinking hearts. Bearing down upon them was a column of Egyptian soldiers. With the sea before them and the army of Pharaoh closing in from behind, the Children of Israel were trapped.

Then, miraculously, a strong easterly wind arose. It drove back the ebbing waters of the sea, making a path of dry land. With joyful hearts, the throng followed Moses to the opposite shore. In fierce pursuit, Pharaoh's soldiers also took the dry path through the Sea of Reeds, but the wind turned and the tide rolled in. Back rushed the waters, engulfing the chariots and drowning the soldiers.

Free at Last

The Bible tells how the Israelites rejoiced when they found themselves safely across

This picture of Pharaoh Tutankhamen in his chariot was found in his tomb. The chariot reins are tied around the pharaoh's waist, freeing his arms and enabling him to shoot his arrows. The Bible describes the pursuit of the Israelites by the "chariot of the king of Egypt."

the sea. Moses composed a poem of praise to God. The women danced joyously to the music of their timbrels and sang a song composed by Miriam, Moses' sister.

Ahead of them lay untold dangers, but on this great day there was but one song in the hearts of the Israelites—a song of gratitude for their newly-won freedom.

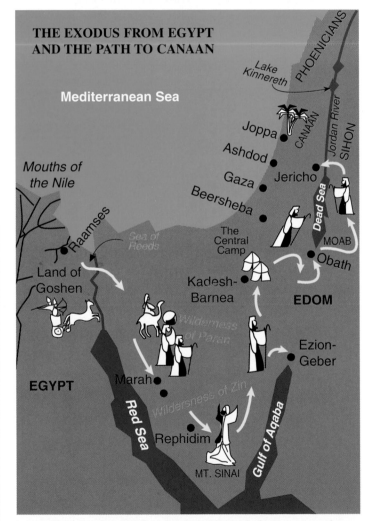

THE EXODUS FROM EGYPT
AND THE PATH TO CANAAN

Mediterranean Sea

Lake Kinnereth

PHOENICIANS

Joppa

Ashdod

CANAAN

Jordan River

SIHON

Gaza

Jericho

Beersheba

Dead Sea

Mouths of the Nile

The Central Camp

MOAB

Obath

Raamses

Sea of Reeds

Land of Goshen

Kadesh-Barnea

EDOM

Wilderness of Paran

Ezion-Geber

Marah

Wildersness of Zin

EGYPT

Red Sea

Gulf of Aqaba

Rephidim

MT. SINAI

According to the Bible, the Israelites left Egypt and traveled along the northern coast of the Sinai peninsula. During the forty years of wandering they passed through many kingdoms and endured great hardships.
The Israelites spent much time at the oasis of Kadesh-Barnea. Moses sent 12 spies into Canaan from this oasis.
At Marah the Israelites found bitter water. According to the Bible God showed Moses a plant which made the water drinkable.
Before the Israelites reached Mount Sinai, they battled the Amalekites at Rephidim.

Miriam and the Israelite women dancing with joy after their liberation from Egypt. This painting is from the Sarajevo Haggadah.

The Ten Commandments

Mount Sinai / ca. 1280 B.C.E.

When the Israelites reached Mount Sinai, Moses ordered them to pitch their tents. Here occurred the most important moment in Jewish history.

After the camp had been made, Moses ascended the mountain. For days, he was hidden from the people. Then, amidst thunder and lightning so intense that the very mountains shook, the voice of God reverberated throughout, proclaiming the Ten Commandments.

The Ten Commandments

Descending from the mountain, Moses brought down the Ten Commandments, carved upon two tablets of stone.

The Ten Commandments sealed a covenant between the young nation of

An artistic rendition of the Ten Commandments.

1. I am the Lord, your God.
2. You shall have no other gods before me.
3. You shall not take the name of God in vain.
4. Remember the Sabbath to keep it holy.
5. Honor your father and your mother.
6. You shall not kill.
7. You shall not be unfaithful to wife or husband.
8. You shall not steal.
9. You shall not bear false witness.
10. You shall not desire what is your neighbor's.

Israel and the one God. No other nation had a code of laws so just and humane. The Israelites now truly abandoned the ways of Egypt and dedicated themselves to live by this lofty code.

The Torah

According to tradition, the entire Torah was revealed to Moses on Mount Sinai. The Torah, also known as the Five Books of Moses, recounts the early history of the Jewish people and lays down the rules, laws, and ethical teachings of Judaism.

The Torah scroll used in the synagogue is written on parchment by a scribe in ancient Hebrew letters. As in days gone by, it is written with a feather pen and specially prepared ink.

In traditional synagogues the Torah is read aloud at services on Sabbaths, holy days, and Monday and Thursday mornings.

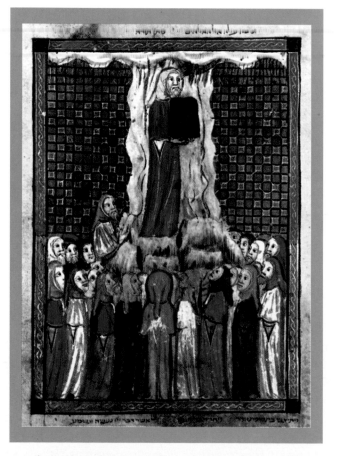

Moses bringing down the Ten Commandments. From the Sarajevo Haggadah.

Since the Torah is divided into 54 sections called Sidrot, it can be read through from beginning to end in one year, at the rate of one section a week (except for two weeks when two sections are read).

The Tabernacle

In order to provide a place where the Israelites could worship God, Moses appointed two craftsmen, Bezalel and Oholiab, to construct a sanctuary.

The sanctuary was designed to be portable. It was a constant reminder to the Israelites of their allegiance and dedication to the service of God. The primary structure was the Tent of Meeting, a large tent with a strong wooden frame. It consisted of an outer court, supported by pillars, and an inner court, separated from the outer court by curtains. In the inner court stood the Tabernacle. This was divided by a curtain or veil into the Holy Place, where the priests would offer sacrifices on the altar, and the Holy of Holies, which contained the Ark of the Covenant. The Holy of Holies symbolized God's mysterious presence.

The Torah vividly describes the Ark of the Covenant in which the two holy tablets brought down by Moses were kept. The Ark was a precious, portable shrine made of acacia wood, with handles for carrying it from place to place. Atop it were two carved angels called cherubim. The Ark and the holy objects used for the service in the Tabernacle were all fashioned by Bezalel.

Aaron and the Priesthood

Moses consecrated Aaron and his sons for the priesthood, anointing their heads with oil in a sacred ceremony. Forever after, Aaron, his sons, and their descendants were to be the priests (kohanim), of Israel. The duties of the priests were many and varied. Most important, they offered sacrifices for the people and raised their voices in prayer. The priestly garb was prescribed in the Torah. For Aaron, the high priest, it included a breastplate bearing the Urim and Tumim, twelve precious stones in four rows, each stone symbolizing one of the tribes of Israel. The high priest wore these garments when he stood before God in prayer.

The Torah describes the clothing and ornaments worn by the high priest. The Urim and Tumim were worn on the priest's chest. It was inlaid with 12 different stones, one for each of the tribes of Israel.

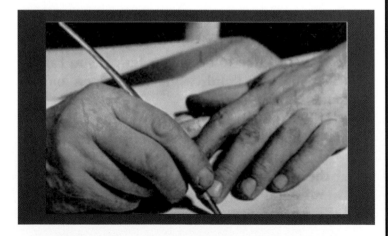

A *sofer*, or scribe, writing a Torah in the traditional way with a feather pen and special ink. In Babylonia, the Torah was divided into 54 sections called Sidrot, so that the entire Torah could be completely read in one whole year. In traditional synagogues the Torah is read on Sabbaths, holy days, and Monday and Thursday mornings.

In the Desert / *ca. 1280–1240*

The Wandering Begins

It was at Sinai that the Israelites first began to observe the laws and religious rituals laid down in the Torah. When the Israelites broke camp and continued their wanderings, they carried with them the Tent of Meeting and the Ark of the Covenant which housed the tablets of the law.

The Israelite wanderers were sincerely dedicated to the new ideals set forth in the Torah. The memory of the Exodus and the courage of their leaders, Moses, Aaron, and Miriam, was ever before them, inspiring them to renewed faith and purpose.

Scouting Canaan

At long last the Israelites drew close to the Promised Land. Moses gave the order for the march to halt, for he wanted time to map his strategy for the conquest of Canaan. Scouts were sent across the border, among them Caleb and Joshua, Moses' able young assistants. The scouts were ordered to find out all they could about the condi-

A reconstruction of the court of the Tabernacle. The large structure is the Tabernacle. In the center of the court is a laver so that the priests could wash their offerings. The altar for the offering is at the other end of the court.

tion of the land, the number of troops, and the strength of the fortifications. The scouts returned with conflicting reports. Some of them spoke in glowing terms of the land's fertility, bringing back luscious fruits as proof. Others spoke in more somber terms of well-armed soldiers and well-fortified cities.

The Years of Wandering

Moses realized that the Israelites lacked the faith and courage necessary for a successful invasion. He led them back into the desert, where they wandered for the next 40 years.

The Torah records the many difficulties the Israelites encountered during this time of wandering. Hunger and thirst stalked their path. Hostile desert tribes were a constant danger, harassing the people by day, and terrifying and robbing them by night.

The New Generation

At the end of 40 years of desert life, a new generation had grown to adulthood. Few remained of the generation who had known the chains of Egyptian slavery. The new generation had lived

The nomadic nature of the Israelite wanderings in the desert made it necessary to build a portable sanctuary for the Holy Ark in which the Ten Commandments were kept. The Book of Exodus describes its construction. It was 45 by 15 feet and was constructed of acacia wood. As pictured, the completed Tabernacle was draped with protective curtains

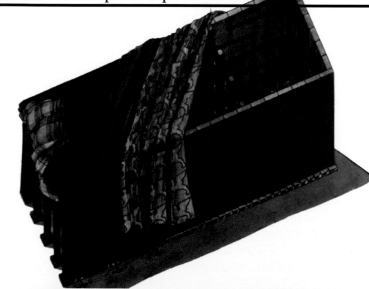

The Torah is divided into 5 books. The Hebrew and Latin titles are:

GENESIS	Bereshit
EXODUS	Shmot
LEVITICUS	Vayikrah
NUMBERS	Bamidbar
DEUTERONOMY	Devarim

no other life than that of the desert and had known no other gods but the one God, no other laws but the laws of the Torah.

Joshua Succeeds Moses

Moses, the great leader, grew old. The time had come to choose someone to take his place after he was gone. Moses' choice fell on Joshua, a man respected by the people and possessing a gift for military strategy. Into Joshua's capable hands Moses placed the task of invading Canaan.

The Death of Moses

Moses knew that he would not live to enter the Promised Land. After he had blessed and consecrated Joshua for his new responsibilities, Moses felt his work was done. From atop Mount Nebo he bade his people farewell. Then the old man gazed out over the rich and fertile land which stretched for miles beyond the mountain.

"This land," God told him, "which I swore to give to Abraham, Isaac, and Jacob, I will now give to your offspring."

"I have let you see it, but you shall not cross into it," ends the account of Moses' life. The Torah records his death with the phrase, "No one knows his burial place to this day."

There would be other great leaders in the years to come, but that unique and special era in their history through which Moses had guided them enshrined him in the hearts of Jews for all time.

From atop Mount Nebo Moses saw the land of Canaan, which God promised to give to the Children of Israel.

The Promised Land

The Invasion Begins / ca. 1240 B.C.E.

When Joshua decided the time was right for entering the Promised Land, he sent his officers through the great throng of Israelites encamped near the river Jordan. The officers instructed the people to prepare themselves. When they saw the Ark of the Covenant being carried across the river by the priests, they broke camp and followed.

The peoples of Canaan—the Canaanites, Jebusites, and Hittites—lived on farms and in fortified towns and cities. The houses of the city dwellers were of stone, and many of the cities were surrounded by strong walls and watchtowers. The tools these people used and their weapons of war were much more advanced than those of the Israelites. Their spears were tipped with iron, a new metal not yet widely used. They even had chariots, drawn by fine, swift horses. The Israelites, on the other hand, used simple spears and bows.

The Fall of Jericho / ca. 1225 B.C.E.

The Hebrew tribes crossed the Jordan near the Dead Sea and took the key city of Jericho, "whose walls came tumbling down." Thereafter, in a series of battles the Israelites captured the fortified cities of Lachish, Ai, Eglon, and many others.

The conquest of Canaan was accomplished by a spectacular invasion in which the Israelite defeated 31 kings. Joshua's campaign employed a series of brilliant maneuvers and surprise attacks.

Many of the Canaanites were panic-stricken by the Israelite onslaught. Six kings from the north joined forces to oppose the Israelite army. So Joshua and his men attacked the combined armies at the Waters of Meron and defeated them.

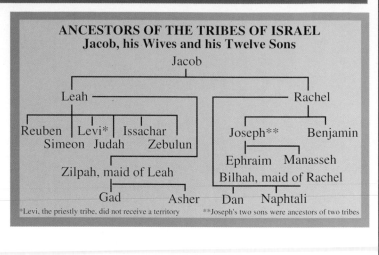

ANCESTORS OF THE TRIBES OF ISRAEL
Jacob, his Wives and his Twelve Sons

*Levi, the priestly tribe, did not receive a territory   **Joseph's two sons were ancestors of two tribes

TRIBAL SYMBOLS AND TERRITORIES

Note that the tribes of Gad, Reuben, and half of Manasseh were allotted territories on the other side of the Jordan River.

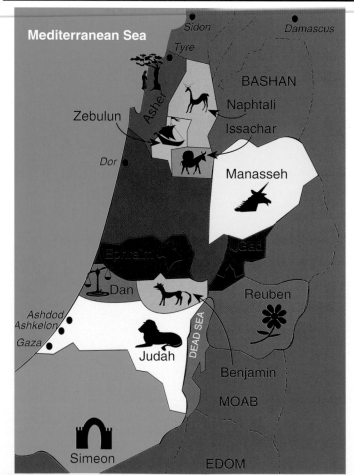

The Israelites Settle Canaan / ca. 1225 B.C.E.

As the conquest of Canaan proceeded, Joshua distributed the land among the Israelite tribes. He assigned portions to all of them except Levi, which was allotted 48 special cities in the territories of the other tribes. The Levites (and the priests, who were members of Levi) had the special assignment of administering the laws of Israel and tending the sanctuary which Joshua had established in Shiloh, where the Holy Ark and the Tabernacle were kept.

It was to Shiloh that the people made pilgrimages, bringing sacrifices and praying there together. The sanctuary was tended by Aaron's son Elazar and grandson Phinehas, assisted by the Levites. Other Levites traveled through the land, making the people familiar with the Torah and instructing them in the worship of the one God.

Israel's Greatest Threat

The gravest threat facing the Israelites was not the superiority of their enemies' weapons nor even the strong walls around their enemies' cities. It was a threat far more difficult to avoid and overcome, a threat to the very foundations of the faith of Israel. Upon entering Canaan, the Israelites found themselves mingling with peoples who worshipped idols.

Fearing that they would fall into the idolatrous ways of their pagan neighbors, Joshua, now an old man and knowing that his death was near, called the twelve tribes together for a great assembly at Shechem, near Shiloh. Gathered together before their leader, the people listened as Joshua impressed upon them the importance of remaining united and faithfully following the laws of the one God.

The people made a solemn promise to put away all the idols and hold steadfast to the Torah. With one voice they cried: "We will obey none but the God of Israel."

The excavations at biblical Shechem have uncovered this 12th century B.C.E. stone monument. Shechem was in the territory allotted to the tribe of Ephraim. Here, Joshua gave his farewell address and formally renewed the covenant made by the Israelites at Sinai.

A Canaanite shrine uncoverd at Hazor, 14th–13th century B.C.E. Note the hands reaching upwards to a disc and crescent, symbols of the Canaanite religion. The city, was a Canaanite stronghold. It was destroyed by Joshua but was later rebuilt by King Solomon.

The Judges of Israel / ca. 1225–ca. 1020 B.C.E.

After Joshua's death, the Israelites were guided by leaders called judges. Both men and women served as judges; among them were warriors, priests, and seers. The first judges led the Israelites in defense against the warlike pagan neighbors who frequently attacked their farms and towns. In times of peace the judges settled disputes and provided religious inspiration.

A Canaanite victory celebration on an ivory plaque. The ruler sits on his throne as a court musician plays a lyre. Behind the musician is a warrior leading two prisoners and an armored chariot.

In periods when there was no judge representing a central authority for all Israel, some of the tribes would fall away from the laws given at Sinai. They would no longer make pilgrimages to the Tabernacle at Shiloh, but would take sacrifices to the Canaanite shrines and lay their offerings before the idols.

The Canaanite Threat

During the centuries after Joshua there were twelve judges. No longer half-starved desert nomads, the Israelites had now become farmers, shepherds, artisans, and city dwellers. Their new way of life, however, was beset with dangers from all sides. Canaanite soldiers often raided Israelite farms and storehouses. Though the Israelites bravely fought off the attackers, their efforts were futile against the armed might of Jabin, the most powerful Canaanite king. Jabin's army, commanded by his general, Sisera, was well-trained and equipped with heavy iron chariots and weapons.

Deborah, Leader and Judge / ca. 1100 B.C.E.

In the hill country of Ephraim lived a female judge named Deborah. People came from far and near to consult her. Deborah held court near her home at a place between Ramah and Bethel. Here she would sit beneath a palm tree and the people would come and tell her their problems.

Deborah resolved that Jabin must be defeated. When the time was ripe, she gathered her allies. Summoning Barak, an able warrior from the tribe of Naphtali, she ordered him to muster every available Israelite soldier and prepare to attack.

Together, Deborah and Barak led the warriors of Israel up the sides of Mount Tabor, a mountain that rises over the great plain of Jezreel near the Kishon River.

JUDGES

The twelve Judges of Israel whose histories are told in the Book of Judges:*

OTHNIEL	DEBORAH	JAIR	ELON
EHUD	GIDEON	JEPHTHAH	ABDON
SHAMGAR	TOLA	IBZAN	SAMSON

*The lives of the later judges, Eli and Samuel, are told in the Book of Samuel, I.

Mount Tabor, where Deborah and Barak defeated the Canaanite general Sisera.

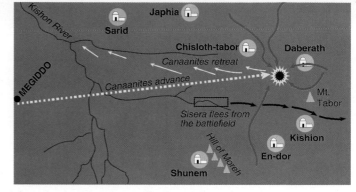

After the battle Sisera fled and found refuge in the tent of Jael.

Victory at Mount Tabor

Confident of an easy victory over this small army equipped with inferior weapons, the mighty King Jabin and his general, Sisera, assembled their troops and their iron chariots and waited beneath Mount Tabor for the Israelites to strike.

Shouting their battle cry, the Israelite warriors charged down the mountain and attacked the Canaanites. In the midst of the battle the skies opened and rain poured down. The Kishon, normally a quiet stream, became a raging torrent, rolling and rushing across the plain. The heavy iron wheels of Sisera's chariots were mired in thick, slippery mud. Weighed down by their heavy armor, the Canaanite solders were no match for the lightly armed Israelites, who seemed to be everywhere at once with lightning speed, cutting down the enemy right and left with their spears and slings.

Complete Victory

The Canaanites fled in utter confusion. Sisera, their general, sought refuge in the tent of Jael, a Kenite woman, begging her for water to quench his thirst. Jael gave the great warrior a dry cloak and some milk to drink, then stood guard at the door of the tent. Unaware that Jael and her husband, Heber, were secret allies of the Israelites, Sisera thought himself safe and fell into a deep sleep. And while he slept, Jael slew him. According to the Book of Judges, Jael took a sharp tent peg, quietly crept close to the sleeping Sisera, then hammered it through his temples.

Deborah's Song

Great was the rejoicing of the Israelites when they learned that Sisera was dead and that the fierce Canaanite warriors had fled in confusion. Deborah, the prophetess who had so fearlessly led her people, sang a song of praise to God.

With the Israelite victory at Mount Tabor, the power of the Canaanites came to an end. The successful conquest of this troublesome enemy gave the Israelites a much firmer hold on their new land. Peace had come to the Promised Land—at least for a time.

A Canaanite clay altar excavated from the city of Tanach. It is dated to the 10th century B.C.E.

Gideon the Judge / ca. 1120 B.C.E.

New Enemies

Out of the east, from across the Jordan, came the Midianites, greedily searching for new grazing grounds and plunder. These desert raiders, warlike and strong, came riding on camels. Borne by the swift ships of the desert, the ruthless Midianites bore down on the land of Canaan, shattering the peaceful existence of the Israelites.

Gideon Fights Back

Once more a leader rose from the ranks of Israel to meet the challenge to freedom. The new leader was Gideon, a farmer from Ophrah. When he called for volunteers to battle the Midianites, the response was immediate. Thousands of Israelites came, but Gideon only chose the 300 most stalwart and God-fearing of them for a surprise attack.

In the dead silence of night the Israelite warriors stealthily approached the camp of the sleeping Midianites. Gideon's small army was equipped with odd weapons— burning torches, jars and pitchers. At a given signal, they held their torches high, shattering the jars and pitchers at the same time in one tremendous crash. The noise was deafening and, to add to the confusion, some of the Israelites blew their rams' horns, shouting, "For God and for Gideon!"

The Midianites were terrified. They tumbled from their tents and fled into the night. The Israelites pursued them and drove them out of the land. Never again did the Midianites attack Israel.

Gideon, a valiant warrior and brilliant strategist, was also a dynamic political leader. In his effort to defeat the Midianites he succeeded in reuniting the tribes of Israel.

God Shall Rule

So great was the people's confidence in Gideon and so sincere their love for him that the elders of the tribes asked him to be their king. To this request Gideon answered, "I shall not rule over you, neither shall my son rule over you. Only God shall rule over you."

Gideon served as judge in Israel for many peaceful years and died a very old man.

The Gezer Calendar Stone was discovered by R. Macalister in 1908. This 10th century B.C.E. limestone plaque is inscribed with the planting schedule of the ancient Palestinian farmer.

1   (Its?) months of ingathering 2 months of sow-
2   ng 2 months of late sowing
3   The month of pulling flax
4   The month of barley harvest
5   The month when everything else is harvested
6   2 months of vine-pruning
7   The month of summer fruit

The Philistines

Dangerous Neighbors / ca. 1200 B.C.E.

A time of great peril came upon the Israelites. Their most formidable enemies, the Philistines, were on the march.

The Philistines had come from far away. Their long trek had led them through Crete, across the Aegean Sea by ship and through Asia Minor on foot and by oxcart. Wherever they passed, they left a trail of pillage and bloodshed in their wake. Their ambitious plan of conquest even included mighty Egypt.

The Philistines

The Philistines marched into Canaan victoriously, for the inhabitants were helpless before them. They conquered the rich coastal cities and established five powerful city-states: Ashkelon, Ashdod, Ekron, Gaza, and Gath. Each of these cities in the southern part of the fertile coastal plain was ruled by an independent Philistine prince, but all five were united as allies in peace and in war. Next the Philistines began to subject the land of Israel to their power. They drove the tribe of Dan out of its territory. The Danites were forced to move on and settle in the far north of the land.

Samson, Man of Strength / ca. 1100 B.C.E.

By the time of Samson, the last of the judges, Israel was desperately trying to hold off the Philistines. Samson's great physical strength was known and admired by both Philistines and Israelites. The story of how this fearless hero was finally brought down by the trickery and deceit of his Philistine sweetheart, Delilah, has been made famous in the world's music and literature. During a Philistine festival, Samson, blinded and in chains, was exhibited at Gaza. Sightless and alone, he exerted the last of his remaining strength to bring down a great Philistine temple, destroying many of his captors and perishing under the crashing pillars himself.

This drawing from an Egyptian stone relief pictures the naval engagement between the ships of Rameses III and the Philistines.

A stone relief from Thebes showing a group of Philistine prisoners of Rameses III. In hieroglyphics, the Philistines were called *peles et*. The name Palestine was derived from this word.

Samuel, Judge and Prophet / ca. 1040–1020 B.C.E.

The Birth of Samuel

In the period after Samson's death, the sanctuary at Shiloh was tended by Eli, who served as both priest and judge.

Eli noticed that a woman named Hannah was a frequent visitor to the sanctuary at Shiloh. When the kindly priest learned that Hannah was there to pray for the birth of a son, he comforted her and told her to be of good faith, promising that God would answer her prayer. Soon thereafter a son was born to Hannah. She called the child Samuel (from the Hebrew *shama el*, "God heard").

A Future Leader

As soon as Samuel was old enough to leave home, Hannah brought him to Shiloh. She asked Eli to make the boy his assistant in the service of God. The priest was delighted to grant Hannah's request, and Samuel proved an apt and eager pupil.

Eli was very pleased with Samuel, for the youngster seemed truly worthy to be a future leader and judge of Israel, even though he was not a descendent of the priestly family of Aaron. Eli instructed Samuel in the ways of the Torah and the faith of Israel.

As the years passed, Hannah's son became well known for his knowledge and great wisdom. In time he was revered as a man of divine inspiration, a judge and a prophet in Israel. Samuel became the national leader and head of the tribes.

The Battle of Aphek

Meanwhile, the Philistines, Israel's dreaded foes, had grown increasingly powerful. At last, the Philistine and Israelite armies met in a bloody battle on the plain of Aphek. The Israelites suffered heavy losses. In desperation, the elders of the tribes went to Eli.

"Let us carry the Holy Ark into battle," they pleaded. "It will inspire us to victory."

With the Holy Ark in their midst, the Israelites fought a brave fight, but the superior arms and training of the Philistines proved overwhelming.

The Holy Ark of the Covenant, with the tablets of the law, was captured by the enemy.

Philistines, Masters of Israel

The Philistines had become masters in the land. They destroyed the sanctuary at Shiloh, and the priests and Levites scattered to different parts of the country.

Samuel's task of keeping alive the faith of Israel was not an easy one in those dark days. Fear and discouragement lay like a

Archaeologists have unearthed the stone relief of the Holy Ark in the ancient synagogue in Capernaum. The original Holy Ark was built by Moses, and was carried from place to place before being permanently enshrined in the First Temple.

heavy yoke upon the people. They were forced to pay heavy tribute to the Philistines. They were not permitted to carry weapons, and their pickaxes and plowshares had to be sharpened in the forges of the overlords.

All Israelites were forbidden to use iron, the precious new metal, for it was to be forged only in the cities of the Philistines. Many Israelites turned away from God in bitterness and began to worship Baal and Astarte, the gods of their pagan conquerors.

However, in the midst of utter despair and defeat, the Israelites won a victory of sorts. The Philistines were afflicted by a terrible plague. Convinced that it was a punishment for having taken the Ark of the Covenant, the enemies of Israel returned it to the Israelites.

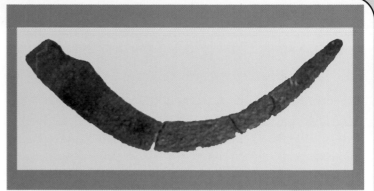

An ancient iron sickle. This sharp knife was used for harvesting grain. Sickles are still used in underdeveloped regions of the world.

The Ark in the Land of the Philistines. Taken from the fresco in the synagogue at Dura-Europos, 3rd century, C.E.

A 13th century French manuscript depicts the Ark of the Covenant being brought out. The Ark of the Covenant was a gold-plated chest in which the Ten Commandments given by God to Moses were stored. It was originally kept at Shiloh, and brought out during battles to encourage the army.

King Solomon placed the Ark of the Covenant in the Holy of Holies, of the Temple at Jerusalem. It disappeared after the destruction of the Temple in 586 B.C.E.

Appoint for Us a King

Voices of Hope

Samuel realized that if Israel was to survive, its people had to be united and inspired. Like the priests and Levites of earlier times, he began traveling through the land, encouraging the people everywhere to hold fast to their faith.

On his travels, Samuel attracted many followers, men who were uplifted by his words and, like himself, felt called upon to talk to the people about God and hope. Samuel's disciples would sing and play the harp, telling the stories of Israel's past and expounding the laws of the Torah.

Idol worship was popular among some of the Israelites. The prophet Samuel and his followers traveled throughout the land encouraging the people to hold true to their faith.

This impression of a Canaanite seal found at Bethel shows the idol Baal and his wife Ashtoreth. The name Ashtoreth is written in Egyptian characters in the center of the seal. Ashtoreth is mentioned several times in the Bible.

"Appoint Us a King"

When Samuel grew old, the elders of the tribes became fearful about the future. The tribes were worn out by the constant warfare with their enemies. They felt the need for a central authority which could mold them into a unified strong nation. The people appealed to Samuel, "Appoint us a king who will rule us, like the other nations." Samuel was deeply troubled when the tribal elders asked him to select a king to rule over them. The wise old judge was well-versed in the laws of Israel and knew the needs of a Israeli society.

Samuel's Leadership / ca. 1040–1010 B.C.E.

Samuel realized that life under a king would be different in many ways. The people would have to maintain a grand style of living for the king. A king would require a royal palace and servants. Hitherto the people had defended the land of their own free will, but with a king a regular army would be needed, with men from each tribe to guard and serve him. Taxes would be levied to meet the government's civil and military expenses. One by one, Samuel

presented these arguments against the establishment of a kingdom, but the elders refused to be discouraged. The people had set their hearts on having a king. Reluctantly Samuel bowed to their wishes.

Saul, Israel's First King / ca. 1020–1004 B.C.E.

Under God's guidance, Samuel chose the first king of Israel with great wisdom and much diplomacy. Because of the competition and rivalry among the more powerful tribes, Samuel turned to the smaller, poorer tribe of Benjamin. By selecting a man from the tribe of Benjamin, Samuel wisely avoided the danger of setting the great rival tribes against one another. The man chosen by Samuel was Saul, who was respected by all and a valiant fighter.

The Bible tells how Saul left home to go in search of his father's runaway donkeys. Traveling through Zuph, he stopped to ask the advice of Samuel, who was speaking there to the people. Samuel took Saul into the hills, where he told the young man that instead of the donkeys which he had gone to seek, he had found a crown.

King Saul's Victory

Saul soon proved himself a forceful leader. Now that Israel was weakened by the yoke of the Philistines, the Ammonites saw their chance to recapture the territory of Gilead. They besieged the city of Jabesh-Gilead. Their king was a cruel, vengeful monarch. As the price of a peace treaty he demanded that the people of Jabesh-Gilead submit to having their right eyes put out, branding them forever with the shame of defeat.

Saul sent messengers from Gibeah throughout the land, asking the tribes to unite at once to help the city of Jabesh-Gilead. The men of Israel responded, and under Saul's capable leadership, Israel attacked the Ammonites, who were besieging the city. Saul's warriors fell upon the Ammonites and sent them fleeing in confusion.

Saul's victory served a double purpose. It vanquished an enemy and, as well, reunited the tribes of Israel. Together, they marched to Gilgal. There, led by Samuel, the people proclaimed Saul their king.

Samuel Is Disappointed

Saul had met Israel's dire need for a courageous and clever military leader; but Samuel was disappointed in the new king. Saul's spiritual values did not always meet the high standards set by the Torah. A rift developed between Samuel the spiritual leader and Saul the warrior king. In his last years Samuel refused even to meet with Saul, and predicted that none of Saul's sons would succeed him on the throne.

The stone remains of Saul's ancient fortress at Gibeah.

Hebrew writing went through several stages before it crystalized into its present form in the 9th or 10th century. Note the early forms of picture writing.

Saul, A Troubled King / ca. 1020–1004 B.C.E.

Search for a New Ruler

Samuel's rejection lay heavily on the mind of King Saul. He became deeply troubled, suffering sleepless nights and days of anguish during which he scarcely spoke to those around him.

Samuel, the aged seer, began to look about secretly for a new king. Inspired by God, his choice fell on David, a shepherd, the youngest son of Jesse of Bethlehem, a farmer of the tribe of Judah. Samuel anointed David in secret and proclaimed him the next king of Israel.

David the Sweet Singer

Saul's advisers had heard about David's outstanding musical talent. Soon after these events they brought the young shepherd to Saul's court to play his harp and sing his songs for the troubled king. In later years, because of his musical gifts, people would call David "the sweet singer of Israel."

The king took a great fancy to the young singer and later gave David his daughter Michal in marriage. David and Jonathan, Saul's eldest son, became very good friends.

David killed the giant Goliath with a stone from a sling. Soldiers with slings fought side-by-side with the archers. A sling consisted of two leather straps and a stone-holder. The sling was whirled until it hummed like a bee. The stone was then released with nearly the speed of a bullet. It hurtled to its target and could cause death or serious injury. This orthostat from the time of David and Solomon shows how the sling was used in battle.

David proved himself as capable in battle as he was with his harp and song. He slew Goliath, a Philistine giant who had terrified the Israelite army. Up and down the land went the stories of David's valiant deeds. "Saul has slain his thousands," the people sang, "but David his ten thousands!" From this, however, David was to learn a bitter lesson: it is always dangerous for a man to become more popular than his king.

Saul Becomes Jealous

Saul became suspicious and jealous of David. The king began to plot to destroy the popular young hero.

Jonathan warns David

Early on Jonathan, the heir to the throne, recognized David's gifts of bravery and leadership. He told David, "You are going to be king over Israel, and I shall be your second."

Musical instruments were common in the ancient Near East. This relief from Ashurbanipal's palace shows a quartet of musicians playing a tambourine, cymbals and a harp.

Jonathan's friendship with David alienated him from his father, King Saul. He secretly warned David when he learned that Saul was planning to kill him. David, accompanied by his most trusted warriors, fled into the mountains of Judah. Saul tracked him down and David realized that he would be safe nowhere in Israel. He was forced to seek refuge in the land of Israel's Philistine enemies. For sixteen months, he and his men were given shelter in the city of Ziklag by King Achish of Gath, who was no doubt secretly elated at this sign of disunity in the land of Israel. Though they were guests of the king, David and his men were closely watched by the Philistines, who did not trust these aliens in their midst.

Saul's Last Battle / ca. 1104 B.C.E.

The Philistine army, encouraged by news of King Saul's troubles, prepared again for all-out attack. Their ranks were greatly reinforced by many fierce mercenaries. The Philistines advanced to the plain of Jezreel. At the foot of Mount Gilboa a bloody battle took place, close to the very spot where Barak and Deborah had once put the Canaanites to rout. There was no glorious victory this time, for the morose and troubled Saul was no longer able to inspire courage and enthusiasm in his warriors. He and his army were overwhelmed by the Philistine onslaught.

The battle at Mount Gilboa was a disastrous defeat for Israel. Many thousands were slain, among them the sons of Saul, including the valiant Jonathan. Saul, dreading the fate of being taken captive, died by his own hand.

The Philistines carried the bodies of Saul and his sons in triumph to their temple at Beth-She'an, where they exhibited them on the temple walls. The loyal men of Jabesh Gilead, remembering how Saul had once so bravely defended them, removed the bodies in the dark of night to save them from further shame.

David, the "sweet singer," composed a song of mourning, one of the Bible's greatest poems, extolling the courage of the two great warriors and lamenting their fall in battle.

Both Saul and Jonathan!
They were together in life and death.
They were swifter than eagles, stronger than lions.
Now, people of Israel weep for Saul,
Jonathan is slain upon the hills.
How I weep for you, my brother Jonathan;
How much I loved you.

The preferred weapon in the ancient Near East was the bow. This Egyptian painting shows instructors teaching their pupils the art of marksmanship with the bow.

The House of David / ca. 1004–965 B.C.E.

A New Era for Israel

The time that followed the death of Saul was difficult and unhappy for the Israelites. The Philistine tyranny weighed heavily upon them. Taxes of tribute were high, and the presence of Philistine soldiers throughout the land was a constant reminder of Israel's bitter defeat. After Saul's death, civil strife disrupted the tribes, for they could not agree on who was to be Israel's new ruler.

Abner, one of Saul's generals, proclaimed Ishbosheth, the last surviving son of Saul, as king. At the same time, David ruled in Hebron, the capital of Judah. The unfortunate Ishbosheth, who proved to be a weak monarch, was slain by his own men after a reign of only two years. In 1006 B.C.E., after his death, the tribes accepted David as their king.

David, now king over all Israel, scarcely had time to take stock of the new situation before the Philistines, eager to prevent Israel from uniting, marched into the territory of Judah. David hastily assembled all available fighting men. The enemy was forced to fight in the Judean hills, a territory well known to David and his soldiers.

With the assistance of his brilliant general, Joab, David forced battle after battle upon the Philistines. David gave them no peace, attacking ferociously whenever they attempted to rest.

The Philistine city of Gath fell to the Israelites. Soon thereafter the war ended and the battle-weary Philistine army began to dissolve. The Philistine mercenaries, ever ready to follow the winner, came over to the side of Israel and found employment with David's army. The crushing power of the Philistines was broken and their heavy yoke was lifted from the people of Israel.

David playing his harp. Painting is from an Italian prayer book, ca. 1450–1470.

The Israeli archaeologist Abraham Biran has excavated the 4000-year-old site of Tel-Dan. He has found a stone inscription which he believes contains the first-ever mention of the royal House of David.

Jerusalem Is Captured

In the midst of the Judean hills there still remained a fortified city which had resisted every Israelite effort to conquer it since the time of Joshua. This was the city of Jerusalem, the ancient stronghold of the Jebusites.

Joab, David's general, found a chink in Jerusalem's invincible armor. He learned of a secret passage—a natural tunnel that led through the rocky mountains into the center of the city. Joab led his troops through this tunnel, taking the Jebusites by surprise. Thus did Jerusalem become an Israelite city.

Israel, a Growing Nation

The tribes of Israel were now firmly united. Jerusalem became the seat of a central government which dealt with the many issues confronting the nation. David made the city his royal residence, and had the Holy Ark brought there. On festivals throngs of joyous Israelites made the journey to Jerusalem to participate in worship services.

The land of Israel had become a thriving nation, with a splendid capital city of which any people might have been proud and a king to whom even the mightiest monarchs paid homage.

Nathan the Prophet

In addition to Saul's daughter, Michal, David had other wives, as was the custom in the Near East. Among them was Bathsheba, who had been the wife of Uriah, an army captain. David had ordered Uriah into combat, where he was slain. The king then married the captain's beautiful widow. The prophet Nathan rebuked King David, making him aware of the seriousness of his deed. Although David realized that he had done wrong and repented his transgression, Bathsheba remained his favorite wife, and her son, Solomon, became his favorite son.

David Instructs Solomon

When David lay dying, he instructed Solomon as follows: "I am going the way of all earth; be strong and act like a man. Keep the laws of your God, walking in his ways and following his commandments and rules as recorded in the Torah, in order that you succeed in whatever you undertake. Then your descendants will be true in their conduct and will walk before me with all their heart and soul, so that your line on the throne of Israel will never end."

David Chooses Solomon

David found it difficult to decide which of his sons was to succeed him as king. He realized that in order to prevent strife over the succession, he had to announce his choice before he died. Summoning Nathan the prophet, he told him that he had selected the wise Prince Solomon, son of Bathsheba. Solomon was anointed by Zadok, the high priest, and proclaimed king. The rams' horns sounded and the people shouted, "Long live King Solomon!"

King David's work was done. When he died, all Israel mourned the passing of the sweet singer whose many accomplishments had included the composition of the beautiful poems that comprise the biblical Book of Psalms. David died in 965 B.C.E.

The Citadel of David stands on the site over which Herod the Great built his palace in the 1st century B.C.E. At the time of the Jewish revolt against Rome the Citadel of David was one of the main fortifications guarding Jerusalem.
The Byzantine conquerors mistakenly thought that this was David's palace. When the crusaders invaded Palestine, they used the Citadel as a residence, and when they were defeated, Saladin used it as his headquarters. The tall minaret was added in 1655.

Solomon, King of Peace / ca. 965–926 B.C.E.

Solomon on the Throne

Solomon took over the reins of government with efficiency. He carefully evaluated Israel's assets, his father's accomplishments, and the possibilities at hand. He completed the fortifications and building projects which David had begun and furthered his trade alliances with other nations.

The friendly alliance between David and King Hiram of Tyre proved advantageous for Solomon, who became a close friend of the Phoenician monarch. Both kings were aware of the importance of Ezion-Geber, Israel's new port on the Red Sea, and both cooperated in enlarging it. Ezion-Geber could open the sea route to India.

With Hiram's assistance, Solomon began building a navy for Israel. Soon Phoenician and Israelite traders were voyaging together, exchanging their wares for the rich offerings of faraway lands. The Israelites exported their most valuable new product, copper from the mines of the Negev. It was the main source of their new wealth.

queen. Finally the Queen of Sheba herself journeyed from her far-distant empire in Ophir to visit King Solomon's court. Solomon also forged strategic, commercial, and political ties with his neighbors. In addition to his commercial relations with Hiram of Tyre, he promoted trade with an Egyptian Pharaoh and married one of his daughters. In fact, Solomon made so many matrimonial alliances with foreign royal families that he was said to have 1,000 wives and concubines. These marriages promoted political and commercial treaties.

An artist's idea of the Bet Hamikdash, the Temple in Jerusalem. The large area, the Temple Mount, was surrounded by a wall.

The Queen of Sheba

Israel's seafarers told many tales about the riches of Arabia and the beauty of its

This potsherd establishes the existence and wealth of Ophir. It reads: "Gold from Ophir for Beth-Horon." The Book of Kings tells us "They came to Ophir and fetched 400 talents of gold and brought it to King Solomon."

A horned altar from the Solomonic period. Altars of this type were used for sacrifices and incense burning. After the Temple was built, sacrifices were only performed at the Temple by the priests. This altar was discovered at Arad, in the Negev.

Solomon's Temple contained a huge bronze water basin called a "sea", which weighed about 30 tons and held about 10,000 gallons of water. The "sea" contained the water which was used to wash the hands of the priests who took part in the ceremonies.

The Holy Temple

Now Solomon turned to the project which would demand his greatest effort, the one most dear to his heart and the hearts of his people—the building of the Holy Temple (Bet Hamikdash), on Mount Zion. Until now, Israel had worshipped God in the simple sanctuary that housed the Holy Ark. Solomon wanted a more fitting House of God, a magnificent Temple that would be the grandest structure in all Jerusalem, indeed in all the land of Israel.

From his close friend and ally, King Hiram of Tyre, Solomon obtained cedar wood of Lebanon for the Temple. He paid for this precious wood with the produce of Israel—grain and oil, olives and figs—and with copper from the mines of Ezion-Geber.

The Temple was built of stone and precious wood, with great pillars and spacious inner courts, with special places appointed for the various rites of the services. The interior was paneled with cedar wood. Gold, newly brought to the land of Israel from other countries in exchange for copper and olive oil, was lavishly used to make Solomon's Temple a dazzling sight to behold.

Moreover, not one iron tool was used in the construction of the Temple, because of iron's association with violence and war.

Solomon acquired a reputation for great wisdom. Three biblical books, Proverbs, Ecclesiastes (Kohelet), and Song of Songs (Shir Ha Shirim) are attributed to him.

Jerusalem Rejoices

When the Temple was completed, Jerusalem was thronged with jubilant people. Many had come merely to marvel, but many others had come to rejoice and rededicate themselves to their faith.

They also brought wares to trade in the busy markets, they presented their problems and disputes to the judges in the king's court, they left their sacrifices and offerings.

The Romans conquered Jerusalem in 70 C.E. and burned the Temple to the ground. All that remained was the Western Wall, which became a sacred place where Jews prayed. All through the centuries of exile Jews worshipped at the Western Wall. The Wall has become a place for Jews to write prayer and requests to place in the cracks between the stone.

The Seeds of Rebellion

Solomon the Builder

Meantime, a change was taking place in Israel's old way of life. Masses of unskilled laborers were needed for Solomon's many projects and to work in the mines. Great masses of Israelites became poor laborers, while only a few of the people grew rich. The latter were mainly merchants, artisans, designers and builders, chroniclers and officials in the civil service, or officers in the king's army.

The Temple in Jerusalem was only one of Solomon's building projects. He also erected a series of fortified towns, among them Hazor, Gezer, and Beth-Horon. In addition he built dams and wells which allowed cities to withstand enemy sieges. For his chariot troops and cavalry Solomon built large garrison towns and store-cities for munitions and food.

One section of the ruins of King Solomon's stables at Meggido.

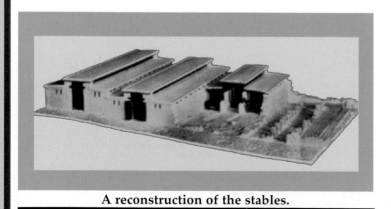

A reconstruction of the stables.

For efficiency Solomon divided the country into twelve taxpaying districts.

Every citizen paid tribute to the king in some way. Taxes were levied on the wealthy for highway construction, building projects, and to pay for the many government officials, soldiers, and royal servants. The poor who had no money to pay their taxes had to contribute their services to the king as laborers or soldiers. Samuel's warning, which had gone unheeded by the people of Israel so long ago, now seemed to echo across the years. The people had chosen to be ruled by a king, and they were paying a heavy price, both in property and in freedom.

Some of the lands which David had conquered became restless under Solomon's rule. They felt confident that Solomon, unlike his father, would not march against them if they revolted. One by one, the outlying territories began to break away.

Discontent Grows

As Solomon's reign proceeded, the northern tribes became discontented, chafing under their heavy burden of taxes and forced labor. They felt that they were not benefiting from Solomon's policies. Trouble exploded when Jeroboam, the official in charge of labor and building projects for the district of Joseph, plotted rebellion.

Solomon, wise and wealthy, was reaping a golden harvest, but the seeds of discontent were sprouting uncomfortably close to the throne. Many of his nobles disapproved of the king's tolerance toward foreign priests and his foreign wives, who prayed to their own idols under Solomon's roof.

A reconstruction of Solomon's Temple.

Throughout the land many who longed for the simpler ways of days gone by. As far as they were concerned, Solomon valued wealth and pomp far too highly, at a price the Israelites were reluctant to pay.

King Solomon Dies / ca. 926 B.C.E.
Solomon died after a reign of 40 years. The combined reigns of David and Solomon covered a span of 80 years, during which Israel grew into an important, wealthy nation.

Rehoboam the Successor
In 928 B.C.E., Rehoboam, the son whom Solomon had named as his successor, was proclaimed king. Yet the throne which Solomon's son ascended was resting on shaky foundations.

Rehoboam lacked the great ability of his father and grandfather, but he was a prince of the House of David and the tribe of Judah followed him loyally. The northern tribes warned Rehoboam that they would not be his loyal subjects unless he met their demands.

The elders of the northern tribes did not go to Jerusalem to pay homage to the new king; instead, they asked Rehoboam to come to an assembly at Shechem in the territory of Ephraim.

Rehoboam Refuses Concessions
When the northern leaders asked the young king to give them assurance that he would lighten their taxes and ease their burdens, Rehoboam kept them waiting three days for his answer. Solomon's old advisors, experienced in the ways of government, strongly urged Rehoboam to grant the request, pointing out that the loyalty of the northern tribes was an important asset to the kingdom. Rehoboam refused to make any concessions. Instead, he arrogantly informed the northern tribes that he would demand even higher taxes and more labor services than his father had required.

The Kingdom Is Divided / ca. 926 B.C.E.

Rehoboam the Arrogant / ca. 926–910 B.C.E.

Angered and offended by Rehoboam's arrogance, the northern tribes rose up in revolt. Had Rehoboam listened to the advice of wiser heads, it is possible that the united kingdom could have been saved. But he insolently rejected the demands.

When the people of Shechem petitioned him for relief, he replied, "My father, Solomon, punished you with a whip, but I will punish you with scorpions." Only the tribes of Judah and Benjamin remained loyal to the young monarch. The other ten tribes chose a new leader—Jeroboam, the veteran rebel from the northern tribe of Ephraim. Jeroboam had been in exile in Egypt, where he had gained the support of Pharaoh Shishak. As the ambitious head of a new dynasty, Shishak was delighted at the prospect of disunity in Israel and encouraged Jeroboam to return home as soon as he learned of Solomon's death.

Taking advantage of the crisis at Shechem, Jeroboam raised the standard of revolt against Rehoboam. The situation

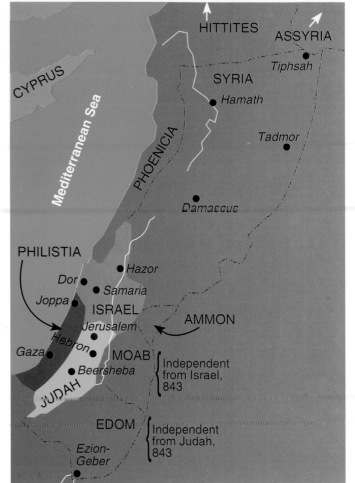

ISRAEL AND JUDAH
The Northern and Southern kingdoms.

became so threatening that Rehoboam and his advisors fled back to Jerusalem.

Two Kingdoms: Israel and Judah / ca. 926 B.C.E.

As a result of the fateful assembly at Shechem, the flourishing kingdom of David and Solomon was divided into two smaller states, the northern kingdom of Israel, under Jeroboam, and the southern kingdom of Judah, under Rehoboam.

A bronze statue from Samaria. The Canaanites were idol-worshippers, and this bull is thought to have been one of their gods.

KINGS BEFORE DIVISION OF KINGDOM		
1020–1004 B.C.E.	SAUL	
1004–965 B.C.E.	DAVID	THE NORTHERN
965–928 B.C.E.	SOLOMON	KINGDOM OF ISRAEL

All dates are approximate

Pharaoh Shishak immortalized his victory over King Rehoboam in a relief on the wall of the great temple in Karnak. In his hands can be seen the ropes by which he leads the captives from the conquered cities of Judah. Each captive represents a different city.

Throughout the reigns of Rehoboam and Jeroboam, there was war between Israel and Judah. Each kingdom fortified its frontier. Judah reinforced many of its fortresses, but despite this, much of its power had been lost and a great deal of its influence weakened. The powerful empire created by David and Solomon was no more, and many former allies abandoned the House of David.

Egypt Attacks Israel / ca. 922 B.C.E.

Judah suffered another great blow when Shishak of Egypt attacked in the fifth year of Rehoboam's reign. The advance of Shishak's army was swift and unexpected. One after another Judah's fortresses fell, and Jerusalem was taken without a struggle. Shishak spared the Holy City the horror of destruction but ransacked Judah's treasury and marched back to Egypt laden with booty. Among the prizes were many of the golden vessels from the Temple and the famous golden shields which Solomon's guards had carried so proudly. Judah was left impoverished.

Jeroboam Abandons Jerusalem

The people of the northern kingdom of Israel still looked to Jerusalem as their sacred city. On festival days they journeyed there to join the people of Judah in prayers, sacrifices, and holiday processions. Jeroboam, ambitious to be recognized as head of a new royal line entirely separate from Judah, looked with misgivings upon the devotion of his subjects to the Temple. He feared that this bond between the two kingdoms would eventually serve to unite them again.

Idol Worship in Israel

Jeroboam had altars and shrines erected in Bethel and Dan to entice his people to offer prayers and sacrifices in their own land rather than in Jerusalem. In open violation of the Ten Commandments he placed images of golden calves in the shrines, proclaiming that they were representations of the God of Israel.

Jeroboam's purpose in introducing idol worship was twofold. He hoped that it would strengthen his power over his own people and serve further to cement his bond with Egypt.

Thoughtful and faithful Israelites were bitterly disappointed in their king and fervently hoped for a time when things would change. Weakened as they were, there was little to do now but bide their time.

Prophetic Voices

The Prophets

Although it seemed that this dark night of disunity would spell the final decline for Israel, faint signs of a new dawn began to appear on the horizon. Strong new voices were heard among the people of Israel and Judah—often in humble places, in caves and on mountainsides, by the roadside or at the city gates. These were the voices of the prophets, explaining how the ways of man should serve the ways of God.

The prophets went from place to place, caring for neither wealth nor physical comfort. Often they traveled in groups, singing and praying together to the accompaniment of their own music. Wherever the prophets went, the people gathered.

The Assyrian Threat

During these unhappy years, a great new power began to assert itself in Mesopotamia. This was the kingdom of Assyria, whose powerful armies were marching out to conquer all the nations from the Mediterranean to the Euphrates, from Egypt to Lebanon. The prophets of Israel warned the people about the threat posed by this new enemy, a cruel master that showed little mercy to those it conquered, and would suppress the worship of the one God.

The Split Between Judah and Israel

The conflict between Judah and Israel resulted in a stalemate. Israel, the northern kingdom, was larger in both land and population. It was also wealthier and more favorably situated on the busy caravan routes connecting Asia and Egypt. Judah was more compact and far less involved in regional contacts and conflicts. Both kingdoms, however, were at the mercy of their neighbors, Egypt, Aram, and Syria, which managed to preserve a power balance between the two.

The Splendor Is Gone

Much of the outer splendor of Jerusalem was gone, but its marketplaces were still crowded and busy. Here farmers and shepherds exchanged livestock, grain, olive oil, and honey for textiles and leather, vessels and tools, spices and imported goods of every kind. The people of Judah were proud of their famous capital, high in the mountains, with its fortifications and palaces, its markets and fine buildings. They were proud, too, that they were still ruled by the same dynasty which had given them such great kings as David and Solomon. Until the very end, Judah was ruled by an uninterrupted line of kings of the House of David.

Idol Worship

The rulers of the northern kingdom of Israel encouraged the people to worship the idols at the shrines established by Jeroboam. The new kingdom was a constant battleground between two ways of

Acient wall drawings of two Assyrians court officials. These drawings were found in the ruins of a palace on the banks of the Euphrates River.

The famous Moabite Stone, discovered by archaeologists in 1868, records how Moab was enslaved by the House of Omri and made to pay tribute.

life: the way of the Torah and the God of Israel against the way of idol worship and paganism. Many people from Israel still made pilgrimages to the Temple in Jerusalem.

Because it never developed a stable succession, the northern kingdom was ruled by nine separate dynasties. It had five different kings within just a few years of the death of Jeroboam.

The Reign of Omri / ca. 871 B.C.E.

Omri, an able general, established order in Israel. He defeated the Moabites and made them Israel's vassals. He built a beautiful new capital, Samaria. It became an important city, well fortified and strategically located in the central hills of Ephraim. From Samaria new trade routes developed to the south and, most important, to Phoenicia in the north.

Omri reverted to the tradition of King Solomon and traded with the Phoenicians. He fortified Israel and brought peace and prosperity to the land. For the first time since its beginning, the northern kingdom was secure among its neighbors and free of bloodshed. But, although he was shrewd in battle and wise in the ways of commerce, Omri was not sensitive to the people's spiritual needs and ideals, and as the Bible says, he "did evil in the eyes of God."

Ahab and Jezebel / ca. 871–852 B.C.E.

When Omri died, Ahab became king. Intent on cementing his pact with Phoenicia, Ahab married a Phoenician princess, Jezebel. She brought her idols and priests to her new home in Samaria. Strongly influenced by Jezebel, his vain and haughty wife, Ahab set up shrines to Baal, the most popular Phoenician god.

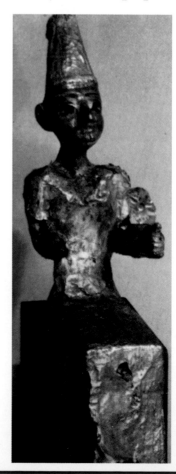

Jezebel, with the priests of Baal, set about teaching the Phoenician way of life to the people of Israel, persecuting anyone who defied her. Many of the prophets were killed at her command. Many others escaped, however, for the people protected them.

Bronze statue of an idol excavated from the ancient city of Megiddo.

Elijah and Elisha

Elijah Fights for Justice / ca. 869–849 B.C.E.

Not many people had the courage to criticize Ahab and Jezebel openly. There was one, however, who would not be silenced. This was the prophet Elijah. Boldly and passionately Elijah spoke out for the poor, who according to the laws of Israel were to be afforded protection from oppression and unjust taxes.

Elijah spoke out fearlessly against the priests of Baal. He fought their influence, upholding and defending the ancient traditions and faith of the people of Israel.

A seal which belonged to an official of King Ahaz, King of Judah. It reads, "Ushana, servant of Ahaz."

Elijah's most famous feat took place on the slopes of Mount Carmel. In order to prove that Baal was a false god, he challenged the Phoenician priests to a contest. While the assembled people watched, he and they prepared to offer sacrifices on wood saturated with water. When the priests urged Baal to set the wood afire, nothing happened. When Elijah asked God to do the same, the thoroughly soaked wood burst into flames.

Wherever he journeyed, Elijah comforted the poor, healed the sick, and encouraged people to serve God. In many places he destroyed the shrines of Baal. From all sides, Elijah heard shocking stories about King Ahab's cruelty.

Naboth's Vineyard

A man named Naboth owned a beautiful vineyard near Ahab's palace. Despite the king's threats, Naboth had refused to sell the vineyard, for it had been in his family for generations. The ruthless Jezebel arranged to have Naboth falsely accused of sacrilege and treason. Naboth suffered the punishment customarily inflicted on those who committed this crime—he was stoned to death.

Elijah was outraged. He went to see Ahab, prophesying the destruction of the House of Omri as a dynasty which had become unfit to rule. Struck with remorse, Ahab mourned, fasted, and asked God's forgiveness. Unfortunately, his repentance and good intentions were no match for the influence of Queen Jezebel.

Elijah in Jewish Tradition

Elijah was greatly loved by the people of Israel. Stories of his bravery, his compassion, his helpfulness to the poor and sick, were told through the length and breadth of the land. In time, he was to become a symbol of the spirit of redemption.

According to the biblical story, Elijah and his disciple Elisha were walking along the banks of the Jordan River when a fiery chariot suddenly descended next to them. Elijah threw his prophetic mantle to Elisha

The stone tower of Jezebel in Jezreel.

and stepped into the chariot, which flew upward and vanished from sight. Elisha picked up the mantle and assumed the leadership of the crusade against idolatry.

Jewish tradition believes that Elijah did not die, but will one day appear to announce the coming of the Messiah. Each year on Passover, on Seder night, when Jews celebrate their deliverance from Egypt, they remember Elijah, the symbol and spirit of freedom.

Elijah Calls Elisha to Prophecy

Elisha was Elijah's disciple. The Bible tells how Elijah recruited him. While passing through the Jordan Valley, Elijah saw Elisha plowing a field with a team of oxen. From a distance, he sensed the extraordinary power in the strong, sweat-soaked farmer. Without hesitation, Elijah removed his mantle and flung it around the young man's shoulders. This was an ancient symbolic call to prophetic service which Elisha eagerly accepted.

Both prophets devoted themselves to the crusade against idolatry, but there was a definite difference between them. Elijah was stern and solitary, while Elisha was gentle and was often found in the company of his disciples.

Elisha performed miracles and was active in the political and military life of Israel. When the Israelite army attacked Moab, he saved the day by finding water for the troops. Elisha also played a major role in the events leading to the seizure of power by Jehu. Determined to dethrone the idol-worshipping King Jehoram, Elisha sent one of his disciples to anoint Jehu, thus inducing him to revolt.

Elisha's fame as a miracle worker was so great that legend attributed power to him even after his death. One day, mourners at a funeral were attacked by Moabite

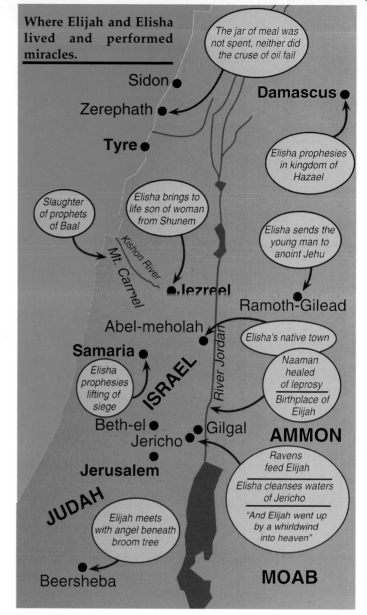

Where Elijah and Elisha lived and performed miracles.

The jar of meal was not spent, neither did the cruse of oil fail

Sidon

Zerephath

Damascus

Tyre

Elisha prophesies in kingdom of Hazael

Slaughter of prophets of Baal

Elisha brings to life son of woman from Shunem

Kishon River

Elisha sends the young man to anoint Jehu

Mt. Carmel

Jezreel

Ramoth-Gilead

Abel-meholah

Elisha's native town

Samaria

River Jordan

Elisha prophesies lifting of siege

Naaman healed of leprosy

Birthplace of Elijah

Beth-el

Gilgal

Jericho

AMMON

Jerusalem

Ravens feed Elijah

Elisha cleanses waters of Jericho

"And Elijah went up by a whirldwind into heaven"

JUDAH

Elijah meets with angel beneath broom tree

Beersheba

MOAB

bandits. The frightened mourners threw the corpse into the nearby tomb of Elisha and fled. On contacting the prophet's bones, the corpse came to life and walked away.

A 12th century miniature shows ravens bringing food to prophet Elijah.

The House of Omri

Ahab's Alliances

King Ahab was successful in his military campaigns and in establishing friendly relations with Israel's neighbors. Like all the rulers of the Middle East, he kept a wary eye on the growing power of Assyria; he was well aware that its armies were advancing closer and closer to his country. Realizing the importance of obtaining allies against these powerful conquerors, Ahab gave his daughter Athaliah in marriage to Jehoram, crown prince of Judah, thus strengthening Israel's bond with that country. When Ahab became involved in a war with Aram, Judah helped him to win the victory.

Ahab's pacts with Judah, Aram, Phoenicia, and Moab were well-timed, for the Assyrian army commanded by King Shalmaneser III was drawing nearer. Ahab and his allies met the Assyrians in battle at Carchemish. The coalition resisted valiantly, and in the end Shalmaneser's host departed.

Ahab was succeeded by his son Ahaziah, but he soon fell ill and died. He was followed by his brother Joram, the last king of the House of Omri.

The End of the House of Omri / ca. 845 B.C.E.

With the support of the prophet Elisha, Jehu, one of the king's officers, led a revolt against Jehoram. Elisha was confident that Jehu, once he became king, would abolish idol worship and govern in accordance with the Torah. Jehu's revolt was successful but bloody. Among the victims was Queen Jezebel, and with her all the members of the House of Omri. Jehu now ascended the throne.

Athaliah Becomes Queen / ca. 851 B.C.E.

Jehu's revolt in Israel had grave consequences for Judah. King Ahaziah of Judah was killed in ambush on his journey home from Samaria, where he had been visiting his cousins of the House of Omri. Ahaziah's mother, the ambitious Queen Athaliah, was a true daughter of Jezebel and Ahab. When Athaliah learned of her son's death, she saw her chance to become ruler of Judah. She had all the princes of the House of David killed, no matter how closely they were related to her; ascending the throne, she proved to be a ruthless and tyrannical ruler.

Unknown to Athaliah, one prince had escaped her henchmen: Joash, her grandson. The child had been saved by his uncle Jehoiada, the high priest, who for seven years kept him hidden.

When the time seemed ripe for revolt, Jehoiada brought the young prince before the elders of Judah and Joash was anointed king. This brought Athaliah's tyrannical reign to an end, and the House of David was established in Judah once more.

An ivory found at Arslan-Tash in Syria shows a woman, possibly the goddess Astarte, framed in a window. It is thought to be part of the booty taken from Aram-Damascus by the Assyrians in the 8th century B.C.E.

Jehu / ca. 845–818 B.C.E.

Jehu, who had overthrown Jehoram to become king of Israel, was the first ruler of the northern kingdom to forbid idol worship. At last the people could worship God openly. However, Jehu was not successful in foreign relations. To ward off an invasion by Damascus, he sent tribute to King Shalmaneser of Assyria and asked for his protection. Despite this, Damascus marched against Israel. Jehu was defeated, and Israel became a tribute-paying vassal of Damascus.

War with Damascus

In the days of Jehoahaz, the son of Jehu, the kingdom of Israel suffered severely under the yoke of the Arameans of Damascus and struggled for many years to free itself.

Jehoash / ca. 802–787 B.C.E.

King Jehoash, the son of Jehoahaz, fought Aram three times and finally was victorious. Now it was the Arameans of Damascus who paid tribute to Israel.

Joash reigned for 40 years. During the first part of his reign he accepted the advice of the high priest Jehoiada, but when Jehoiada died, Joash permitted and fostered the worship of idols. Joash was intensely disliked for his religious laxity and military failures. He was slain in his bed by his servants and was succeeded by his son Amaziah.

The black obelisk was set up by Shalmaneser III in his palace at Nimrod. It is inscribed with the story of his battles.

One of the panels on the obelisk shows King Jehu of Israel surrendering to the Assyrian king. Jehu is on his knees, bowing before the victorious Shalmaneser.

Relief on the black obelisk set up by Shalmaneser III shows Israelites bringing tribute to Shalmaneser. The tribute consists of gold, silver, and lead bars.

A Time of Prosperity

A time of prosperity now began for Israel. Samaria, its capital, was a flourishing city. The reign of Jeroboam II, son of Jehoash, saw foreign merchants coming once more to Israel's markets. New trade pacts were signed with the Phoenicians of Tyre.

Unfortunately, Israel's new prosperity was limited to the nobles and the merchants, who failed to remember that the poor were their brothers. Workers were underpaid and rich farmers dealt unfairly with their help. The builders exploited the masons. Workers and small farmers paid high taxes and lived in huts, while the rich lived in luxury.

Jeroboam II (784–748 B.C.E.), like other rulers before him, restored Israel's material wealth and power but had no understanding of people's inner needs. He neglected the laws of the Torah and encouraged his people to adopt the idol-worshiping ways of Damascus and Tyre. The kingdom of Jeroboam appeared strong and powerful, but inwardly it was weak and unjust.

Amos Speaks for Justice / ca. 780–760 B.C.E.

Now another strong voice arose in the land, crying out against the oppressors who were forcing the greater part of the people to endure poverty and injustice. Amos, a shepherd from Tekoa, spoke openly in the streets of Samaria, declaring that the sacrifices made by the rich on the altar at Bethel were meaningless as long as the donors did not act justly.

Amos possessed great knowledge of the political problems of the day. He warned that all the wealth of Samaria would be useless against the Assyrian threat unless the kingdom of Israel was united and strong. This would only come about, he declared, if the nation kept the laws of the Torah.

Israel's wealthy class was annoyed by the prophet. They forced Amos to leave Samaria, but he continued to speak out fearlessly, telling the rich that God would be more pleased by acts of justice than by costly offerings.

Hosea the Prophet

Soon another, younger prophet began to speak in Israel. This was Hosea, who was to witness not only the prosperity of Israel under Jeroboam II, but also a time of

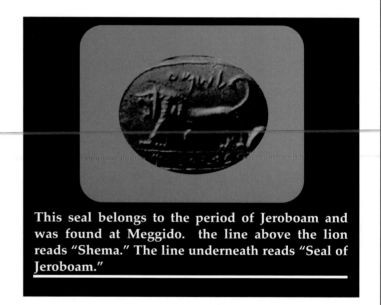

This seal belongs to the period of Jeroboam and was found at Meggido. the line above the lion reads "Shema." The line underneath reads "Seal of Jeroboam."

unhappy changes. The death of Jeroboam was followed by a quick succession of kings and a time of greed, murder, and decay which hastened the destruction of the kingdom.

Hosea's Warnings / ca. 760–755 B.C.E.

Like Amos, Hosea possessed both spiritual and political vision. He foresaw Assyria's invasion of Israel and warned the people to arm themselves morally against the coming time of danger.

Assyria the Conqueror

Assyria had conquered all of Babylonia, and its mighty armies were drawing ever closer. In the light of this threat, Israel, Judah, Aram, and Tyre drew closer to one another. They were in a strategically difficult position, for they stood on the road from Mesopotamia to the Nile Valley. Assyria, they knew, would inevitably attack Egypt, its strongest rival, and before it could do so would have to overrun them. Egypt attempted to persuade the smaller nations to join in an anti-Assyrian alliance. King Menachem of Israel faced with a tough decision: which of the two giants would be a better ally, or, rather, which would be the less ruthless overlord? He made his choice—and sent his tribute to Assyria.

This drawing of the ruthless Assyrian king Tiglath Pileser III, was discovered in the ruins of a palace on the banks of the Euphrates River. The king subjugated the people of Israel and Judah. In his annals the king lists the payments of tribute by King Menachem of Israel and King Ahaz of Judah.

Tiglath-Pileser III / ca. 734 B.C.E.

Meanwhile, another revolt took place in Israel. Menachem's son, Pekahiah, perished in the rebellion, and Pekah, one of the soldiers who had led the uprising, became king. Pekah joined the alliance of small nations along the Mediterranean coast that planned to resist Assyria. Israel was now allied with Edom, the Philistine city-states, Phoenicia, and the Arameans in a desperate effort to ward off Assyria.

A new king named Pul now sat on the Assyrian throne. Better known as Tiglath-Pileser III, he was a soldier who had risen from the ranks. He and his sons were cruel rulers, dedicated only to conquest.

King Ahaz of Judah / ca. 742–725 B.C.E.

Pekah invited King Ahaz of Judah, who was already a vassal of Assyria, to join the coalition. Ahaz firmly refused, for he did not believe Assyria could be defeated. He chose to stay out of the war, but the allies, bent on winning his support, marched against Jerusalem to force him to change his mind. Ahaz asked for Assyria's help in ridding Judah of the invaders.

At this dark moment, Israel again was torn by revolt. King Hoshea (733–724 B.C.E.), a rebel who had taken Pekah's throne, ruled over the remnant of what had once been the northern kingdom. He hoped for an opportunity to shake off the Assyrian yoke and win back Israel's northern lands. When Tiglath-Pileser died, Hoshea made an alliance with Egypt and refused to pay further tribute to Assyria.

Hoshea survived this time, but the allies who attempted to withstand Assyria fared badly. The Assyrians had already begun their march to Egypt. The people of Israel were filled with forebodings about the future.

Israel Falls / ca. 721 B.C.E.

The Reign of Shalmaneser V / ca. 727–722 B.C.E.
Shalmaneser V, the new Assyrian king, would tolerate no rebellion. He invaded Israel at once and laid siege to Samaria, the capital. Samaria had been wisely planned and well-fortified by Omri, however, and for three years its valiant defenders withstood the invaders. Shalmaneser died during the siege, but his successor, Sargon II, continued the campaign. Samaria finally fell to Sargon in the first year of his reign (721 B.C.E.).

As always, Assyria dealt ruthlessly with the conquered nation. Israel's leaders and best-educated, most skilled people were deported. All signs of opposition were suppressed. The region that had once been the proudly independent kingdom of Israel was made part of the Assyrian province of Syria.

The Ten Lost Tribes
Sargon deported 27,290 Israelites to distant countries far from their homeland. Scattered in strange lands and broken in spirit, the conquered people posed no threat of revolt to their captors and eventually lost their religious identity. Ever since they have been referred to as the Ten Lost Tribes.

To repopulate the areas left desolate by the war and the deportations, people from other lands conquered by the Assyrians were moved to Israel. The foreigners brought their own customs and religions with them. As they mingled with the surviving Israelites, a new people known as the Samaritans eventually emerged.

The northern kingdom of Israel was no more; its glory had vanished, its people were gone. Those few who had escaped to Judah told tales of suffering and defeat.

A stone tablet with the victory inscription of Sargon II. " I besieged Samaria and carried off 27,290 of its people as booty."

The kings of Israel in order of succession. The list starts with Jeroboam in 937 B.C.E. and ends with the destruction of Samaria in 722 B.C.E.

937–722 BCE

1. JEROBOAM
2. NADAB
3. BAASA (BAASHA)
4. ELAH
5. ZIMRI
6. OMRI
7. AHAB
8. AHAZIAH
9. JEHORAM (JORAM)
10. JEHU
11. JEHOAZ
12. JEHOHASH
13. JEROBOAM II
14. ZECHARIAH
15. SHALLUM
16. MENAHEM
17. PEKAHIAH
18. PEKAH
19. HOSHEA

The Assyrians destroy Samaria and lead the Ten Tribes into captivity.

They now realized that the warnings of Hosea and Amos had indeed been prophetic.

Religion played a key role in Judea and in Israel. Despite its defeats, Judah remained loyal to the God of Abraham, Isaac, and Jacob.

In what had been the northern kingdom, however, the worship of Baal and other gods was prevalent. The remaining Israelite inhabitants were demoralized; they had no religious shield to protect them from their idol-worshipping neighbors, the foreign settlers brought in by the Assyrians. Before long they blended with the pagan population and disappeared as a nation.

After a long and bloody battle, Lachish was captured by the Babylonians. To instill fear, the Judean captives were impaled on stakes and hung on the walls. This event was recorded on a relief in Shalmaneser IV's palace at Nineveh.

THE END OF THE KINGDOM OF ISRAEL

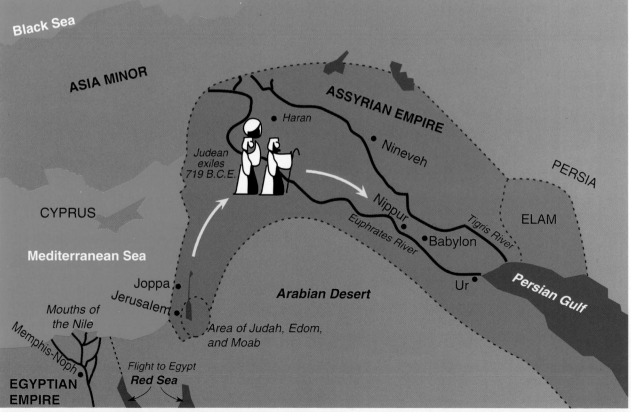

The annals of Sargon II, king of Assyria, state, "I besieged and conquered Samaria. I led away 27,290 of its inhabitants as captives."

Isaiah, Statesman and Prophet

In contrast to turbulent Israel, the little kingdom of Judah lived rather peacefully for many years. Since it was remote from the main caravan routes, it did not seek important trade and military pacts and most of its kings tried to avoid war. The splendor of Solomon's days was gone, but the real glory still remained—the Temple on Mount Zion in Jerusalem. Here the people of Judah brought their offerings and celebrated their festivals.

When King Ahaz (742–725 B.C.E.) faced the difficult choice between appeasing Assyria and joining the other small nations in an anti-Assyrian alliance, he turned for advice to a man of great brilliance and wisdom. This was the prophet Isaiah, who had counseled the royal family for three generations. Isaiah was well-educated, born into a noble family. Drawing on his wide knowledge of Judah's political problems, he advised Ahaz not to join the alliance, for he was positive that the allies would be no match for the mighty Assyrian war machine. Ahaz followed Isaiah's advice.

Ahaz Appeases Assyria

Soon after this came the news that the alliance had been defeated. All Judah mourned the destruction of Israel and the plight of the helpless thousands lost in captivity in far-off Assyria. Frightened lest Judah share the same fate, Ahaz tried in every way to win the favor of the Assyrians. He began to follow the Assyrian way of life and worship, even installing idols in the Temple. Isaiah, who had advised neutrality, not submission, was bitterly disappointed and criticized Ahaz severely. He foresaw that the king's policy would bring nothing but disaster to Judah.

The Isaiah Scroll, one of the scrolls discovered in a cave in the Dead Sea area. This is one of the oldest parts of the Bible ever found.

The grave of King Uzziah is marked by this engraved stone tablet. The inscription reads:
To this place (lit. hither) were brought the bones of Uzziah King of Judah. Do not open!

Stone encased in its original copper setting. On the face is carved the figure of a ram. Above the ram is the name of the owner, Jonathan. This name was borne by a Judean king. Uzziah's son was named Jonathan.

Prophets of Peace

Foreseeing the destruction of Judah, Isaiah wrote prophecies of great comfort and compassion during these dark days. Inspired by visions of hope and longing for the happiness of all humankind, the prophet wrote of the day when all peoples would live together in harmony, serving the one God—the God of peace.

Today, high on a marble wall opposite the United Nations Building in New York City, are engraved the words of Isaiah's ancient prophecy of peace, for all the peoples of the world to read and ponder:

They shall beat their swords into plowshares, and their spears into pruning hooks. Nation shall not lift up sword against nation, neither shall they learn war any more (Isaiah 2:4).

The prophet Isaiah and his younger contemporary Micah shared the same ideals of faith and peace. Their voices were heard throughout Judah, and while the people often seemed indifferent, the inspiring words of these two great prophets left a deep impression.

This Khorsabad painting shows Sargon and an officer before an Assyrian god.

The marble wall opposite the United Nations Building.

Micah the Prophet

Another prophet who spoke in those days was Micah, a young man of humble birth from the small village of Moresheth-Gath in the Judean hills. Micah grieved for Samaria and wept for the sufferings of the people of Israel. He warned the people of Judah not to forsake the Torah. As Amos had done before him. Micah reminded the people that God wanted more of them than sacrificial offerings.

"What does God require of thee," cried Micah, "save to do justice and to love mercy and to walk humbly with thy God!"

This is the opening page to the Book of Isaiah, from a Bible copied in Portugal, in the 15th century.

King Hezekiah Rebels

Hezekiah Rules / ca. 725–697 B.C.E.

Ahaz was succeeded by his son Hezekiah. Heeding Isaiah's warnings, Hezekiah rid Judah of the idols his father had installed and strengthened the nation by upholding its laws and traditions.

Unrest was breaking out among the countries which had been conquered by the Assyrians. Hezekiah joined the general spirit of revolt and refused to pay further tribute to Assyria. Egyptian envoys came to Jerusalem and secret conferences were held. Envoys from the Babylonian king in far-off Mesopotamia also came to seek Hezekiah's aid against the hated Assyrian giant. Egypt and Babylonia had already formed an alliance.

Quietly and efficiently, Hezekiah prepared Judah for revolt. He devised a major engineering project to increase the city's water supply. The waters of the river Gihon were diverted into a reservoir, called the Pool of Siloam, and an underground tunnel was constructed to bring the water into the city.

The Hebrew inscription found in the tunnel of Siloam. "The tunnel (is completed). And this is the story of the boring through: While yet they plied the pick, each toward his fellow, and while yet there were three cubits to be bored through, there was heard the voice of one calling to another, for there was a crevice in the rock on the right hand. And on the day of the boring through, the stone-cutters struck, each to meet his fellow, pick upon pick; and the waters flowed from the source to the pool for a thousand and two hundred cubits, and a hundred cubits was the height of the rock above the heads of the stone-cutters."

Sennacherib Invades Judah / ca. 701 B.C.E.

When Sargon died, the rebellious allies thought the time had come to strike against Assyria. However, Sargon's successor, Sennacherib, learned that rebellion was brewing, and went forth with a large army to crush it. Hezekiah's preparations had been made just in time, for Sennacherib invaded Judah, storming its fortresses and smashing great holes in their walls with his battering rams.

Sennacherib laid siege to Jerusalem. Guided by Hezekiah and the prophet Isaiah, the people of the city bore up bravely, but as the siege wore on, food became so scarce that surrender seemed inevitable.

Then an unexpected ally came to the beleaguered city's rescue. Plague, that dread disease of ancient times, providentially struck

Underground tunnel leading to the pool of Siloam.

the Assyrian camp. Thousands of Assyrian soldiers perished in the epidemic and were buried in hastily-dug mass graves.

The prophet Isaiah mourned for the ravaged land of Judah. Towns and cities were burned or lay in ruin. Yet, even in the midst of the ruins there were prayers of thanksgiving, for the people had survived the Assyrian onslaught.

Assyria Rules

Sennacherib returned to Nineveh, where all his energies were now required to defend his empire. Uprisings had broken out close to his capital, in Mesopotamia itself. Sennacherib finally suffered the same fate as his father. In 681 B.C.E. he was assassinated. He was succeeded by his son Esarhaddon, who had to fight almost continuously to maintain his power. The great Assyrian Empire, seemingly about to crumble, was still a force to be reckoned with.

When Hezekiah died, his son Manasseh submitted completely to Assyrian rule, even reinstating idol worship to appease the foreign overlords.

Manasseh, an Obedient Servant / ca. 696–642 B.C.E.

The aging Isaiah, whose voice had been heard for so many years, now foresaw Judah's destruction and fall, and again warned of the consequences of abandoning the Torah's ancient laws. But the words of the old man went unheeded.

Manasseh was an obedient Assyrian vassal. The country was impoverished by the high taxes he collected for his Assyrian masters. Foreign idols stood in the Temple of God, and corruption reigned among the nobles of Judah, even reaching into the lives of the Levites and priests. After Isaiah

died, and his voice was no longer a comforting and inspiring force, many Judeans turned to the Assyrian idols.

Despite Manasseh's submissiveness, Assyrian officials began to doubt his loyalty. They summoned him to Nineveh to punish him. In exile he suffered great indignities. When he returned to Jerusalem he had changed completely. His deep remorse is shown by a prayer he composed around this time, which is preserved among the postbiblical writings known as the Apocrypha:

You (before) whom all things fear and tremble;
(especially) before your power.
Because your awesome magnificence
cannot be endured;
none can endure or stand before
your anger and your fury against sinners!
But unending and immeasurable
are your promised mercies;
Because you are God,
long-suffering, merciful, and greatly compassionate;
and you feel sorry over the evils of men.

At the end of his long reign, Manasseh was succeeded by his son Amon (642–640 B.C.E.). This unfortunate king was soon assassinated by a group of palace officials. The plotters were quickly captured and executed, and Amon's son Josiah was placed on the throne.

Victory monument of King Esarhaddon. He is leading two captive kings on a leash attached to hooks which pass through their lips.

Decline of Assyria

More and more new threats of revolt plagued the successors of Ashurbanipal. While Assyria was busy keeping its many rebellious vassals in check, the empire was suddenly invaded by the Scythians, a people from the Black Sea region. Wild and fearless riders, they came on horseback, plundering and looting wherever they went. Hordes of Scythian horsemen raced through Assyria's territories, and throughout the entire Fertile Crescent.

Josiah the Reformer / ca. 639–609 B.C.E.

While the Scythian hordes swept through ancient empires, a new king had come to the throne of Judah. Josiah, the son of Amon, was a very different man from his father. Josiah heeded the words of the prophet Zephaniah, who had criticized the corruption that prevailed in Judah in the days of Amon. The new king rid the land of idols and corrupt officials, and returned to the laws of Israel and the worship of one God. Josiah had all the idols destroyed and the Temple thoroughly cleansed.

A Great Discovery

During the process of cleansing the Temple, a great discovery was made. A scroll was found which had lain forgotten and lost for generations. When examined the scroll was found to be the Book of Deuteronomy, the last of the Five Books of Moses. It summarized and explained the Ten Commandments and the laws of Israel. Hilkiah, the high priest, and Huldah, a prophetess, encouraged the king to study this long-lost book and read it aloud to the people of Judah. Standing before a large assembly, Josiah read from the Book of Deuteronomy, as the people, young and old, stood listening in awe to the ancient words.

All over Judah priests assembled the people and read to them from the book. The people became familiar with their history and traditions. Most important of all, the Book of Deuteronomy taught the people the meaning of their laws. Strengthened by this new knowledge, the people of Judah regained faith and dignity.

Such was the state of Judah when Assyria was dealt its final blow. Two prophets, Nahum and Zephaniah, had prophesied that the destruction of Assyria was at hand. Josiah had heard and believed these prophecies. Now they came true. After the death of Ashurbanipal, the Medes and Babylonians attacked Assyria from both the north and the south.

Assyria Falls

Assyria was like a wounded animal. Its massive structure was held together by sheer force. Enemies within and without circled the weakened giant hoping to bring it to its knees and destruction.

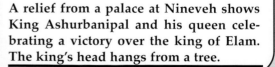
A relief from a palace at Nineveh shows King Ashurbanipal and his queen celebrating a victory over the king of Elam. The king's head hangs from a tree.

55

An Assyrian stele showing King Ashurbanipal carrying upon his head a basket filled with gifts.

A bloody and desperate battle was fought at Nineveh, after which the city finally fell in 612 B.C.E. and was completely destroyed by the victors.

The Battle of Megiddo / ca. 609 B.C.E.

In its final days, Assyria turned for help to Egypt, its old enemy and rival. Egypt's Pharaoh, Necho, prepared to take his army to Mesopotamia to aid the dying giant. He hoped that after he defeated Assyria's enemies he would be rewarded with a share of Assyria's territory. Confident that his armies would be able to pass freely through the lands which lay between him

and the Assyrian forces, the ambitious Egyptian ruler began his march. But Josiah had no intention of allowing Egyptian soldiers to march unmolested through Judah, nor did he wish to see Assyria assisted.

Josiah summoned Judah's small army to halt the Egyptians. Although the Egyptian troops were superior both in numbers and arms, Josiah hoped that the high morale of his own soldiers would bring victory.

Josiah's army met the Egyptians at Megiddo, the gate to the plain of Jezreel and the site of many battles in the past. It was a bloody, desperate battle and Judah suffered a disastrous defeat. Josiah, the courageous king, perished at Megiddo with many of his brave men.

After Judah's defeat, Pharaoh Necho's army joined the Assyrian forces in Mesopotamia to fight for the city of Haran. But here the Medes and Babylonians were victorious, defeating Assyria and its Egyptian ally. Bitterly disappointed, the Pharaoh withdrew from Mesopotamia, and his army retreated through the lands which it had so recently conquered.

The Gladd Chronicle is a Babylonian clay tablet which recounts the battles of the Chaldean ruler Nabopolassar (625-605 B.C.E.) and his victories over Assyria.
The chronicle describes the capture of Nineveh by the Chaldeans and their allies the Medes, "They launched a powerful attack on the city and in the month of Abu the city was captured. They slaughtered the princes . . . They took much booty and turned the temple and the city into a ruin."

The Babylonian Empire

The Medes and the Babylonians divided the Assyrian Empire. The Medes took the territories in the north and the northeast; the Babylonians those in the south and southwest—the lands of the Fertile Crescent.

Judah the Vassal

In Judah, a sad time followed the death of King Josiah. After the defeat at Megiddo, Judah became a vassal of Egypt under Pharaoh Necho, a harsh master who forced it into utter submission. The reign of Josiah's son, Jehoahaz, lasted less than a year. He was taken captive to Egypt and died in exile. In 608 B.C.E., Necho appointed Jehoahaz's brother, Jehoiakim, as king of Judah. Jehoiakim was an obedient vassal. He installed Egyptian gods in Judah, followed Egypt's laws, and paid heavy tribute.

Belonging to Eliakim

Steward of Yaukin

The owner of this seal, Eliakim, was one of the officals of King Jehoiachin. "Yaukin" is one of the many variations of Jehoiakim's name.

Like a bone between two huge ferocious dogs, Judah found itself a small, weak nation with Egypt on one side and the advancing armies of Nebuchadnezzar of Babylon on the other. Fortunately for Judah, Nebuchadnezzar interrupted his victorious march when he received news of

A relief from Carchemish showing two heavily armed soldiers.

his aged father's death, returning to Babylon to receive homage as the new king. Thus little Judah was granted a brief time of peace.

Egypt now sought to undermine the power of Babylonia by encouraging its new vassals to revolt. King Jehoiakim of Judah, encouraged by Egyptian promises of assistance in case of a Babylonian attack, refused to pay tribute to Nebuchadnezzar. The Babylonian king promptly sent an army. but little Judah stood firm under Jehoiachin, who was only 18 years old when he succeeded his father, Jehoiakim.

Judah Invaded

Nebuchadnezzar himself finally took command of his troops, destroyed many cities of Judah, and marched up to the gates of Jerusalem. The promised Egyptian assistance never materialized, and in 597 B.C.E. Nebuchadnezzar took the city by storm, carrying young Jehoiachin and many important families into captivity.

One of a group of cuneiform texts listing the rations for captive kings and their retinues living in the vicinity of Babylon. Among the peoples listed are Philistines, Phoenicians, Judeans, Elamites, Medians, and Persians. These texts are basic for our knowledge of the treatment of captive foreigners by the Babylonians. This text is dated in the 13th year of Nebuchadnezzar II reign (592 B.C.E.). Jehoiachin and his sons are mentioned.

The First Exiles / ca. 597 B.C.E.

Judah's attempt to cast off the Babylonian yoke had only made matters worse. Jehoiachin was now exiled in Babylon along with many of his country's craftsmen, musicians, soldiers, and nobles.

Zedekiah, an uncle of Jehoiachin, another of Josiah's sons, ascended Judah's throne.

Zedekiah faced the same problem that had confronted his predecessors: should he rebel and shake off bondage, or should he allow Judah to remain a Babylonian vassal?

Most of the king's advisors favored rebellion, confident that Babylonia was not interested in further expansion. This confidence was strengthened by news reaching Judah that the captives in Babylon were being well treated. Unlike the Israelite captives in Assyria after the fall of Samaria, the exiles in Babylonia were not dispersed over various vassal lands, nor were they persecuted. Many of them had found useful employment and sent letters and messages home to their friends and relatives reporting how well they were faring. Encouraged by these stories, the members of Judah's war party urged Zedekiah to revolt.

An Assyrian relief showing Jewish prisoners of war playing lyres.

Jeremiah, Advocate of Peace

King Zedekiah / ca. 598–587 B.C.E.

Zedekiah had another advisor who urged him to cease all thought of revolt and devote himself solely to ensuring Judah's peace and welfare. This advisor was the aged prophet Jeremiah. Born in Anathoth, a small village near Jerusalem, Jeremiah was the son of a wealthy family of priests and had been given a good education. Before he received the call to prophecy he had lived a studious and quiet life. But the call to prophecy proved stronger than his misgivings, and Jeremiah, still a very young man, went forth to Jerusalem to declare the word of God.

Jeremiah had gone to the Temple of Jerusalem and prophesied that the House of God would be destroyed if the people did not willingly bear the Babylonian yoke. The people had been shocked by what seemed to them disloyalty, and Jeremiah became very unpopular. He was finally arrested and thrown into prison. After his release the prophet retired to his native town, Anathoth, with his loyal disciple Baruch.

Jeremiah in Disgrace

Baruch journeyed to Jerusalem to bring the words of the prophet to the king's attention. Jehoiakim refused to listen and scornfully burned the scrolls containing Jeremiah's message.

For ten years Judah had been wavering between revolt against Babylonia and peaceful acceptance of vassaldom. Zedekiah and his allies were about to decide in favor of revolt. Again the courageous Jeremiah raised his voice against this plan.

The people listened to the aged prophet when he appeared among them. He

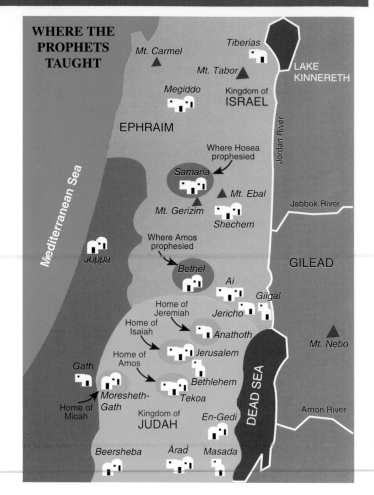

WHERE THE PROPHETS TAUGHT

warned that Judah was far too small and weak to challenge the mighty Babylonian empire. He begged them to preserve what freedom remained and comforted them by predicting that someday the captives would return from Babylon and Judah would be rebuilt.

Meanwhile, Egypt continued to support all efforts at revolt against Babylonia and sought allies for a last stand against the new empire.

When Judah's neighbors approached Zedekiah to form an alliance against Babylonia, he veered back to the side of the war party and began preparing his country for a long siege. Fortifications were strengthened, food and arms were stored, and all able-bodied men were trained for defense.

Jeremiah in Prison

In despair over these preparations for another war, the prophet Jeremiah renewed his warnings. He was denounced and again cast into prison.

An alliance was formed between Judah, Edom, Moab, Ammon, and the Phoenician cities of Tyre and Sidon. Pharaoh Apries of Egypt assured the allies of his support.

In the ninth year of his reign, after a long period of indecision, Zedekiah, the last king of Judah, revolted against Nebuchadnezzar of Babylon. The year was 586 B.C.E.

Judah Is Invaded Again

Nebuchadnezzar dealt swiftly with the rebellion. His army of charioteers, infantry, and cavalry far outnumbered the combined forces of the allies.

The Babylonian tidal wave rolled on to Jerusalem, the last fortified city of Judah. No help came from Judah's allies, for they were busy defending their own cities. The siege of Jerusalem began on the 10th day of Tevet in the year 586 B.C.E. It was briefly interrupted while Nebuchadnezzar marched off to do battle with the Egyptian army. When the Egyptians evaded him by retreating to their newly-won Phoenician ports, the Babylonians marched back to Judah and laid siege to Jerusalem once again.

Jerusalem Falls / ca. 586 B.C.E.

The people of Jerusalem valiantly defended their city against the battering rams, spears, and firebrands of the enemy. For 18 long months the walls around the city withstood the attack, but on the 10th day of Tammuz, the Babylonians managed to break through. After three more weeks of fighting, the Babylonians won a total victory. They destroyed the Temple and set fire to the rest of the city. The fateful day on which this tragic event occurred was the 9th of Av.

Zedekiah Captured / ca. 586 B.C.E.

On the 9th day of Av, Nebuchadnezzar entered Jerusalem in the morning, while his soldiers continued the destruction and plundering. Zedekiah was taken captive. He was forced to witness the death of his children. Then he was blinded and put in chains. Nearly all of the people of Judah were deported to Babylonia. By the end of the year the land of Judah was desolate. Its farms and vineyards lay barren. Its towns were in ruins.

With the fall of the kingdom of Judah, 400 years of rule by the House of David came to an end. Many more Judeans were deported to Babylonia in punishment of this violent act of rebellion.

Tisha Be-Av

The holiday of Tisha Be-Av is the saddest day of the Jewish year. On this day many Jewish tragedies took place. On the 9th of Av in 586 B.C.E., Solomon's Temple was destroyed; six centuries later in 70 C.E., on the same day, the Second Temple was destroyed; and in 1492 C.E., again on the same day, the Jews were driven out of Spain.

This miniature from a 14th century French Bible shows the blinded king Zedekiah being led into captivity. Zedekiah's desperate rebellion against Nebuchadnezzar led to the Babylonian invasion of Judah in 587 B.C.E.

Judah Falls / *ca. 586 B.C.E.*

Life In Babylonia

It is not difficult to imagine the homesickness and the bitter sorrow which must have filled the hearts of the exiles as they walked by the rivers of Babylon. The fame of Judah's musicians and singers had spread far and wide, and the Babylonians often asked the captives to sing them the songs of Zion. From the depths of their despair the exiles sang new songs, rising from glorious memories of desperate struggles of the past and the stark tragedy of the present:

> *If I forget thee, O Jerusalem,*
> *Let my right hand forget her cunning*
> *Let my tongue cleave to the roof of my mouth*
> *If I remember thee not: If I set not Jerusalem*
> *Above my chiefest joy. (Psalm 137)*

Babylonia's most beautiful city was its capital, Babylon. Babylon was graced with paved streets, gardens, temples, and palaces. Even the city gates were adorned with multi-colored, glazed bricks. This is a reconstruction of the Ishtar Gate in Babylon. The designs of lions, bulls, and dragons are made of baked bricks, covered with glazes of blue, gold, and white.

This painting from a German manuscript of 1344 decorates *Eycha*, the first Hebrew word in the Book of Lamentations. It shows a Jew, wearing a tallit, preparing to read the text.

The Book of Lamentations was written in response to the destruction of the First Temple. On Tisha Be-Av, it is read in the synagogue to a sad chant.

The exiles built a new life in Babylonia. Some continued to be farmers, others went to work on the irrigation and canal-digging projects which turned dry stretches of clay into fertile land. Most of the exiles, however, settled in the great cities of Babylonia, such as Babylon and Tel Abib.

From the many Babylonian records unearthed by archaeologists, we know that life in the Babylonian cities was on a high level of civilization. Among the records were found the books of a Jewish firm of merchants, Murashu and Sons, of the city of Nippur. These books were preserved in large clay jars much like those which held the Dead Sea Scrolls, written 600 years later. Judging from the records, Murashu and Sons was apparently known throughout Babylonia.

Jewish Observances in Babylonia

In the midst of Babylonia's strange and foreign ways, the Jewish exiles held fast to their own traditions. They kept to themselves in their own communities, observing the Sabbath, the holidays, and the religious laws. Each community conducted services in its own house of prayer. Precious Torah scrolls had been rescued from the destroyed cities of Judah, and from these the priests read portions from the ancient laws and history. Levites sang the old melodies, the psalms. Prophets spoke of God and gave renewed courage to the people. Thus did the exiles keep alive their faith and their traditions.

While the rulers and nobles of Babylon complacently admired their jewels and held feasts to honor their gods, the spirited young nation of Persia was on the march to the west, in the mountains of Iran. The Persians had been vassals of the Medes, but under the leadership of their young king, Cyrus, they gained their independence. Cyrus, the son of a Persian prince and a Median princess, was a brilliant and ambitious general.

The Handwriting on the Wall
As the rumble of Persian conquest grew louder, the rulers of the uneasy nations

formed an alliance against Cyrus. He marched on to challenge the armies of Belshazzar, crown prince of Babylonia. The Bible records that during a feast, Belshazzar summoned Daniel, a Jewish seer, to interpret strange signs which had appeared on the wall of his palace. His most learned advisors had been unable to decipher this "handwriting on the wall," but Daniel explained that it foretold the conquest of Babylonia and the death of Belshazzar. And indeed, soon after Daniel's dire predictions, Belshazzar was murdered.

The writing on a 5th century clay tablet from the city of Nippur. It is a rental agreement from the archives of the Jewish banking and commercial family Murashu. The language is primarily Babylonian with an Aramaic summary.

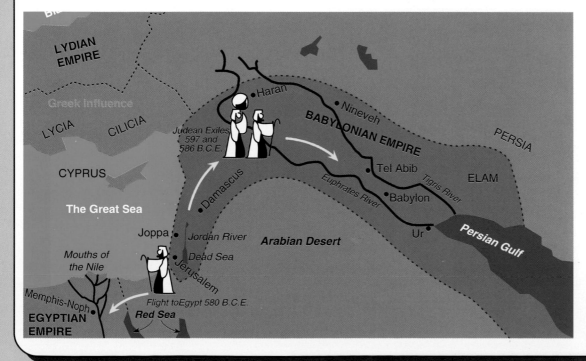

The route of the exiles to Babylon, following the destruction of the Temple in Jerusalem.

Cyrus, King of Persia

Cyrus the Conqueror / ca. 539 B.C.E.
Babylon's army was routed by the disciplined, well-organized Persian troops. The Babylonians fearfully awaited the plundering and devastation which they believed would inevitably follow. Cyrus, however, was unlike the conquerors of old. He entered the Babylonian capital with a minimum of harm to life and property. The entire ancient world marveled at the peaceful way in which this new lord took over the mighty Babylonian Empire.

Cyrus proved to be an efficient administrator and a monarch of great tolerance. He granted religious freedom to all, believing that a nation flourished best under such conditions. Many of the peoples of Babylonia regarded Cyrus as their liberator. Under his rule, Persia became a great nation.

The armies of Babylon were defeated by the Persians. The Persians were good to the Jews. They allowed Ezra and many Jews to return to Judea. Persian soldiers escorted the Jews. These are Persian soldiers. They are armed with spears and bows.

The Persian conquest of Babylonia in 539 B.C.E. was a great boon for the Jewish exiles. Cyrus was sympathetic to them and soon issued a decree permitting them to return to Jerusalem and restore their Temple. Great was the rejoicing in the Jewish communities. Scores of exiles prepared to make the long-dreamed-of journey back to their homeland.

From the biblical Book of Ezra we learn that about 42,000 Jews from all over Babylonia joined in the exodus to Judah. Their long, difficult journey took them through the lands of the Fertile Crescent, retracing Abraham's trek of ancient days.

Inscribed cylinder recording the capture of Babylon by Cyrus. It tells how "without battle and without fighting Marduk (the god of Babylon) made him (Cyrus) enter into his city of Babylon; he spared Babylon tribulation, and Nabonidus the (Chaldean) king, who feared him not, he delivered into his hand." Nabonidus, the Chaldean king of Babylon, was not in favor with the priests, and they assisted in delivering the city to Cyrus.

The Exiles

The Second Commonwealth / ca. 520 B.C.E.

The land of Judah lay barren. Fields and vineyards were deserted; villages and towns were in ruins. Jerusalem was a city of desolation. The magnificent Temple of Solomon had been destroyed, and grass was growing on its site.

The pioneers from Babylonia wasted no time lamenting the past. All their energy was needed now for rebuilding. Amid the ruins of the Temple they erected an altar for the worship of God. They plowed the barren fields and tended the cattle they had brought with them. They were joyfully assisted in their labors by the few Jews who had escaped deportation and had remained in Judah, living in great poverty in the hills, where they had fled for safety.

The head of the community was Zerubbabel, a prince of the House of David. Zerubbabel had led the returning pioneers back to their land and was appointed governor by Cyrus. The priest Joshua, son of an ancient priestly family, assisted Zerubbabel. The Second Commonwealth, founded by the returning Babylonian exiles, was called Judea.

When Assyria conquered the northern kingdom of Israel and deported most of its people, a small number of Jews had managed to remain there. They had intermarried with the non-Jewish newcomers whom the Assyrians had settled in the territory around Samaria. Their descendants were called Samaritans. The Samaritans considered themselves Israelites, but followed some of the customs of their non-Jewish ancestors. When they learned of the exiles' return, they wanted to be part of the new commonwealth and offered to help rebuild the Temple.

The tomb of Cyrus, who allowed the Jews to return to Jerusalem.

The newly returned pioneers feared that the Samaritans might introduce idolatrous ways and even bring idols into the new Temple.

THE RESTORATION

Cyrus was a liberal ruler and allowed the worship of the God of Israel in Jerusalem.

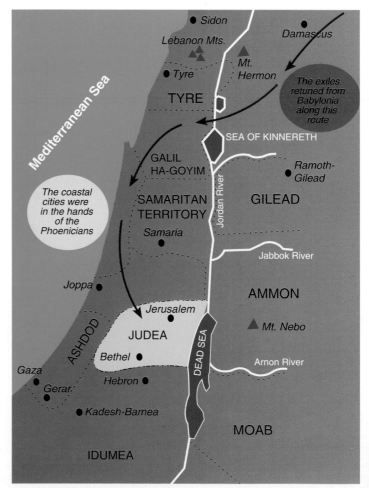

The Samaritans

The Samaritans Accuse the Jews

The Samaritans were bitterly offended by the Jews' refusal of their assistance. They subsequently built a temple of their own on Mount Gerizim and worshipped in their own territory. Thenceforth the two peoples were enemies.

The Samaritans sought to hinder the Jews from rebuilding the Temple in Jerusalem. They wrote to the government in Persia, false claiming that the Jews were planning to revolt and persuading King Cambyses II, the son of Cyrus, to put a stop to the reconstruction.

In their despair the Judeans turned to their prophets. The prophets bade them be of good faith, foretelling that the building of the Temple would be resumed soon—even in their own day. For several years no further work was done on the Temple, for the Jews dared not defy the order of the Persian king. During these years the prophets Haggai and Zechariah

were a source of great help and strength to the community.

Darius Encourages the Jews

When Darius (522–486 B.C.E.) succeeded to the throne, the Jews sent letters of petition

Mosaic in an ancient Samaritan synagogue, showing the Greek influence.

to the new king. Darius considered their case. Upon reading the original decree issued by Cyrus, he declared the Jews innocent of the charge brought against them and sent messengers to encourage the building of the Temple.

Unfortunately, the Samaritans were not the only enemies of the Jews. Edomites,

The Torah of the Samaritans is housed in the synagogue in Nablus. It is written in ancient Hebrew and is extremely old.

Page from Samaritan Bible. Damascus, 1485.

King Darius of Persia (521–486 B.C.E.), seated on the throne; his son Xerxes stands behind in attendance.

Moabites, and Ammonites attacked the poorly-armed settlers. Raiding parties seized their meager harvests and attacked their homes.

Despite these harassments the Jews toiled on. They worked night and day, living in poor huts and sparing time from the building only to provide the barest necessities of food and clothing for themselves.

In comparison to the magnificent Temple of Solomon, the new Temple was unimposing indeed. However, the Levites sang the same sacred old melodies and the priests offered the same prayers and sacrifices as they had in the First Temple. Again, the people came and assembled in the courts to worship.

The task of reconstructing the Temple completed, the people could now turn to the rebuilding of the land.

Cylinder seal with the name of Darius in three languages, Persian, Assyrian, and Scythian.

A gold coin (daric) named after Darius I. Darics continued to be minted under Alexander and his successors. This coin is dated to the 4th century B.C.E.

Rebuilding the Temple / ca. 458–445 B.C.E.

Ezra the Scribe

Among the Jews in Babylonia who were distressed by the news of Judea's troubled state was Ezra, a learned Jew of priestly descent. Ezra was a dedicated teacher and had many disciples whom he instructed in the Torah. Because he was highly skilled in the art of writing Torah scrolls, he is often referred to as Ezra the Scribe (Ezra Hasofer).

When Ezra applied to King Artaxerxes I for permission to go to Jerusalem with his disciples, his request was granted. The king and the Jewish community of Babylonia generously gave Ezra many gifts for the Temple and also the supplies he needed for the long journey.

Approximately 1,500 Jews, eager to return to their homeland, accompanied Ezra to Judea. They arrived in Jerusalem in the summer of 458 B.C.E. and were warmly welcomed by the people of Judea, who

Hebrew coin dating back to the 4th century B.C.E, the period of Ezra the Scribe. The coin is inscribed *YHD* (in ancient Hebrew script), which stands for Yehud, the Persian name of Judea.

had gone forth to meet the new group of pioneers.

Ezra began his task without delay. He traveled through the land visiting and teaching, but was saddened and disturbed to find among most of the people a lack of knowledge of the Torah.

Patiently, he reasoned with them, reminding them of their great struggle to regain their homeland and their high purpose in doing so. A great many were deeply impressed by Ezra's words and promised to give up the heathen ways which were undermining their character.

Nehemiah, Governor of Judea / ca. 445 B.C.E.
The next major task was to fortify Jerusalem against the hostile bands of raiders by rebuilding the city's walls. Building fortifications, however, would make the Persians suspicious and open the Judeans to the charge of planning a revolt.

In this relief from a palace in Persepolis Phoenicians are presenting tribute to a Persian king.

Help came in 445 B.C.E. when Nehemiah, a Babylonian Jew, was appointed governor of Judea. Nehemiah had been the trusted cupbearer of King Artaxerxes I in Shushan (Susa), the Persian capital.

The two great leaders, Ezra and Nehemiah, combined their efforts to restore the commonwealth of Judea. Ezra was Judea's spiritual guide; Nehemiah, the governor, was its political leader. Inspired by Nehemiah, the people set about rebuilding the walls of Jerusalem with great enthusiasm.

"Come," they said, "let us go and rebuild the walls of Jerusalem. Let us end our shame. We shall work in the daytime and stand watch during the night."

The walls and fortifications were completed in just 52 days. The men of Judea defended the walls fiercely, and the raiders soon began to think twice before they attacked.

The tomb of Darius I at Naqsh-i-Roustem, Persia.

The Commonwealth of Judea

Nehemiah was well versed in Jewish law, and with the help of Ezra he laid the foundations of the new Jewish commonwealth. The Torah was its constitution, the fundamental law of Judea. Ezra and his disciples, traveling among the people, instructed them in Torah and saw to it that they lived by their own laws and not by those of their heathen neighbors or of Persia.

The new commonwealth of Judea began to thrive. Farmers and shepherds harvested in peace and took their oil and wool, their fruits and grain to the market in Jerusalem. Traders came again from the neighboring countries to sell their wares in the city.

The Festival of Sukkot

Ezra and Nehemiah together brought about the political reconstruction and spiritual rejuvenation of Judea. On the day before the festival of Sukkot in the year 445 B.C.E., numerous Judeans made their way to Jerusalem. They assembled in the ancient City of David and built their tabernacles. The people gathered to hear the proclamations of their two great leaders. Nehemiah and the priests and Levites of the Temple stood before the assembled Judeans while Ezra read to them from the Torah.

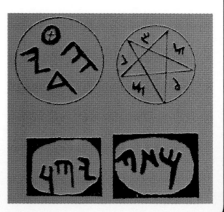

Official seals of the province of Judah during the 5th-4th centuries B.C.E.

The Spiritual Revival

Ezra and his disciples continued their travels through the land. They carried Torah scrolls with them and taught not only the judges in the courts but everyone who wanted to learn. During this time a new way of writing Hebrew was adopted. The ancient Hebrew script was replaced by one very much like the Hebrew script we use today.

Ever since the time of Moses and Joshua, a body of unwritten interpretations of the Torah, known as the Oral Tradition, had been handed down by the elders, prophets, and scribes. The Oral Tradition was revived by Ezra and his disciples. After the time of Ezra, it continued to be passed down from generation to generation by word of mouth. Over the years, many new interpretations were added, since each generation applied the Torah to its own times and its own problems. This process culminated many centuries later when the Oral Tradition was put into writing in the Mishnah, Talmud, and Midrash.

The Synagogue

The work of Ezra and Nehemiah was followed by an era of peace for Judea. Towns and villages were rebuilt; land was tilled and cultivated. Many towns built their own small marketplaces and houses of prayer. The latter, which grew into the institution that we now refer to as the synagogue, were the centers of communal life. In them the priests and scribes taught the Torah and led the people in observing the festivals. Here the people met to celebrate Sabbaths and holidays, to conduct meetings and discuss community problems. Here judges held court and marriages were celebrated.

In the course of centuries, especially after the destruction of the Second Temple, the synagogue became the heart of every Jewish community. It was a place where strangers could seek shelter, where the poor received alms, and where those with problems or disputes could come for counsel.

Modern Hebrew	Old Hebrew	Phoenician	Early Greek	Later Greek	Latin	English
א					A	A
ב					B	B
ג					C G	C G
ד					D	D
ה					E	E
ו					F V	F V U
ז					...	Z
ח					H	E H
ט					...	TH PH
י					I	I
כ					...	K KH
ל					L	L
מ					M	M
נ					N	N
ס					X	X
ע					O	O
פ					P	P
צ					...	S
ק					Q	Q
ר					R	R
ש					S	S
ת					T	T

Table showing how the Hebrew and Phoenician letters passed through Greek and Latin forms to their present English forms.

The Targum

Throughout the Near East, and especially in Babylonia and Syria, Aramaic was the dominant language. After the return from the Babylonian exile, it also became the everyday spoken language of Judea. Since the Torah was written in Hebrew, it was necessary to provide a translation for the many people who were no longer able to understand it.

Ezra solved the problem by providing a translator who stood right next to the Torah reader during services and translated the Hebrew into Aramaic for the congregants. Eventually the oral translations provided in this manner were set down in writing. The Aramaic translation of the Torah is called the Targum. Note the close similarly between the name Targum and the word *meturgeman* (translator).

The Talmud mentions that in some synagogues the Torah was read twice, once in Hebrew and once in Aramaic.

There are three major Aramaic translations of the Torah: Targum Onkelos, Targum Jonathan, and the Palestinian Targum (Targum Yerushalmi).

Page from a Hebrew Bible with commentaries. The narrow column at the upper left is the Aramaic translation by Onkelos, the most widely-used Targum. It is still printed side by side with the original Hebrew text in modern editions of the Torah. Some Jews recite it with the regular weekly portion. Onkelos was a convert to Judaism.

A page from the Palestinian Targum of the Torah. This translation may have originated in the Second Temple period. It was lost, until a copy was discovered in the Vatican Library. This page contains Genesis 4:14-5:1.

The Story of Purim / ca. 486–465 B.C.E.

Persia was a generous ruler. Although Judea was a province of the Persian Empire, it was allowed to govern itself. During this period, the Jews of Babylonia also fared well under Persian control.

A dramatic glimpse of Jewish life under Persian rule is provided by the biblical story of Esther, which took place in Shushan (Susa), the capital of Persia, in 486–485 B.C.E. The king in the story is named Ahasuerus, probably a form of Xerxes. According to the Bible, his kingdom extended from Ethiopia to India and he ruled over 127 provinces.

Mordecai Defies Haman

Ahasuerus asked his wife, Vashti, to dance for the drunken guests at a palace party. When she refused, he decided to punish her disobedience by finding a new queen. A beauty contest was held to choose a successor; the winner was a Jewish girl named Esther. Her uncle Mordecai was an employee of the king.

The names Mordecai and Esther are similar to the Persian names Marduk and Ishtar. The fact that the Jews of Persia had Persian names, just as Jews in America today have English names, shows that they

This gold cup with a lion base is from the 5th and 6th century. Such cups were in use during the reign of Xerxes.

A fresco found at the 3rd century Dura Europos synagogue shows Ahasuerus and Esther. The king is being given a letter by one of his attendants. Esther, the queen, is seated on the throne to the king's left. Esther's head is covered with a tall crown

The palaces of the Persian kings were very large and ornate. Archaeologists at Persepolis have uncovered several stone palaces dating from the time of Darius and Xerxes. This is the Hall of Pillars with its 72 giant pillars. It is calculated that it was large enough to accommodate 10,000 celebrants.

were fully assimilated into the nonreligious aspects of the dominant culture.

Sometime after this, Mordecai refused to bow down to Haman, the king's grand vizier. Haman was very angry; he went to Ahasuerus and accused the Jews of plotting against the government.

He said, "Their laws are different, and they do not obey the king's rulings. If it pleases the king, let them be destroyed." Just as the Nazis tried to destroy all the Jews in Europe, Haman wanted to wipe out all the Jews in the Persian Empire. Ahasuerus agreed to his proposal.

Esther Saves the Jews

When Mordecai found out about the impending pogrom against the Jews of Persia, he urged Esther to save her people. Bravely violating a law that prohibited anyone from approaching the king without an invitation, Esther went to Ahasuerus. She revealed that she was Jewish and that Haman's bloodthirsty plot would destroy her people. The king ordered Haman hanged on the very gallows he had built for Mordecai. He appointed Mordecai one of his advisors and as a token of trust gave him Haman's signet ring. The Jews of Persia were given permission to defend themselves against their enemies. The holiday of Purim was instituted to commemorate this series of events.

The Holiday of Purim

Jews all over the world celebrate Purim by reading the story of brave Queen Esther in the Megillah. They exchange *shalah manot* gifts and sing and dance and conduct masquerades.

The name Purim comes from the Hebrew word *pur,* meaning "lot." Haman set the day for the pogrom against the Jews by casting lots (*purim*). Purim, the Feast of Lots, is celebrated on the 14th day of the Hebrew month of Adar.

Persia Falls

Far to the west of Shushan, a great civilization, with its center in Athens, was growing up in Greece. Perhaps inevitably, the Greeks and the Persians came into conflict. In the 5th century B.C.E. Persia invaded Greece.

Although the Persians were defeated at Marathon and Salamis, their resources were so huge that they continued the struggle even after their armies withdrew, using their vast wealth to bribe Greek traitors and finance wars among the Greek city-states.

An 18th century, artistically illustrated Scroll of Esther (Megillah) from Alsace, France.

Timeline—The Age of the Tanak

JEWISH HIGHLIGHTS

Patriarchs and Matriarchs 2000–1700 B.C.E.	Israelites in Egypt 1720–1280 B.C.E.	Exodus from Egypt 1280 B.C.E.	The Desert 1280–1240 B.C.E.	Promised Land 1240–1080 B.C.E.	King Saul 1020–1004 B.C.E.	King David 1004–965 B.C.E.

JEWISH • EVENTS PERSONALITIES • LITERATURE • HOLIDAYS

One God	Joseph	Moses Aaron Miriam	Shavuot Sukkot Ark of the Covenant Tabernacle	Joshua Judges Twelve tribes	Samuel the Priest	Jerusalem capital
Ivrim–Hebrews	Moses	Sea of Reeds	Ten Commandments	Deborah	Saul unites tribes	Ark to Jerusalem
Promised Land Canaan	Children of Israel	Passover	Torah	Gideon	Jonathan	Psalms of David
			Mount Sinai	Samson	David	Bathsheba
				Samuel		

WORLD HISTORY

Hittites	Hyksos	Merneptah	Babylon	Canaanites	Aram	Philistines
Hammurabi	Rameses II			Medianites	Damascus	
Babylon	Assyria			Philistines		

*All dates are approximate

Timeline—The Age of the Tanak

JEWISH HIGHLIGHTS

| King Solomon 965–926 B.C.E. | Division of Israel and Judah 928 B.C.E. | House of Omri 871–845 B.C.E. | Fall of Israel 721 B.C.E. | Fall of Judea 586 B.C.E. | Ezra and Nehemiah 460–515 B.C.E. | Queen Esther 486–465 B.C.E. |

JEWISH EVENTS • PERSONALITIES • LITERATURE • HOLIDAYS

▷ SOLOMON builds First Temple	▷ Rehoboam Jeroboam	▷ Ahab	▷ Hosea	▷ ISAIAH	▷ Temple rebuilt	▷ Purim
▷ Queen of Sheba	▷ Egypt attacks Israel	▷ Jezebel	▷ Amos	▷ Micah	▷ Hebrew language	▷ Mordecai
		▷ Athaliah	▷ Ten lost tribes	▷ Jeremiah	▷ Jewish Commonwealth	▷ Haman
		▷ Elijah		▷ King Zedekiah	▷ First synagogues	▷ Ahasuerus
		▷ Elisha		▷ Tisha Be-Av	▷ Bible completed	
					▷ Samaritans	

WORLD HISTORY

▶ Hiram of Tyre	▶ Assyria	▶ Assyria	▶ Assyria	▶ Egypt	▶ Cyrus	▶ Persia
	▶ Egypt	▶ Aram	▶ Sargon	▶ Medes	▶ Artaxerxes	▶ Xerxes
	Shishak	▶ Phoenicia	▶ Tiglath Pileser III	▶ Assyria	▶ Samaritans	▶ Darius
			▶ Shalmaneser V	▶ Babylon	▶ Persia	
				▶ Esarhaddon		
				▶ Nebuchadnezzar		
				▶ Sennacherib		

Alexander the Great / ca. 336–323 BCE

The Macedonians

A new threat loomed in Macedonia, the rugged country to the north of Greece. Under King Philip, the Macedonians conquered Greece. Philip's son, known to history as Alexander the Great (356–323 B.C.E.), set out to conquer the sprawling and unbelievably wealthy Persian Empire.

A mosaic showing a likeness of Alexander the Great.

Alexander was a brilliant general. In the next few years he conquered all the Persian lands---a vast territory that included the modern countries of Turkey, Syria, Israel, Egypt, Iraq, and Iran---and pushed on into Arabia, Afghanistan, and Pakistan. When his troops marched into Judea in 332 B.C.E., Alexander was kind to its people, for he knew that the Jews had a remarkable civilization of their own, and he loved and respected culture and scholarship.

Alexander founded many cities in the territories he conquered. The most famous of these was Alexandria in Egypt. Built on the Nile delta, Alexandria became a great trading port and center of Greek culture. People from Judea were invited to settle there, and from then on Jews always constituted a substantial part of its population.

The Empire Is Divided

Alexander's huge empire was destined to be short-lived, for the young ruler died of a fever in 323 B.C.E., when he was only 33 years old. His three most powerful generals conspired against his heirs and brutally murdered them. One of the generals, Antigonus, took over Macedonia and Greece. Another, Seleucus, took Babylon, Persia, Syria, and the adjoining territories. The third, Ptolemy, ruled over Egypt.

The Jews of Alexandria

Judea was part of Ptolemy's kingdom and remained under Egyptian rule for a century. A flourishing Jewish community developed in Alexandria, the most important city of the Ptolemaic kingdom. Jewish settlers had helped to build the city, and Alexander had granted them the same rights and privileges as its Greek citizens. Jews flocked to Alexandria from other parts of Egypt and from the rugged Judean hills. In this city on the Mediterranean coast, they found not only new opportunities but a new way of life.

Alexander the Great being greeted by the high priest Jaddua. From a 14th century French picture.

Under the rule of the Ptolemies, Alexandria became one of the most important cities of the ancient world. Although the Jews of Alexandria practiced their own religion and conducted their own communal life in their synagogues, they were attracted to the ways of the Greeks. They adopted the Greek language, and many took part in Greek sports and debates. For centuries the Jews of Alexandria had to wrestle with one of the gravest problems facing Jews of their era: Greek civilization versus the Jewish way of life.

A reconstruction of the famous lighthouse in the harbor of Alexandria.

The Ptolemies were kind to the Jews, and for more than 100 years Judea was at peace under the protection of Egypt. The Ptolemies did not demand unreasonable taxes and seldom interfered with the Judean government.

Mosaic found at Pompei records the battle of Issus between the Macedonians and the Persians. Alexander the Great, bareheaded (at left), charges the bodyguard surrounding the Persian king, Darius III.

The Septuagint / ca. 285–246 B.C.E.

The Bible in Greek / ca. 285–246 B.C.E.

Under Ptolemy II Philadelphus, the Bible was translated into Greek. This came about, we are told, because the library at Alexandria had a copy of every book in the world except the Bible. Wanting its collection to be complete, Ptolemy sent to Jerusalem for a Bible and asked the high priest for permission to have it translated. He invited 72 Jewish sages to Alexandria and set each of them to work by himself. The 72 sages had no contact with one another, but when they finished, all 72 translations were identical. We do not know whether this story is fact or legend, but whatever may be the case, the first Greek translation of the Bible came to be known as the Septuagint, meaning the translation "by the seventy."

The Septuagint created a great stir. By that time Greek had become the most widely used language in the ancient world.

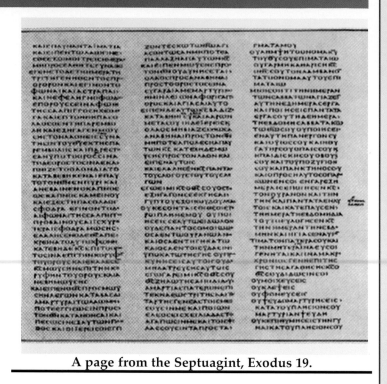

A page from the Septuagint, Exodus 19.

The Septuagint translation also enabled non-Jews to read the Bible. Before long the entire ancient world became acquainted with the history and ideas of the people of the little land of Judea. Many non-Jews, known as "God-fearers," began attending synagogues or adopting Jewish customs.

Bust of Ptolemy IV (285–246 B.C.E.)

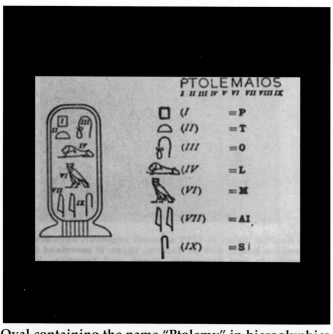

Oval containing the name "Ptolemy" in hieroglyphics.

Many Jews in Egypt and other countries no longer knew Hebrew. Their knowledge of Judaism had suffered as a result, but now they were able to read the Holy Scriptures and study the laws of the Torah.

Torah Prophetic History—Tanak

In Judea itself, the people continued to live peacefully, abiding by the laws of the Torah as explained by the high priest and by the members of the Great Assembly. The Torah was not a secret book to be read only by scholars. It was the law and the way of life for the entire nation. Almost all Jews could read and write, and beginning in the time of Ezra, the Torah was studied in depth by people of every background—farmers and shepherds, merchants and artisans. The scribes, teachers, and scholars who made up the Great Assembly were not a tiny elite, but represented the entire populace.

When necessary, the Great Assembly interpreted the laws of the Torah to fit new conditions and situations. This body, known also as the Great Synagogue and as the Sanhedrin, was at one and the same time a legislature, a court, and a national council. In addition, it served as a training ground for the leaders who went out to teach in the synagogues of Judea's towns and villages.

The Bible Is Compiled / ca. 200 B.C.E.

The scribes collected and carefully examined all the holy writings. These were put together in the great collection of sacred literature that eventually came to be known as the Hebrew Bible. Among the writings they included were the Five Books of Moses, or Torah; the books of the prophets; historical works like the books of Samuel, Kings, Chronicles, Ezra, Nehemiah, Esther, and Ruth; and philosophical and poetic works like Psalms, Lamentations, Ecclesiastes, Job, and Proverbs.

The Bible was the repository of the Jewish historical and religious experience, the highpoint of ancient Hebrew literary

Note: except for TORAH books with the same color are counted as one unit.

THE TANAK (BIBLE)

The complete Hebrew Bible is called TaNaK. It is divided into three divisions; Torah (Five Books of Moses), Neviim (Prophets), and Ketuvim (Writings).

The name Tanak comes from the first letters of each of the three divisions. T is for Torah, N is for Neviim and K is for Ketuvim.

There are a total of 24 separate books in the Tanak. The Torah consists of 5 books, the Prophets 8 books, and the Writings 11 books.

The chapter divisions and the numbering of the verses were introduced into the Tanak to make quoting from it much easier.

The language of the Tanak is Hebrew except for portions of the books of Daniel and Ezra, which are in Aramaic.

achievement, and the foundation of Judaism. In addition to the writings gathered in the Bible, many other books were written in Hebrew throughout this period. Some of them were lost with the passage of time. Others were preserved in later collections such as the Apocrypha.

78

The Seleucids Rule Israel / ca. 198 B.C.E.

The Seleucid kings of Syria sought to win Palestine from the Ptolemies of Egypt. After many battles the Syrian king Antiochus III defeated Ptolemy V of Egypt in 198 B.C.E. Antiochus III reduced taxes and guaranteed that Jewish religious law would be respected. When his son, Antiochus IV, ascended the throne in 175 B.C.E., conditions worsened, for he doubled the tax burden on Judea and abused the Jewish religion.

A bust of Antiochus III (223–187 B.C.E.)

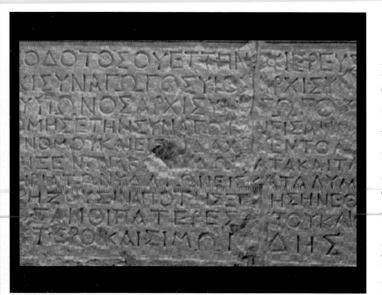
A Greek inscription from a Jerusalem synagogue, in the time of Herod. The inscription reads: "Theodotus, priest and leader of the synagogue, built it to recite the Torah and study the commandments . . . and the water system for the comfort (of strangers)."

Hellenism and Judaism
Gradually, the people of Judea divided into two factions. Those who adopted the Greek way of life and Greek religious practices were called Hellenists. The majority who continued to adhere to the laws of the Torah were called Hasidim ("pious ones"). Whereas the Hellenists were willing to abandon Judaism in order to be accepted by their pagan rulers, the Hasidim adhered to the traditional Jewish ideal of living as servants of the one invisible God—acting justly, showing mercy, and obeying the commandments of the Torah.

The Seleucid kings were Greeks, and like the Ptolemies of Egypt, they promoted and spread Greek culture. Antiochus took steps to induce the Jews to adopt Greek customs. All the important government posts went to those who complied. Before long, Greek ideas and the Greek way of life had become very fashionable among many of Judea's wealthy nobles and merchants.

Bronze bust of Seleucus I which was found near Pompeii, Italy.

Judaism Threatened

The Greek way of life opened the doors to a new world for the affluent pleasure-seekers who adopted it. Many Judeans were willing to cast aside their ancient traditions and lose themselves in the new life. The conflict between the Hellenists, who advocated assimilation to Greek paganism, and the Hasidim, who upheld the ways of Judaism, was a bitter one.

Judaism was threatened abroad as well as at home. Because Judea was a small country that could not support a large population, many of its people had left their homeland and settled in other countries. Known collectively as the Jews of the Diaspora (Dispersion), they were exposed to strong Greek cultural influences in the cities where they lived. In Alexandria and other places, many of them adopted Greek as their primary language. Knowledge of Hebrew began to die out. Although the majority remained committed to Judaism, they were unable to study the Torah, a serious problem that was finally solved by the Septuagint translation of the Bible.

The Hasidim

The Hasidim believed that Greek paganism and social practices would lead to immorality. Greek idol worship, love of conflict, and tolerance of drunkenness would weaken the Jewish way of life. At times there were violent confrontations between Hasidim and Hellenists.

The most extreme Hellenists urged their fellow Jews to use the Greek language and worship Greek gods.

A Greek relief of naked wrestlers at a gymnasium. The gymnasiun was a sport stadium where games and concerts were held. Before an exhibition there was a special opening ceremony in which the athletes paraded naked and then offered sacrifices to the pagan gods.
To the Greeks, it was a way of life. To the Jews, it was a road to idol worship and assimilation.

The Reign of Antiochus IV / ca. 175–163 B.C.E.

The situation came to a head during the reign of Antiochus IV. He hoped to build his kingdom into a great power, but his dreams were threatened by a new empire rising in the west.

The Romans had conquered Greece and Macedonia and marched on to Asia Minor. The Seleucid army was unable to stop them, and as a result Antiochus lost some of his western territories to Rome.

In order to raise funds to defend his kingdom against the growing Roman threat, Antiochus imposed high taxes on Judea to help defray the expense of hiring mercenary soldiers, equipping his vast army, and maintaining his splendid court at Antioch, the Syrian capital.

In addition, Antiochus humiliated the Jews by placing a statue of himself in the Temple.

Antiochus and the Jewish Religion / ca. 168 B.C.E.

Eventually, Antiochus outlawed Judaism altogether. It became a serious offense to observe Jewish laws. The Torah was a forbidden book; the Sabbath, festivals, and holy days could no longer be celebrated in public.

Antiochus added the Greek word Epiphanes ("God made manifest") to his name. Many Judeans, however, referred to him as Antiochus Epimanes—"Antiochus the Madman." Although Antiochus had proclaimed himself a god and decreed that those who opposed him would die, many brave men and women in Judea refused to pay homage at the Greek shrines.

The Maccabees

The first stirrings of revolt came in the village of Modin, near Jerusalem. Syrian officials and soldiers had come to Modin to collect taxes and force the people to worship the Greek gods. There was an old priest in the village, a man called Mattathias, of the Hasmonean family. Mattathias, surrounded by his five sons, walked up to the heathen altar. A Jew who collaborated with the Syrians had just bowed to the idols. Mattathias raised his sword high and his voice came out loud and clear:

"He who is with God, let him come to me!" he cried, and slew the traitorous idol worshipper.

The old priest's bold act inspired his sons and followers. They fell upon the Syrian soldiers and officials and killed them. Only a few escaped.

The Revolt Begins

The long-awaited revolt had begun! News of the incident at Modin spread like wildfire until all Judea was inflamed. Mattathias, his sons, and their followers fled to the mountains and joined forces with the Hasidim.

Marble bust of Antiochus IV (175–163 B.C.E.)

Statue of Zeus (Jupiter) found at Caesarea. Throughout Judea, Syrian overlords forced the Jews to worship before such idols at public altars.

A Greek soldier under attack. He wears a metal helmet and breastplate. This painting was found on an ancient stone coffin.

Mattathias died soon after the beginning of the revolt, but his five sons—Judah, Yohanan, Simon, Eliezer, and Jonathan—took over. The commander was Judah, who was called HaMakkabi, "the Hammerer." The letters of his name are said to have stood for the rebels' password and battle-cry: *Mi kamokah ba'elim, Adonai!* ("Who is like you among the gods, O Lord!").

The people of Judea rallied to the cause of the sons of Mattathias, now known as the Maccabees. In 1995 a road-building crew near Modin uncovered several tombs. Israeli archaeologists are excavating and cataloguing the objects in the tombs.

These newly discovered tombs were discovered while expanding a highway in the vecinity of Modin, ancestral home of the Maccabees. The Hebrew sign indicates that this dig is sponsored by the Israel Department of Antiquities.

The Battle for Freedom / ca. 168–165 B.C.E.

Although the revolutionary movement in Judea was growing day by day, Antiochus refused to take it seriously. He felt sure that his highly trained, well-equipped army could handle any threat.

An enameled picture of Judah Maccabee. It was painted in the 15th century by a French artist.

Judah Maccabee, an able general and a fine strategist, avoided an open battle with the main Syrian forces. Biding his time, he conducted a classic guerilla campaign, striking here and there, attacking whenever feasible. He defeated a Syrian unit based in Samaria and later ambushed a sizable Syrian column passing through the narrow pass of Beth-Horon. The Syrians, taken by surprise, were routed. They fled in wild disorder, leaving their weapons and equipment behind.

Judah Maccabee's Army

Judah Maccabee's army consisted of 6,000 untrained men armed only with equipment taken from the enemy and a few weapons made in Judea's crude forges. But the rebels had two advantages over the Syrians. First, they knew the terrain, since it was their homeland. Second,

they were fighting for a prize of untold value—their religion. They were determined to make a firm stand against the enemy no matter what the cost.

Still avoiding open battle, Judah and 3,000 men made a surprise attack at night on the Syrian encampment at Emmaus. Unable to rally in time, the Syrians again took flight. Their losses were heavy and their camp went up in flames. The Jews had won another great victory against overwhelming odds.

The Temple Is Restored

Now the triumphant Jews marched on Jerusalem. A dismaying sight greeted them, for the Temple was defiled by dirt and refuse and desecrated by idolatrous images.

Together, the victorious Jews set about cleaning their house of worship. Judah Maccabee and his men were assisted in this task by the priests and by the people of Jerusalem.

A Syrian war elephant. These huge beasts with sharp-shooting bowmen were the armored tanks of the ancient world.

Joyfully the army of cleaners and polishers worked, erecting a new altar to the one God in order to rededicate themselves to their faith.

The Miracle of Hanukkah / 165 B.C.E.

On the 25th day of Kislev, 165 B.C.E., three years after its desecration, the Temple was rededicated. The golden Menorah was lit once more. The Temple Menorah had only seven branches. It may still be seen today, in a relief on the Arch of Titus in Rome and on the official emblem of the State of Israel.

Tradition tells us that the victors found only enough oil in the Temple to keep the Eternal Light burning for one day. Yet miraculously the golden Menorah burned for eight full days. The eight-branched menorah of today and the annual eight-day celebration of Hanukkah, the Festival of Lights, commemorate the victory won for freedom by Judah Maccabee and his courageous followers.

Aware that the Seleucid state was still strong enough to threaten Judea, Judah Maccabee shrewdly decided to make a pact with Rome. For a time, this kept the Syrians at bay, for they were afraid to attack an ally of a power as mighty as Rome. Gradually, however, this fear lessened and Syria again invaded Judea, regaining some of its old strongholds.

Death of Judah Maccabee

The Syrians did not win all the battles, however, for Judah Maccabee defeated the Seleucid elephant corps near Beth-Horon. A month later, however, the Syrians returned with a fresh army of 22,000 men. Against this overwhelming force Judah Maccabee pitted an army of 800. Sheer bravery was not enough and the Judeans suffered a grave defeat.

Judea suffered a terrible loss; Judah Maccabee fell in battle. The beloved leader was carried home to Modin by his retreating soldiers and laid to rest beside his father.

Despite the loss of their great warrior leader, the Judeans stubbornly refused to submit to Syrian rule. Death had now taken all but two of the five brave brothers. Jonathan and Simon Maccabee still lived to carry on the struggle for independence.

Jewish ritual objects, including two seven-branched candlesticks, are shown on the base of a gold goblet of the 2nd century C.E. found in a Jewish catacomb in Rome, where it was hidden from the Romans. The objects shown on the goblet are believed to have been taken from the Temple in Jerusalem when it was desecrated by Antiochus IV of Syria.

The word *menorah* refers specifically to the huge seven-branched golden candle-holder that stood in the Temple of Jerusalem. It was removed by the Romans when they destroyed Jerusalem in 70 C.E. This bronze 4th century menorah was found in Egypt.

The Torah (Exodus 25:31–40) provides the construction details of the Temple menorah. It was made by Bezalel and hammered out of a solid slab of gold. According to the Torah it stood seven feet tall, weighed 100 pounds, and was seven-branched.

The Great Assembly

Meantime, the Seleucid state was torn apart by inner confusion and strife. King Antiochus had died and the Syrian nobles were fighting each other over the right to the throne. Each contender, hoping to gain Judean support, sent an envoy to Jonathan with messages of friendship, gifts, and promises of peace.

Simon Rules Judea / 145–134 B.C.E.

Simon, the last of the Maccabean brothers, succeeded Jonathan as high priest. He expelled the last remaining Syrian soldiers from the country. Garrison by garrison, the Syrians were forced to abandon their strongholds. At last Judea was free from the Syrian yoke.

Independence at Last

For the first time in centuries, Judea was no longer ruled by foreigners. The people rejoiced. Simon convened the Great Assembly, a representative body of priests and other communal leaders. This body, which is also known as the Sanhedrin, proclaimed Simon and his descendants high priests and rulers of Judea.

Simon's reign brought happiness and prosperity to Judea. Jews came from Babylonia, Egypt, and many distant lands to visit Jerusalem and the Temple. Traders came once again with their wares and greatly increased Judea's commerce.

Like his brother Judah, Simon realized that Rome was a power to be reckoned with. As Judah had done before him, Simon sent a delegation to Rome to negotiate a pact renewing the alliance between the two states.

John Hyrcanus Seeks Conquest

When Simon died in 134 B.C.E., he was succeeded by his son, John Hyrcanus. An ambitious man, Hyrcanus wanted to extend the borders of Judea by conquering other lands. Taking advantage of the confusion that prevailed in Syria, John Hyrcanus began by capturing Gaza and other coastal cities. His troops went on to conquer Idumea (Edom) and Nabatea in the area that is today Jordan.

Hyrcanus struck new coins to commemorate his reign. Under his rule, Judea grew prosperous and expanded its borders. But many people were dissatisfied with his policies.

A temple in the rock-cut city of Petra, the capital of Nabatea. John Hyrcanus expanded the borders of Israel and conquered Idumea and Nabatea, in Jordan.

Pharisees and Sadducees

As a result of the discontent with John Hyrcanus, two opposing parties developed in Judea, the Pharisees and the Sadducees.

The Sadducees were named after Zadok, the high priest of Solomon's time. Most of them were high-ranking priests, noblemen, and wealthy merchants. They supported John Hyrcanus and his stern, literal interpretation of the Torah, which often worked for the benefit of the upper classes.

They were opposed by the Pharisees, who took their name from the Hebrew word *perushim* ("separatists"). The Pharisees favored a more democratic approach and were concerned about the welfare of the common people; they advocated a more flexible interpretation of the Torah.

All the Hasmoneans until now had ruled Judea as high priests and hereditary princes. After the death of John Hyrcanus in 105 B.C.E., his son Aristobulus declared himself king. But Aristobulus died after ruling for one year. He was succeeded by his brother Alexander Jannai. Like John Hyrcanus, Jannai was a worldly man.

The aristocratic Sadducees gave Jannai their full support. During his 27-year reign, Judea was involved in many military campaigns.

The struggle between Pharisees and Sadducees grew very bitter during this time. With the help of Alexander Jannai, the Sadducees obtained a majority in the Great Assembly, Judea's supreme court.

The Oral Tradition

The Pharisees and Sadducees disagreed about the Oral Tradition. More interpretations were needed, and added, to meet the requirements of changing political, economical, and social conditions.

The Pharisees regarded the Oral Tradition as having equal status with the written Torah. The Sadducees did not. As a result, there were many differences between them in practice, holiday, and theology. The Pharisees believed that knowledge of the Torah should be spread throughout the populace, whereas the Sadducees felt that it was unnecessary for the people to understand all aspects of the Torah. They held that knowledge of the Torah should be reserved for the priests. Most of the people of Judea sided with the Pharisees.

The Majority Party

When Alexander Jannai grew old, he realized that the Pharisees had become a strong force. He advised his wife and successor, Salome Alexandra, to grant them a more active part in the government. Accordingly, Queen Salome appointed a Pharisee, her brother Simon ben Shetah, as the new president of the Sanhedrin (Great Assembly). The choice was a wise one, for Simon ben Shetah was a learned, able man who instituted many good laws.

An Era of Peace / ca. 76–67 B.C.E.

Queen Salome's reign was an era of peace. She established a fairer balance between the two parties in the Sanhedrin.

Pleased by this separation of state and priesthood, the Pharisees loyally supported the queen. They were now the majority They saw to it that only responsible men, familiar with Jewish law, were appointed as judges. Guided by Simon ben Shetah, the Pharisees improved the Judean school system. During the seven years of Salome Alexandra's reign, Judea prospered and flourished.

Civil War in Judea

After Salome's death in 67 B.C.E. her two sons, Aristobulus II and Hyrcanus II, contended for the crown. Jew fought Jew in a bitter civil war which lasted for five years. Finally, the warring factions turned to Rome to arbitrate their dispute. The Roman general Pompey had just taken Damascus. To this great general came three separate Judean delegations seeking protection and help. One group represented Hyrcanus, another represented Aristobulus, and the third, a delegation of Pharisees, represented the Judean people.

Bust of Julius Caesar.

Roman Legions Overrun Judea / 63 B.C.E.

The Pharisees asked Pompey to choose neither of the sons of Salome but to restore rule by the high priest, who would be aided by the Sanhedrin. Pompey, thinking first of what would be best for Rome, decided in favor of Hyrcanus, the weaker contender. Soon afterward Pompey's legions overran Judea, capturing Jerusalem after a three-month siege. Thousands of Jews lost their lives and many others were enslaved. Aristobulus was carried off to Rome along with scores of other Jewish captives.

After almost 80 years of independence, Judea was once again under the domination of a foreign power. The Judean coastal cities and Mediterranean ports now became part of the Roman province of Syria.

Under Roman rule Judea was divided into five districts, and Hyrcanus was left to govern only Jerusalem itself and the immediately surrounding area. Meanwhile, a bitter struggle broke out between Pompey and Julius Caesar for control of the Roman Empire. Caesar marched against Pompey and defeated him. Pompey fled to Egypt, where he was murdered by his own men in 48 B.C.E.

This 15th century French painting shows Pompey and his soldiers desecrating and looting the Holy Temple.

Julius Caesar and the Jews

Hyrcanus II Supports Caesar

Although Pompey was gone, Caesar still faced opposition in Rome. In Judea he won the support of Hyrcanus II and his chief advisor, Antipater. The latter was a clever, scheming man from Idumea whose parents had been converted to Judaism.

A Jewish army of 3,000 men fought alongside Caesar's legions during the campaign in Egypt in which he defeated Ptolemy XII, the husband of Cleopatra. In gratitude for the help the Jews had given him, Caesar reinstated Hyrcanus II as high priest and appointed him ethnarch (secular ruler) of Judea. Caesar rewarded Antipater with the high honor of Roman citizenship.

In addition, he reinstated the rights of the Jewish community of Alexandria, which had been taken away some years earlier by a hostile government.

Antipater Becomes Procurator

In 47 B.C.E., Caesar appointed Antipater procurator (governor) of Judea. Since most Judeans resented Antipater as an outsider because he was an Idumean and the son of converts, this caused great dissatisfaction. Antipater, in turn, appointed his older son, Phasael, as governor of Jerusalem. The governorship of Galilee he gave to his brilliant but ruthlessly ambitious younger son, Herod.

This is the well-preserved amphitheater in Caesarea. It was built by King Herod for the Roman procurators.

The Romans were brilliant engineers and prolific builders. They left their imprint on the civilizations of the countries they conquered. Many Roman roads, monuments, aqueducts, and amphitheaters have survived the ravages of time and war.
This is one of the high-level aqueducts built by the Romans in Caesarea. It brought water from the local spring to the city.

Herod the Cruel Becomes Ruler / ca. 37–4 B.C.E.

Under the leadership of a man named Hezekiah, a band of rebels was organized in Galilee to fight for Jewish independence from Rome. When Herod learned about their activities, he had the entire group arrested and executed.

The news of Herod's cruelty shocked the Sanhedrin. Herod was summoned to stand trial. Accused men usually came before the Great Assembly dressed in black as a sign of humility. Herod, however, entered the court dressed in the purple garments of a prince and escorted by soldiers.

The members of the Sanhedrin wanted to punish Herod, but they had to be lenient because he was under the protection of Hyrcanus, the high priest.

In 44 B.C.E. Julius Caesar was assassinated by his political opponents. This had unfortunate consequences for Judea. Caesar had been its protector, but Mark Antony, the ruler of Rome's eastern territories, was a friend of Herod. Jewish delegations repeatedly went to see him to complain about Herod's cruelty, but Antony ignored them.

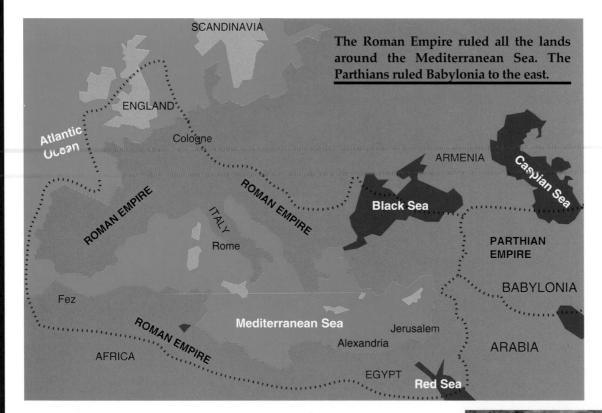

The Roman Empire ruled all the lands around the Mediterranean Sea. The Parthians ruled Babylonia to the east.

SCANDINAVIA

ENGLAND

Atlantic Ocean

Cologne

ROMAN EMPIRE

ARMENIA

Caspian Sea

Black Sea

ITALY

Rome

ROMAN EMPIRE

PARTHIAN EMPIRE

BABYLONIA

Fez

Mediterranean Sea

Jerusalem

ROMAN EMPIRE

Alexandria

ARABIA

AFRICA

EGYPT

Red Sea

King Herod built the city of Caesarea as a seat of government for the Roman procurators. He named it in honor of Caesar Augustus. All that now remains of this once busy deepwater port are fragmented stone pillars awash in the Mediterranean Sea.

Instead, he made Herod and his brother Phasael tetrarchs, or co-rulers, of Judea and executed the members of the Jewish delegations.

Antigonus Overthrows Herod / ca. 47 B.C.E.
In 40 B.C.E. the Parthians, an Iranian people who now ruled the former Seleucid territories in Persia and Mesopotamia, invaded Palestine. Taking advantage of the situation, Antigonus, a grandson of Alexander Jannai and Hyrcanus' nephew gathered all the discontented groups under his leadership and joined forces with the invaders. For about three years, Antigonus ruled as king of Judea, and he remained in power after Rome drove back the Parthians. The politically shrewd Herod,

Portrait coin of Mark Antony, 41 B.C.E.

Herod's Reign of Terror / ca. 37–4 B.C.E.
With the help of Roman legions, Herod entered Judea, his new kingdom. He laid siege to Jerusalem, and after five months of fighting, the city surrendered. Herod immediately executed the leaders of the opposition. Antigonus, too, was executed.

Herod proved to be a cruel ruler. He was very ambitious, and craved splendor and fame. Deeply suspicious, he saw signs of rebellion and danger everywhere. Many people had to pay with their lives because of his fears.

Constantly fearing that a member of the Hasmonean family would take the throne from him, Herod sought to make his position secure by a reign of terror and murder. He executed two prominent Hasmoneans, Hyrcanus, who had returned from Parthian captivity a broken old man, and his own wife, Mariamne, as well as their two sons.

Memorial inscription of the Roman 10th Legion, which was stationed at Jerusalem after the city was conquered by Titus in 70 C.E.

however, sailed for Rome. Combining bribes and personal charm, he persuaded Mark Antony and Octavian, the co-rulers of the Roman Empire, that only he could keep the Jews under control. He returned home as king of Judea. Technically Judea was again an independent state, but for practical purposes it was a Roman dependency.

Herod's family tomb in Jerusalem. Here the monarch buried his wife Mariamne and his two sons after murdering them in a maniacal rage.

Economic Prosperity

Herod the Great

Despite his cruelty, history refers to Herod as Herod the Great. While the Judeans hated and feared him, the Romans admired him as a loyal ally and efficient administrator and for keeping the peace. In addition, he implemented policies to increase Judea's trade and prosperity.

Situated between Syria and Egypt, Judea was crossed by the great trade routes that ran east and west. Caravans from Arabia and Persia with goods for the west made their first stop in Judea. Traders even came from distant India. And ships from Greece and Africa landed at Judea's Mediterranean ports.

Herod gained control of several free cities on the Judean coast which had been built by Greek and Roman settlers. These cities had been part of a confederation called the Decapolis, or "League of Ten Cities." As part of Judea, they brought new wealth to the country.

Herod collected high taxes from his people. Some of the money went to Rome, and some paid for his own Judean projects.

Herod the Builder

Herod delighted in building elaborate structures and founded two new cities named in honor of his Roman friends: Tiberias, in honor of the emperor Tiberius; and the coastal city of Caesarea, in honor of Caesar Augustus. He also built amphitheaters and arenas, where gladiators and captives had to fight and wrestle with untamed beasts, as was the custom in the arenas of Rome.

The Temple / ca. 20 B.C.E.

Unquestionably, Herod's most ambitious project was the improvement and enlargement of the Temple. For 500 years the

The Herodium fortress, near Bethlehem. It is situated on a mountaintop and is highly defensible. The fortress also served as a palace. After the Great Revolt in 70 C.E., it provided a refuge for rebels who managed to escape from Jerusalem.

Temple built by the returning Babylonian exiles had served as the nation's sanctuary. In no way like the splendid Temple of Solomon's reign, it was a small, simple building, and was deteriorating with age. Herod spared no cost or effort in rebuilding the Temple. Portion by portion, his workmen and architects restored and improved it. Throughout his reign, Herod continued work on the Temple compound. The project was begun in 20 B.C.E. and was not finished until several years after Herod's death.

Herod's Temple was a magnificent structure. Throughout Asia Minor people marveled at its beauty and splendor. Like all of Herod's buildings, it was built in the classic Greek style. Herod raised a strong wall around the Temple compound, and above the main gate he placed an eagle, the golden emblem of Rome.

This deeply offended the people. How could a warlike emblem be allowed to disgrace God's peaceful sanctuary? Thus, while the beauty of Herod's Temple gave him prestige abroad, it did not win him the love of his people.

Masada, the Fortress

The ruins of the synagogue on Masada. The round pillars in the center of the photograph supported the synagogue's roof.

The fortress of Masada was built by King Herod. It has been excavated and a large part has been reconstructed.

Masada

To guarantee internal security and protect the borders of his kingdom, Herod built a number of fortresses, including Antonia in Jerusalem, Herodium near Bethlehem, and Masada near the Dead Sea.

Masada is situated on a high rock in the Judean desert. The cliffs that surround it are steep and make the fortress easy to defend.

One of Herod's first projects on Masada was the creation of a system to ensure an adequate supply of water. He built a series of cisterns which stored rain water for use during the dry season. Almost the entire summit was enclosed with a thick fortified wall, with 30 watchtowers and four gates.

Herod constructed several palaces at Masada, containing many rooms, bathrooms, and a cold-water pool paved with mosaics. In addition, there were a series of storehouses where oil, flour, wine, and foods were kept in special jars. Other storehouses contained munitions and weapons.

Two mikvot (ritual baths) and a synagogue have also been uncovered on Masada.

Masada was the last Zealot stronghold during the Jewish war against Rome in 66–72 C.E.

The Leaders of Judea

The Sanhedrin

Distrusting Herod because he was an Idumean, and distrusting the high priests because they were now appointed either by Herod or by the Roman government, the people of Judea turned for leadership to the religious teachers and scholars who made up the Great Assembly, or Sanhedrin.

Students and scholars from the Jewish communities of Egypt and Babylonia, Syria and Persia, North Africa and Rome, came to Jerusalem, the center of Jewish learning, to learn Torah from them.

The Chain of Tradition

The Sanhedrin was the institution where the laws of the Torah were expounded, interpreted, and codified in accordance with the Oral Tradition.

According to tractate Avot of the Mishnah, the chain of tradition started with Moses. He handed it on to Joshua, who in turn passed it on to the elders. From them it came down to the prophets, who handed it over to the Men of the Great Assembly. The latter, sometimes referred to as scribes, were the true spiritual leaders of Judea and world Jewry.

How the Sanhedrin Functioned

The Great Sanhedrin had 71 members, most of whom were Pharisees. It was presided over by two leaders, known as *zugot* ("pairs") One of the zugot was the *nasi* ("prince" or "chief"); the other was the *av bet din* ("presiding judge").

The most famous of these "pairs" of scholars were Hillel and Shammai. The discussions in the Sanhedrin were often sharp and brilliant, and many of the debates and legal decisions of the zugot became famous.

The stone *cathedra* (chair) of Moses from the 3rd century synagogue at Korazim, in Galilee. Chairs of this kind were installed in ancient synagogues for the principal teacher of the law, or for a person the community wished to honor.

Hillel / 1st cent. B.C.E.

Hillel was a brilliant young man who came to Judea from Babylonia. Although very poor, he loved learning. He earned the money to pay for admission to the lectures at the academy by cutting wood.

One cold winter's night when he did not have the admission fee, Hillel lay atop the roof of the schoolhouse and listened to the lectures until he fell asleep from exhaustion. The next morning, when the academy assembled, the scholars found the hall

These catacombs are called the Tomb of the Sanhedrin. Inside are a large number of burial chambers carved into the rock. It is the traditional place where the members of the Sanhedrin were buried. The tomb is in Jerusalem.

exceptionally dark. Looking up at the sky-light, they saw Hillel's body blocking the sun. Touched by the young man's great devotion to learning, the teachers provided him with a scholarship.

Hillel became a renowned sage. He returned to Babylonia to teach, but was invited back to Jerusalem to join the Great Sanhedrin. His wisdom and learning were recognized by Jewish scholars everywhere.

Once Hillel was asked to tell what he considered the fundamental principle of Judaism. His famous answer was: "What is hateful to you, do not do unto others. All the rest of the Torah is merely an explanation of this rule." Hillel said that the way to the Torah, and to God, was to love peace and love mankind. He valued the unity of Israel above all, and warned his students never to set themselves apart from the community of the Jewish people.

So greatly respected was Hillel that the office of nasi of the Sanhedrin became hereditary in his family. He became the founder of the school of Torah interpretation known as Bet Hillel ("House of Hillel").

Shammai / 1st cent. B.C.E.

Hillel's colleague Shammai, the av bet din, was a brilliant scholar who came from one of Jerusalem's wealthy, noble families. Stern and conservative, he often differed on questions of law with Hillel. While Hillel usually took the more lenient, flexible view, Shammai interpreted the law strictly. He was a pious scholar, devoted to preserving the Torah and the Jewish way of life.

The famous debates between Hillel and Shammai caused a great stir in the Jewish communities of their day. Wherever Jews

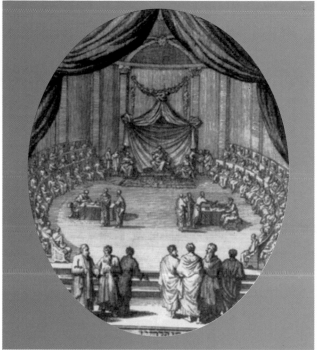

An engraving in a Hebrew-Latin edition of the Mishnah (1744). It illustrates a session of the Sanhedrin.

assembled, studied, and prayed, the teachings of Hillel and Shammai were discussed.

An oil press from talmudic times. Ripe olives were crushed and olive oil was extracted. Olive oil was a basic food in ancient Israel.

Revolt in Judea / ca. –14 CE

Under Roman Rule

Herod died in 4 B.C.E. Soon afterward, Augustus, the Roman emperor, divided his kingdom among his three sons, making each of them an ethnarch. Judea, Samaria, and Idumea were now Roman possessions ruled by officials called procurators. The procurators were cruel and ruthless. They collected high taxes, taking a good portion for themselves before sending the rest to Rome. Garrisons of Roman soldiers were stationed throughout the land.

Although Rome seemed all-powerful, the people never gave up the hope of regaining their independence. In the hills of Galilee, guerilla fighters rallied to Judah, the son of Hezekiah, the leader executed by Herod.

The Pharisees Oppose Rebellion

The Pharisees and the Great Sanhedrin in Jerusalem opposed this uprising. They advocated passive resistance and steadfast devotion to Jewish law. Like the earlier revolts against Assyria and Babylon, they warned, open rebellion against Rome would end in utter destruction.

The Zealots Form a Party

Violently opposed to the pacifism of the Pharisees, the rebels founded their own party, calling themselves Zealots. Many of the more extreme Zealots formed partisan bands in the Galilean hills. They ambushed Roman transports and attacked Roman patrols.

This was a terrible time for the people of Judea. Those who were suspected of anti-Roman activities were tortured in Roman prisons. Many others were executed by crucifixion.

The Essenes

More and more people began to yearn for the coming of the Messiah, a savior whom God would send to defeat their enemies and institute a golden age of peace, prosperity, and piety in an independent Jewish state. Some formed groups or sects which adopted a pious lifestyle designed to prepare them for the Messianic era and perhaps even to bring it closer.

The Essenes were the best-known of these sects. They were dedicated to a life of purity, study, and charity. They owned no property as individuals, but held everything in common. Most of them lived together in secluded communities, following their own strict rules. They were extreme pacifists, totally opposed to war and bloodshed. They ate no meat and lived frugally. Many of them went out into the desert for long periods of fasting, meditation, and prayer.

The famous Dead Sea Scrolls, which were discovered in a cave near Qumran, are a rich source of information about the beliefs and rituals of the Jewish sects of this period.

The Dead Sea Scrolls are the oldest Hebrew manuscripts in existence. They are housed in the Shrine of the Book, in the Israel Museum, Jerusalem. The scroll of Isaiah is displayed fully opened around a drum.

Birth of Christianity

John the Baptist / 1st cent. C.E.

Around this time a wandering preacher named Yohanan, known in history as John the Baptist, made his appearance. John spoke of the coming of the Messiah, called for repentance, and bathed his followers in the waters of the Jordan River as a symbolic act of purification. This act, which resembled the ritual bath of the Essenes, is now known as baptism.

Before long Herod Antipas, the tetrarch of Galilee, learned about John's activities. Fearing that John's sermons would stir the people to revolt, he had him arrested and executed.

Jesus of Nazareth / ca. 29 C.E.

Among those influenced by John's sermons and baptized by him was a young man from Nazareth named Joshua, known to history as Jesus. He too traveled through the land with a band of disciples, preaching to the people.

Jesus was familiar with the teachings of the great sages and frequently quoted them. But his own teachings differed from those of the Pharisees. Whereas the Pharisee scholars based their opinions on the Oral Tradition, Jesus often spoke in his

The remains of the synagogue at Capernaum on the shores of the Sea of Galilee.

own name and challenged the accepted religious and political authorities.

Pontius Pilate Crucifies Jesus

In the year 29 C.E., at the time of Passover, Jesus went to Jerusalem. During festivals, when the city was crowded with pilgrims, Jerusalem was a hotbed of revolt. Amid the tumult in the crowded streets, Jesus' disciples proclaimed that he was the Messiah. From the Roman standpoint this was a serious matter. It meant that he might try to overthrow their government.

Roman soldiers arrested Jesus and brought him to the procurator, Pontius Pilate. Accused of rabble-rousing and of pretending to be the "King of the Jews," Jesus was condemned to death by crucifixion.

The Followers of Jesus

The followers of Jesus remained together after his death. Many of them believed that he had risen from the grave and would return in glory as the Messiah. Within a few years, from this small group, emerged the new religion of Christianity.

The limestone rock, excavated in Caesarea, is inscribed with a dedication to Pontius Pilate, the Roman governor who authorized the crucifixion of Jesus.

The Zealots Resist

The Zealots were Jewish patriots. They hated Rome and all it stood for. They considered everyone who collaborated with the Romans to be an enemy. Seeing themselves as successors of the Hasidim and the valiant Maccabees, they conducted a guerrilla war against Rome and its supporters.

The Zealots were a serious problem for the Roman government. Many members of the Great Sanhedrin, feeling that it was important to keep the peace, also opposed them. The Jewish people were not united and often disagreed about which policy to follow.

Rebellion Against Florus / 64–66 C.E.
Florus was the last Roman procurator of Judea. When he came to Judea, he took no interest in the problems of the Jews. He increased taxes, which were already high. He even seized a great sum of gold from the Temple treasury.

The Jews were indignant. The Temple funds had been raised by voluntary contributions and were intended for charitable purposes, not to build up the Roman treasury.

An Independent Jerusalem
The people of Jerusalem, led by the Zealots, armed themselves and rose up against the Romans. Men, women, and children joined in the fighting. The Roman garrison, unable to put down the rebellion or to hold the city, was forced to retreat.

Soon another Roman army appeared before Jerusalem, but it was ambushed and

This ancient block of stone was a part of the wall of a building in the Temple compound in Jerusalem. The Hebrew inscription reads, "To the place of trumpeting."

The Essenes were a religious sect in Palestine at the end of the Second Temple period. They lived a severe, mystic life in isolated monastic communities. Each member of the sect worked and contributed manual labor for the benefit of the group. They believed in personal and ritual purity.

The Roman army marched through Palestine, destroying Jewish cities and strong points. They leveled the Essene settlement at Qumran.

Most scholars attribute the Dead Sea Scrolls to the Essenes. Excavations at Qumran have enabled archaeologists to reconstruct their lives.

defeated. Many of its weapons fell into Jewish hands. Thus, in the fall of 66 C.E., Judea began its last brief period of independence. Once more the Jews ruled themselves.

The Romans Attack / 67 C.E.

The people were overjoyed, even though they knew that Rome would not give up easily. They were ready to fight to preserve their freedom.

In the spring of 67 C.E., a Roman army of 60,000 well-equipped soldiers commanded by Vespasian, the greatest general of the day, invaded Galilee. Vespasian was aided by his son, the able young general Titus, who brought reinforcements from Egypt. One by one, the Jewish strongpoints in Galilee fell. Led by Yohanan (John) of Giscala, the few remaining Jewish fighters fled to Jerusalem.

Revolt in Rome / 66 C.E.

While Vespasian was preparing to besiege Jerusalem, he received news of a revolt in Rome. The emperor Nero had committed suicide, and three contenders, one after another, had seized the throne. All three had been murdered within a year, and the Roman army had proclaimed Vespasian as the new emperor. Leaving his troops under the command of Titus, Vespasian left for Rome to take control of the government.

For five centuries, Rome dominated the ancient world. Among its conquests were Spain, France, England, Greece and the Balkans, Mesopotamia, Armenia, Egypt, Judea, and North Africa. At its height the Roman Empire controlled an expanse which included 100 million people.

The Roman armies were well equipped and led by talented commanders. Success in battle came easily to this well-disciplined fighting machine.

These Roman soldiers belonged to the Praetorian Guard, the emperor's personal bodyguard

The ancient city of Gamla is located in the Golan. It is called Gamla, because it is situated on a hill that is shaped like a camel (Gamla). During the war against Rome it was besieged and captured by Vespasian, and after a month of severe fighting.

In revenge for their loses, the Romans massacred all the inhabitants. The above are the ruins of the synagogue in Gamla.

Portrait coin of Vespasian, 69-79 C.E.

Judea Is Defeated / 70 C.E.

Jerusalem Under Siege

In the year 70 C.E., Titus began the siege of Jerusalem. It went on for several months. In the final hours of their resistance, the defenders of Jerusalem were united. Despite hunger and hardship, they held out courageously. Day and night they heard the heavy thud of Roman battering rams and the terrifying ballistas, which shot 100-pound boulders into the city. The outer walls of Jerusalem gave way; so did the third, northern wall. Many still hoped that some miracle would happen and the city would be saved.

On the 17th of Tammuz, conditions in Jerusalem grew worse. The fighting in the Temple area was so heavy that for the first time since the days of Judah Maccabee, the sacrifices had to be discontinued. Yet the defenders fought on. Their leaders, Yohanan of Giscala and Simon Bar Giora, gave them courage.

Josephus as Historian / ca. 38–ca. 100 C.E.

Outside the walls, Titus spurred his soldiers on to make an end to the bloody siege. Titus had a strange companion in those days, Josephus Flavius, a descendant of the Maccabees whose Hebrew name was Joseph ben Mattiyahu ha-Kohen. From the enemy camp, Josephus watched the defeat of his people.

At the age of 26, Josephus had been was sent on a diplomatic mission to Rome, where he remained for two years at the court of Nero. On his return in 65 C.E. he found Judea in revolt against the Romans. Despite Zealot suspicions of his loyalty, he was given command of the Jewish forces in Galilee. In 67 C.E., when his troops were defeated by Vespasian's army, Josephus saved his life by surrendering. During the

The Arch of Titus in Rome.

siege of Jerusalem, he helped Titus by trying to demoralize the city's defenders. After the city's fall, he was rewarded for his treachery and took a Roman name.

Josephus wrote several books which serve as our main source of information about the very important period of Jewish history in which he lived.

This Roman coin, inscribed *Judaea Capta,* "Judea is captured," recalls the Roman victory in the first Jewish revolt.

The Temple Is Destroyed / 70 C.E.

On the 9th of Av in the year 70 C.E., on the anniversary of the day Nebuchadnezzar had destroyed the Temple of Solomon, Titus stormed the Temple area. A Roman soldier climbed the wall and hurled a burning torch. In moments, the Temple was in flames. Some of the fighters tried to escape, to make a stand in another Judean fortress. But they did not succeed. Yohanan of Giscala and Simon Bar Giora, with many of their brave men, were taken captive.

The Arch of Triumph

When Titus returned to Rome, the Jewish captives were paraded in front of the populace. They were forced to march in a procession into the Roman Forum, carrying the treasures that Titus had taken from Judea.

The Romans customarily erected an arch of triumph whenever a victorious general returned from a military campaign. The Arch of Titus, commemorating the defeat of Judea, can still be seen in Rome. One of the reliefs on the arch shows the Jewish captives marching in Titus' triumphal procession.

A copy of the carving on the Arch of Titus, showing the Menorah and other furniture of the Temple being carried in triumph through the streets of Rome.

The Destruction of Judea / 70 C.E.

Judea was destroyed and its people conquered. More than a million people died in the war, and thousands were carried off into exile and slavery. The Jews lost their independence. Palestine was again governed by a representative of the Roman emperor.

Jewish communities throughout the world mourned for Judea, for Jerusalem, and above all for the Temple, which had been the spiritual center of their lives.

Judea was a land of desolation. Nothing of the Temple was left except the ruins of its western wall. Year by year, Jews assembled there in prayer, conducting services, reading from the Torah. Many wept as they stood by the ruined wall. On the 9th of Av, the anniversary of the destruction, Jewish pilgrims would come from many lands to mourn for the lost Temple.

Despite the loss of their land and their Temple, the Jews continued to live in accordance with the laws of the Torah. It gave them hope and courage to face the future.

After the revolt Josephus wrote *The Jewish War*. In it he graphically describes the heroism of the Jewish soldiers. This 11th century drawing is from the Latin version of *The Jewish War*. Joseph, wearing a crown and seated on a throne, is presenting his book to Vespasian.

The Fall of Masada / 73 C.E.

The Romans had captured Jerusalem in 70 C.E., but some Jewish soldiers refused to give up. These valiant resistance fighters took refuge in Masada, Herod's palace-fortress on a flat-topped rock plateau in the desolate Judean desert, overlooking the Dead Sea. Although the Temple had been destroyed and Jerusalem had fallen, they stood their ground. For seven months, the Romans battled against the last Jewish stronghold. Finally, they managed to breach the wall of Masada and were poised to storm the fortress in overwhelming strength.

On the first day of Passover in 72 C.E. the Jewish leader, Eleazar ben Yair, called together all his soldiers. He advised them to take their own lives rather than be taken prisoner.

During Roman victory celebrations, thousands of prisoners, many of them Jews, were thrown into the arena and died battling wild, hungry beasts. The Jews atop Masada did not wish to become slaves and participate in the deadly spectacles in the Roman arenas.

Catapults of various sizes were used to hurl large stones into enemy lines. The silently falling stones from above instilled fear in the hearts of the enemy. They were also used in teams of batteries to rain death on the exposed enemy. The heavy stones could easily kill or maim a combatant.

The Jewish defenders who faced the might of Rome were poorly armed. On the other hand, the Romans were equipped with the most modern armaments of the period. Roman catapults could hurl heavy boulders with great force. The Romans also employed battering rams, which destroyed defense walls and paved the way for the Roman infantry.

Roman battering ram.

"We know in advance that tomorrow we shall fall into the enemy's hands," he said, "but we still have the free choice of dying a noble death together with our loved ones. Let our wives die undisgraced, and our children free from the shackles of slavery!"

Eleazar ben Yair's soldiers agreed. When the Romans entered the fortress the next day, their victory was an empty one.

In *The Jewish War*, Josephus records their astonishment at what they found.

"The Romans, expecting further resistance, were under arms at daybreak and advanced to the assault. Not a single defender was to be seen. On all sides there was an awesome silence. They were at a loss to guess what had happened. At last they called out to any one within. Their shouts were heard by the old women, who emerged from the caverns and informed the Romans of the deed and how it was done. When they came upon the rows of the dead, the Roman enemies admired the nobility and utter contempt for death displayed by so many.

"Masada being thus taken, the Roman general left a garrison on the spot and departed. For not an enemy of Rome remained throughout the country, the whole having now been subdued by this protracted war."

A clay fragment with the name "Yair" found atop Masada. It may refer to the Jewish leader Eliazar ben Yair.

During the revolt against Rome, the rebels minted bronze and silver coins. The inscriptions read: "Freedom of Jerusalem" or "For the Redemption of Zion." Coins such as this one were found in Masada.

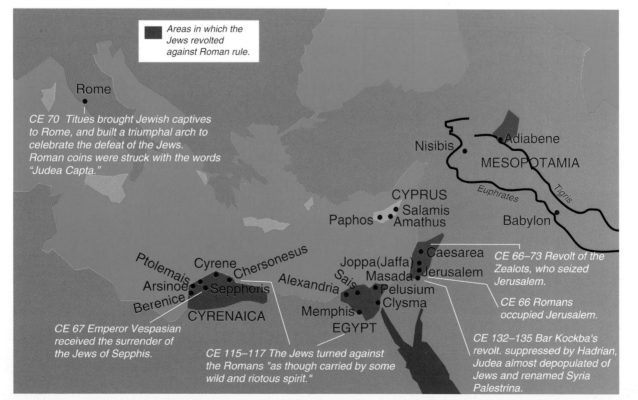

Areas in which the Jews revolted against Roman rule.

Rome

CE 70 Titues brought Jewish captives to Rome, and built a triumphal arch to celebrate the defeat of the Jews. Roman coins were struck with the words "Judea Capta."

Nisibis

Adiabene

MESOPOTAMIA

CYPRUS

Salamis

Paphos • • Amathus

Euphrates

Tigris

Babylon

Ptolemais • Cyrene • Chersonesus

Arsinoe • • Sepphoris

Berenice

CYRENAICA

Alexandria

Sais

Memphis

EGYPT

Joppa(Jaffa)

Caesarea

Masada • Jerusalem

Pelusium

Clysma

CE 66–73 Revolt of the Zealots, who seized Jerusalem.

CE 66 Romans occupied Jerusalem.

CE 67 Emperor Vespasian received the surrender of the Jews of Sepphis.

CE 115–117 The Jews turned against the Romans "as though carried by some wild and riotous spirit."

CE 132–135 Bar Kockba's revolt. suppressed by Hadrian, Judea almost depopulated of Jews and renamed Syria Palestrina.

Roman rule was harsh, and under the rule of cruel Roman procurators, law and order broke down. Riots flared up all over Israel, and Roman troops were frequently attacked by bands of Jewish rebels.

The Struggle for Survival / 1st century C.E.

In the days before the siege of Jerusalem, many felt that Rome was sure to win. They feared that the Jews would not survive as a people if the Romans destroyed their country.

But there were others who believed that the Jews did not need a land or a Temple to be united. They felt that the Torah was a sufficiently strong bond. Among those who held this view was Rabban Yohanan ben Zakkai, a scholar who had been a member of the Great Sanhedrin and now became one of the great leaders of Jewish history.

A Plan for Survival

Yohanan ben Zakkai knew that Judaism would survive if the Torah lived on in the hearts of the people. Like most of the Pharisees, he had opposed the war with Rome. Hating bloodshed, he believed in passive resistance. He had taught that true dignity would come not from rebellion but from faithful observance of the Torah

When the Romans prepared to lay siege to Jerusalem, Yohanan ben Zakkai thought of a way to preserve the Torah. He decided to start a school—an academy of Jewish learning—away from Jerusalem, where the Torah could be studied and questions of Jewish law discussed.

In those days it was impossible to leave Jerusalem. With the city preparing for the Roman attack, the Zealots were on the lookout for traitors. Many people were falsely accused of treason.

Determined to start his school. Yohanan had himself put into a coffin. His disciples, pretending he was dead, carried him out of Jerusalem under the watchful eyes of the Zealots, presumably to bury him.

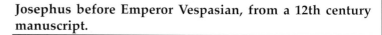

Josephus before Emperor Vespasian, from a 12th century manuscript.

Once they were outside the city, Yohanan ben Zakkai emerged from the coffin, very much alive. Before long he and his companions were stopped by a Roman patrol. Yohanan asked to be brought before their commander, Vespasian.

Portrait coin of Vespasian (69–79 C.E.)

Vespasian and Yohanan

The Roman general granted the scholar an audience, for he knew that Yohanan had opposed the war. Yohanan told Vespasian that he would soon become emperor of Rome. Very pleased by this prediction, Vespasian promised to grant anything Yohanan might request. This was exactly what Yohanan ben Zakkai had hoped for. He promptly asked for permission to set up a school in Yavneh, a small town on the seacoast. Vespasian agreed.

The School at Yavneh

Yohanan ben Zakkai at once set up a school in Yavneh. There the scholars continued their studies and conducted services in the synagogue. Eventually, Yohanan formed a Sanhedrin modeled after the Great Sanhedrin of Jerusalem, a court of 71 scholars who decided on all questions of law and learning, and on the proper interpretation of the Torah.

When the news came that Jerusalem had fallen and the Temple had been destroyed, Yohanan wept and tore his clothes in mourning. Yet he did not allow his disciples to despair.

Yohanan ben Zakkai

Rabban Yohanan ben Zakkai was the first nasi, or president, of the Sanhedrin in Yavneh. He was beloved for his humility, his love and respect for everyone. Yohanan ben Zakkai realized that new judges, teachers, and scholars had to be trained and ordained, as had been the practice in the days of the Great Sanhedrin. These scholars would have the title of rabbi, which literally means "master." Once ordained, after completing the necessary studies, the rabbi would

cease to be a disciple and himself become a teacher. The rabbis educated at Yavneh would be links in the great, unbroken chain of teachers of the Torah.

Yohanan and those who followed him were called tannaim, meaning "repeaters" or "teachers." The period in which they were active is known as the tannaitic era. It ended around 200 C.E.

A Roman soldier with his combat equipment. The short sword was called a *gladium* and the shield was called a *scutum*.

The interior of the Yohanan ben Zakkai Sephardic synagogue in the Jewish Quarter of Old Jerusalem. It is one of the oldest synagogues in the Meah Shearim section of Jerusalem. In 1948 the synagogue was destroyed by the Arab Legion. It was rebuilt in 1972.

Christianity Begins / ca. 65 CE

Paul of Tarsus / ca. 65 C.E.

Some years after the death of Jesus of Nazareth, the sect that followed his teachings found a new leader in Paul of Tarsus. Paul, a Jew from what is now southern Turkey, had come to Jerusalem to study Torah. He opposed the Christians at first but then became a zealous adherent of the sect. Determined to spread the new creed, he traveled widely throughout the Diaspora, preaching to both Jews and non-Jews.

Paul regularly sent letters about the new religion's doctrines to the communities he had visited. Later these were gathered together with various other Christian writings, including the accounts of Jesus' life known as the Four Gospels, in a collection of books called the New Testament. The Christian Bible is made up of both the New Testament and the Hebrew Bible, which Christians refer to as the Old Testament.

The Christian Church

According to Christian tradition, Paul died in Rome during the persecution of the new religion that followed the great fire that consumed much of the city in 65 C.E. He left a major legacy, however. The small groups of converts he organized during his missionary journeys made new converts of their own and founded houses of worship which later became known as churches. Before long there were churches throughout the Roman Empire. They all felt themselves bound to one another in a single large community, the Christian Church.

Earliest known manuscript of the letters of Paul, 200 C.E.

A painting of Mark the author of one of the New Testament gospels. It is dated about 800 C.E.

Gamaliel II / late 1st century C.E.

Gamaliel Becomes Nasi

When Yohanan ben Zakkai retired as nasi of the Sanhedrin, his place was taken by Gamaliel II, a descendant of Hillel. Gamaliel applied all his energy to the task of preserving Judaism under the new conditions confronting the Jewish people.

Gamaliel was particularly concerned with devising ways for people to worship now that the Temple was destroyed and the local synagogues had to take its place. To this end he supervised the formulation of many new rituals and prayers, including prayers for the restoration of the Temple.

In addition, Gamaliel and his colleagues in Yavneh decided that portions from the Torah and the Prophets should be read in the synagogues every Sabbath and on the holidays. Shorter sections of the weekly Sabbath portions were to be read on Mondays and on Thursdays, when the farmers came to town to market their produce. Jews everywhere still follow this custom.

Since festival pilgrimages to Jerusalem were no longer possible, Gamaliel and the scholars also arranged the prayer services for Sukkot, Pesach, and Shavuot. They included readings about the rituals that had taken place in the Temple on these days.

Gamaliel was troubled by the bitter differences of opinion that often occurred in the Sanhedrin. Fearing that disputes would destroy its authority, he wanted the nasi to be the final arbitrator whenever the scholars differed. Many of the scholars angrily felt that Gamaliel was trying to make himself too powerful.

Gamaliel Is Dismissed and Reinstated

The opposition voted to remove Gamaliel from office. Gamaliel took his dismissal gracefully. He did not withdraw from the Sanhedrin but continued to attend its sessions, although his opinions were never shared by a majority. He also continued his teaching duties. Eventually, Gamaliel was reinstated as nasi of the Sanhedrin. But never again did he, or any other nasi, attempt to interfere with the Sanhedrin's democratic procedures.

Rabban Gamliel the Elder with three of his disciples, an illumination from the 13th century in the Sarajevo Haggadah.

Rabbi Akiva and the Mishnah / ca. 40–135 CE

Rabbi Akiva was the most outstanding of the many scholars and rabbis who taught at Yavneh. As a young man, Akiva had been an uneducated shepherd. He had married Rachel, the daughter of his wealthy master, and over the years she made many sacrifices to enable him to fulfill his ambition of learning Torah. Thanks to her efforts, he was able to attend the academy of Eliezer and Joshua, who were carrying on the work of Yohanan ben Zakkai. Akiva became the most brilliant scholar of the time. His decisions were concise and clear. He was not only a great scholar, but also a great teacher, and students eagerly flocked to his lectures at B'ne B'rak, where he founded his own academy.

The Mishnah of Rabbi Akiva

Rabbi Akiva initiated one of the most important projects in the history of Jewish law. With the aid of his colleagues, he set about systematically organizing the vast body of laws, discussions, and cases comprising the Oral Tradition. Akiva did not put all this down in writing, for it was not yet the custom to do so, but he originated the idea of classifying material by subject, arranging Sabbath laws, marriage laws, and laws of property as separate categories. Thanks to this system, which is now known as the Mishnah of Rabbi Akiva, scholars found it much easier to locate important information when researching questions of Jewish law and practice.

Rachel and Akiva

Not only did Rachel consent to Akiva's leaving her to attend the academy, but she even cut off her hair and sold it to a wig merchant in order to pay his tuition. Though she had no children at this time, and had to support herself,

she was willing to make the sacrifice to help her husband become a learned man.

Akiva stayed away 24 years. By the end of that time he had become the best student in the academy and was able to expound the Torah better than his teachers. He returned home as a great scholar attended by thousands of students.

The people crowded around to see the visiting scholar. Among them was an old man dressed in fine clothing but with a sorrowful appearance. "Many years ago," he said to the rabbi, "I made a vow. Now I am old and do not have many years left. I am sorry and would like to know if I can be released from my vow."

"What was the vow you made?" asked Rabbi Akiva.

"When my daughter enraged me by marrying a poor shepherd," said the man, "I swore I would never speak to her or help her in any way."

"Why did you make the vow?" asked Rabbi Akiva.

"Because he was an ignorant man who could not even read or write," said the old man.

"Vows cannot easily be broken," said Akiva, "but this one was made because of a certain condition. If the condition has changed, the vow need no longer be kept. You may consider your vow null and void, because I am that same ignorant shepherd."

Rachel's father was delighted to learn that his son-in-law was now a distinguished scholar. Weeping with joy, he embraced his long-lost daughter and his grandchildren. Respected leader and teacher of his people, Akiva never forgot to give credit to Rachel. When asked, "Who is really a rich man?" Akiva answered, "He who has a good wife."

Rabbi Akiva instructing his pupils. From the Sarajevo Haggadah.

A New Rebellion

Trajan's March of Conquest / 98–117 C.E.

Following the revolt, Judea went through a period of peace and reconstruction, but this changed when Trajan became the emperor of Rome in 98 C.E.. Filled with dreams of surpassing Alexander the Great's achievement, Trajan began a new march of conquest. His great ambition was to conquer far-off India. He began by invading Dacia (modern Romania) in 101 and 105 C.E., and in 113 he attacked the Parthian Empire.

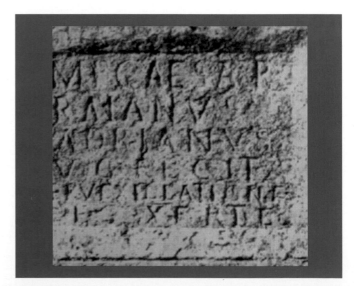

Fragment of an ancient Torah scroll. It belongs to a Jewish family in the Israeli village of Peki'in in the Galilee. Peki'in has a record of Jewish settlement from the 1st century C.E. The inhabitants of this tiny agricultural village escaped Roman exile.

While Trajan was embroiled in these wars, rebellions broke out in many parts of the empire. The Jews of Cyprus, Egypt, and Cyrene revolted in 115–117, but the uprisings were cruelly suppressed. For the survivors, the only result was disappointment and hardship.

Hadrian Rebuilds Jerusalem / 117–138 C.E.

Trajan's campaign of conquest ended suddenly in 117 C.E. when he died on one of his expeditions. His successor, Hadrian, abandoned Trajan's policy of conquest. The Roman Empire was already huge and unwieldy, and Hadrian felt it was dangerous to add more territory. His legions were already hard-pressed putting down revolts in many areas—Germania, Gaul, and Britain; Spain, Egypt, Mesopotamia, Parthia, and Palestine. There was hardly a province that did not cause Hadrian worry.

Hadrian decided to rebuild Jerusalem. But how disappointed the Jews were when they realized what he had in mind! He was not building the Jerusalem of the past, the setting for the Temple of God. Instead, he was building a heathen city, with a circus and stadium, and with a temple for the gods of Rome. Hadrian visited the city and supervised the building projects himself. On the site of the Holy Temple he built an altar dedicated to the god Jupiter. At the same time he outlawed circumcision and issued other new laws that made it difficult to practice Judaism.

Engraved stone with the name of Emperor Trajan, found in Caesarea.

Bar Kochba's Revolt / *ca. 132–135 CE*

Judea had been at peace. The people had made no trouble even during the stormy days of Trajan's invasion of Parthia or when their fellow Jews in other countries revolted. But now the country seethed with anger and a rebellious spirit. Many Jews were impatient to rise against Rome and fight once more for freedom. The rebellious spirit spread even to the academy, where the scholars usually favored peace. Rabbi Akiva was one of the leaders of those who wanted to rise against Rome.

The Romans developed a wooden catapult that could throw giant stones very far. Because of its kicking action it was called an onager. An onager is a wild donkey which defends itself by kicking wildly.

Son of a Star

By the time Hadrian came to Palestine in 129 C.E. to supervise the rebuilding of Jerusalem, Akiva was very old. Despite his advanced age, he still hoped to see his people living in freedom again. When he heard about Simon Bar Kozeba, a brave young man of great magnetism and religious fervor who was organizing a guerilla force to fight the Romans, Akiva felt that the time was at hand. He gave Bar Kozeba his support and renamed him Simon Bar Kochba ("Son of a Star"), a title that heralded his extraordinary strength and spirit. Like many others in this era of turmoil and expectation, Akiva came to believe that Bar Kochba might actually be the Messiah, sent by God to restore the political independence of the Jewish people.

Bust of Hadrian.

The Revolt Begins / 132 C.E.

Hadrian's departure from Palestine was the signal for revolt. The insurrection began in 132 C.E. and lasted for three and a half years. Striking from secure hiding places in the caves and valleys, the Jewish fighters conducted lethal hit-and-run raids against the Romans. Everywhere, Roman outposts were attacked, Roman patrols were ambushed, and Roman supplies were taken. Revolt had broken out! Hadrian sent an army to reinforce the Palestine garrison, but his troops were defeated. Bar Kochba went from victory to victory, liberating one town after another, and the Roman army was chased into Syria.

A Period of Independence

Bar Kochba and his victorious army entered Jerusalem. Everyone rejoiced! They were free again, as in the days of the Maccabees. An altar was erected on the site of the Temple. An uncle of Bar Kochba, the priest Eleazar, officiated at the services. Bar Kochba was declared head of the state, to be assisted by Eleazar. Under the leadership of Bar Kochba, Judea had two short years of independence.

In 1960, Yigal Yadin, professor of archaeology at the Hebrew University in Jerusalem, launched an expedition to explore the caves in the mountains near the Dead Sea. A member of the expedition, exploring one of the narrow tunnels of a cave, discovered a basket filled with objects. Further inspection revealed a treasure trove of artifacts which included sandals, knives, mirrors, jugs, bowls, and the greatest treasure of all—papyrus rolls containing about 40 letters from Bar Kochba.

Bar Kochba had special coins struck to commemorate Judea's newly won independence. One side of the coins showed the Temple gate with a star above it, the other side was inscribed with Bar Kochba's name and the date (ca. 131–132 C.E.).

Rome Strikes Again

When Hadrian learned that Judea had declared its independence, he summoned Severus, his most able general, who was then engaged in a campaign in Britain. Severus appeared in Judea with a powerful army. But in the mountain passes and valleys, Jewish fighters swooped down upon his men. The Romans were repeatedly ambushed and beaten, and Severus suffered heavy losses.

Hadrian now came to Judea in person, bringing reinforcements to replace those who had been killed. Hadrian had decided to use Judea as an object lesson for the many other subjugated nations that made up the Roman Empire. In the end, Severus was victorious. Suffering huge losses, his army doggedly followed the Jewish fighters into the rugged terrain where their strongholds were located, destroying them one by one.

Bar Kochba's Defeat / 135 C.E.

Bar Kochba and his brave fighters made a final stand in the mountain fortress of Betar, southwest of Jerusalem. The Jewish soldiers fought desperately, inflicting heavy losses on the Romans, but Severus' army was much larger, and in the end Betar fell.

The land of Judea was laid waste. Fifty fortresses had been destroyed and a thousand villages lay in ruins. Jerusalem was completely destroyed, and the Jewish population of the land had been decimated. Hundreds of thousands of Jews had been killed, just as many were sold into slavery. Many towns and villages were almost deserted. Within a few years non-Jews began moving in. Areas that had once been entirely Jewish soon became mixed; some even had a non-Jewish majority.

In Jerusalem, as was their custom, the Romans cleared away the rubble and plowed up the ground. On the site they built the new city Hadrian had planned—a heathen city with temples for the worship of Roman gods. It was named Aelia Capitolina.

The Romans concluded that the people of Judea derived their strength from their religion. If Torah study was outlawed and the religious leaders were eliminated, they reasoned, the ordinary people would yield to Roman authority. Accordingly, soldiers hunted down the most important leaders. Rabbi Akiva was condemned to be skinned alive. With his last breath, the saintly hero proclaimed the words of the Shema, "Hear, O Israel, the Lord is our God, the Lord is one."

A silver coin issued by the revolutionary government of Bar Kochba. He and his followers set up a Jewish state in 132–135 B.C.E. which was soon crushed by the Romans.

Judah HaNasi / 2nd century C.E.

A Spiritual Center in Galilee / ca. 140 C.E.

When the Roman persecution came to an end, a new academy was founded in the Galilean town of Usha by Rabbi Judah ben Ilai, one of Akiva's students. It was patterned on the academy at Yavneh. The scholars who studied and taught at Usha were the heirs of the rabbis who had expounded the Torah at Yavneh. As had been the case after the first revolt, the nasi acted as spiritual head of the Jewish community and was recognized as patriarch by the Roman government.

Judah HaNasi

The literal meaning of the Hebrew word *nasi* is "prince." It was a very fitting title for the head of the Sanhedrin, for the nasi had to be a man of learning and fine character whose everyday life would set an example for the people. The nasi most beloved and best-remembered for these qualities was Judah HaNasi, known in English as Judah the Patriarch or Judah the Prince, and often referred to in Hebrew simply as "Rabbi." Judah succeeded his father, Simon, who became nasi after the second revolt, and held the office for almost 50 years.

An outstanding scholar, Judah HaNasi is regarded as the last of the tannaim, for with him the great tannaitic era came to an end. Judah HaNasi set up the Sanhedrin and the academy in Beth-She'arim, and later in Sepphoris. He was very eager to unify the scattered Jewish communities throughout the world. As nasi, he had the sole authority to ordain rabbis and judges even for posts in faraway lands.

A Byzantine mosaic from the 6th century synagogue of Beth-She'an.

Bar'am, high up in the mountains of Upper Galilee, is the site of the best-preserved ancient synagogue in the country, dating to the end of the 2nd or beginning of the 3rd century C.E.

With the destruction of Jerusalem in 70 C.E., Jewish political and military life was crushed. Only towards the end of the 2nd and beginning of the 3rd century, however, were Jews allowed to engage in serious rebuilding programs. This was due largely to the attitude of Emperor Septimius Severus, more benevolent than his predecessors and more tolerant toward the Jews of Palestine.

The Hebrew Language Survives

In Judah HaNasi's time, most Jews, even in the land of Israel, spoke Aramaic, the language of their neighbors, the non-Jewish peoples of Palestine, Babylonia, and Persia. Judah was greatly concerned about the survival of Hebrew. He wanted it to be a living language, used everyday in Jewish homes. To set an example, he and his household spoke only Hebrew. It was said that Judah's servants spoke better Hebrew than many scholars. He also composed his great law code of the Mishnah, in Hebrew.

Judah's love of the Torah and of Hebrew went hand in hand with wide cultural interests. He knew many languages. He spoke and read Greek and Latin, and was learned in many subjects. He had many non-Jewish friends, including Marcus Aurelius (121–180 C.E.), a Roman emperor who was very interested in philosophy.

The academy at Sepphoris was a great success. Students from Babylonia and other faraway places came there to study with Judah and his colleagues. He used to say, "I have learned much from my teachers, more from my colleagues, but most of all from my students." He gave freely of his wealth to needy students and scholars, and to the poor of the land.

Recording the Oral Tradition

Judah HaNasi dedicated his whole life to the great task of compiling, editing, and preserving the Oral Tradition. Over the centuries, a huge quantity of unwritten

Tombs of the Just—Joseph in Shechem, Saul in Gilboa, Rabbi Akiva in Tiberias, etc.—in the eyes of a Jewish pilgrim. Manuscript dating from 1598.

material—laws and legal decisions, biblical commentary, legends and historical narratives—had been accumulating. Some of this had been organized by Rabbi Akiva, but none of it had been set down in writing. Judah HaNasi knew that this material might be lost and forgotten unless it was put in writing.

After the destruction of Jerusalem in 70 C.E., the center of the Jewish religious and national life shifted to the Galilee. Beth-She'arim, about 10 miles from Haifa, became an important Jewish city. Rabbi Judah HaNasi made it the seat of the Sanhedrin. He also compiled the Mishnah there, and in 220 C.E. was buried there in the family tomb.

In 1953, Israeli archaeologists discovered a giant necropolis, an underground city of the dead. The numerous vaulted catacombs are cut out of the soft limestone hills around which the city was built.

After the destruction of Jerusalem, Jews could not use the traditional cemetery on the Mount of Olives, so the necropolis became the central burial ground. The necropolis is a series of long, vaulted interconnected catacombs with thousands of marble and stone coffins, some of which weigh up to five tons. The entrance to the underground city is from stone courtyards dug out of the hills. One of the catacombs contains burial sites with inscriptions that mention the talmudic sages Gamliel and Hanina.

The Oral Tradition

The Mishnah / 1st–2nd century C.E.

The Oral Tradition had grown to such a huge size that very few could possibly remember all of it. In years past, scholars had felt that putting the Oral Tradition in writing would violate the spirit of Jewish law, but now they believed that this step had to be taken if the Torah was to survive. With the assistance of his colleagues and students, Judah set to work on the great task. The entire Oral Tradition was edited and logically arranged according to subject. Around 200 C.E. it was finally put into a permanent written form that would ensure its survival. The work that resulted from their efforts is called the Mishnah. Several centuries later the Mishnah became the basis of the vast encyclopedia of Jewish law and lore known as the Talmud.

In this gigantic task, Judah and his colleagues were aided by the contributions of earlier scholars. Since the time of Yohanan ben Zakkai and the academy at Yavneh, efforts had been made to organize some of the vast material of the Oral Tradition.

In the days of the tannaim, it had been customary in legal discussions to refer to the decisions of Hillel, or the decisions of Shammai, or the decisions of other scholars. Rabbi Akiva and Rabbi Meir were not content with this personalized way of classifying decisions, and proceeded to organize them instead on the basis of what area of law they referred to.

Divisions of the Mishnah

Judah HaNasi codified the legal commentaries and decisions of the Oral Tradition according to subject matter, grouping them into six main divisions:

1. Zeraim (Seeds): Laws of agriculture & prayer.
2. Mo'ed (Festivals): The observance of the Sabbath, festivals and fast days.
3. Nashim (Women): Marriage and divorce.
4. Nezikin (Damages): Civil and criminal laws.
5. Kodashim (Holy Matters): Temple services, sacrifices, and Shehitah (Kosher slaughter).
6. Tohorot (Purities): Ritual purity and cleanliness.

Each of these divisions in turn is subdivided into tractates (*masekhtot*), chapters (*perakim*), and paragraphs (*mishnayot*).

The End of an Era

For many years Judah HaNasi suffered from a painful ailment, but he worked on and devoted himself fully to this task. He also continued with his teaching and other activities. When Judah died around 220 C.E., he was mourned deeply by his friends, colleagues, and students, and indeed by the whole community of Israel. He was one of those rare men who embodied the spirit of a kind father for an entire people. "Not since Moses," the people said, "has there been a man like Judah, who so combines leadership with Torah." Crowds of people paid the last honors as Judah's body was brought to burial at Beth-She'arim. Everyone seemed to feel that a great era of Jewish history had come to an end.

With the death of Judah HaNasi the period of the tannaim ended. The work of the tannaim was preserved in the Mishnah, which served as a groundwork of Jewish law for generations to come.

This page from a manuscript of the Mishnah was written between the 12th and 14th centuries.

Rabbi Heller

Rabbi Bertinoro

A page from tractate Ketubot. The Mishnah is in the center. To the right is the commentary of Rabbi Obadiah Bertinoro, who lived in Italy and then in Jerusalem in the 15th century. To the left is the commentary of Rabbi Yomtov Lipman Heller, of the 17th century.

Halakhah: A Way of Life

The rabbis from the time of Yohanan ben Zakkai to that of Judah HaNasi are known as tannaim, which means "teachers" in Aramaic. The period in which they lived and worked is called the tannaitic age. During this period, with all hope of Jewish independence destroyed as a result of the two disastrous revolts, the center of Jewish life changed from governmental institutions to religious institutions like the synagogue and the academy. The nation's religious leaders formulated a body of regulations for daily life. These regulations are called halakhot.

The word halakhot is the plural of halakhah, which comes from the Hebrew verb *halakh*, meaning "to walk." The halakhot are a series of laws that teach observant Jews how to "walk" through life. By observing the halakhot, all of which ultimately derive from the Torah, the pious Jew lives in accordance with God's will.

The scholars in Israel and Babylonia who followed the tannaim are known as amoraim, which means "spokesmen" or "interpreters." The period in which they were active extended from the 3rd through the 6th century C.E.

Yohanan and Simeon

Yohanan bar Nappaha / 225 C.E.

One of the outstanding scholars in the academy at Tiberias was Yohanan bar Nappaha. The son of a blacksmith, Yohanan was a disciple of Judah HaNasi. He helped to establish a satisfactory method for studying the Mishnah and commenting on its sources. He was much admired by Jewish scholars everywhere.

Simeon ben Lakish / 225 C.E.

One day, Yohanan bar Nappaha met a stranger who impressed him very much. The stranger was a man of outstanding physical appearance, strongly athletic and full of vitality. His name was Simeon ben Lakish. Simeon told Yohanan that he had once been thrown into the arena with Roman gladiators, and had survived. He also had been a trainer of wild animals. Simeon talked at length about his many experiences. He even hinted that he had been the head of a band of highwaymen.

Eventually, Yohanan persuaded Simeon to change his way of life and join him in the academy. Simeon ben Lakish followed this new road and in time became a great rabbi. Many of his discussions with Yohanan on important points of Torah interpretation were recorded by later scholars. There is a romantic side to the story. Simeon married Yohanan's beautiful sister.

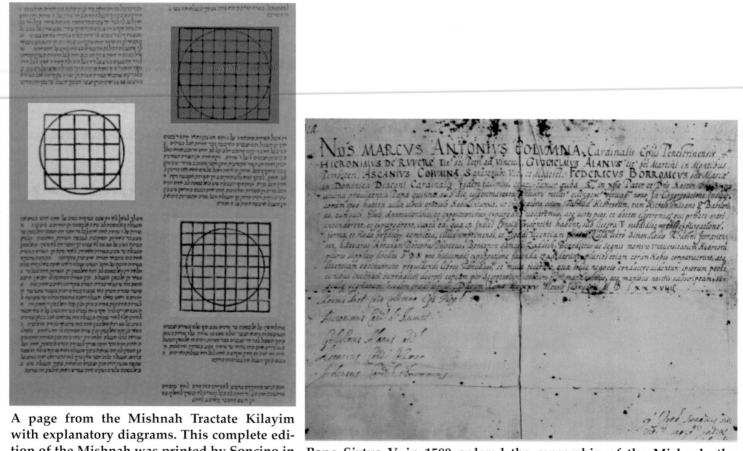

A page from the Mishnah Tractate Kilayim with explanatory diagrams. This complete edition of the Mishnah was printed by Soncino in Naples, Italy in 1492

Pope Sixtus V, in 1589 ordered the censorship of the Mishnah, the Talmud, and other Jewish books. Above is the Pope's edict.

Roman Christianity

Constantine Embraces Christianity / 285–337 C.E.

Developments in Israel were interrupted by an event which deeply affected Jews everywhere: the Roman emperor, Constantine, embraced Christianity. By the year 300 C.E. there were so many Christians in the Roman Empire that the emperor found it politically advantageous to seek Christian support.

With the power of the government behind them, the Christians set out to

The Arch of Constantine in Rome. This arch is decorated with panels and statues taken from other monuments from the reigns of Trajan and Hadrian.

Byzantine coin with a likeness of Emperor Constantine the Great. Constantine converted to Christianity and established his capital at Byzantium, which he rebuilt as a purely Christian city, renamed Constantinople.

destroy Judaism. They regarded it as a rival religion and resented the fact that the Jews, among whom Jesus had first lived and preached, had never accepted the new faith built around him.

Constantine was soon persuaded to enforce a series of anti-Jewish laws. The empire had become weak, and he thought that its strength might be revived if its people were united under the Christian banner. Looking with disfavor on Judaism, he sought to undermine it.

Under Constantine II, Constantine's son, new anti-Jewish laws were issued and a revolt broke out among the Jews of Galilee. The Romans crushed the uprising, destroying Sepphoris and Tiberias, the seats of the academies. Everywhere, Jews had to flee for their lives.

A Period of Peace

In 361 C.E., Constantine's successor, Julian the Apostate, treated the Jews more kindly. The academies were reopened and peace again reigned in the land. Julian had rejected Christianity and hoped to restore paganism to its former dominance. He did everything he could to weaken Christianity. He even sent a letter to the nasi, Hillel II, in which he addressed him as his "Venerable Brother, the Patriarch," and announced that he intended to rebuild the Holy Temple.

Christianity the Official Religion

Julian's reign was short, and after his death in 363 C.E. the Roman Empire again came under the rule of a Christian emperor. Henceforth, Christianity was the empire's official religion. Many other restrictive laws forced the Jews into a position of disadvantage. They were forbidden to own Christian slaves. Intermarriage between Jews and Christians was also forbidden.

In 399 C.E. the government prohibited the sending of emissaries (*apostoli*) to Jewish communities in other parts of the empire to raise funds to support institutions in Palestine.

The Gemara

The Talmud

In the days of Hillel II's son, Gamaliel V, and grandson, Judah IV, the end of Jewish authority in Palestine drew near. Working under great pressure, the last of the Palestinian amoraim collected and codified all the important legal discussions, teachings, and decisions that had taken place in Palestine since the completion of the Mishnah. This work was called the Gemara. The Mishnah and Gemara together make up the Talmud; the Mishnah is the foundation; the Gemara, the superstructure.

The Amoraim

Outside of Palestine, new academies were rising and flourishing in the faraway land of Babylonia. In the town of Nehardea, two students of Judah HaNasi, Rav and Samuel, started to teach and make independent decisions. They based their work on the Mishnah. The generations of scholars after Judah HaNasi, both in Palestine and in Babylonia, were called amoraim, meaning "speakers" or "interpreters." A wealth of new discussions, decisions, stories, and allegories accumulated, both in Galilee and in the new academies of Babylonia. Many Babylonian scholars still went to the academy at Tiberias in Palestine to study with the masters and judges of the academy and the Sanhedrin.

The Palestinian and Babylonian Talmuds

There are two versions of the Talmud, one compiled in Palestine, the other in Babylonia. Both of them are built upon the Mishnah, but the Palestinian Gemara, the work of the Palestinian amoraim, is shorter and does not cover all the tractates of the Mishnah. The Babylonian Gemara, the work of the amoraim in Babylonia, is much more extensive. The Palestinian Talmud (sometimes called the Jerusalem Talmud) was completed around 400 C.E. The Babylonian Gemara continued to grow for another century.

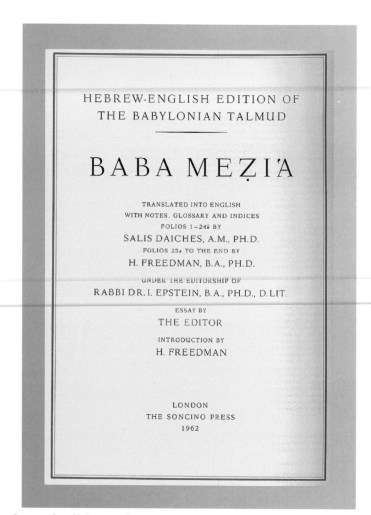

HEBREW-ENGLISH EDITION OF
THE BABYLONIAN TALMUD

BABA MEZIA

TRANSLATED INTO ENGLISH
WITH NOTES, GLOSSARY AND INDICES
FOLIOS 1–24b BY
SALIS DAICHES, A.M., PH.D.
FOLIOS 25a TO THE END BY
H. FREEDMAN, B.A., PH.D.

UNDER THE EDITORSHIP OF
RABBI DR. I. EPSTEIN, B.A., PH.D., D.LIT.

ESSAY BY
THE EDITOR

INTRODUCTION BY
H. FREEDMAN

LONDON
THE SONCINO PRESS
1962

Several editions of the Talmud have been translated into English. This is one of the title pages of the Soncino edition, published in England.

In 1923 Rabbi Meir Shapiro decided to found a course of Talmud study which he called Daf Yomi. The word *daf* means "page" and *yomi* means "daily." Rabbi Shapiro's plan envisaged the study of all 2711 pages (*dapim*) of the Talmud in seven and a quarter years.

Today, many people all over the world participate in the Daf Yomi program. Some study the Talmud individually, some in groups which use both the original and the English translation. There are Daf Yomi groups in Hollywood, the Senate in Washington, and the boardrooms of Wall Street.

The heading starts with the page number, the name of the chapter, the number of the chapter, and the name of the tractate.

Rashi, whose full name was Rabbi Solomon ben Isaac, was an eleventh century French scholar. Rashi's commentary on the Talmud is one of the most influential contributions to rabbinic literature ever written.

The text of the Talmud consists of the Mishnah and the Gemara. The Mishnah is the six-part legal code which was developed in Israel during the first and second centuries C.E. It was written in Hebrew and was completed by Rabbi Yehudah Ha-Nasi. The Gemara is written in Aramaic and is a summary of the legal debates on the meaning of the Mishnah. It was compiled in the Babylonian academies between the third and sixth centuries C.E.

This commentary to the Talmud, called *Ayn Mishpat*, lists the sources of the laws and quotations cited in the Talmud. *Ner Mitzvah* lists the legal literature relevant to the talmudic passage.

The disciples of Rashi, called Tosafists, lived in the twelfth, thirteenth, and fourteenth centuries, and composed a talmudic commentary called Tosafot. The word "Tosafot" means commentary.

This is a commentary on the Talmud by Rabbenu (Hananel ben Hushi'el). Rabbenu lived in Kairouan, Morocco, in the tenth and eleventh centuries.

There are numerous other commentaries in this edition of the Talmud, but they do not appear on this page.

אלו מציאות פרק שני בבא מציעא

A page of the Talmud with some of the commentaries. The selection is from Baba Batra, first tractate of the Order Nezikin.

The Byzantine Empire

The Split in the Roman Empire / 303 C.E.

Although the Roman Empire had one official religion, Christianity, it was torn by strife and disunited. In the 4th century C.E. the empire was divided in two for administrative purposes. The western part had its capital at Rome. The eastern part had its capital in the city of Byzantium, which was rebuilt and renamed Constantinople. The eastern portion of the Roman Empire soon became an independent entity, the Byzantine Empire.

During the Byzantine period, numerous churches were built in Israel. Above is a photo of the ruins of the 6th century church of St. Theodorus at Avdat.

The End of the Patriarchate

The governing apparatus of the Jewish community of Palestine was headed by the nasi, who had been given the title of patriarch by the Romans. It was supported by contributions from Jewish communities throughout the Roman Empire. After the empire was divided, however, the western Roman government prohibited fund-raising by Palestinian emissaries in order to prevent money from being drained off to an area under Byzantine control.

Deprived of financial support, the nasi, the academy, and the Sanhedrin became impoverished. When Gamaliel VI died in 426 C.E., leaving no sons, the Byzantine emperor, Theodosius II, decided to abolish the patriarchate. This was the end of Jewish autonomy in Palestine, and under Byzantine rule it now became a Christian country. Some of its remaining Jewish inhabitants emigrated to Babylon or other places, but many continued to live there even under the increasingly adverse conditions.

Although there were still Jews living in Palestine, the spiritual leadership of world Jewry now passed to the Babylonian Jewish community. Babylonia was a rich, fertile country situated between the Tigris and Euphrates rivers. Jews had been living there ever since 597 B.C.E., when Nebuchadnezzar had deported thousands of people after he conquered Jerusalem.

The Byzantines discovered the secret of making flamethrowers. By 675 C.E. the Byzantine fleets with their deadly flamethrowers had won control of the seas. In the 9th century the Arabs also learned the secret and used flamethrowers against the Christian crusaders.

Babylonian Jewry

The Babylonian Jewish community had grown and prospered. By the 1st century C.E. there were more Jews in Babylon than in Judea. The Babylonian Jews maintained their own synagogues, their own houses of study, and their own courts where Jewish law was observed.

Palestine as Spiritual Center

Like Jews everywhere, the Jews of Babylonia regarded Palestine as the spiritual center of Judaism. Babylonian students, including the great Hillel, flocked to the teachers in Jerusalem. After the destruction of the Second Temple, Jews from Babylonia continued to study with the tannaim at Yavneh, Tiberias, and Sepphoris.

In Roman times Babylonia was ruled by the Parthians, able warriors from Persia who had conquered the old Seleucid kingdom. They were tolerant toward the Jews, and welcomed the stream of refugees from Judea who poured in after each of the revolts against Rome.

The Exilarch

The Jewish community in Babylonia was headed by an official known as the *resh galuta*, meaning "leader of the exile." The office of the exilarch, as it is often called, was hereditary, and the exilarchs were descendants of King David, tracing their descent back through Jehoiachin, who was king of Judea at the time of Nebuchadnezzar.

The exilarch ruled over all the Jewish communities in Babylonia, collecting the taxes assessed by the government as well as the taxes the Jews imposed on themselves to support their communal institutions. Until its destruction in 70 C.E., the exilarch also collected the voluntary tax Jews everywhere paid to support the Temple. In addition, the exilarch had the authority to supervise markets and schools, maintain law and order in predominantly Jewish towns, and enforce rulings by Jewish courts. The exilarch was, in short, the powerful ruler of a rich and important autonomous community.

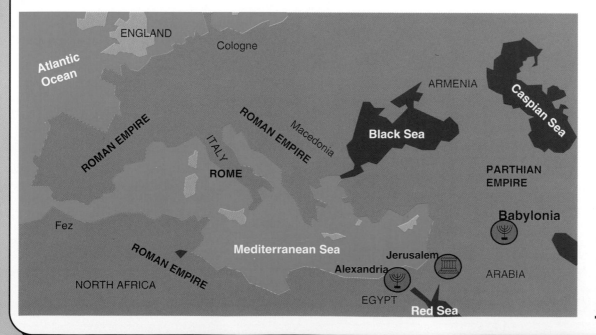

The largest Jewish communities are circled Alexandria in Egypt; the land of Israel; and Babylonia.

Rav and Samuel

Abba Arikha / early 3rd cent. C.E.

In the early centuries, Babylonian Jewry's brightest young men went to study in Palestine, and as a result there were not enough trained rabbis and scholars to staff the schools and religious institutions it needed. One of these young Babylonians, Abba Arikha (Abba the Tall), was among the most gifted of Judah HaNasi's students. Abba Arikha is usually known simply as Rav, meaning "Master." (Rav eventually became the title of all ordained rabbis.)

When Rav returned to Babylonia, he brought with him a copy of the newly composed Mishnah. Rav was appointed inspector of markets and of weights and measures for the Jewish communities of Babylonia. As he journeyed through the land, he saw how slack the people's spiritual life had become. He began to reorganize the schools and synagogues. Eventually, he was appointed head of the academy at Nehardea, but he declined this post so that it could be given to a younger colleague, Mar Samuel, also known as Samuel Yarhina'ah (Samuel the Astronomer), another gifted student of Judah HaNasi.

Rav went on to found an academy of his own in Sura, near the city of Pumpeditha. His new school attracted many scholars and students.

The Month of Kallah

Rav instituted a revolutionary new plan of study, open to anyone who wanted to take advantage of it. Every year during the months of Adar (March-April) and Elul (September), when the farmers could be spared from their work and when artisans and merchants could take a rest during their slack season, Rav would give a special course in Jewish law. These months were called the months of Kallah ("Assembly").

During the months of Kallah and the weeks preceding the holidays, people would stream into Sura from all corners of the surrounding provinces to attend the popular courses at the academy. A thirst for learning took hold of Babylonian Jewry; throughout the land synagogues and schoolhouses were improved and Jews met in great numbers to study and learn.

With the help of the Mishnah, Babylonian scholars were able to apply the Torah's teachings to life in exile. By introducing the Mishnah to their students, Rav and Samuel succeeded in their great purpose of making the Torah a living guide that would enable the Jews of Babylonia to deal with the many problems they faced.

Fragment of an ancient manuscript Siddur showing the Ahabah Rabbah prayer.

The Siddur Is Revised

Samuel and Rav remained close friends and collaborators throughout their lives. Together, they revised the Siddur (prayer-book). Rav wrote the beautiful Alenu prayer for Rosh Hashanah; it is still part of our daily service. Samuel wrote a shorter version of the Shemoneh Esreh (or Amidah)—the Eighteen Benedictions.

Mar Samuel / ca. 177–257 C.E.

Samuel's last years were darkened by trouble. In 226 C.E., the Parthians were overthrown by the Persians. The new rulers of Babylonia were Zoroastrians. Their priests tried to force their religion on all the inhabitants of the territories they had conquered. Since the Jews were not willing to accept Zoroastrianism, a time of persecution began.

After Samuel's death, Nehardea was plundered by desert invaders. Nehardea never regained its former importance. Its academy was rebuilt, but the centers of Jewish learning were thenceforth at Sura and Pumpeditha.

The fire altar depicted on this Sasanian coin was the focal point of Zoroastrian religion. These perpetually burning fires were set up all over Iran. Some burned in the open air, while others were enclosed in fire-temples.

A relief from Persepolis dating from the early Second Temple period depicts Ahura Mazda, god of Zoroastrianism, the religion of ancient Persia. Zoroastrianism taught that the world was torn between two deities: Ahura Mazda, the Wise Lord, creator of heaven and earth, light and life, who embodied the spirit of goodness, truth, and law; and Ahriman, the Evil Spirit, whose essence was falsehood and death.

Rava and Abaye / early 4th century

The Academy of Pumpeditha attracted the brightest and most dedicated students in Palestine and Babylon. The methodology and sharp disputations between the amoraim (teachers) and the students created keen, knowledgeable scholars who made great contributions to halakhic principles.

Among the students were two colleagues, Rava and Abaye, who became the two greatest amoraim of the 4th century.

Abaye / 4th century

Abaye, orphaned as a child, was raised by his uncle, Rabbi bar Nahmani, who lovingly nicknamed him Abaye, meaning "Little Father." Abaye perpetuated the memory of his foster-mother, whom he referred to as "Em," by publicly quoting her proverbs and folk remedies.

In the field of halakhah and Torah learning, Abaye emphasized the importance of traditional sources. He supported the plain meaning of the biblical text (*peshat*) against the midrashic (non-literal) interpretation.

Abaye was known for his willingness to help others. He took special pride when one of his students satisfactorily completed a section of the Mishnah. Although he was poor, he would make a party to celebrate the event, so as to encourage the student. His peaceloving disposition is recalled by the saying "Be mild in speech, suppress your anger, and maintain goodwill to everyone."

Abaye headed the Academy in Pumpeditha from 333 to 338 C.E., at which point he was succeeded by his boyhood friend Rava.

Rava / 4th century

Rava, the son of Rabbi Joseph bar Ham, married a granddaughter of the great talmudic sage Rav, who founded the academy in Sura. His real name was Abba, but he was called Rava, which is the contraction of Rabbi plus Abba. In addition to being a brilliant scholar, Rava worked hard to maintain good relations with the Persian government.

Rava was on friendly terms with the exilarch of Persia, King Shapur II's intermediary in dealing with the Jewish community. He also enjoyed the special protection of Shapur because he had secretly contributed large sums of money to the king. As a result, Rava succeeded in easing the oppression against the Jews of Babylonia.

The debates between the two Talmud luminaries which formed the foundation of halakhah are known as "the investigation of Rava and Abaye." Eventually these debates became a major part of the Babylonian Talmud.

This drinking bowl dates from the 7th century. It depicts King Shapur II on a hunt.

Later scholars, who studied the debates, decided all the cases in favor of Rava except for six which were won by Abaye. It is thought that Rava's conclusions and thought patterns were more logical and clearer than Abaye's.

Abaye (333–338 C.E.) and Rava (338–352) successively headed the academy at Pumpeditha. Both amoraim, because of their brilliance, drew the brightest minds of Palestine and Babylonia to their academies.

THE TALMUDIC AGE

SOFERIM (scribes)
5th to 3rd cent. B.C.E.

The generations of scholars and teachers who carried on the work of EZRA.

ZUGOT (pairs)
2nd cent. B.C.E. to
about 10 C.E.

The two leaders of the great Sanhedrin who carried on the teachings and interpretations of the Torah after the period of the Soferim. HILLEL and SHAMMAI were the last and most brilliant of the Zugot.

TANNAIM (Teachers)
1st and 2nd cent. C.E.

The scholars and teachers whose works are recorded in the Mishnah.
- GAMALIEL I, Nasi and last president of the Great Sanhedrin.
- YOHANAN BEN ZAKKAI, founder of the academy of Yavneh.
- GAMALIEL II, Nasi and head of the Sanhedrin and of the academy of Yavneh.
- RABBI AKIBA.
- RABBI MEIR and SIMEON BAR YOHAI.
- JUDAH HANASI (Judah I), Nasi, head of the Sanhedrin and the academy, compiler of the Mishnah.

AMORAIM (speakers)
3rd to 6th cent. C.E.
(about 200-499)

The scholars and teachers whose work is recorded in the Gemara.
- GAMALIEL III, son of Judah Hanasi, head of the academy and of the Sanhedrin.
- ABBA ARIKHA (RAV) and MAR SAMUEL founded the Babylonian Talmud.
- YOHANAN BAR NAPPAHA and SIMEON BEN LAKHISH.
- HILLEL II, Nasi and head of the academy and of the Sanhedrin, introduced the fixed calendar.
- Completion of the Palestinian Talmud.
- GAMALIEL IV, last Nasi. End of Patriarchate.
- ASHI and
- RABINA, compiled the Babylonian Talmud.

SABORAIM (reasoners)
500 to 530 C.E.

The scholars and teachers who completed the editing of the Babylonaian Talmud. Until the tiime of the Gaonate great Babylonian scholars bore the title of SABORA.

Rav Ashi / ca. 352–427 C.E.

The troubled Jewish community of Babylonia found a new leader in Rav Ashi, a highly gifted scholar of a noble and wealthy family. When still a young man, he had been appointed head of the academy of Sura. He immediately set about revising the course of study and making it more meaningful to his listeners. Again people streamed into Sura during the Kallah months and before the holidays.

The Babylonian Talmud

Rav Ashi also turned his attention to the Gemara that had been developed by the amoraim of Babylonia. Aided by his students and colleagues, he codified this vast accumulation of oral material according to the system used in the Mishnah by Judah HaNasi. During the months of Kallah, many students contributed their own discussions and decisions, together with stories and allegories they had heard from earlier teachers.

For 60 years Rav Ashi presided over the academy of Sura, earning the distinction of being called Rabbana, "Our Master," an honorary title ordinarily conferred only on the exilarchs.

Rabina succeeds Rav Ashi / 427 C.E.

After Rav Ashi's death a time of persecution began again under a cruel Persian king. Rabina, who succeeded Ashi as head of the academy of Sura, con- tinued the work of editing and codifying, but it took another generation of scholars to complete the work. This next generation, known as the saboraim ("reasoners") further edited the Babylonian Gemara. By the year 530 C.E. the Babylonian Talmud, consisting of the Babylonian Gemara together with the Mishnah, was completed.

The Gaonim

In 531 C.E. a new king, Khosru I, ascended the throne of Persia. During his reign the academies of Sura and Pumpeditha reopened. From then on, the heads of the great academies were called gaonim, the plural form of *gaon* ("excellency"). Since the patriarchate in the land of Israel had come to an end, the gaonim were the spiritual leaders of world Jewry. In the reopened academies the newly completed Babylonian Talmud was studied and became the basis for further work.

A productive new period of Jewish life began. The Persian Empire was at peace. Its people prospered, and its cities were filled with beautiful gardens and palaces. Poets and painters, architects and sculptors, created many beautiful works. Craftsmen fashioned handsome objects of metalwork and made lovely materials of cloth and silk. After the death of Khosru II in 628 C.E., however, Persia went into a decline.

Magic bowl with Hebrew inscription found in the ruins of Babylon.

The Jews of Arabia

Jews had settled in Arabia as early as 70 C.E., when the Second Temple was destroyed. Escaping from the devastation brought on by the first revolt against Rome, some of them settled on the oases in the northwestern part of the Arabian peninsula, where they became farmers and planters. According to some sources, it was orchard keepers and planters from Judea who first introduced the date palm to Arabia. Jewish settlers also helped found the cities which lay along the strip of oases through which merchant caravans laden with precious incense and spices traveled between east and west. Jewish merchants and artisans sold their wares in the cities of Yathrib and Mecca.

A Passover Seder as conducted by a Yemenite family.

The Kingdom of Yemen

In Yemen, in the southwestern corner of Arabia, Jewish planters and artisans helped to bring wealth and prosperity to the land. Many Jews settled there, and in the 5th century C.E., the king became a convert to Judaism. The Jewish kingdom of Yemen flourished. Its merchants traded goods in many lands, its artisans forged lovely vessels of silver, copper, and gold, and its poets wrote beautiful songs. In 525 C.E., however, the Jewish kingdom was destroyed by the Byzantines and the Abyssinians. Although many Jews left Yemen, a sizable Jewish community remained there.

In 575, Yemen became part of the Persian Empire, but the Jewish community never regained its former splendor. Often there was bitter poverty and persecution. In spite of these hardships, the Yemenite Jews held fast to their beliefs and preserved their skills. They continued to do fine metalwork, and to plant and trade.

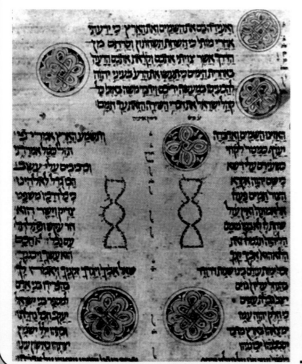

A page from an illuminated Yemenite Five Books of Moses. This manuscript was completed in 1496 C.E for Ibrahim ibn Yusuf ibn Sa'id ibn Ibrahim al-Israili. The text is a section of the Song of Moses.

Islam Begins / 570 C.E.

Meanwhile, in the deserts of Arabia, a new power was preparing for conquest---a people driven on by a new religion and a need for fertile land.

The Rise of Muhammad / ca. 570–632 C.E.

Around the end of the 6th century, an Arab camel driver named Muhammad was profoundly influenced by the concepts of Judaism. Although Muhammad was poor and uneducated, he possessed extraordinary intelligence and energy. He worked his way up untiringly until he became a caravan master, and eventually one of the wealthy merchants and importers of the city of Mecca.

Like other Arabs, Muhammad believed himself to be a descendant of Abraham, the patriarch of the Jews, through Ishmael, his elder son. Deeply occupied with religious questions, Muhammad began to develop his own ideas. Finally he came to look upon himself as a great prophet like Moses and the prophets of old. Muhammad

An old painting showing Muhammad preaching to the non-believers.

affirmed the belief in the one God, whom he called Allah. "There is no god but Allah, and Muhammad is his prophet," he declared. He proclaimed a new religion, and devoted all his intelligence and energy to the task of spreading it. Muhammad called his new religion Islam, meaning "submission" to the will of God.

A New Religion

The religion of Islam was founded on the basic principles of Judaism. Muhammad's prophecies contain pronouncements against idol worship and sacrifice, and uphold the worship of one God. He promised his followers that if they followed the commandments of Islam they would be rewarded with eternal bliss in an afterlife in heaven.

Muhammad won no following in his own city of Mecca. The people there were enraged at his attempt to convert them to Islam and considered him a fanatical rabble-rouser. In the year 622 C.E. Muhammad was forced to flee from his home.

The Hegira (flight) of Muhammad was the key event in Muslim history. It was so important that on the Muslim calendar, all dates are A.H. ("year of the Hegira"). Thus, 1 A.H. is the same as 622 C.E.

This 16th century Turkish painting shows an angry mob of the citizens of Mecca throwing stones at Muhammad. Because of their opposition he was forced to flee the city, but eight years later he returned in triumph. Note the halo around Muhammad's featureless face.

The golden dome of the Mosque of Omar in Jerusalem is a highly visible landmark. It was built by Caliph Abdul Malik Ibn Marwan in 691 C.E.

The 29 letters of the Arabic alphabet. Each letter is accompanied by its Arabic name and sound. Arabic, like Hebrew, is written from right to left.

Islam Spreads

Muhammad preached his faith and sought followers among the many Arab tribes. Gradually the new religion took root throughout the Arabian peninsula. Yathrib, to which Muhammad fled when he was driven out of Mecca, became a holy city and was renamed Medina (Medinat-en-Navi, "City of the Prophet"). Mecca, his birthplace and long regarded as holy even before the advent of Islam, became the main shrine and object of pilgrimage for his followers.

Limits for the Jews of Arabia

Muhammad expected the Jews of Arabia to accept his new religion. After all, had it not been founded on the principles of Judaism, and was not he, Muhammad, a prophet in the great tradition of the prophets of Israel? When the Arabs of Mecca rejected Muhammad and he fled to Medina, he expected to find a friendly reception among the three Jewish tribes in the area. But the Jews of Medina rejected him.

Muhammad angrily abandoned the effort to convert the Jews and changed the direction of Muslim prayer from Jerusalem to Mecca. When he attained power he revenged himself on the Jewish tribes. Some were put to death, some were sold as slaves, and some were forced to convert. Those who survived, together with the Jews of Yemen, were taxed excessively and forced to obey humiliating laws.

Jews (wearing their traditional colored costumes) consult a 120-year-old elder in Damascus, who tells them that Muhammad was a Messiah and the last prophet to come into the world—a 16th century Turkish miniature based on 10th century Arab text. In this period there was constant theological discussion about the respective roles of the three monotheistic religions—Judaism, Christianity, and Islam.

The Holy Wars

Muhammad died in the year 632. His successors held the title of caliph. Muhammad was succeeded by Caliph Abu Bakr, who died two years later and was followed by Caliph Omar. As princely ruler of Arabia and religious leader of all Muslims, Omar declared a holy war. He and his followers rode across the desert into the lands of the Fertile Crescent. His army, recruited from all over Arabia, was made up of warriors united and fanatical in their faith.

Jerusalem Conquered / 638 C.E.

Omar and his generals conquered Egypt, Palestine, Syria, and Persia, spreading the faith of Islam in those lands. Omar laid the foundation of a vast Arab empire, often referred to as the caliphate. The Muslim empire ultimately spread over the entire

A page from an ancient copy of the Koran. Illuminated copies of the Koran were skillfully handwritten and illustrated in gold and bright colors.

An ancient painting showing Muhammad with the leader of a Jewish tribe in Arabia. He condemned the whole tribe to death because they refused to convert to the Muslim religion.

Fertile Crescent, across North Africa to Spain, and from the Nile delta eastward as far as India.

The Koran

During the reign of Omar's successor, Caliph Othman (644–656 C.E.), a son-in-law of Muhammad, the Koran, Islam's holy book, was put together in written form.

At Othman's command, all of Muhammad's prophecies were arranged and written down, based on notes taken by Muhammad's secretary at his master's dictation. The Koran is divided into chapters arranged in order of length. Written in beautiful classical Arabic, it begins with a short passage in praise of Allah.

The Nonbelievers

As the new Arab Empire grew, a body of laws known as the Pact of Omar was instituted in 640 C.E. to regulate Muslim relations with Jews and Christians. The rights of "nonbelievers" were severely reduced. They were forced to pay a humiliating poll tax; they were not allowed to ride on horseback and were forced to wear clothes that would make them conspicuous and set them apart from Muslims; and they were not permitted to bear arms. But they were not forbidden to observe their own religion.

As time passed, the Arab conquerors became more tolerant. The Jews of the Arab Empire followed their religion and way of life. Jewish poets wrote Arabic poetry, and Jewish physicians, mathematicians, and astronomers contributed to the growth of the sciences. Jewish merchants helped establish trade routes throughout the Middle East. They followed the Arab conquerors into North Africa, and eventually across the Mediterranean to far-off Spain.

A pilgrim caravan on the way to Mecca. The happy pilgrims are accompanied by music of horns and drums. Painted in 1237, in Baghdad.

Palestine Under the Caliphate

After Omar's conquest of Palestine in 638 C.E., conditions there improved. The Arabs established a Muslim sanctuary in Jerusalem, which had now become holy to three religions. Once again the Jews were permitted to enter the city and pray at the ruined western wall of the Temple. Soon there was a small Jewish community in Jerusalem.

The holy city of Mecca and its mosque. Near the center of the mosque is a small shrine called the Kaaba. Muslims believe that the Kaaba was built by Abraham and Ishmael. In the Kaaba is a black stone. Muslims believe the stone was given to Adam by an angel. Each year thousands of Muslim pilgrims come from far away to kiss the sacred black stone.

Timeline—The Age of Learning

JEWISH HIGHLIGHTS

Great Assembly of --- 250 BCE	Rededication of Temple 164 BCE	Judea expels Syrians 134 BCE	Jerusalem Falls 63BCE	Herod the Great 37 BCE	Birth of Christianity first century CE	Jerusalem Falls 70 CE

JEWISH • EVENTS PERSONALITIES • LITERATURE • HOLIDAYS

Septuaguint	Maccabean revolt	High priest, SIMON	Civil war	Temple enlarged	John the Baptist	Zealots
Bible standardized	JUDAH MACCABE	Sadducees	Judea becomes Roman province	Masada	Jesus crusified, 29 CE	Tish B'av
	Hanukah	Pharisees		Sanhedrin	Essenes	Johanan ben Zakkai
		Sanhedrin		Hillel	Dead Sea scrolls	
		Great Assembly		Shammai		
		Salome		Economic prosperity		

WORLD HISTORY

Alexander the Great	Selucid empire	Syria	Romans	Romans	Romans	Romans
Ptolemies	Antiochus IV	Hellenism	Pompei	Parthians	Pontius Pilate	Vespasian
Antiochus III			Julius Caesar			Titus

Timeline—The Age of Learning

JEWISH HIGHLIGHTS

Masada falls
73 CE

Sanhedrin
Nasi
85 C.E.

Bar Kochba Revolt
132 C.E.

Tannaim
1st–2nd century C.E.

Amoraim
3rd–6th century C.E.

Age of Gaonim
starts 589 C.E.

Arabs conquer Jerusalem
638 C.E.

JEWISH EVENTS • PERSONALITIES • LITERATURE • HOLIDAYS

- Eleazar ben Yair
- Jews commit suicide
- Josephus

- Gamaliel II
- Prayer services
- Torah readings

- Bar Kochba
- Rabbi Akiva executed
- Betar falls, 135 C.E.

- Mishnah
- Responsa
- Halakhah
- Judah HaNasi
- Siddur

- Yohanan bar Nappaha
- Simeon ben Lakish
- Rav
- Samuel and Rav Ashi
- End of Patriarchate
- Jerusalem Talmud
- Early synagogues

- Babylonian Talmud
- Exilarch
- Responsa
- Halakhah
- Masorah

- Muhammad
- Islam begins, 622
- Forced conversion of Jews
- Omar
- Koran
- Pact of Omar

WORLD HISTORY

- Romans
- Trajan
- Hadrian

- Romans

- Romans
- Severus

- Parthians and Persians
- Romans

- Babylon
- Byzantines
- Constantine
- Rome

- Persia

- Muslims
- Persia
- Caliphate

The Gaonim

Although the Jewish community in Jerusalem had been restored after the Muslim conquest, the center of Jewish life was still in Babylonia. Conditions had deteriorated during the persecution by the Persians, but under the Arabs, who conquered the area in 660, the situation of Babylonian Jewry improved. The schools of Sura and Pumpeditha reopened, presided over by the gaonim. Once again the Jewish community was led by the exilarch, a descendant of King David. The exilarchs were now authorized to collect taxes both for the caliphate and for the Jewish community. The gaonim was given the right to select the exilarch, but their choice had to be approved by the caliph.

Bustanai / ca. 620–675

The first exilarch under Muslim rule was Bustanai, a wise and beloved leader. The exilarchs who followed over many generations looked back to him as their spiritual ancestor. As heads of the academies, the gaonim had great prestige and often acted as advisors to the exilarchs, especially on matters of Jewish law and scholarship. Even the far-off communities of North Africa, Spain, and France turned to the gaonim for advice.

Whenever Jews anywhere were in doubt on questions of Jewish law (halakhah), they would send messengers to the gaonim in Babylonia. The Babylonian scholars sent their answers and legal decisions in clear, concise letters known as *teshuvot* (responsa). Ever since, decisions on legal questions by Jewish scholars have been set down in accordance with the form used in the gaonic responsa. Nowadays responsa are still written by prominent rabbis who are experts on the halakhah.

The Age of the Gaonim

The gaonic period extended from the 7th to the 11th century. During this era the gaonim sent emissaries to acquaint Jews in far-off communities with developments in Sura and Pumpeditha, and to teach the Talmud. By this means knowledge of the Talmud was spread far and wide, and a bond was established among the many groups that made up world Jewry.

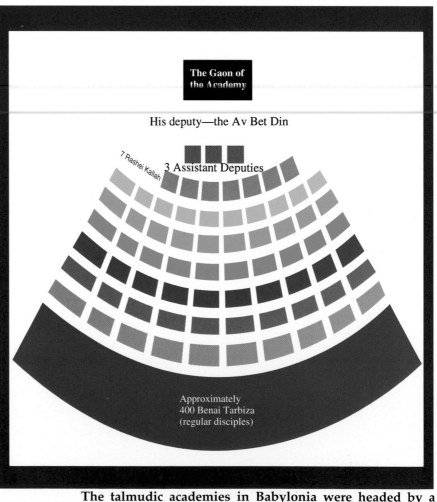

The Gaon of the Academy

His deputy—the Av Bet Din

7 Rashei Kallah   3 Assistant Deputies

Approximately 400 Benai Tarbiza (regular disciples)

The talmudic academies in Babylonia were headed by a gaon. It consisted of 70 sages whose places in the hierarchy were fixed. The sages closer to the gaon, were generally the more advanced.

The Karaites / ca. 762 C.E.

In the 8th century a group opposed to the gaonim arose in Babylonia and became a powerful threat to Jewish unity. Its ideas resembled those of the Sadducees of old. This new movement rejected the Oral Tradition, claiming that the written Torah was the only valid source of Jewish law.

By rejecting the Oral Tradition, it was also rejecting the Talmud, in which the Oral Tradition had been codified.

Anan ben David / ca. 750

One of the foremost leaders of this movement was Anan ben David. As a member of the Davidic family, he had expected to become exilarch, but instead the gaonim of Pumpeditha and Sura chose his younger brother, Hananiah. Bitterly disappointed, Anan challenged his brother's right to the high office.

The caliph endorsed Hananiah as exilarch and, fearing unrest, had Anan arrested. Anan had to stand trial. On the advice of a Muslim lawyer, he testified that he did not care whether or not he became exilarch but was merely the founder of a new religion. As a result, he was acquitted.

Anan Combats the Talmud

Anan condemned the Talmud and the complicated legal system based upon it, emphasizing that every Jew had the right to interpret the Torah. For many people this approach had great appeal, even though its extreme form sometimes led to silly excesses. For example, the Talmud permitted the use of heat and light on the Sabbath if they were initiated before the Sabbath, but Anan did not. As a result, his followers were obliged to sit in the dark and cold on the day of rest.

Under Anan's successors, the movement he began named itself the Bnai Mikra ("Sons of the Scripture"). They were also called Karaites ("Scripturists").

In the 9th and 10th centuries the Karaite sect was an active, growing movement. Its leaders wrote eloquent defenses of their approach. Before long there were Karaites in Babylonia, Palestine, Egypt, and North Africa.

A 10th century Karaite manuscript of the Bible.

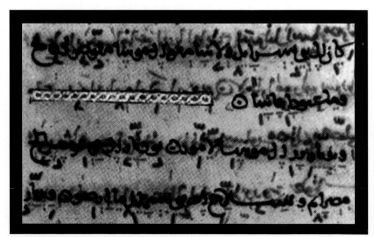

A 10th century Karaite manuscript. Through it is written in Hebrew and has vowel points, the characters are Arabic. Arab and Jewish cultures were closely linked in this period

Saadia Gaon / 882–942 C.E.

Saadia ben Joseph (882–942) was an Egyptian Jew. His brilliant treatises against Karaism helped many people to understand the issues at stake in the conflict between the new sect and talmudic tradition.

Saadia as Gaon

Concerned about the inroads being made by Karaism, the exilarch summoned Saadia to become the gaon of the academy at Sura. He proved to be the greatest, most capable of all the gaonim. During his tenure he taught a whole new generation of scholars and wrote numerous responsa dealing with religious and legal questions from Jews in many lands. In addition, he succeeded in exposing the weaknesses of Karaism and restoring faith in the talmudic tradition. As a result, the unity of world Jewry was preserved.

To teach the alphabet to young Hebrew scholars, this book was produced in 10th century Egypt. This page was found in the Cairo Genizah.

the days of Saadia Gaon, the prestige and power of the gaonim reached their highpoint. After the death of the great master, however, the importance of the Babylonian schools slowly diminished, and with it the influence of the gaonim.

The Siddur

Saadia was an accomplished poet in both Arabic and Hebrew. He translated the Bible into Arabic and compiled one of the first Jewish prayerbooks. It was called the Siddur, meaning "order," as our prayerbooks are called today. Saadia's Siddur was a very important achievement, because until his time the synagogue service had no fixed order or content.

Saadia the Thinker

Saadia Gaon was a profound religious philosopher. One of his greatest works was *Sefer ha-Emunot ve-De'ot* ("The Book of Beliefs and Opinions"), it explains Judaism's fundamental beliefs and ideas. Written in Arabic, it was helpful to the many Jews in Arabic-speaking countries who no longer spoke or read Hebrew. In

Title page of the *Emunot ve-De'ot* by Saadia Gaon. This edition was printed in 1562, in Constantinople.

The Masorah

An absorbing task that now occupied the scholars of Tiberias was the establishment of the Masorah. The term Masorah literally means "handing down." It designates the establishment of the correct, standard text of the Holy Scriptures, to be "handed down" to future generations. Establishing the correct text was necessary because in ancient times every copy of the Bible had to be written by hand, and over the centuries errors of various kinds had slipped in. The scholars who performed this task are called Masoretes. The Masoretic text is followed by soferim (scribes) to this day when they copy scrolls of the Torah.

True Text and True Meaning

In order to preserve the true text and meaning of the Scriptures, the Masoretes carefully compared different versions of each biblical book and decided which corresponded to the pure, original form. They laid down the text word for word, letter for letter, and worked out a system of punctuation. They devised a system of vowel signs to ensure that every word was pronounced properly. In addition, they provided a system of accentuation and punctuation that also serves as musical notation for the chanting of the Torah and other parts of the Bible in the synagogue.

The Masoretes were active from the 7th through the 10th century. Their most outstanding scholars were Ben Asher and Ben Naphtali.

Page from the *Rules of Accents* by Jacob ben Asher in the 10th century. This momentous work established the rules of punctuation and spelling in the Bible

Colophon of the Masoretic Codex of Moses ben Asher (897 C.E.).

The Golden Age / 10th–12th century

Spain Is Conquered

The Moors of North Africa were converted to Islam when the wave of Arab conquest spread westward during the early years of the caliphate. Under their rule, the Jews of North Africa prospered. In the city of Kairouan, near the site of ancient Carthage, a talmudic academy was established and a center of learning flourished.

Spain Under the Arabs

In 711 C.E., the Moors, driven by religious fervor, crossed the Straits of Gibraltar. Within four years they had conquered most of Christian Spain. In 755, the city of Cordova became the capital of the Spanish caliphate.

The Moors were tolerant rulers who wanted all their subjects, whether Muslim, Jewish, or Christian, to participate in the life of the new commonwealth they had founded. Although the language of the land was Arabic, and Islam was the religion of the court and the ruling class, opportunity was open to everyone.

The Jews of Spain

The Jews of Spain entered many professions. They worked as farmers and vintners, goldsmiths, tailors, and shoemakers. They were small merchants and large-scale traders. Spanish Jews also entered the sciences, becoming physicians, astronomers, and mathematicians. Many Jews were well-traveled, highly educated, and achieved high positions in the new society. Jews were government officials, and acted as ambassadors and interpreters, carrying out commercial and diplomatic missions in distant lands. Under the Moors a golden age dawned for Spanish Jewry. Schools of Jewish learning were founded. Scholars from Babylon came to Cordova with copies of the Talmud, and taught the Jews of Spain.

Hasdai Ibn Shaprut / ca. 915–970 C.E.

One of the most famous Jewish figures in Cordova was Hasdai Ibn Shaprut. An eminent physician, Hasdai counted the caliph himself among his patients. The caliph considered Hasdai a trusted friend and advisor. Hasdai Ibn Shaprut knew Latin, the language of the learned in Christian Europe, and often acted as the caliph's interpreter. When ambassadors from other countries came to Cordova, he represented the caliph in discussions with them.

As a leading member of the Jewish community of Spain, Hasdai supported the academies, purchase prized copies of the Talmud, and gave fincial assistance to scholars and students, poets and writers.

The Muslim invaders were spurred into battle by the belief that heavenly angels protected them. The Christians adopted St. James, the Moor Killer, as their protector. He was believed to ride a great white horse and wield a deadly sword. This Spanish painting pictures St. James in battle with the Moors.

The Khazars / 8th to 11th C.E.

An ambassador from Persia told Hasdai Ibn Shaprut about the Kingdom of the Khazars on the shores of the Black Sea. This far-off kingdom, ruled by a king named Joseph, stretched to the shores of the Caspian Sea. The Khazars were valiant warriors but they lived as Jews, following the laws of the Torah. Hasdai was greatly excited by this news; could these strange Jews be descendants of the Ten Lost Tribes?

A Letter to King Joseph

Hasdai sent a letter to the Khazar king. It passed through many hands on its journey, and three years went by before Hasdai received a answer. In his reply the Khazar king told Hasdai about his land and people, recounting the story of how they had come to accept the Jewish faith. The Khazars, he explained, were not one of the lost tribes. During the 8th century one of his ancestors, Bulan, had decided to abandon paganism. He invited a Christian, a Muslim, and a Jew to his court, and asked them to describe their respective religions. After hearing their presentations Bulan chose Judaism. Many of his courtiers followed his example, and eventually many other Khazars also became Jews.

The story told by Joseph captured the imagination of many Spanish Jews. It formed the background for one of the classics of medieval Jewish philosophy, Judah Halevi's *Kuzari*.

The Khazar kingdom survived until the 11th or 12th century, when conquering Russian princes destroyed it and scattered its people over the great steppes of Russia.

A letter in Hebrew from a Khazar Jew, dated 950 C.E. It recounts the incidents that led to the conversion of the Khazars to Judaism and events that took place in Khazaria during the 10th century.

The Alcázar castle in central Spain was built by the Moors in the Middle Ages.

Samuel Ibn Nagrela / 993–1056 C.E.

In 1031 C.E. the Cordova caliphate broke up into several smaller Muslim kingdoms. New cities gained importance, among them Malaga, the capital of the caliph of Granada.

The Scholarly Merchant

In the city of Malaga there lived a most unusual man named Samuel Ibn Nagrela (993–1055). Samuel had come to Malaga from Cordova. He earned his living as a spice merchant but was a well-educated man—a philosopher, mathematician, and a fine Hebrew scholar, and knew several languages, including Hebrew, Spanish, Arabic, Greek, and Latin. Many of the city's nobles came to him for advice or to write letters for them.

Even the grand vizier had heard about the scholarly merchant. He so admired Samuel that he appointed him his secretary. When the vizier died, Caliph Badis appointed Samuel in his place. Henceforth, Samuel lived in the palace in Granada. In addition to his other duties, he became the commander of the caliph's army.

Like Hasdai Ibn Shaprut, Samuel Ibn Nagrela always took a deep interest in the Jewish community. He had the most complete and valuable Hebrew library in Spain. He wrote essays on the Talmud, composed poems on both religious and secular subjects, and even worked on a Hebrew grammar.

Samuel, the Prince in Israel

Also like Hasdai, Samuel was very generous. He helped many poets and writers, students and scholars to find work and to support themselves. He aided the charitable collections that supported the poor Jews of Malaga and raised funds for the talmudic academies of Spain, Babylonia, and Palestine. The Jews of Malaga, regarding Samuel Ibn Nagrela as the head of their community, conferred the title of *nagid* ("prince") upon him. Thus he is known in history as Samuel HaNagid.

The Great Mosque of Cordova with its nineteen naves, each with a double layer of vaults, dating from the 8th to 10th century.

Solomon Ibn Gabirol / ca. 1021–1056

Among the many writers whom Samuel HaNagid encouraged and supported was Solomon Ibn Gabirol (1020–1057). During his short life Solomon wrote many beautiful poems in Hebrew and Arabic, as well as philosophical works that were widely read by both Jews and non-Jews. He wrote hymns for the Sabbath, festivals, and fast days, many of which found their way into the prayerbook. His most celebrated poem was the ethico-philosophic hymn Keter Malkhut ("Royal Crown"), which became part of the liturgy for the Day of Atonement.

The "Fountain of Life"

Ibn Gabirol's most important philosophical work, *Mekor Hayyim* ("Fountain of Life") explains his personal faith and his view of

The poem "Grief and Desire" by Solomon Ibn Gabirol. The page is from a 12th century manuscript.

The Court of Lions in the Alhambra of Granada, Spain. This fountain is mentioned in one of the poems of Solomon Ibn Gabirol.

God's relationship to the physical world. In the Middle Ages it was translated into Latin under the title *Fons Vitae*. Since it is characterized by a general philosophical approach, with no special emphasis on Judaism, it was long thought to have been written by a Christian philosopher. Ibn Gabirol's authorship was established in 1846 by a scholar doing research on old manuscripts in a Paris library.

A Golden Age

The life of Ibn Gabirol marks a high point in Arabic-Jewish culture, a golden age that began in the 10th century and continued until the 12th. During this period, scholars, poets, scientists, and philosophers flourished in the Jewish communities of Muslim Spain, despite the political strife which surrounded them.

Isaac Hakohen Alfasi / 1013–1103 C.E.

The Jewish academies of Spain produced many talmudic scholars. The founder of the most important Spanish academy was Isaac ben Jacob Hakohen Alfasi (1013–1103). Born in North Africa, Alfasi studied and taught at the academies in Fez and Kairouan for many years. He moved to Spain in 1088 and settled in Lucena, where he became head of the Jewish community and established a center of talmudic learning which became famous throughout the country.

A Guide for Talmud Students

In order to guide judges who had to rule on questions of Jewish law, Isaac Alfasi wrote a great code and commentary on the Talmud in which he concentrated on those parts of the halakhah which seemed most important. This work, the *Sefer Halakhot*, is often referred to as the *Rif*, from the initials *Rabbi Isaac Fasi*. It is still used by students of the Talmud.

Alfasi's method of codifying the laws did not please everyone, however, and many scholars criticized his work. Despite his sharp and precise opinions, Alfasi was a mild and forgiving man. When one of his most bitter opponents was about to die, he made his peace with Alfasi by sending his son to study with the master. Alfasi took the orphaned boy into his own household and taught him together with his own sons and favorite students.

Alfasi's academy in Lucena was attended not only by talmudic scholars but by students who became writers, poets, and communal leaders. Among them were the poets Moses Ibn Ezra and Judah Halevi.

Rabbi Isaac ben Jacob Hakohen Alfasi.

Title page of *Rav Alfas,* the code of Isaac Alfasi. It was printed in 1552, in Venice.

Judah Halevi / 1075–1141 C.E.

To this day, Judah Halevi (1075–1141) is the most beloved of the Spanish-Jewish poets. Born in Toledo, Halevi studied at Alfasi's academy in Lucena, where he received an intensive Hebrew education. A scholar of Arabic literature, he was learned in astronomy and mathematics, and was an eminent physician.

Judah the Poet

Eventually Judah returned to Toledo to practice medicine. Though he was one of the most famous physicians of his day, he felt that he was only a humble assistant to God, the true healer. He wrote:

My medicines are of Thee and bespeak
Thy art—whether good or evil, strong or weak.
The choice is in Thy hands, never in mine:
Knowledge of all things fair and foul, is Thine.
I heal not with some power in me,
But only through the healing sent from Thee.

Although his medical career kept him busy, Judah wrote hundreds of poems of prayer and thanksgiving, many of which are included in the prayerbook. After he married, the light of his life was his one daughter, who became as learned as Rashi's daughters. When she later had a son, she named him in honor of his famous grandfather.

As he grew older, Judah Halevi developed a passionate longing for the Land of Israel and wrote a number of beautiful poems famed as the "Songs of Zion."

The Kuzari

Like most of the other Spanish-Jewish poets, Judah Halevi was interested in philosophy. His most important philosophical work was a book in Arabic called *Kuzari* ("The Khazar"). Based on the letter from King Joseph to Hasdai Ibn Shaprut, it presents a dialogue in which a rabbi explains Judaism to the Khazar monarch. At the end of the book, the rabbi bids farewell to the king and sets out on a journey to Palestine.

Judah Halevi Travels to Israel

In his old age, Judah Halevi set out to see the Land of Israel. His friends tried to dissuade him, for the journey was long and dangerous. But the poet would not change his mind. He crossed the Mediterranean Sea and traveled through North Africa, visiting the Jewish communities along his route. In Fostat (Cairo), Egypt, many urged him to give up the idea of going on to Israel. But the old man was determined to see his dream fulfilled.

The Death of Judah Halevi

Judah Halevi never returned from his journey. When he reached the gates of Jerusalem, he fell upon his knees and kissed the holy ground. As he knelt there, he was trodden to death by the horse of a hostile Arab rider. And so the poet Judah Halevi died—standing at last on the soil of the Land of Israel.

A page from the *Kuzari*. The dialogue form of the work can be seen. On the right side of the page stand the words:

"Said the Kuzari,"

and

"Said the *Haver*" (meaning rabbi), introducing their statements.

Moses ben Maimon / 1135–1204

The Almohades Rule Spain

In the 12th century, when the Almohades, a fanatical Muslim sect from North Africa, invaded Spain, the golden age for Spanish Jewry began drawing to an end.

Unlike Spain's earlier Muslim rulers, the Almohades sought to convert everyone to Islam. They persecuted Jews and Christians alike, forcing them to become Muslims or leave the land. But where could the Jews go? The northern part of Spain was ruled by unfriendly Christian kings. The Crusades, the Christian march to rescue the Holy Land from the Muslims, had begun, and the Jews in Christian lands now faced new dangers.

Moses Maimonides / 1135–1204

Many Spanish Jews set out for North Africa. Among the emigrants was a scholar named Maimon and his family, who fled from Cordova to Morocco. Maimon's son Moses, who was 13 at the time, is today known as Maimonides; in Hebrew he is often referred to as Rambam, an acronym for *Rabbenu Mosheh ben Maimon*.

Maimonides was an eager student, well-versed in Hebrew, the Bible, the Talmud, and other Jewish writings. He also studied mathematics and astronomy, Arabic literature, and the philosophy of the ancient Greeks. Although he had to go to work at an early age, he managed to study medicine and became a skilled physician.

Maimonides Gives Advice

Even as a very young man, Maimonides wrote brilliant books and essays. When the Jews of Morocco were hard-pressed by the Almohades to forsake their religion and become Muslims, they asked Maimonides what they should do. He advised them to leave the place of forced conversion. "Whoever remains in such a place," he said, "desecrates the Divine Name and is nearly as bad as a willful sinner."

The Jews of Morocco heeded his advice. Maimonides himself was forced to leave Morocco for having spoken out so courageously and frankly. He and his family tried to settle in Palestine, but could not do so because conditions there were very unstable.

Portrait of Maimonides.

מסף ברבי מיימון

The autograph of Maimonides.

The gravestone of a grandson of Moses Maimonides, found in Cairo, Egypt. The inscription reads: "This is the grave of David, grandson of Rabbenu the Gaon Moses ben Maimon, Light of the Exile.

Maimonides in Egypt / 1166

Maimonides and his family went to Egypt, where he set up a medical practice in the city of Fostat, near Cairo. His fame spread quickly, and before long he became the personal physician of Sultan Saladin and the royal family. Rich and poor, Jew and Muslim alike, patients of every background consulted him, and the great physician found time to see them all. The wealthy paid for his services, but the poor were treated free of charge.

At the request of the nagid, the leader of the Jewish community, Maimonides also took on the responsibility of providing religious guidance to the Jews of Egypt. He became a greatly beloved teacher. After Sabbath services each week, he gave public lectures on Talmud and Torah.

The Mishneh Torah

Despite his many duties, Maimonides managed to write the most important code of Jewish law since the completion of the Talmud. This great code is called the *Mishneh Torah* ("Repetition of the Torah") or *Yad Hahazakah* ("The Strong Hand").

The *Mishneh Torah* codifies all the laws in the Mishnah and the Talmud, together with the commentaries of the gaonim and the scholars in the generations following them.

Guide for the Perplexed

Maimonides' best-known philosophical work is the *Moreh Nevukhim* ("Guide for the Perplexed"). In it he clearly explains the principles and ideas of Judaism.

Maimonides had to defend himself against critics who disliked his philosophical views and his approach to the Bible. But he was beloved by many scholars and Jewish leaders, and by the many simple people whom he had helped or advised in one way or another. When he died in Fostat in 1204, he was mourned throughout the Jewish world. People compared him to the great leader who had led Israel out of Egypt in ancient times, saying: "From Moses to Moses, there was none like unto Moses."

The city of Cordova, in 1964, honored the memory of Maimonides by erecting a statue in his honor.

The Crusades

The Rise of Islam

Christian Europe felt threatened by the rise of Islam. The leaders of the church supported any effort to drive the Muslims out of Spain and were very concerned about Muslim domination of Palestine. To Christians, as to Jews, Palestine was the Holy Land. They regarded it as holy because it was the place where Jesus, the founder of their faith, had lived and preached.

This painting shows the crusaders besieging Jerusalem. The giant catapult was able to throw a 100-pound stone into the city.

The First Crusade / 1096–1099 C.E.

In 1095 a church council met in the South of France and proclaimed the First Crusade, a holy war to liberate Palestine from the Muslim "unbelievers." Bands of knights and their followers assembled, accompanied by monks, to march to the Holy Land.

As the feeling against unbelievers grew stronger, roused to a fever pitch by inflammatory sermons, a bitter period began for the Jews of Europe. Christian mobs demanded that they accept baptism and massacred those who refused. Several popes issued bulls prohibiting conversion by force, but they did nothing to restrain the clergy from spreading anti-Jewish libels. The accusations resulted in the murder of thousands. When the crusader army captured Jerusalem, it massacred the city's Jewish and Muslim inhabitants.

The Second Crusade / 1146–1147 C.E.

In 1144, during the preparations for the Second Crusade, a monk named Rudolph inflamed the masses in the Rhine valley against the Jews of Germany. People began to believe that killing Jews was God's will. Bernard of Clairvaux, an important Christian leader, rose to the defense of the Jews and tried to stop the campaign against

them. Due to his courageous stand the loss of Jewish life and property was relatively mild in that part of France.

Hospitaller, Teutonic Knight, Templar.
The most dedicated crusaders were members of quasi monastic military orders. The Knights Hospitaller guarded the Hospital of St. John in Jerusalem. The Knights Templar guarded the palace of the king of Jerusalem.

Belvoir Castle was built by the French Knights Hospitaller. It was destroyed in the 13th century by the sultan of Damascus, who was afraid that the crusaders would return. The stone arches are a part of the ruins of Belvoir.

physician was the great Maimonides. In contrast to the Christian crusaders, Saladin was a tolerant, moderate ruler. Several minor attempts to reconquer Palestine followed, but enthusiasm for Crusades soon petered out.

The Crusades had serious consequences for the Jews of Europe. Even though the Holy Land remained under Muslim domination, life in Europe changed when the crusaders returned. On their journeys, they had learned about distant lands. Many became traders and travelers, taking advantage of the valuable contacts they had established in other lands.

The Jews of York

The Jews of England fared as badly as those on the European continent. The courage of the Jews of York is still remembered. They took refuge in a tower and were besieged by a fanatical mob. Led by their rabbi, Yomtov ben Isaac of Joigny, they chose to take their own lives rather than submit to the forced conversions which the mob had in store for them.

A page from a French history book written in 1337. The painting shows the crusader attack on Jerusalem.

The End of the Crusades / 1189–1192

In 1187, the crusaders were defeated by Saladin, the Egyptian sultan whose court

This illustration from the *Luttrell Psalter* shows Richard the Lion Heart fighting Saladin during the Third Crusade.

Saladin (1137–1193) captured Jerusalem from the Crusaders. The sultan then summoned the Jews and gave them permission to resettle the Holy City.

Jewish Changes

Bankers and Moneylenders

In the era before the Crusades, much of the commerce between cities and countries in Europe had been carried out by Jews. But now more non-Jews entered the field.

No longer safely able to engage in large-scale commerce, the Jews were forced to enter other occupations. One area was banking and moneylending, activities in which Christians were forbidden to participate by church law. Jewish bankers and moneylenders managed the financial affairs of princes, bishops, nobles, and kings. But most Jews now had to make their livelihood by keeping pawnshops, lending small amounts of money, or dealing in second-hand goods.

No longer could Jews be craftsmen. The world of medieval Europe had become highly organized and restricted. All craftsmen were organized into guilds, and applicants for membership had to be of the Christian faith. In addition, Jews were no longer permitted to own land or vineyards.

Protectors of the Jews

Some Christian nobles and princes protected the Jews in their territories. This was less often due to tolerance than to the fact that the ruler usually collected higher taxes from the Jews in his domain, who thus were a steady source of income for him.

Since borrowers would sometimes refuse to repay money obtained from Jews, moneylending was often a risky business. In many instances debtors would organize mobs to plunder the Jewish quarter. Often an entire community would be expelled.

Expulsion from England / 1290

King John of England and his son Henry III viewed their Jewish subjects as a source of income. They imposed taxes so severe that

Aaron's house in Lincoln, England.
Aaron of Lincoln (1123–1186) was an English financer whose moneylending clients included bishops, barons and the king of Scotland. Aaron financed the building of ten English churches. After his death, his estate was seized by the king and the state collected the moneys owed to him.

the Jews begged for permission to leave the country. Permission was refused, and further taxes were imposed. In 1290, when the country's 16,000 Jewish inhabitants had nothing left to tax, the entire community was expelled. John confiscated their homes and personal property.

The king furnished ships so that they could return to France, where their families had originated. On the voyage many of the Jewish passengers were robbed and some were thrown to a watery grave in the English Channel. This was the end of English Jewry until the year 1657.

Edict of Louis VII banishing the Jews from France in 1145.

Rabbi Solomon ben Itzhak—Rashi / 1040–1105

A Child Is Born

Despite the grim situation in the Middle Ages, the continuity of Jewish scholarship was assured by the birth of a Jewish child in the year 1040 in the French city of Troyes. This child was destined to become the most popular and important figure of rabbinic Judaism—Rabbi Solomon ben Itzhak, universally known as Rashi (Rabbenu Shlomo Itzhaki).

It is told that Rashi's father was once offered a large sum of money for a valuable gem he owned. He refused to sell it, because he knew it would be used to embellish a Christian religious image. Fearing that the Christians might take the gem by force, he threw it into the sea. As a reward for this deed of loyalty to his faith, he was blessed with a son who would brighten the light of the Torah.

As a youth Rashi studied at the academy of Jacob ben Yakar in Worms, Germany. On his return to Troyes he earned his living from his vineyards, but devoted most of his time to study and writing. Before long his influence radiated throughout the world's Jewish communities.

Rashi's Commentaries

Rashi wrote a commentary to the Torah based on a sound understanding of the plain meaning of the text and of the interpretations incorporated in the talmudic and midrashic literature. Rashi's commentary on the Torah is the most beloved and valuable ever written. In traditional circles, studying Torah without Rashi is virtually unthinkable. Rashi's commentary on the Talmud holds an equally important place. For centuries it has been printed on the same page as the Talmud text, for the convenience of scholars.

The Rashi chapel in the city of Worms, the synagogue where the great commentator worshipped and taught.

Rashi's work of commenting on the Bible and Talmud was continued by his grandsons. The most prominent of them were Rabbi Shemuel ben Meir (1080–1174), known as Rashbam, and Rabbi Jacob ben Meir (1100–1171), known as Rabbenu Tam.

THE RASHI SCRIPT

Mem Sofit	ם	ם	Alef	א	ה
Nun	נ	כ	Beit	ב	ב
Nun Sofit	ן	ן	Gimel	ג	ג
Samech	ס	ס	Daled	ד	7
Ayin	ע	ע	Hay	ה	כ
Fay	פ	פ	Vav	ו	ו
Fay Sofit	ף	ף	Zayin	ז	ו
Tzadi	צ	ל	Chet	ח	ח
Tzadi Sofit	ץ	ץ	Tet	ט	ט
Quf	ק	ק	Yud	י	י
Resh	ר	ר	Khaf	כ	כ
Sin	ש	ש	Khaf Sofit	ך	ך
Tav	ת	ת	Lamed	ל	ל

Rashi was a prolific scholar and was constantly writing new commentaries. It was difficult and very time-consuming to write using the regular Hebrew alefbet. So Rashi used a cursive script that was much easier and faster to write.

Most of the early commentaries on the Torah and the Talmud were printed in Rashi script.

The Tosafists

Despite the difficult times they had to face, the generations following Rashi continued to study the Talmud and the Torah. The writings of these scholars are called Tosafot ("additions, supplements"), because they were added on to Rashi's commentaries, and the scholars themselves are known as the tosafists.

Rabbenu Tam / 1100–1171

The period of the Tosafot began immediately after Rashi wrote his commentary. Rashi's son-in-laws and grandsons were the first tosafists.

The Tosafot are records of talmudic discussions held primarily in the yeshivot of northern France during the 12th century. Rabbis and students would analyze and discuss talmudic questions. Their conclusions are summarized in notes (also called glosses) printed in all editions of the Talmud on the outer margin opposite Rashi's comments.

The most famous tosafist of the 12th and 13th centuries was Jacob ben Meir, known as Rabbenu Tam, a name which means "Our Perfect Master." Like many other scholars in that era, Rabbenu Tam lost all his belongings in the dark days of the Crusades. Undaunted, he continued with his studies and gave advice and leadership to his fellow Jews. Rabbenu Tam called together a synod or council of rabbis at which rules of conduct and questions of internal government were discussed. The purpose of the synod was to find ways to protect the Jewish community, especially those who were poor and who suffered most from the persecutions.

This synod was followed by other assemblies. The Jews of the Rhineland arranged their communal life as best they could. They helped one another, so that their religious and communal life could continue and those in need could receive help.

Jews were required by law to wear pointed hats and yellow badges.

A page of the Talmud with some of the commentaries. This selection is from tractate Berachot. *Tosafot* means "commentary." The Tosafot are in yellow.

Badges, Blood Libels, and Black Death

The Yellow Badge

In 1215 Pope Urban II decreed that Jews had to wear some means of identification to distinguish them from Christians. From then on, all Jews were required to wear a yellow badge on their garments. In some localities they were also ordered to wear pointed hats.

King Philip the Fair

In 1306, the Jews of France were expelled by King Philip the Fair (1268–1314), who confiscated their money and real estate. But the Christian moneylenders who replaced the banished Jews were so greedy and pitiless that the king soon recalled them to his realm.

Expelling the Jews was financially profitable, however, so the same scenario was played out twice more. After the second time, during the reign of Philip of Valois in 1394, they were not allowed to return. For a thousand years Jews had lived in France. But from then until the time of the French Revolution, there were no Jews in France, except in Avignon, Carpentras, and Cavaillon, which were under the direct rule of the pope, and in Bordeaux and Alsace.

The Black Death / 1348

In the middle of the 14th century, a terrible plague called the Black Death befell Europe, killing millions. A rumor began to circulate that the Jews had poisoned the wells to bring about the disaster. In September of 1348, the Jews of Chillon on Lake Geneva were arrested and forced to confess that they had poisoned wells.

In Strasburg, France, on February 14, 1349, large numbers of Jews were burnt to death. Similar scenes took place in many other areas.

In the German city of Nordhausen, the mob ran wild through the Jewish quarter. To avoid worse tortures, the town's Jews, led by their rabbi, committed suicide by throwing themselves into a fire and burning themselves to death. Scores of persecutions occurred throughout Europe in the wake of the Black Death. Despite efforts by Pope Clement VI to protect them, hundreds of Jewish communities were destroyed and tens of thousands of Jews were slaughtered.

Blood Libels

Exploiting the fear and superstition of the common people, some members of the clergy began spreading a rumor that Jews used the blood of Christian children in their rituals. During Passover, they alleged, Jews had to kill a child and drink its blood or use the blood to make matzot. The first pogrom caused by this libel occurred in 1171 C.E.. The Jews of Blois, in France, were accused of killing a Christian child. In the aftermath, 30 innocent Jews were burned at the stake.

In 1475 the city of Trent, in northern Italy, was the scene of another blood libel incident. The body of a child was found near the home of a Jewish community leader. After questioning under torture, 17 Jews confessed and were executed. As a consequence, no Jews were allowed in Trent until the 18th century. Despite condemnation by the popes, the blood libel accusation has persisted. In 1903, a massacre occurred in Kishinev, Russia, after a blood libel accusation. Forty Jews were killed and hundreds were seriously injured. In 1993 the blood libel once again appeared in Leon, France. The accusation seems to raise its ugly head in different parts of Europe during the Passover season.

Meir of Rothenburg / 1215–1293

Rabbi Meir ben Baruch

One of the great German rabbis of the Middle Ages was Meir ben Baruch of Rothenburg. He was born in 1215 in the city of Worms, where Rashi once had studied. As a young man, Meir was taught by the great rabbis of France and witnessed the burning of the Talmud in Paris in 1242. Returning to Germany, he established a talmudic academy.

In the days of Rabbi Meir, Rudolph I of Hapsburg became the emperor of Germany. Rudolph began his reign as a powerful ruler, endeavoring to control his domain with an iron hand. Previously the nobles had enjoyed complete power over the Jews; now they became subjects of the crown and responsible to the emperor alone. Rudolph raised their taxes and confiscated their property whenever he felt it necessary to punish them.

Rabbi Meir Is Arrested

Many Jews decided to emigrate. A large group, led by Rabbi Meir, set out for Palestine. Rudolph had Rabbi Meir arrested. He felt that the Jews had no right to leave, because they were valuable subjects whose high taxes helped to swell the funds of the royal treasury.

When Rabbi Meir was thrown into prison, the Jews begged the emperor to release him. Rudolph asked them for a large cash ransom.

A Martyr for His People

Rabbi Meir implored his people not to pay the outrageous sum, for he knew that if they did, it would place an even heavier financial burden on

Tombstone of Rabbi Meir.

the Jewish community. For years he remained in his prison cell. His students often visited him there, bringing letters in which he was asked for legal advice by Jewish courts throughout the land. In 1293 Rabbi Meir died in prison, a martyr by his own choice; he had put the well-being of the Jewish community above his own.

The emperor refused to release the body of Rabbi Meir unless the Jewish community paid a large sum of money for its return. Years later, a German Jew named Alexander Wimpfen paid the ransom on the condition that he would be buried alongside the rabbi. When Alexander died he was buried next to Rabbi Meir.

Flight to the East

The Jews of Germany somehow managed to survive these dark days. Temporary expulsions occurred, but in many instances the Jews were eventually able to return. Doggedly they set about rebuilding their homes, synagogues, and schools, resuming their pattern of study, work, and Sabbath and festival observance.

By the end of the 15th century, new territories in Eastern Europe opened up to immigrants. Poland, Russia, Ukraine, Lithuania, and Hungary all welcomed Jewish settlers from Germany because of their advanced commercial, technical, and industrial skills. The Jewish immigrants who settled in these lands brought their religious heritage, their institutions of learning and self-government, their love of home, and their will to survive.

Christians in Spain

The Christians Regain Control / ca. 1230

Meanwhile, the Christians were slowly regaining control of Spain. King Alfonso VI of Leon and Castile united the three Christian kingdoms of the north. Alfonso ruled his realm with foresight and tolerance equal to that of the Muslim rulers of an earlier day. Cities again began to flourish. Merchants brought goods from distant lands, and artisans fashioned their wares. Farmers tilled their fields, and shepherds tended their flocks. The Jewish community of Spain benefited from the improved conditions, living in freedom and prosperity.

By the 15th century the rest of Spain had been wrested from the Muslims and the Christian reconquest was practically complete. The church now intensified its efforts to convert the country's Jews.

Christianity Debates Judaism

The friars of the Dominican order were charged with the task of winning over the Jews. One of them, a convert from Judaism named Pablo Christiani, was very eager to make converts. He persuaded King James I to hold a public debate at Barcelona. In the debate Pablo would pit his arguments for Christianity against the arguments of a learned rabbi.

This altar relief shows the forced conversion of Jewish women. The women were forced to choose between conversion and exile.

Bullfighting was a popular Spanish sport. This 13th century painting shows the spectators throwing darts called banderillas at the bull.

Spain enjoyed an economic boom and the affluent public demanded luxuries. Enterprising merchants, some of them Jews, established trading companies which imported luxuries from the Orient, India, Russia, Venice and France. These Spanish women are shopping for luxuries at a country fair.

Nahmanides / 1194–1270

Rabbi Moses ben Nahman

The rabbi chosen to defend Judaism in the debate before the king's court and many high-ranking church dignitaries was Moses ben Nahman (1194–1270), also known as Nahmanides and as Ramban (from Rabbi Moses ben Nahman).

Nahmanides was Spanish Jewry's most important scholar and rabbinic leader. He earned his living as a physician and served as rabbi of the town of Gerona. His responsa on questions of Jewish law were circulated to Jewish communities throughout the world.

Nahmanides' synagogue in Jerusalem. From the *Casale Pilgrim*, a 16th century guide to the holy places of Palestine.

The Debate

Nahmanides stood undaunted before the court and the king to face the fanatical Pablo and the other Dominican friars. In the debate Pablo tried to prove that Jesus was the Messiah, citing isolated talmudic statements to support his claim. Nahmanides easily refuted him. The statements quoted by Pablo, he explained, were legends and tales that had no bearing on what Jews believed. The important part of the Talmud was its legal portion, the halakhah, and that contained nothing whatsoever to support Pablo's arguments.

Nahmanides asked a very important question. How, he inquired, could Jesus have been the Messiah if wars were still being waged between nations? The coming of the Messiah was supposed to usher in an era of peace and goodwill, but this had still not come to pass.

The wisdom of the aged Nahmanides impressed the king, who adjourned the debate without declaring Pablo the victor. On parting with Nahmanides, the king gave him a generous gift. Nahmanides published the text of the debate. When Pablo heard about this he reported it to the

king. Again Nahmanides was summoned. This time he was sentenced to two years in exile.

Nahmanides in Israel

Nahmanides went to Palestine. He was grieved by the state of the Jews there. Wars and invasions had impoverished the Jewish communities of the Holy Land. Schools no longer existed, and only a very few synagogues still stood intact.

The aged scholar devoted the last years of his life to the Jewish community in Palestine. He built a synagogue in Jerusalem and opened a school. Scholars and students gathered around him. Before his death, Nahmanides could see the results of his work. The spiritual life of the Jews in Palestine had been enriched and rejuvenated through his efforts.

Seal of Nahmanides found near the city of Acre.

The Kabbalah

A system of thought based on mysticism began to gain ground among Spanish Jewry. This system, known as Kabbalah, sought hidden meanings in the Torah that would explain difficult religious problems. Among these were such questions as how the world could have been created out of nothingness, how God, who is perfect, could enter into relations with imperfect human beings, and where evil came from.

Moses de Leon / 1250–1305

The most important kabbalistic work was the Zohar ("Brilliance"), a mystical commentary on the Torah that was supposed to have been written in Palestine in the 2nd century C.E. by Simeon bar Yohai.

The work remained unknown until the 13th century, when a copy was found by a man named Moses de Leon.

Most scholars believe that Moses de Leon himself was the author of the Zohar, although it may contain some material dating back to Simeon's time. The book de Leon produced was full of strange and wonderful ideas. It explained how God had created the world through ten steps and suggested how man could purify his soul and rise to a higher level of understanding. For adherents of Kabbalah it seemed to be an inexhaustible source of profound knowledge about spiritual matters of compelling importance.

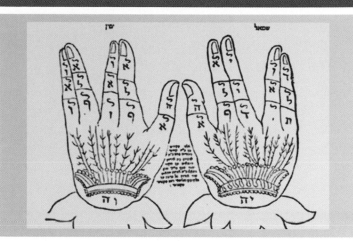

Most Jews believed that Hebrew letters and the Hebrew language were sacred, since they were used by God to create the world. The kabbalist Abraham Abulafia (1240–1300) believed that combinations of letters could help an individual achieve prophetic vision and knowledge of God.

The above is a kabbalistic drawing showing the channels of divine emanation and letter combinations in the form of hands.

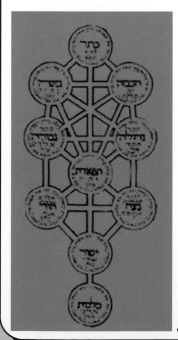

The ten mystic spheres of God. From a book of Kabbalah printed in Mantua, Italy, 1562.

Title page of the first edition of the Zohar, Mantua, 1558.

The Marranos

Samuel Abulafia / 1320–1361

Christian Spain was divided into two kingdoms, Aragon and Castile. Under King Pedro the Cruel, who ruled in Castile, a Jew named Samuel Abulafia became the royal treasurer. Abulafia helped build the Sinagoga del Transito in Toledo, a magnificent synagogue which is still in use as a church.

When Henry of Trastamara, Pedro's half-brother, revolted, the Jews of Castile fought valiantly for their king. Pedro was defeated, however, and his half-brother ascended to the throne of Castile and Leon as Henry II.

Baptism or Death

Henry hated the Jews because they had fought against him. During his reign, zealous monks incited mobs to sack Jewish homes throughout Castile. For the first time, Jews in Spain were required to wear the yellow badge, a humiliation already familiar to Jews in the rest of Europe. A wave of anti-Jewish feeling and riots swept through Spain. The Jews were given a choice—baptism or death. Unlike their coreligionists in northern Europe, many of them chose baptism and became Christians. Some of Spain's most respected Jewish leaders were among the baptized. Frequently entire communities converted together. The baptized Jews, officially known as New Christians, were never fully accepted into Spanish society, as shown by the fact that they were usually called Marranos, which means "pigs."

The New Christians

The Old Christians of Spain detested the New Christians. Competition was one of the main reasons. Now that the Jews were Christians, they were able to compete openly in fields that had been closed to them when they were Jews. In addition, many Spaniards feared that the new converts were not sincere Christians.

Throughout the 15th century riots broke out—not against Jews but against Marranos. The government was forced to ban Marranos from holding public office. Many Marranos remained Jews at heart, or turned to Judaism again when the Christians did not treat them fairly. They attended church and had their children baptized, but began to practice their old faith in secret. They met in secret places to hold services. They observed the festivals and the Sabbath, and studied the Torah.

Isabella and Ferdinand witness the conversion of a Jew. Note that the kneeling Jew has crossed his arms into the shape of a cross.

The Inquisition

The infamous
Torquemada.

Ferdinand and Isabella

When Isabella of Castile and Ferdinand II of Aragon married in 1469, the two great kingdoms of Spain were united. At that time three different religions were still practiced in the land, Christianity, Judaism, and Islam. But Queen Isabella yearned to make Spain an all-Christian nation. She delegated great powers to the dreaded Inquisition, headed by the infamous Tomas Torquemada, and many of its victims were burned at the stake.

Torquemada

Torquemada, the soul of the Inquisition, was determined to rid Spain of the Marranos. He published a series of instructions called *Constitutions* for the guidance of judges. In it he detailed how accused New Christians were to be tortured and how to dispose of their properties.

Persecution of the Marranos

Distrusted by the Old Christians, the New Christians were constantly watched by spies and informers. Anyone suspected of secretly practicing Judaism was arrested and brought before the Inquisition, which confiscated their property and subjected them to torture to make them confess. Many of the Marranos brought before the Inquisition "repented." Many others, however, bravely refused, remaining loyal to the religion of their ancestors even though this meant a terrible death by burning at the stake.

It gradually became clear to Isabella and Ferdinand that the continued presence of Jews in Spain was one of the factors causing Marranos to backslide from Christianity. They decided to give the Jews of Spain a simple choice: either become Christians or leave the country.

New Christians Fight Back

The New Christians did not surrender without a fight. Influential Marranos protested to the king and the pope. But Ferdinand was resolute in his determination to use the Inquisition to acquire the property of the victims.

Juan Perez Sanchez and Juan de Abadia organized a team to assassinate Pedro Arbues, the chief inquisitor of Aragon. The assassination was successful, but it brought a vast number of new victims into the hands of the inquisitors. More than 200 supporters and conspirators were rounded up, dragged through the streets of Saragossa, and hanged.

Juan de Abadia, the chief conspirator, was caught, but escaped torture by killing himself in prison.

The city of Granada in Southern Spain was the last outpost of Moorish control. It was captured by the Christians in 1492. This painting shows Ferdinand and Isabella triumphantly entering the city.

The Expulsion from Spain / 1492

Isaac Abrabanel / 1437–1508

Isabella and Ferdinand had several trusted Jewish advisors. Among them were Isaac Abrabanel, Luis de Santangel, Gabriel Sanchez, and Abraham Senior. Abrabanel was not only an excellent financier but a wise man whose opinion was valued at court. In addition, he was a

Isaac Abrabanel

scholar, philosopher, and author, and a leading member of the Jewish community. When the king and queen issued the order expelling the Jews from Spain, Isaac Abrabanel asked them to rescind it, offering a large sum of gold and silver if they did so. But his plea was in vain. Had he chosen, Abrabanel could have stayed in Spain as an exception to the royal edict because his services were appreciated and needed. He chose instead to leave, casting his lot with his friends and brethren, the Jewish people.

The Jews Leave Spain

The date of the expulsion on the Hebrew calendar was the 9th day of the month of Av in the year 1492 C.E. This was the very same day on which the First Temple had been destroyed by the Babylonians in 586 B.C.E. and the Second Temple had been destroyed by the Romans in 70 C.E.

Each destruction had been followed by a period of exile. Now, Jews already living in exile from their true homeland in Israel had to go into a third exile, from the adopted land in which they had once been so happy. Once again, the Jews of exile were being forced into exile. Spanish Jewry, which had

lived through a golden age unsurpassed in the history of the Jewish dispersion, was now coming to an end.

Everything had to be left behind. Jews who had property traded it for sturdy traveling clothes. Precious jewels were exchanged for food for the long and perilous journey. The exodus was so terrible a catastrophe that it even shocked Spanish and Italian witnesses who detested Jews. Many of the exiles died from the hardships of the journey or were robbed and murdered. All suffered from a terrible sense of shock and dislocation.

King Ferdinand, Queen Isabella, and Torquemada, the Grand Inquisitor, kneel in prayer.

Christopher Columbus

On August 3, 1492, just one day after the expulsion took place, the *Nina*, the *Pinta*, and the *Santa Maria*, under the command of Christopher Columbus, set sail westward across the Atlantic Ocean in search of a sea route to India. Columbus had received much of the money needed to finance his expedition from Marranos. Many of his maps were made by Jews who knew the art of map-making and the routes across the great seas. It is said that some members of his crew were Marranos. Indeed, the famous navigator himself may have been of Jewish origin, according to some scholars.

As his three ships hoisted anchor that day, Columbus made a note in his log of the Jewish refugee ships which he sighted as he began the journey which was to alter the map of the world.

Christopher Columbus was convinced that he could reach the Orient by sailing westward. He failed to identify America as a new continent, thinking it was part of India.

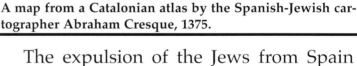

A map from a Catalonian atlas by the Spanish-Jewish cartographer Abraham Cresque, 1375.

The expulsion of the Jews from Spain marked the end of a memorable epoch. The journey of Columbus, however, signified a beginning, for it set the stage for the birth, centuries later, of a new nation in a far-away land, where Jews would live in freedom.

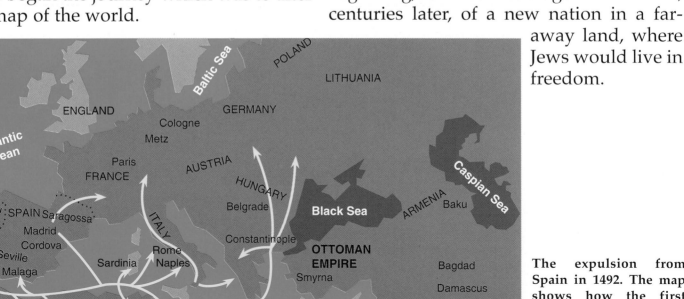

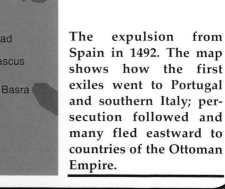

The expulsion from Spain in 1492. The map shows how the first exiles went to Portugal and southern Italy; persecution followed and many fled eastward to countries of the Ottoman Empire.

Timeline—The Age of Europe Begins

JEWISH HIGHLIGHTS

Age of Gaonim
7th–11th century

Karaites
founded 762 C.E.

Khazars
8th–11th century

Golden age of Spain
9th–12th century

Moses ben Maimon
1135–1204

Christian Crusades
11th–13th century

JEWISH EVENTS • PERSONALITIES • LITERATURE • HOLIDAYS

▶ Saadia Gaon

▶ First Siddur

▶ Sura

▶ Pumpeditha

▶ Halakhah

▶ Responsa

▶ Bustanai

▶ Masorah

▶ Saadia Gaon

▶ Anan ben David

▶ Hananiah

▶ Gaonim

▶ Khazar kingdom destroyed in 11th century

▶ Moors conquer Spain 715 C.E.

▶ Hasdai Ibn Shaprut

▶ Samuel Ibn Nagrela

▶ Solomon Ibn Gabirol

▶ Isaac Alfasi

▶ Judah Halevi

▶ Mishneh Torah

▶ Guide for the Perplexed

▶ Jews massacred

▶ Saladin defeats Crusaders

WORLD HISTORY

▶ Muslims

▶ Khosru

▶ Babylonia

▶ Russia

▶ Arabs

▶ Moors

▶ Caliph of Cordova

▶ Morocco

▶ Egypt

▶ Fostat

▶ France

▶ Germany

▶ England

▶ Italy

Timeline—The Age of Europe Begins

JEWISH HIGHLIGHTS

English Jews
10th–12th century

Rashi and family
11th–12th century

European expulsions
13th–15th century

Christians conquer Spain
12th–15th century

New Christians
14th–15th century

Spanish Expulsion
1492

JEWISH EVENTS • PERSONALITIES • LITERATURE • HOLIDAYS

- English Jews expelled, 1290

- Bible and Talmud commentaries
- New script
- Rabbenu Tam
- Tosafists
- Synods

- Yellow badges
- Black Death
- Blood libels
- Meir of Rothenburg
- Economic restrictions

- Christian/Jewish debates
- Nahmanides

- Inquisition
- Auto da fé
- Marranos
- Samuel Abulafia

- Isaac Abrabanel
- Tisha Be-Av
- Torquemada
- Columbus
- Sephardim

WORLD HISTORY

- England
- King John
- King Henry

- France
- Troyes
- Rhineland

- Popes
- France
- Rhineland

- Spain
- King Alfonso VI
- King James I

- King Pedro

- King Ferdinand
- Queen Isabella
- Portugal

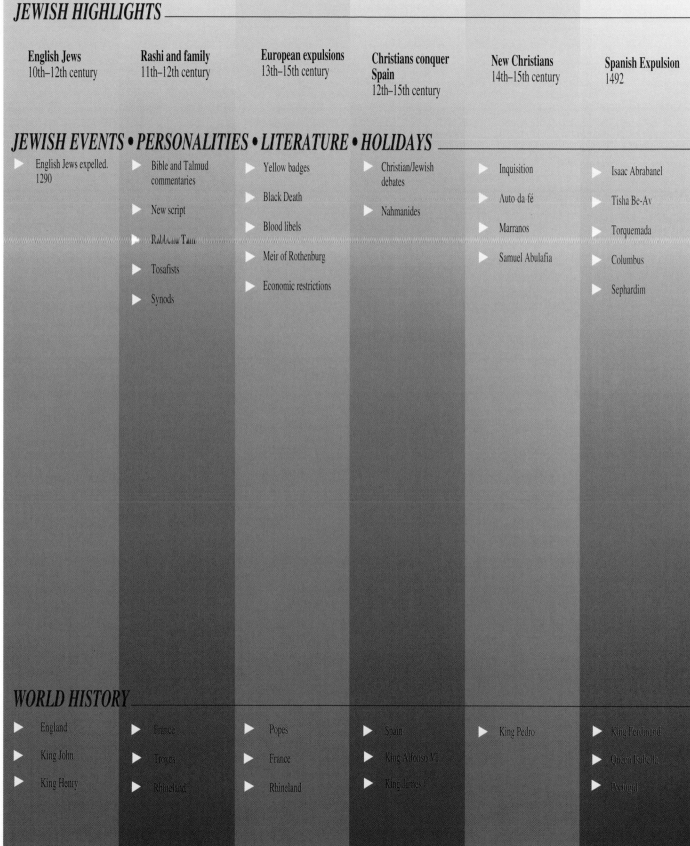

The Jews Leave Spain

Where were the Spanish refugees to turn? England had expelled her Jews; so had France. In German lands Jews fared badly, subject to suspicion, persecution, and expulsion. Many Jews from Germany had already sought new homes in the east, in Poland and Lithuania. Some German Jews, especially those who were scholars and successful merchants, had gone to Italy, where Jewish communities were said to prosper under the influence of the free spirit of the new learning encouraged by the Renaissance.

A Haven in Portugal

Closest to Spain was the kingdom of Portugal. Here, for a short span of time, many of the refugees found a haven. They had to pay a poll tax but were permitted to practice their trades and crafts. Their new home was of short duration, however. The king of Portugal had married Princess Isabella of Spain, the daughter of Ferdinand and Isabella. They had agreed to the marriage only on the condition that Portugal become a Christian country free of all heretics and Jews.

In 1497, the king of Portugal the country's Jews expelled. However, when they reported to the port cities, they were all forcibly converted to Catholicism.

New Homes in Muslim Countries

Some of the Jews driven out of Spain went to North Africa. There they found new homes in Tunis, Fez, and Algiers, or in the great cities of Cairo and Alexandria in Egypt. Many other Spanish Jews found a refuge in the Ottoman (Turkish) Empire, which welcomed them because of their skills and treated them tolerantly. Under Ottoman rule, many became merchants, scholars, and physicians. Sultan Bajazet, pleased with his new subjects, reportedly said, "How can you call Ferdinand of Aragon a wise king, when he has impoverished his land and enriched ours?"

"The Dutch Jerusalem"

So many Portuguese and Spanish Marranos settled in Holland that the city of Amsterdam was often called the Dutch Jerusalem. This name was coined in 1596, when a group of Portuguese Marranos there returned to Judaism in a solemn, public ceremony. From that time on, Amsterdam was a great center of European Jewry.

1492 EXPULSION
New Homes for Spanish Jews

To Turkey	90.000
To Holland	25.000
To Morocco	20.000
To France	10.000
To Italy	10.000
To America	5000
Total emigrated	160.000
Died while seeking new home	20.000
Baptized, remained in Spain	50.000

The old synagogue of the Sephardic community in Amsterdam, Holland. The reader's desk is in the center of the synagogue.

The Renaissance

The Coming of a New Age

The 15th and 16th centuries—the period during which the tragic expulsion of the Jews from Spain and Portugal took place—witnessed many great social, technical, and religious changes.

New inventions radically transformed life everywhere. One of these was the printing press. As a result of the increased availability of books, people became more interested in learning and many were eager to read the Bible. Indeed, the Bible (in Latin) was the first book to be printed. This revolutionary first edition was produced in 1456 by a German printer, Johann Gutenberg, in the city of Mayence (Mainz). Many scholars now wanted to read the Bible in the original language, and they turned to Jewish teachers in their efforts to learn Hebrew.

Jews, too, enthusiastically took up the craft of printing. Jewish immigrants from Germany brought it to Italy, where the first printed Hebrew book, an edition of Tractate Berakhot of the Talmud, was published in 1484 by Joshua Solomon Soncino. Many other Hebrew works soon followed.

New Ideas

The Jews of Italy were greatly stimulated by the free spirit of the Renaissance. Just as Christian writers, poets, composers, artists, and scientists began to express new ideas and a new view of the world, many Jewish artists and scientists also became active. Despite the restrictive laws still in force against Jews during the early Renaissance, the Jewish communities of Italy flourished.

In the Netherlands, struggling to win independence from Spain, and in Germany, France, and eventually England, the spirit of the Renaissance stimulated the growth of

An illuminated page from Gutenberg's Bible.

Emblem of the Venetian printer Marco Antonio Giustinani.

new life. All over Europe the misty Middle Ages were coming to an end.

The Reformation

In Germany the new learning gave rise to a religious movement known as the Reformation. Martin Luther, the first to translate the Bible into German, opposed the power of the Catholic Church and strove to replace it with a reformed form of Christianity. Luther, Calvin, Zwingli, and other reformers were the founders of Protestant denominations which taught that every individual human being had a personal relationship with God and could find his way to God without the help of intermediaries.

Martin Luther, as depicted by the artist Lucas Cranach.

The Shtadlanim

The rulers of Europe in the 17th and 18th centuries needed people who were loyal and had the skills to supply their financial needs.

They also needed people to represent them on confidential diplomatic missions, provide military supplies, and supply difficult-to-locate luxury items. This delicate and difficult role was often filled by court Jews (*shtadlanim*), who were dependent upon the monarch for protection and remained neutral in the power struggles raging between the clergy, nobles, and rising expectations of the general populace. The presence of a shtadlan at a royal court helped the Jews return to cities and countries from which they had been expelled.

Shtadlanim were the spokesmen for the Jewish community in dealings with town councils and governments. The shtadlanim sought to prevent persecution and defended the interests of the Jewish community. Some were rabbis, others were linguists, and some had widespread business connections and diplomatic skills.

Some of the shtadlanim used their skills and connections to establish banks and trading companies. A great many had far-flung financial connections with Jewish and non-Jewish commercial and industrial trading houses.

Joseph Suess Oppenheimer

Court Jews faced great opportunities and great dangers. Samuel Oppenheimer (1630–1703) loyally served Emperor Leopold I of Austria for 30 years, yet died penniless.

**Joseph Suess Oppenheimer
(1698–1738)**

Joseph Suess Oppenheimer (1698–1738) was shtadlan for Duke Charles I Alexander of Wuerttemberg, managing his estates and business enterprises.

After the duke's death, Jude Suess, as he was called, was imprisoned and hanged in a public ceremony. Oppenheimer refused the offers of the clergy to save his life on the condition that he convert to Christianity. He died reciting the Shema Yisrael.

Yossel of Rosheim

The outstanding shtadlan of 16th-century German Jewry was Yosel (Josel or Joselmann) of Rosheim, a town in Alsace (1480–1554). When still a young boy, he had seen all the members of his family perish as martyrs. Yosel traveled throughout Germany to carry out the task entrusted to him—the defense of the Jewish communities against attack.

Yosel was an active and talented financier, with an excellent background of Jewish learning. In addition to his practical work on behalf of his people, he managed to write two scholarly works, and in the course of his many diplomatic missions he engaged in debate with princes and priests who attacked the Talmud and other Jewish writings.

During the reign of Charles V, ruler of the Holy Roman Empire, when the Jewish communities were threatened with persecution and expulsion by both the Catholics and the Protestants, Yosel traveled hundreds of miles on diplomatic missions. He was not always successful, but many communities owed their peace and indeed their very lives to his efforts. The great community of Prague, in Bohemia, was saved from expulsion by Yosel. He kept a diary in which he recorded many of his experiences during his 40 years as shtadlan of the Jews of Germany. These notes have been preserved to this day.

The lives of Yosel of Rosheim, the Jewish shtadlan, and Martin Luther, the leader of the German Protestant Reformation, covered almost the same span: Luther's from 1483 to 1546 and Yosel's from 1480 to 1554.

Jost Liebmann was a shtadlan in the court of King Frederick William I of Prussia. When he died his wife Esther inherited the position and became the shatadlanit. However, after the death of her benefactor, King Frederick William, she was imprisoned and fined for accumulating excessive profits.

These were stormy times, during which the lands of Western Europe were faced with a challenging crisis—the struggle between the Roman Catholic Church and the Reformation.

Anti-Semitic picture of Yosel of Rosheim, the Court Jew of Emperor Charles V. In one hand is a Hebrew Bible, in the other, a bag of money.

Yet, behind their ghetto walls, following their own traditions and their own way of life, Jews weathered the storms of the centuries that followed, the struggles between Christians, between the church and princes, and the wars and revolutions set off by the new conditions and new ideas.

The public hanging of Joseph Suess Oppenheimer, whose corpse was then displayed in an iron cage. The anti-Semites used accusations against Oppenheimer to spread their message of hate.

The Ghetto

During the Renaissance Jews were forced to live in segregated districts. Residential areas of this kind were called ghettos, probably because the first of them, established in Venice, was located next to a cannon factory and was designated with the Italian word for "factory," *getto*. Some, however, believe that ghetto comes from the Hebrew word *get*, meaning "divorce," indicating that ghettoization separated and divorced the Jews from the general population.

Pope Paul IV

Paul IV argued that it was foolish for Christians to be friendly to a people who had not accepted Christ as their savior. In a papal bull he decreed that Jews living in areas controlled by the church were to be confined in ghettos. They would be permitted to leave the ghetto in daytime to go to work, but forbidden to be outside at other times. The ghetto gates were to be closed at night and on Christian holidays. The pope also decreed that Jews were to wear yellow stars and pointed hats for quick identification. In a short time these practices spread from Italy to the rest of Europe.

The ghetto was usually located in the worst part of town. The ghetto walls confined a large number of Jews into a small confined area. To accommodate this mass of humanity, houses were multistoried and built close to each other. The ghettos were surrounded by a wall and gates, guarded by non-Jewish watchmen who controlled the entry and exit of those imprisoned inside. Outside the ghetto Jews had to wear yellow badges and specially designed hats. These opened them to ridicule and attack.

Economic Restrictions

Economic regulations reduced the ability of Jews to earn a livelihood. Restrictions on commerce and banking deprived them of the ability to compete. Only two occupations were unrestricted: trade in second-hand merchandise and pawnbroking. People who for one reason or another needed a small loan brought something to sell or to leave in pawn. Poor people were thankful for a chance to buy good second-hand clothing cheaply. However, the Christian merchants who sold expensive new clothing objected to the competition.

The Forces for Ghetto Existence

There are several reasons why the ghetto came into existence and for its popularity in Europe. The expulsion from Spain triggered the idea that Jews should not be permitted to live in a Christian country.

In 1417 the Jews of Constance, Germany, offered a Torah scroll to Pope Martin V, with a request that their privilege be restored. He replied, "You have the law but do not understand it. The old has passed away and the new has been found."

While Christian merchants and artisans wanted to eliminate their Jewish competitors, government officials saw the Jews as a source of income and did not wish to expel them. The installation of the ghetto was an ideal compromise.

A third reason was related to the religious competition between Catholics and Protestants. Both groups competed by teaching hatred of the Jews. The Catholics, in fact, often accused the Protestants of favoring the Jews and being under their influence.

Starting in the 15th century, these three forces had an important detrimental effect on Jewish life in Eastern and Western Europe.

The Communal Structure

Ghetto communities were usually governed by a council elected by the residents. The council was responsible for the ghetto's relations with the city government, and in particular was charged with collecting whatever taxes the government levied on the Jews. In addition it supervised the ghetto's synagogue, schools, courts, charities, and other communal institutions.

Medieval painting of a Hebrew teacher and his young pupil. Notice the whip and the hourglass. Germany, 13th cent.

Gate of the Jewish ghetto in Vienna.

Painting by Hieronymus Hess, in the art museum of Basel, Switzerland. The Jews were forced to attend conversion sermons by Catholic priests. Note the priest slapping a Jew for snickering or for falling asleep.

Religious Intolerance

Protestants and Catholics

The new Protestant denominations that came to life in the Reformation had separated themselves from the Roman Catholic Church and now represented a grave threat to its unity. As a result, the church adopted stern measures to guard against the spread of Reformation influences.

Protestants and Catholics became involved in a bitter struggle, each faction bent on proving itself more truly Christian than the other and vying with the other in performing pious acts. Both Catholic and Protestant rulers persecuted heretics and imposed new restrictions on the Jews.

Wherever Jews were permitted to live in Western and Central Europe, except in the tolerant Netherlands, there were ghettos. Jews were set apart and crowded into these confined residential areas, their freedom restricted. Of course, the bait of conversion was always held out to anyone who would accept it. But nearly all Jews disregarded this alternative and steadfastly clung to the heritage of their ancestors.

The Jews of Italy

Although ghetto walls had been erected in Italy, the Italian Jews lived under far better conditions than did their brethren in the rest of Europe. Sometimes, they became traders or bankers, although their commercial activities were restricted, as was true all over Europe, to moneylending and the second-hand trade. According to some scholars, the family of Christopher Columbus was among them.

Italy attracted persecuted Jews from both Spain and Germany. Spanish Jewish merchants, seafarers, mapmakers, doctors, bankers, and scholars all settled in Italy. Jewish printers from Germany settled in northern Italy, where they produced editions of the Talmud, the Bible, and the prayerbook. The most famous of these printers was the Soncino family, whose name was revived by a group of Jewish bibliophiles in Germany before World War II, and adopted by a London publishing house that still prints Jewish books, including an English translation of the entire Talmud.

Jews fared best in the Kingdom of Naples, where Don Isaac Abravanel and many other Spanish Jews found a new home after the expulsion in 1492.

A street in the Jewish ghetto in Venice.

Hebrew emblem of the Italian printer Abraham Usque.

Title page of Don Isaac Abravanel's commentary to the Later Prophets.

The Jews of Turkey

In the 14th and 15th centuries the Ottoman Turks conquered Anatolia, the Fertile Crescent, and many European lands, including Greece, Albania, Bulgaria, Rumania, Bosnia, and Serbia. Their capture of Constantinople in 1453 ended the long history of the Byzantine Empire.

There had been Jews living in the Ottoman territories since ancient times. After the expulsions from Spain and Portugal, their numbers were greatly increased by exiles seeking a new home, and in the 16th century a flourishing Jewish community developed in the Ottoman domain. The port of Salonica in northern Greece became a major center of Jewish life and commerce.

The Turkish sultans welcomed the Jewish merchants, bankers, and physicians from Spain, and put their talents to good use. Jews rose to high positions at the Ottoman court, serving as ambassadors and advisors.

Solomon Ashkenazi / 1520–1600

It was as if the golden age of Spanish rule had returned once more in the lands of the East. Jewish diplomats were sent from Constantinople to the courts of Europe. Solomon Ashkenazi, a learned Jewish physician, became Turkey's ambassador to Venice, where he negotiated a peace treaty in 1571. Later, he offered Turkey's help to Venice in case of war with Spain.

When the Jews of Venice were threatened with expulsion, Ashkenazi pressured the Venetian government to revoke the order. Thanks to his efforts, the Jewish community was saved.

The Mendes Family

Gracia Mendes (1510–1569) was a Portuguese Marrano who sought refuge in Italy. The beautiful widow of a wealthy and famous banker, she had taken over her husband's business after his death. When she left Portugal, she was accompanied by her daughter Reyna and her nephew and business advisor, Joseph Nasi. They had settled in the great port of Antwerp in Belgium, which was then under Spanish rule. But when they were denounced to the Inquisition as heretics, Gracia Mendes and her family fled from Antwerp and found refuge in Venice. There again Gracia Mendes was denounced as a heretic who had abandoned the Catholic Church. She was imprisoned and all her wealth was confiscated. Many of her debtors cancelled their obligations, including the king of France, who owed the Mendes family great sums of money, but declared he would not pay his debt.

Joseph Nasi was determined to rescue his aunt and his cousin. He went to Constantinople and enlisted the help of Sultan Suleiman I. The sultan, impressed by Joseph Nasi's ability and connections, sent a letter to Venice demanding the release of Gracia Mendes.

Doña Gracia Mendes

Joseph Nasi / 1520–1579

Thanks to the sultan's intervention, Gracia Mendes was released from prison and her confiscated property was returned. She went from Venice to Ferrara, where she openly rejoined the Jewish community. When her confiscated property was returned, she proved to be a generous and compassionate woman, giving much of her time and fortune to aid troubled Jews and Marranos who were returning to Judaism. From Ferrara, Gracia Mendes and her daughter journeyed on to Turkey, where Joseph Nasi and Reyna were married.

Joseph in Palestine

Joseph Nasi became the sultan's financial advisor. The young man's intelligence, tactful counsel, and charming manner made him one of the most respected personalities at the sultan's court. He became a skilled diplomat. His knowledge of languages and his connections in many lands made him an ideal diplomat, so that Joseph Nasi was appointed to represent Turkey in conferences with many foreign ambassadors.

After the death of Suleiman, Joseph served his son, Selim II. The new sultan heaped many honors upon Joseph. In addition to making him duke of Naxos, a beautiful island in the Aegean Sea, he granted him the ancient city of Tiberias, in Palestine, where once the rabbis of the Mishnah had taught. Joseph hoped that large numbers of Jews and Marranos would settle in Tiberias, where they would be free from fear and oppression, and could build a new life in the land of their ancestors.

Joseph Nasi's vision had a practical side. In Tiberias he hoped to found a new industry that would bring profit to both the Jewish settlers and the Ottoman Empire—the manufacture of silk. He rebuilt the houses and streets of Tiberias, and planted mulberry trees for the silkworms to feed upon. However, his plans were not realized. Only a few Jews were able to reach the Holy Land, for a war had broken out between Venice and Turkey and ships could not sail the Mediterranean safely. Yet Joseph Nasi was not discouraged. At a time when few wealthy men put the ideals of charity into action, he continued to devote much of his wealth and energy to the service of his suffering brethren.

Suleiman the Magnificent receiving Christian vassals as his army besieges the Hungarian town of Szigetvar.

View of Istanbul, 17th cent.

Pioneers and Mystics

Immigrants to Palestine

The dream of returning to the Land of Israel was ever present in the hearts of all Jews. On the ninth of Av, Jews everywhere wept and fasted in mourning for the destruction of the Temple. Throughout the centuries a trickle of Jewish settlers made their way to Palestine from Germany, France, Italy, and Turkey. In the aftermath of the expulsion from Spain, new immigration came to the ancient communities of Galilee in northern Palestine. A few of the Spanish refugees established themselves in Tiberias. Others went to Jerusalem, most beloved of the cities of the Holy Land. But it was in the town of Safed, in the mountains of Galilee, that the most renowned new community was founded.

Safed: City of the Kabbalah

In this poor little town, a new type of learning blossomed. Schools of mysticism arose, and rabbis steeped in arcane lore passed through the ancient streets discussing the deeper meaning of the Torah. Safed's scholars devoted themselves to the study of Kabbalah—the doctrines and lore of Jewish mysticism. The kabbalists of Safed were concerned primarily with questions relating to the coming of the Messiah. How could evil play such a predominant role in a world created by a benevolent God? What was the nature and means by which a transcendent God interacted with His limited creations?

Most important among the esoteric books that the kabbalists studied was the Zohar. To the kabbalists of Safed, Simeon bar Yohai, the tanna to whom the book was attributed, was a beloved figure. On Lag Ba-Omer, said to be the day of Simeon's death, the Jews of Safed made a pilgrimage to his grave in Meron to honor his memory with prayer, song, and dance. This practice is still followed in modern Israel.

The kabbalists of Safed sought the joy of intense contemplation and a pure life. On the Sabbath, they would dress in special garments and devote themselves to joyously celebrating the day of rest. The famous hymn Lekha Dodi, "Come, My Beloved," which is still chanted in the synagogue on Friday nights, was composed by Solomon Alkabetz (1505–1584), one of the great kabbalist teachers of Safed. In this poem he compared the Sabbath to a beautiful bride, and the people of Israel to her devoted bridegroom.

Lag Ba-Omer is celebrated on the 33rd day of the counting of the Omer. It is a time for singing, dancing, bonfires, picnics, hiking, and playing with bows and arrows.

On Lag Ba-Omer Jews remember the heroes who fought the Romans, especially Simeon bar Yohai. He and his son studied Torah in a cave high on Mount Meron. Students carried bows and pretended to be hunting so the Romans would not arrest them.

For 13 years Rabbi Simeon bar Yohai was hidden in his cave. This brave rabbi died on Lag Ba-Omer.

Today in Israel many Jews travel to Meron on foot and by car to visit his grave.

The Zohar

Moses de Leon / 1250–1305

The body of mystical lore that comprises the Kabbalah developed over several centuries. In the 13th century, all these teachings were compiled in a book called the Zohar by Moses de Leon of Castile, Spain. According to Moses de Leon, however, the Zohar dated back to the 2nd century C.E. and had been written by Simeon bar Yohai. He claimed to have found it in the cave in which Simeon bar Yohai and his son Eliezer had hidden for 13 years during the Hadrianic persecution. Throughout this period, the Talmud records, Simeon and his son ate the fruit of a carob tree and spent their time studying the mysteries of the Torah.

The Zohar fascinated Jewish scholars, and in the next few centuries interest in the Kabbalah spread from Spain to the other countries of the diaspora.

The Sefirot

The kabbalists maintained that every aspect of the Torah, even including the shapes of the letters and unusual spellings, has a secret meaning that can be uncovered through study and spiritual discipline. The hidden meanings embodied in the sacred text are set forth in the Zohar, written in Aramaic and organized as a commentary on the Torah.

The doctrine of the Sefirot has an important place in the Zohar. According to the mystics, there are ten divine aspects of God's interaction with the world; these mediate between between the Infinite God and the finite material universe. The ten Sefirot are:

Keter = Crown, Hokmah = Wisdom,
Binah = Understanding, Hesed=Mercy,
Gevurah = Strength, Tifarah = Beauty,Netzah = Might,
Hod = Splendor, Yesod = Foundation, Malkut = Kingdom.

According to the Kabbalah, each of the Sefirot of the Tree of Life corresponds to a part of the human body. These power centers are energy spheres which control the physical, mental, and psychological functions of the human being. When they are operating properly they provide the individual with special abilities of perception and creativity.

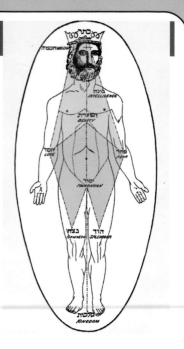

The Zohar retells biblical stories and events, such as the creation of the world, the divine chariot of Ezekiel, the various names of God, and the powers of angels, explaining them in a mystical way.

In kabbalistic studies the Sefirot are combined, and the letters are then reassembled and given new meanings and significance.

Individual Responsibility

The Zohar also teaches that every act of every human being on earth has an effect on the world above. When we perform good deeds, we crown the day with goodness and it becomes our protection in the world-to-come and in our hour of need. But if we sin, it has a negative effect on the day and will destroy us in the world-to-come. Thus, good and bad deeds can build or destroy the balance of the earth.

Some of the formulas and symbols developed by the mystics have been utilized in the prayerbook. The blowing of the shofar is introduced with a kabbalistic prayer. The prayer before reading the Torah, the Berikh Shemei, is from the Zohar.

Rabbi Isaac Luria / 1534–1572

Rabbi Isaac Luria

The greatest teacher of Kabbalah in Safed was the brilliant young Rabbi Isaac Luria (1534–1572). Born in Jerusalem, he lost his father when he was a child but was brought to Cairo, where he was educated under the care of his uncle. Luria made rapid progress in his rabbinic studies and became acquainted with the Kabbalah, to which he applied himself fervently.

Magic formulas from *Sefer Raziel*. This kabbalistic book was printed in Amsterdam in 1701.

When Rabbi Isaac Luria came to Safed, he found many devoted, enthusiastic students there. By devoting themselves to the joys of mystical speculation, prayer, and concentration, they hoped to hasten the coming of the Messiah and the time of eternal peace. Rabbi Luria's charismatic personality and unique approach to kabbalistic study soon won him the affection and loyalty of Safed's mystical community. After he died at the early age of 38, they preserved his teachings and transmitted them to later generations.

Luria's disciples referred to him as the Ari, an acronym for Adoneinu Rabbi Yitzhak ("Our Master Rabbi Isaac"). *Ari* is the Hebrew word meaning "lion," and indeed, the disciples of Rabbi Isaac considered him to be mighty as a lion in mystical knowledge.

Two Approaches to Judaism

Many talmudic scholars at first regarded the kabbalists as dangerous. The kabbalists, they said, did not show much interest in legal problems. Their way of life differed from the life of the scholars. As time went

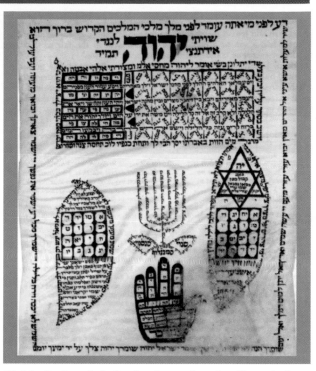

Kabbalistic alphabetic formulas in *Ilan Sefirot* ("A Tree of Emanation") by Abraham Cohen Herera, published about 1600.

on, the conflict between these two approaches to Judaism diminished and Kabbalah became widely accepted. But in Safed, in the days of Rabbi Isaac Luria, they existed peacefully side-by-side.

Interior of the Ari Synagogue in Safed, Israel.

The Shulhan Arukh

Rabbi Joseph Caro

Safed was also the home of Rabbi Joseph Caro (1488–1575). Born in Spain just a few years before the expulsion, Rabbi Joseph wandered through many lands before finding peace in Safed. In Turkey he had been the head of an academy of Jewish learning. After settling in Safed, he undertook a gigantic task: the compilation of an encyclopedic code of talmudic law that would be easier for Jews everywhere to use and follow than earlier legal codes and the original books of the Talmud.

A Handy Reference Book

Caro based his explication of Jewish law on the *Turim*, a code composed by Rabbi Jacob ben Asher (1270–1340) in Spain. He brought the *Turim* up to date by adding rabbinic decisions made in the two centuries since Jacob ben Asher and including Sephardic legal decisions and customs as currently enforced. For 30 years Joseph Caro worked on his commentary on the *Turim*. He then prepared a shorter, well-defined version in which he discussed every phase of Jewish life and all its rituals. Joseph Caro's code is called the *Shulhan Arukh* ("Prepared Table"). It proved a

handy reference work for those seeking guidance on specific details of Jewish practice and custom. In spite of initial opposition among Ashkenazic rabbis, particularly in Poland, it finally won full recognition after the glosses of Rabbi Moses Isserles (1530–1572) were added to it.

The *Shulhan Arukh* was used by Jews in many lands. It was especially helpful in small communities where there was no scholar to turn to for guidance.

Title page of the *Shulhan Arukh*. It lists 20 different commentators. Included is the commentary by Moses Isserles.

Model of Rabbi Moses Isserles' Rema synagogue, Cracow, 1553 (Museum of the Diaspora, Tel Aviv).

False Messiahs

David Reubeni / 1490–1537

One day in the year 1524, a strange, dark man rode into the city of Rome on a white Arabian steed. Jews and Christians alike gaped in amazement and ran after him as he went to the palace of the pope for an audience. This man, who called himself David Reubeni, claimed to be the son of the king of the ancient Israelite tribe of Reuben. In a strange Hebrew dialect that was difficult for the Jews of Rome to understand, Reubeni told tales of the tribe of Reuben, deep in the lands of Arabia. Reubeni proposed a daring alliance to Pope Clement VII. If the pope would equip a Christian army to liberate Jerusalem and place him in command, Reubeni would muster the fighting men of the tribe of Reuben to join forces with it. Together they would free the Holy Land from the Ottoman yoke.

The pope was impressed by Reubeni. Times were difficult for the Catholic Church. The Reformation was taking hold in many lands and curbing the power of Rome. A new crusade that would take the Holy Land from the Turks seemed a worthwhile project. The pope arranged for Reubeni to visit the king of Portugal, who was expected to aid in this ambitious plan. In Portugal Reubeni was received with honor and the king gave serious consideration to his plan.

Solomon Molcho / 1500–1532

The Marranos of Portugal derived some benefit from Reubeni's arrival, for in his honor the Inquisition seems to have suspended its persecutions—a sign that its officials considered his mission authentic. Diego Pires, a prominent young Marrano, was deeply moved by Reubeni. Openly returning to Judaism, Diego left Portugal and went to Palestine to study the Kabbalah, changing his name to Solomon Molcho. In time he became convinced that he was meant to be a messenger of God on earth, sent to proclaim the coming of the Messiah. Solomon Molcho captured the imagination of many Jews, traveled to many lands, and finally appeared in Rome. There Molcho and Reubeni met. Reubeni, for reasons of his own, did not want to speak to Molcho, who was convinced of the righteousness of the cause he had embraced.

By this time, Charles V of Spain had decided that both men represented a danger since they were inciting both Christians and Jews to rebellion. Molcho was imprisoned by the Inquisition and put to death. Reubeni too seems to have died as a prisoner of the Inquisition.

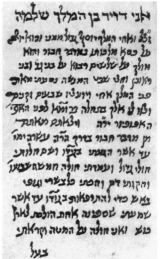

The false Messiah David Reubeni, presented this letter to Pope Clement VII: "I am David, the son of King Solomon (may the memory of the righteous be blessed), and my brother is King Joseph, who is older than I, and who sits on the throne of his kingdom in the wilderness of Habor (Chaibar), and rules over thirty myriads of the tribe of Gad and of the tribe of Reuben and of the half-tribe of Manasseh. I have journeyed from before the king, my brother and his counselors, the seventy elders. They charged me to go first to Rome to the presence of the pope, may his glory be exalted."

David Molcho, another false Messiah, excited the imagination of Jews everywhere. Molcho's signature with a victory pennant.

The Netherlands

In the 15th and early 16th centuries, the Netherlands were under the dominion of Spain. The Protestant Dutch hated the Catholic Spaniards and their ways. Charles V, who ruled both Spain and the Holy Roman Empire, was determined to suppress any stirrings of revolt; he wanted his far-flung domains united in loyalty to church and crown, and therefore sought to crush Protestantism wherever he encountered it.

But Spanish rule could not maintain its grip on the freedom-loving Dutch. The people of the Netherlands fought Spain bitterly, and in 1581 declared their independence.

Meanwhile, Protestant England, also wary of Spain, was on the way to becoming a nation of seafarers, merchants, and colonists. Spain set out to conquer England, but in 1588, under Queen Elizabeth I, the English navy defeated and destroyed the Spanish Armada.

Marranos in Holland

After the Netherlands won their independence, large numbers of Marranos from Portugal and Spain fled to Amsterdam and Antwerp, where they reverted to their ancestral religion. The local Christians treated them with friendliness and tolerance, and before long major Sephardic communities had developed in the great trading cities of Holland and Belgium.

The Dutch Jerusalem

Throughout this era the city of Amsterdam was often called the Dutch Jerusalem, a name coined in 1596, when a group of Portuguese Marranos there returned to Judaism in a solemn public ceremony. From that time on, Amsterdam was one of the great centers of European Jewry. Jewish communities also grew up in the other cities of the Netherlands. Many Portuguese and Spanish Marranos became successful and respected traders in their new homeland and contributed to the growing power of the Netherlands.

Engraving by Adolf van der Laan (ca. 1710) showing the Portuguese synagogue on the left and the two Ashkenazic synagogues on the right in Amsterdam.

Jews in Germany

The Portuguese Marranos who settled in Amsterdam had trade connections with Jewish merchants in the German city of Hamburg. At first the Marranos in Hamburg were simply known as Portuguese, but after a time they openly professed their Judaism. Since they had become very useful to the merchant city, they were permitted to remain, although they had to accept the restrictions imposed on all Jews in Germany. Under the influence of the Portuguese immigrants, Hamburg became a center of active Jewish life.

Resolution of the Amsterdam Portuguese Jewish community granting pioneer Isaac da Costa a Sefer Torah for Curaçao in the West Indies, 1659. The Jews of Holland helped the new overseas communities in many ways.

Jews in the Dutch Colonies

Holland eventually gained a foothold in the New World, both in the West Indies and in Brazil, which was a Portuguese possession until the Dutch conquered it in 1631. There were many Marranos in Brazil, especially in the city of Recife. Under Dutch rule, they openly returned to the Jewish faith, dedicating a synagogue where they proudly worshipped in the Sephardic tradition and bringing a rabbi from Amsterdam to serve their community.

When Portugal began the reconquest of Brazil, the Jewish settlers fought side by side with their Dutch neighbors and many of them died in battle.

Rabbi Jacob Sasportas (1610–1698). In 1681 he was appointed Chacham in Amsterdam. He was a bitter opponent of Shabbatai Zevi.

Minute book, written in Portuguese, of the Spanish and Portuguese Jewish congregation in Amsterdam, 1656.

Rabbi Manasseh Ben Israel / 1604–1657

One of the most important rabbis in the Dutch Jerusalem was Manasseh Ben Israel. The son of Spanish Jews, he was steeped in Jewish learning. Many Christians in those days wanted to study the Bible in its original language rather than in translation, and they often turned to Manasseh Ben Israel for guidance.

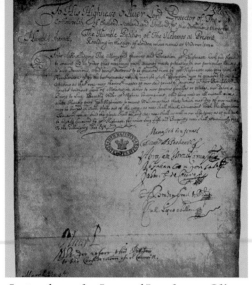

Portrait of Rabbi Manasseh Ben Israel, painted by Rembrandt.

Letter from the Jews of London to Oliver Cromwell, dated March 24, 1655, pleading that "we may with security meet privately in our houses for our devotions."

Rembrandt the Painter

Among Rabbi Manasseh's many Christian friends was the great Dutch painter, Rembrandt van Rijn. Rembrandt was fascinated by the strong facial types and Mediterranean appearance of the Dutch Jews of Spanish and Portuguese descent, so different from the fair, northern Dutch. He asked many Jews to pose for him, among them Manasseh Ben Israel.

Manasseh was a student of the Kabbalah. Like many Jews of his day, he believed that the coming of the Messiah was near. A keen observer of political developments, he noted the great changes that had taken place in England since its break with Catholicism. In 1649, Oliver Cromwell and the Protestant Puritans had come into power and deposed the king. Many of England's political leaders looked to the Bible for inspiration. They seriously studied the workings of the Sanhedrin for guidance in conducting their own Parliament.

Manasseh Meets Cromwell

No Jews had lived openly or legally in England since the expulsion in 1290, but Manasseh Ben Israel felt the time for change was nigh. In 1655, after a difficult journey, he arrived in London and met with Cromwell. England's Protestant ruler was inclined to grant the rabbi's request, but many of his political associates were not so favorably disposed. As a result, the rabbi's plea was rejected. Still, his journey had not been wholly in vain. The following year a group of Marranos who were already living secretly in England returned to the religion of their ancestors and were granted the right to worship as they pleased. Eventually they were joined by other Jews, and Jewish communities arose again all over England.

Portrait of Oliver Cromwell.

Shabbatai Zevi / 1626–1673

As the 17th century progressed, messianic fervor spread among Jews everywhere, steadily intensifying because the kabbalists had calculated that 1648 was the year that would see the coming of the Messiah. Among those affected by the messianic yearning was Shabbatai Zevi, the son of refugees who had settled in the Turkish town of Smyrna (Izmir) after the expulsion from Spain. As a boy he studied the Kabbalah and became deeply involved in unraveling its intricate mysteries.

Shabbatai Zevi

Shabbatai the Messiah

In 1648, the year which was supposed to bring the Messiah, 22-year-old Shabbatai stood up in the synagogue of Smyrna and pronounced the Ineffable Name of God, something only permitted to the High Priest on the Day of Atonement. By this revolutionary act Shabbatai clearly declared himself to be the Messiah. The congregation was awed and stunned.

Shocked by what Shabbatai had done, the rabbi who had guided his studies excommunicated him. Shabbatai was forced to leave Smyrna. He had gained some loyal disciples, however, and accompanied by these followers, he set out for Jerusalem. After winning the support of the Jewish community of the Holy City, the group journeyed on to Cairo.

Even rabbis and scholars came under the spell of Shabbatai Zevi. New prayerbooks with prayers for Shabbatai as Messiah were printed in Amsterdam. Many Jews settled their affairs and prepared to leave for Palestine on Shabbatai's command. Even the Christian world watched attentively, for many Christians hoped that Shabbatai's messianic claims might be a portent of the eagerly awaited Second Coming of Christ.

Shabbatai and the Sultan

In 1666 the Ottoman sultan, concerned about the unrest spreading through his empire, had Shabbatai Zevi thrown in prison. He gave Shabbatai a choice between death and conversion to Islam. To everyone's amazement the would-be Messiah, who had sparked a fire of hope in Jewish hearts throughout the world, accepted conversion and became a Muslim!

Jewish communities everywhere were dumbfounded. Many found it impossible to believe that Shabbatai Zevi had really been nothing but an impostor, and many people, including some prominent scholars, continued to believe in him. Scholars and rabbis, who had disapproved of the Kabbalah even before Shabbatai Zevi's appearance, concentrated on the Talmud and urged the people to do likewise.

Title page of a Shabbatean prayerbook called *Tikkun*, printed in Amsterdam in 1666. It contains readings for each day and night of the year.

Baruch Spinoza / *1632–1677*

Lens Grinder and Philosopher

Among the Jewish merchants and craftsmen in Amsterdam there were many brilliant and unusual people. Some were learned in the Talmud; others were immersed in the study of the Kabbalah. One of them was Baruch (Benedict) Spinoza (1632–1677). The son of refugees from Spain, Spinoza had studied the Torah and the Talmud like all the other Jewish boys of his day. He had also studied not only the great philosophers of Judaism but the secular works of the philosophers of ancient Greece and Rome. Spinoza was a brilliant young man, and his teachers, the rabbis of Amsterdam, hoped he would become their brightest disciple and successor.

But Spinoza gradually isolated himself from Jewish life. He did not follow all the laws of the *Shulhan Arukh,* and some of his ideas seemed shocking and sacrilegious. Spinoza wrote brilliant philosophical works in which he stated that God was present in all things and that humans could serve Him by being just and righteous to one another.

Spinoza also rejected the divine origin of the Torah, and that was considered shocking by the Jewish community of the 17th century. Spinoza's ideas seemed to threaten Jewish unity and survival. Hence he had to be rejected.

Baruch Spinoza (1632–1677) was a Jewish philosopher. In 1656 he was excommunicated for his shocking ideas.

Spinoza Is Excommunicated

In 1656 the rabbis of Amsterdam excommunicated Spinoza, and as a result he was regarded as an outsider by the official Jewish community.

Spinoza earned his living by making lenses for spectacles. He liked this work, and after his excommunication he took his tools and moved to the little village of Rijnsberg on the outskirts of Amsterdam. Here he lived quietly, devoted to his studies and writings. Many of the great scholars of the time came to visit the humble lens grinder. He died at the age of 45, a lonely man. In later years Spinoza came to be universally recognized as one of the greatest philosophic minds.

Spinoza's house in The Hague. The plaque records that he lived there from 1671 to 1677.

Moses Hayim Luzzatto / 1707–1747

A Poet and Mystic

Another unusual personality who caused a stir in the Jewish community of Amsterdam, some years later, was the poet and mystic Moses Hayim Luzzatto (1707–1747). Like Spinoza, he too earned his livelihood as a lens grinder. Born in the Italian city of Padua, Luzzatto made a name for himself by the age of 20 with a book of poetry patterned on the biblical psalms. Inspired by the spirit of the Renaissance, he wrote plays on biblical themes that had a lasting influence on the development of modern Hebrew literature. As he grew older, Luzzatto turned more and more to Kabbalah and the Zohar.

The Kabbalah Forbidden

In Luzzatto's time, the rabbis of Italy forbade young Jewish scholars to study the Kabbalah, because they felt that only mature men would be able to do so without falling victim to confusion and doubt. The rabbis strongly disapproved of Luzzatto's interest in mysticism. They were shocked when the poet ignored their warnings and wrote a book which he entitled *The Second Zohar*. As a result Luzzatto was compelled to leave Italy in 1733. He went to Amsterdam to begin a new life, grinding lenses for a living, but here too he was not able to write works on Kabbalah.

Luzzatto in Israel

As Luzzatto grew older he began to see the Holy Land as his salvation, as the place in which he could pursue his kabbalistic studies, and write in peace. He and his family managed to translate their yearning into reality and, after an arduous journey, settled in Tiberias. Unfortunately, soon after their arrival the entire family was wiped out by an epidemic of plague that ravaged the country.

Besides his psalms, poems, and plays, Luzzatto also wrote a book on Jewish ethics called *The Way of the Righteous* (*Mesillat Yesharim*). This much-studied book has become a classic and has been translated into several languages.

MESILLAT YESHARIM

THE PATH OF THE JUST

by

MOSHE CHAYIM LUZZATTO

Newly Prepared According to the First Edition
Complete with Vowel Marking and Source References

English Translation by
SHRAGA SILVERSTEIN

Title page of the English edition of *Mesillat Yesharim*.

In Eastern Europe

Early Russian Beginnings

According to some traditions, the first Jews to settle in areas that later became part of the Russian Empire arrived there after the destruction of the Temple in 586 B.C.E. They were brought to these regions when Nebuchadnezzar of Babylon deported large numbers of Jews to territories in Armenia, the Caucasus region, and along the shores of the Black Sea.

A sprinkling of Jewish settlers settled in Eastern Europe in Roman times, when Jewish traders traveled along the great rivers and brought their wares to many distant lands. Others moved into Russia from Persia and Arabia. Around 800 C.E., some the Khazars, a Turkic people who lived beyond the Black Sea, converted to Judaism. It is possible that only the royal family, and some of the nobility converted. They continued to practice the Jewish religion until the mid-10th century, when the Russians overran their kingdom.

Beginnings of Polish Jewry

Most of the Jews of Eastern Europe, however, came from Germany. Toward the end of the Middle Ages, they began wandering eastward to Poland, which at that time included Ukraine and Lithuania, in order to escape persecution in the cities and towns of Germany. The Polish kings eagerly welcomed them, for there were many merchants and artisans among the Jewish migrants, and Poland badly needed their commercial and technical expertise.

The populace of Poland at the time consisted of two classes—nobles who owned the land and peasants who worked it; there was virtually no middle class. The kings of Poland hoped that the newcomers would build cities and bring commerce and industry to their realm. To encourage the Jewish immigrants, they made them directly subordinate to the crown rather than to the nobles in the regions where they settled. This gave the Jewish settlers a special legal status that protected them from many manifestations of anti-Semitism and enabled them to live under their own laws.

Drawn by the opportunities Poland offered, ever greater numbers of Jews moved eastward. As cities grew, Jewish communities sprang up. In time, large and prospering Jewish communities flourished in Warsaw, Vilna, Lublin, Posen (Poznan), and Cracow, as well as many smaller towns.

The Old-New Synagogue (Altneuschul) in Prague, built in the late 13th or early 14th century, in the heart of the Jewish quarter. Brick gables were added in the 15th cent.

A Russian cavalryman

King Casimir the Great

The charter granted to the first Jewish settlers was renewed by King Casimir the Great, who reigned from 1333 to 1370. Casimir was renowned for building many new cities, and was often referred to as king of the serfs and the Jews, for he was a very tolerant ruler who was genuinely concerned about the welfare of the serfs and his Jewish subjects.

With the arrival of so many skilled immigrants, Poland experienced an era of rapid progress and development. Many non-Jews joined the movement eastward, and unfortunately they brought to their new homes not only their skills but also their traditional prejudices. They were eager to restrict their Jewish neighbors, whom they regarded as rivals, just as they had done in Germany, and often found allies in the church. But Poland's kings defended the Jews, and for some 300 years Polish Jewry enjoyed an era of peace and freedom.

A model of a wooden synagogue built about 1600.

The Jews as Assets

The Jews proved to be an asset to Poland. They set up a banking system and printed Poland's first paper money. Some of these early banknotes bear the names of the Polish kings of the time printed in Hebrew letters.

Many Jews in Poland were employed as managers of estates, tax collectors, and financial advisors to the nobility, and the nobles valued their services. Jews were also active in the export of grain, salt, timber, and other natural resources, and imported goods needed from abroad. In addition, they owned and operated many of the country's inns, taverns, and stores, were active in transporting merchandise from place to place, and played a major role in many of the skilled crafts so essential to a pre-industrial economy.

Polish coins with Hebrew inscriptions.

Stately house in Lvov, of Simha Menahem, Jewish physician to King John III Sobieski of Poland.

The Jews of Poland

The Kahal

The Jews of Poland constituted a separate social class distinct from the four "estates" of medieval society. They were neither nobles nor peasants, nor city-dwelling burghers like the Christian merchants and artisans. And, of course, they did not belong to the clergy. In recognition of their status, King Sigismund Augustus issued a charter in 1551 that guaranteed the Jews of Poland the right to govern themselves.

The Jews of the four provinces ruled by the Polish kings—Greater Poland, Little Poland, Volhynia, and Lemberg—were organized into self-governing communities headed by a Kahal (assembly) known as the Va'ad Arba Aratzot (Council of the Four Lands), whose members were the elected representatives of Poland's many Jewish communities.

The Council of Four Lands

Whereas the Jews of ancient Babylonia had been ruled by an individual, the exilarch, Polish Jewry was ruled by an elected council. The Va'ad Arba Aratzot negotiated with the king's representatives and collected the taxes levied on the country's Jews. It enforced the law in the Jewish communities and was in charge of Jewish courts, schools, trade guilds, and communal char-

The Jewish community enjoyed a self-sufficient economy and had its own merchants, farmers, and tradesmen. These paintings by Arthur Szyk picture a Jewish blacksmith and baker at work.

ities. When necessary, it appointed a spokesman or advocate (shtadlan) to represent it in dealings with Christian officials.

Although the Jews of Poland were only allowed to live in certain areas, they managed to build up an active and independent communal life. They had their own bankers and merchants, farmers and laborers, and their own craft guilds of butchers, bakers, printers, and locksmiths.

The Yiddish Language

Gradually, the Jews of Poland evolved a language of their own. In medieval Germany their ancestors had spoken German with a significant admixture of Hebrew. The migrants from Germany who settled in Poland continued speaking this language in their new homeland. Over time Polish words and expressions were added. The language that evolved from these developments is known as Yiddish.

The Yiddish language, written in Hebrew letters but ultimately derived from medieval German, soon came to be the main form of intercommunication among the Jews of Eastern Europe. By 1700,

Meeting place of the Council of the Four Lands, Lublin, 16th and 17th cent.

Yiddish was playing an important role in religious, intellectual, literary, and personal correspondence. In some quarters, in the 18th and 19th centuries, especially among those who opposed Zionism and the use of Hebrew for secular purposes, Yiddish came to be regarded as the Jewish national language.

Jewish Education

The Jewish communities of Eastern Europe organized their own school systems. Boys from 4 to 13 years of age attended the heder (elementary school). The better students went on to the yeshiva for advanced studies. Many communities had more than one yeshiva, each headed by a learned rabbi. Great care was taken to provide boys with a thorough Jewish education. Those who had neither time, money, nor aptitude for advanced learning became workers, craftsmen, or businessmen.

Rabbi Moses Isserles

As we have already learned, Rabbi Joseph Caro's *Shulhan Arukh* gained universal acceptance among Sephardic Jews. However, it lacked information on the customs and modes of observance evolved by the Ashkenazim. Rabbi Moses Isserles, a saintly scholar who lived in Cracow, remedied this lack by compiling all the decisions handed down by Ashkenazic rabbis and scholars into a supplement to the *Shulhan Arukh.* Since the title of Caro's work means "The Prepared Table," Isserles called his supplement the *Mappah,* or "Tablecloth." With this addition the *Shulhan Arukh* was accepted by Jews everywhere.

The four volumes of the *Shulhan Arukh* are very detailed. In the years that followed, to make its laws more accessible to general readers, several scholars edited popular, easy-to-understand abridgements of the text. One of the most popular of these is the *Kitzur* ("Short") *Shulhan Arukh,* published by Rabbi Solomon Ganzfried in 1864. It has been translated into many languages.

The Jews in this Polish synagogue are wearing fur hats called streimels that were worn on holidays and special occasions. This rabbi and his disciples are praying in front of a desk called a shtender. The texts are located in shelves above them. The Yiddish word for "standing" is *shtayt,* hence the Yiddish word *shtender.*

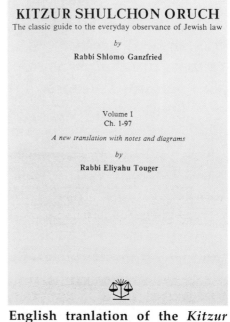

KITZUR SHULCHON ORUCH
The classic guide to the everyday observance of Jewish law

by

Rabbi Shlomo Ganzfried

Volume I
Ch. 1-97

A new translation with notes and diagrams

by

Rabbi Eliyahu Touger

English tranlation of the *Kitzur Shulhan Arukh.*

Revolt and War

Russian Unrest

The 17th century was a time of unrest all over Europe. There were conflicts between Catholics and Protestants, and between members of different Protestant denominations. In the social-political sphere, the revived interest in learning, coupled with the spirit of the Reformation, gave rise to new ideas and new demands. The burghers of the cities wanted more freedom. The serfs—the poor, dependent peasants—developed a sense of self-respect and struggled to break loose from the bondage in which they were held by the nobility.

The peasants of Ukraine hated their Polish overlords. They were members of the Orthodox Church, whereas the Poles were Roman Catholics. The unfortunate Jews were caught in the middle, especially because most of the contact the peasants had with their masters was through Jewish tax-collectors and estate managers. Thus, the Jew was identified with the hated landlord. When the Ukrainians revolted, they launched their first attacks against the Jews.

The Cossacks Spread Destruction

The Ukrainian uprising was spearheaded by fierce peasant-soldiers known as Cossacks. Their commander, Bogdan Chmielnicki, led his troops against the hated Polish landlords and the Jews of Ukraine and Poland. Very often, the terrified Poles abandoned the Jews and left them to their fate. Although the isolated Jewish communities took up arms and bravely tried to defend themselves, many thousands of Jews were killed within a few months. Even in the few instances where Poles and Jews united in defense of their towns, it was to no avail, for the Cossacks swept through the land like a wild hurricane, spreading death and destruction wherever they struck.

In the town of Nemirov, on June 10, 1648, the Cossacks, with the collaboration of the Poles, massacred more than 6,000 Jewish men, women, and children. Similar scenes occurred in many other towns.

Expulsion from the Ukraine

The king of Poland, in order to make peace with Chmielnicki, named him prince of Ukraine. As a condition of this deal, Chmielnicki stipulated that the Jews were to be expelled from Ukraine. But peace did not come to the torn country even then, for the Cossacks were still not satisfied. They received aid from hordes of Russians who rode through the land, leaving death and ruin in their wake.

The Cossack leader, Bogdan Chmielnicki, killed thousands of Ukrainian Jews in the revolt he led in 1648.

By the time the Cossacks and the Poles finally signed a peace treaty in 1654, 700 Jewish communities had been destroyed and more than 100,000 Jews killed. The Council of the Four Lands had disintegrated. The surviving Jews were left impoverished and scattered.

To make things worse, the Orthodox Church increased its hostility toward the Jews, accusing them of meddling in its affairs. Blood-libel accusations fanned by the church began to spread in which the Jews were accused of using the blood of Christian children in making matzot for Passover. Anti-Jewish riots terrorized the Jews in eastern Poland.

In order to obtain a feeling of hope that conditions would someday improve, many Jews turned to the Kabbalah. According to the calculations of the kabbalists, the time was ripe for the Messiah to appear and put an end to war and hatred. As a result, many Jews were easily swayed by the messianic claims of Shabbatai Zevi and his followers.

A street in Lublin, a major economic center for the Jews of Poland from the 16th cent. Lublin also became a center for the study of Torah, and was nick-named Jerusalem of Poland.

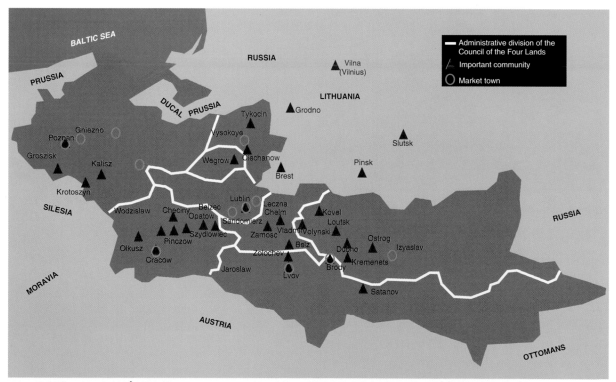

The territory administered by the Council of Four Lands. The area was divided into districts to simplify its administration.

Pale of Settlement

The last half of the 18th century was another stormy era both for Poland and for its Jews. Three times the land was invaded and partitioned by its more powerful neighbors. By 1796 nothing remained and Poland lost its independence altogether. Depending on where they lived, the Jews of Poland now became subjects of either Russia, Prussia, or Austria. To further compound their difficulties, even before the partitions Poland's last king, Stanislaw II Poniatowski, had abolished their two institutions of self-government, the Council of the Four Lands and the Council of Lithuania.

Several hundred wooden synagogues were built in Poland during the 17th and 18th cent. Unfortunately they were vulnerable to arson, and almost none remain.

Stanislaw II Poniatowski, the last king of Poland.

Catherine the Great

The ruler of Russia at this time, Catherine the Great, regarded herself as a progressive and liberal empress, but her subjects lived under extremely primitive conditions. Russia had a wealthy nobility and a merchant class composed of immigrants from Germany. The rest of the people were mostly serfs. The partitions of Poland brought Catherine the lion's share of Polish Jewry. In order to prevent this mass of Jews from expanding into other parts of the Russian Empire, she and her successors restricted their right of residence to the areas taken from Poland in which they were already living.

Life in the Pale

The Pale of Settlement, the area in the Russian government allowed Jews to live, included eastern Poland, Ukraine, and Lithuania. In addition to its Jewish residents, it had a much larger population of Christians, many of whom were quite hostile to their Jewish neighbors.

Catherine the Great was the daughter of a minor German ruler. In 1745 she married the Russian Tsar Peter III and soon after his mysterious death, in 1761, made herself the ruler of the greatest state in Europe. Domestically, she ruled with an iron hand and militarily advanced Russian power. She acquired Lithuania and the Ukraine from the Polish kingdom, and the Black Sea territories from the Ottoman empire. Envious statesmen saw Catherine's success as the work of the Devil.

It was here, in the little towns and villages of the Pale, in a few crowded cities and lonely inns along the highway, that most of Europe's Jews were to live for the next 200 years. Many harsh restrictions were placed upon them: they had to pay high taxes and could not move or travel without permission; they did not attend Russian schools or academies of higher learning and were barred from many other public institutions. Nonetheless, Jewish life in the Pale was active and full. While all but a few of the Russian nobles were illiterate, even the humblest Jewish family sent its sons to the heder to learn to read and write and engage in studying the Torah. The very restrictions that had been forced upon them served to unite the Jews of the Pale to a way of life based on brotherhood, neighborliness, and genuine affection for one another.

Ukrainian woodcutters drink in a Jewish-owned tavern. Note the costumes of the Jews. Painted in 1870 in Poland, by F. Lewicki.

Jewish Life in Poland

After the Chmielnicki revolt, the Cossack wars, and the general disillusion that set in after the exposure of Shabbatai Zevi and his false messianic claims, Jewish life in Poland went into a decline. The institutions of self-government were abolished. Many thriving communities disappeared; others were greatly reduced in size. Many communities could not even maintain their school systems.

Despite these serious problems, and the accompanying demoralization, this period was to produce two great religious leaders, each quite different from the other and each concerned with a different way of life. One was Israel ben Eliezer, known as the Baal Shem Tov; the other was Elijah ben Solomon, the Gaon of Vilna.

The Russian general Roumantsov leading his troops to victory over the Turks, August 1, 1770

The Baal Shem Tov / 1700–1760

Israel ben Eliezer

Israel ben Eliezer was born in a small town in Ukraine about 1698. When still a small child he lost both his parents and was cared for by the community. After graduating from the heder he became the assistant to his teacher. Israel liked children, and they, in turn, loved to listen to his stories. Although he was not known as a talmudic scholar, Israel was a bright young man with a charismatic manner and mystical disposition. He was also known as a healer and wonder-worker.

Israel married a young woman called Anna. From contemporary Polish records it appears that the two were given a house in Mezhbozh by the community, along with a small stipend.

The Worship of the Heart

All around him Israel could behold the beauty God had created. The humble lime digger was convinced that the holiness, or Shekhinah, of God dwelt within every living thing. All human beings, he believed, had the ability to see and experience the Shekhinah within themselves and around themselves. Everyone, scholar and simple laborer alike, he asserted, could reach spiritual heights by prayer and communing with God. The "worship of the heart" through joy and ecstasy, he taught, is of greater importance than dry, routine, ritual observance. Israel infused religious zest and vigor into the hearts of the physically downtrodden and spiritually impoverished masses.

Israel learned to make healing salves and ointments from plants and herbs, for he wanted to help the sick and the suffering. He also kept an inn which his wife managed while he devoted himself to teaching and healing. Faithful and inspired students flocked to him.

Day of Atonement in a Shtetl Synagogue. **Oil painting by Maurycy Gottlieb, 1878.**

Israel's Teachings

Israel ben Eliezer's teachings appealed not only to students but also, in the next generation, to the humble classes of the Jewish community.

He wrote no books; his wisdom was spread by word of mouth among rabbis and among the tradesmen, artisans, and laborers who were his followers. His followers told one another many wonderful stories about the wondrous deeds he performed, and before long the kindly Israel ben Eliezer was known as the Baal Shem Tov, the Master of the Good (Holy) Name, for it was said that he could heal people by wearing amulets. He is also known as the Besht, an acronym made up of the first letters of Baal Shem Tov.

Hasid and his wife in holiday dress.

The Hasidim

The followers of the Baal Shem Tov, who called themselves Hasidim ("pious ones") would dance with joy in their synagogues when they welcomed the Sabbath. Even in the midst of fervent prayers they would dance and sing niggunim, wordless melodies in praise of God. The leaders of the Hasidim in the generations after the Baal Shem Tov were known as Tzaddikim ("righteous ones"), and their disciples followed them with great fervor. As time passed, some of the Tzaddikim became men of great power and influence.

The synagogue of the Baal Shem Tov.

Hasidic scholar wearing a *streimel*. A *streimel* is a fox fur hat worn by some Hasidic sects on holidays and special ocasions

The Gaon of Vilna / 1720–1797

Elijah ben Solomon

The rabbis who fought against Hasidism were called Mitnagdim ("opponents"). Their leader was the Vilna Gaon—Elijah ben Solomon (1720–1797), the greatest among the many scholars of Vilna, a city known as the Jerusalem of Lithuania because of the great schools that flourished there. Elijah never accepted an official position as rabbi. He spent many hours in his quiet study at scholarly work, and, on occasion, teaching a small circle of disciples—advanced scholars who wanted to acquire his approach to talmudic study. His method was one of exacting detail. He would first study each passage thoroughly, and then refer to its original sources in the Mishnah and in the Torah itself. This thorough method made for a much clearer understanding of the Law.

Like the great scholars of earlier days, the Vilna Gaon studied mathematics and astronomy in addition to the works of Jewish mysticism. A few of his disciples encouraged the study of the sciences as essential for a proper understanding of Torah. This was unusual, for in those days most yeshiva scholars confined themselves strictly to teaching the Babylonian Talmud and the commentaries of Rashi and the tosafists.

The Vilna Gaon never held public office. Unofficially, however, he was the acknowledged spiritual leader of Lithuanian Jewry.

Conflict Between Hasidim and Mitnagdim

In the days of the Vilna Gaon the conflict between Hasidim and Mitnagdim became very bitter. The Tzaddikim had become very powerful, for their followers had come to regard them as intermediaries between the ordinary Hasid and God. The Mitnagdim, on the other hand, maintained that all human beings were personally responsible to God and therefore no intermediary was needed.

The Vilna Gaon took up the fight against Hasidism, going so far as to excommunicate its leaders and forbidding his followers to intermarry with its adherents. In time, however, this ban was lifted. As it became evident that the Hasidic faith fully followed the laws and commandments of the Talmud and the *Shulhan Arukh,* the two ways of Judaism made peace with one another. Hasidim and Mitnagdim still persisted in their different ways, as they do to the present time, but each group came to respect the other and to have a sense of appreciation for its contributions to Judaism.

The Vilna Gaon

New Horizons

First Stirrings of Democracy

During the 18th century more tolerant ideas first advanced in the Renaissance took on new life. Europe was slowly outgrowing the idea of absolute monarchy in which a king ruled supreme and an aristocracy had the right to subject the rest of the people. A new class of citizens had arisen—burghers who lived in the cities. Many of them were merchants, who helped build connections with other countries and with the faraway colonies of the New World. Also among the burghers were doctors and teachers. Universities began to rise in the cities of Europe, attended by the sons of nobles and wealthy burghers. Writers and poets put forth new and stimulating ideas.

The Reformation had stimulated widespread interest in the Bible, and many Christians had become aware that the Hebrew Scriptures were part of their religious heritage. Despite this, the Jews, whose ancestors had given gave the Bible to the world, were among the most despised people in Europe.

The Court Jews

Occasionally an individual Jew would rise to a position of high honor. At many a European royal court, especially in the many princedoms of Germany, a Jewish banker, often referred to as a court Jew, managed the sovereign's financial and business affairs. The court Jew usually enjoyed respect and prestige, but his position was precarious, for in many instances the kindness of the prince would turn to wrath.

Frequently a court Jew would speak to his prince on behalf of his community. Sometimes Jewish merchants who had helped a free city in time of war would be

The old synagogue in Berlin.

invited to settle there with their families and friends. In this way some Jewish communities increased in size. But there also were small communities surrounded by the high walls of the ghetto from which a Jew could go forth only when he had to do business. No social relations existed between the world outside and the ghetto Jews.

Developments outside the ghetto were foreign to the Jews of the 17th and 18th centuries, except insofar as they affected their lives directly in the form of persecution or war. So isolated was the life of the Jews in Germany that their spoken language was not the German of everyone else but Judeo-German, medieval German closely interwoven with Hebrew words, the same dialect that in Eastern Europe had evolved into Yiddish.

The writers and thinkers of Germany had little occasion to meet Jews. But as they became interested in the theories of human equality and natural rights, they began to turn their attention to the minority that suffered so much discrimination in their own country.

Moses Mendelssohn / 1729–1786

Moses Mendelssohn was a small man who spoke with a slight stammer, but he had a dynamic spirit and a brilliant mind. The son of a Torah scribe, Mendelssohn was born in the German town of Dessau and studied with a rabbi there. When he was a boy of 14 his beloved teacher moved to Berlin. The boy followed him, and on paying the tax required of Jews, he succeeded in gaining admission to the city.

Moses Mendelssohn

Mendelssohn Finds a New World

Mendelssohn found a new world in Berlin. Even though most of the city's Jews lived much as their brethren did in other German communities, there were quite a few enterprising Jewish merchants and financiers in Berlin who enjoyed special privileges and were in contact with the world outside the ghetto. Young Mendelssohn continued his Jewish studies with his mentor, but broadened his education by taking up a variety of other subjects as well. He found willing teachers with whom he studied the writings of the philosophers.

Mendelssohn secured employment as tutor to the children of a wealthy silk manufacturer. In his spare time he began to write on philosophy and current issues, expounding his ideas in a pure, flowing German. Moses Mendelssohn was the first German Jew of his day whose writings and intellectual interests transcended the ghetto walls. Berlin's intellectual and cultural elite became very much interested in this unusual man.

Difficulties in Germany

All through the German lands Jews were still confined to ghettos. In the great and ancient communities of Frankfurt, Mayence, Worms, and Hamburg, as well as in the new community of Berlin, they lived under severe restrictions. Usually only the eldest son of a Jewish family was permitted to marry, and then only after paying a special tax. Jews also had to pay taxes for such acts as entering a walled city. Often families would be separated by these cruel restrictions, because their daughters and sons had to go to distant communities to marry and have families of their own.

It was difficult for Jews to earn a living, for most of them were only permitted to engage in small-scale businesses like moneylending and dealing in second-hand goods. They were not allowed to own land or real estate outside the crowded ghettos.

Title page of Book of Psalms, translated into German by Moses Mendelssohn.

A Protected Jew

Moses Mendelssohn became a privileged, or "protected," Jew—a status normally reserved for the most important Jewish merchants and financiers, and for a few Jewish physicians who

193

treated influential non-Jewish patients. Thanks to the freedom provided by this status, Mendelssohn met many of the writers and scholars of the day. He even met Frederick the Great, the king of Prussia, who was very much interested in philosophy and the arts.

Mendelssohn's main concern, however, was the Jewish community. Convinced that German Jewry had to break down the ghetto walls and participate in the life outside, he devoted himself to the task of bringing his brethren the modern learning and culture that would make this possible. Mendelssohn knew that to participate fully in life outside the ghetto the German Jews would first have to learn the German language. He had no intention of sacrificing Jewish education, however, and participated in publishing a magazine that carried articles, poems, and commentaries in Hebrew. But he insisted that in addition to traditional Jewish studies, Jews must learn German and become acquainted with the world around them.

At that time few German children went to school. Most of the common people were illiterate. But the Jews all knew how to read and write in Hebrew. Under Mendelssohn's influence, new schools were founded in Berlin where Jewish children were given their Jewish and secular education under one roof. He insisted, too, that the children receive trade and vocational training to prepare them for life as free citizens among their non-Jewish neighbors.

The First German Torah Translation

Facility in German, Mendelssohn felt, was essential. Few German Jews knew the language well, and virtually none could read it. To provide them with a learning resource, Mendelssohn translated the Five Books of Moses into German. He had it printed in Hebrew characters, however, so that Jews could read it even if they did not know the German alphabet. The translation appeared with a Hebrew commentary prepared by Mendelssohn in collaboration with a biblical scholar.

The new translation was published with the permission of the rabbis of Germany, and at first it was widely accepted. Since most Jews already knew and had read the Bible in Hebrew, the translation satisfied an important need. It became a learning tool for everyone who wanted to learn German; copies found their way even to the Yiddish-speaking villages of far-off Russia where isolated students sought to master German as the first step on the road to enlightened self-improvement.

Before long, however, the rabbis decided that Mendelssohn's German Bible and modern commentary were dangerous innovations; the old, traditional way of teaching was safer and more desirable. This did not deter those who were eager to learn German from continuing to rely on Mendelssohn's Bible.

Moses Mendelssohn playing chess.

Edict of Frederick the Great with regard to the conversion of Jews.

Edict of Tolerance / 1782

No explicit laws to better the lot of the Jews were passed in the German states during Mendelssohn's lifetime. But new ideas had paved a path for new hopes and attitudes.

Wilhelm Dohm

Among Mendelssohn's many Christian friends who were favorably disposed toward the new concepts of liberty and tolerance was Christian Wilhelm Dohm, a Prussian lawyer. When the Jews of Alsace asked Mendelssohn to write a petition requesting the authorities to remove some of the heavy restrictions placed upon them, it was to Dohm that Mendelssohn turned, asking him to draft the text of the memorandum. Dohm not only complied with his friend's request, but also wrote a plea for freedom and equality for all the Jews of Western Europe.

Dohm's plea brought Joseph II, the emperor of Austria, to proclaim the famous Edict of Tolerance (1782). While this law did not lift all restrictions from the Jews of Austria, it eased their burden considerably and opened doors hitherto closed to them. They no longer had to pay special poll taxes and wear the yellow badge; they were allowed to engage in trade and manufacturing and to become appren-ticed to Christian master craftsmen. However, when Joseph died in 1790, most of the restrictions were revived.

Other Proclamations of Freedom

Meanwhile, in the New World across the ocean, the American colonies had revolted against England. Their Declaration of Independence and Constitution stimulated much discussion among thinking people throughout Europe. The laws of the new land incorporated many of the same ideas that Mendelssohn and his friends had helped formulate in Berlin.

Freedom and Assimilation

Moses Mendelssohn fought not only for enlightenment and religious freedom but also to ensure the survival of Judaism and its traditions. He was by no means an assimilationist. He did not want the Jewish people to merge into the other nations of the world and lose its distinctive identity. His goal was to enable his brethren to make a contribution to civilization outside the ghetto and to live in peace and harmony side by side with their Gentile neighbors.

Medal commemorating Joseph II's Edict of Tolerance, Vienna, 1782.

Revolution and Reform

The French Revolution / 1789

For a hundred years France had set the trends in Europe. In Germany, Poland, and Austria, and even in Russia, French was the language of the nobility, the educated, and the wealthy. French ideas and styles were adopted and imitated.

When French philosophers, writers, and poets first began to speak out for religious and political freedom, the rulers of France were greatly disturbed, for they needed obedient subjects who would willingly supply the immense sums of money necessary to support the elegant French court and powerful French army.

On July 14, 1789, the people of Paris stormed the Bastille, a fortress in which many of those who had been unable to pay the high taxes were imprisoned. This was the start of the French Revolution, an upheaval in which the people came to power.

In 1789, the year the Revolution began, the French Assembly proclaimed the Declaration of the Rights of Man. This document, which is similar to the American Declaration of Independence, declared that all human beings are born free and entitled to equal rights.

In 1790, the Jews of Bordeaux were granted equality. A decree passed in 1791 gave all French Jews the rights and privileges of full citizenship. But then the new French republic became involved in war. First, it had to defend itself against the monarchs of Europe, who were afraid that the spirit of revolt would spread to their lands.

A short time later, the French armies themselves became armies of conquest. They were led by a young general named Napoleon Bonaparte.

The Reign of Napoleon

Napoleon was a brilliant strategist. A highly ambitious man, he had dreams of great conquest. He hoped to carry the ideals and the new freedom of the young republic of France to every country in Europe.

Wherever his conquering armies took over, serfs and Jews were freed. The ghetto walls of Germany, Austria, and Italy fell. Many Europeans regarded Napoleon as a great liberator. The laws he promulgated, known as the Napoleonic Code, lent legal force to the concepts of freedom and civil liberties. His ambition was to be the undisputed ruler of the French state, the crowned conqueror of Europe. In 1804 he became emperor of France.

In 1806 Napoleon convened an assembly of Jewish notables and announced that Jews were now officially citizens of the French nation. The emperor is shown raising the Jewess while the rabbis kneel at his feet.

Freedom and Citizenship

Napoleon Convenes a Sanhedrin

Eager to gain the loyalty of the Jews and also to exercise a measure of control over them, Napoleon convened an assembly patterned on the ancient Sanhedrin. Altogether, 71 representatives, 46 rabbis and 25 laymen, were chosen to settle legal and religious questions and to demonstrate loyalty to Napoleon's France.

Napoleon Bonaparte

The Sanhedrin was soon dissolved, but it served to emphasize some of the fundamentals of Judaism to the non-Jewish world.

Reaction

Eventually the allied countries of Europe defeated Napoleon. With Napoleon defeated and banished, the Jews lost many of the freedoms he had granted them. In some parts of Germany and Austria they had to return to the ghettos, and the peasants were forced to revert to serfdom.

Having had a taste of freedom, the Jews found it difficult to readjust to the old restrictions. Some German and Austrian Jews had attended universities and embarked upon brilliant careers; they were now respected bankers and merchants, or high-ranking government officials. Some of them, concluding that there were many advantages to be gained from converting to Christianity, underwent baptism in order to be able to keep their positions.

Changes Within

Most of the Jews of Germany and Austria continued to follow the ways of their ancestors. But, like everyone in the 19th century, they, too, had to adjust to the radical changes that were occurring in their time.

Patriotism and nationalism reached new heights. The Jews were proud of their newly won rights of citizenship in the countries in which they lived. And this brought them face to face with a new problem: how to remain faithful to the traditions of Judaism and still be loyal, active citizens of the countries that had accorded them freedom and equality.

Impelled by a desire to eliminate the differences between themselves and those in whose midst they lived, many Jews were anxious to change Judaism itself.

Napoleon became the ruler of France after the turmoil of the French Revolution. During his regime France conquered much of Europe. In 1821 he died in exile on the tiny island of St. Helena.

Changes and Resistance in Germany

Reform Judaism

Those calling for radical changes in Judaism founded the Reform movement. They felt that if Judaism was to have a meaningful function in the modern world, it was necessary to eliminate old ceremonies and ideas which seemed antiquated or inappropriate, or which reflected the sensibility of the narrow life of the medieval ghetto.

Rabbi Zechariah Frankel

One of the leaders of this new movement, headed by Rabbi Abraham Geiger (1810–1874), proposed a different form of service. They introduced sermons and prayers in German, the everyday language of the people, and shortened Hebrew prayers that seemed too long. References to the return to Zion and the coming of the Messiah were omitted. Believing that a "reformed" Judaism would adjust Jewish life to the demands of the times, they set aside the authority of the Talmud and the *Shulhan Arukh.* The Reform movement took root in some of the larger German cities and the first Reform temple was dedicated in Hamburg.

Orthodoxy

Many Jews steadfastly resisted the changes proposed by the reformers, maintaining that any break in the chain of tradition would endanger the very foundations of Judaism. Their approach is now known as Orthodox Judaism. The most influential early opponent of reform was Rabbi Moses Schreiber (1763–1839), who was born in Germany and later became known as the Chatam Sofer, after the title of many of his works. From his position as rabbi in Pressburg, Hungary, he rallied traditionalist-minded Jews against any changes in the synagogue service. Orthodoxy, which held the loyalty of most German Jews, had a number of brilliant spokesmen. In the next generation, the most prominent among them was Rabbi Samson Raphael Hirsch (1808–1888). Hirsch was convinced that Jews could be good citizens, steeped in the culture and learning of their country, and still remain loyal to the laws that had come down through the ages in the Bible and Talmud.

The Historical School

A third group took a midway position between Reform and Orthodoxy. Led by Zechariah Frankel (1801–1875), the president of the rabbinical seminary in Breslau (Wroclaw), this movement was known as the Historical School, and eventually became what is today called Conservative Judaism. It emphasized the importance of the historical continuity of the Jewish heritage. The adherents of the Historical School knew that change was inevitable and acknowledged that Judaism had undergone changes throughout its history, but they insisted that innovations had to be within the framework of Jewish tradition. Radical reform, they felt, was not in keeping with the evolving spirit of Judaism.

A German army War Haggadah used during World War I.

Judaism and Civil Liberties

The "Science of Judaism"

A group of young German Jewish universi-ty graduates believed that the best way to ensure the survival of Judaism was to make its history and values better known. To this end, they began to apply the same analytical methods to the study of the Jewish heritage that were used in studying any other ancient culture. This group, headed by Leopold Zunz (1794–1886), called itself the Society for the Scientific Study of Jewish Culture; its approach is often referred to as the "Science of Judaism" (*Wissenschaft des Judentums*).

Printed handkerchief showing an open-air service on the Day of Atonement, 1870, outside Metz.

Heinrich Graetz, Historian

Among the adherents of Zunz's school was Heinrich Graetz (1817–1891), a man of great talent and imagination. Graetz, a pro-fessor at the rabbinical seminary of Breslau, devoted 17 years of his life to the task of writing a well-documented history of the Jews. The first work of its kind, based on solid research and analysis of sources, it is still widely read to this day.

The Struggle for Democracy

As the first half of the 19th century drew to a close, Europe was shaken by uprisings and revolts. When the Revolution of 1848 in Germany was crushed, many of the dis-appointed freedom fighters left their homeland. Thousands of them crossed the Atlantic to settle in the United States.

The cause of civil liberties in Germany was greatly advanced by the unification in 1871 of all the German lands and provinces into one nation, under the leadership of Prussia. All Germans were recognized as free citizens with equal rights and liberties, including the freedom to worship as they chose. At last the Jews of Germany were free.

A Jewish Wedding by Moritz Oppenheim, 1861. Painting of a German marriage ceremony, showing a tallit serving as a huppah canopy.

Heinrich Graetz, professor and leading modern historian.

The Jews Resettle in England / 1656

Rothschild and Montefiore

Across the Channel from France, England had become a major world power. This land of seafarers and merchants had attracted many Jewish immigrants since the days when Rabbi Manasseh Ben Israel had first come from Holland to plead for the readmission of Jews. Even before his meeting with Oliver Cromwell, individual New Christians had managed to find their way to England. In 1594 one of them, Roderigo Lopez, the personal physician of Queen Elizabeth I, was executed for plotting to poison her.

The first Jews to settle in England in the 17th century were Marranos. They were followed by Sephardic Jews from Italy and Ashkenazim from Germany and Poland. By the 19th century a sizable Jewish community existed in England.

Moses Montefiore

Another prominent British Jew serving in the war against Napoleon was Nathan Mayer Rothschild's brother-in-law, Moses Montefiore (1784–1885), whose family had come to England from Italy. After his discharge from the British army, Montefiore returned to his business. At the time of the battle of Waterloo, he was a successful stockbroker. Through some of their agents on the continent, Rothschild and Montefiore learned of Napoleon's defeat at Waterloo before this good news reached England.

Rothschild and Montefiore were far-sighted financiers. When the British stock exchange appeared on the verge of collapse during the war, they helped stabilize the market with their financial talents.

Brothers-in-Law

Among the leading members of Britain's Jewish community was Nathan Mayer Rothschild (1776–1836). His father, Mayer Amschel Rothschild (1743–1812), had built up a major banking business in the German city of Frankfurt. The oldest of Nathan's five brothers had remained in Frankfurt to run the bank there, while the other three had established branches in Paris, Vienna, and Naples. Nathan Rothschild had settled in London, where he became a major figure on the stock exchange and acted as a financial agent for the British government during the Napoleonic Wars.

New Synagogue, Great Helen Street, London, 1860. It is Sukkot. The man on the left is carrying the Torah. The person next to him is holding a lulav and etrog. On each side of the sanctuary is a prayer for the Royal Family, in English and Hebrew.

Jewish Champions of Liberty

Champions of Civil Liberties

Rothschild and Montefiore were both ardent champions of freedom. When England decided to abolish slavery, they assisted the government with a large loan to make the enforcement of the new law possible.

In 1835, David Salomons was elected sheriff of London, and two years later the same post was occupied by Montefiore. At that time Jews in England still could not receive academic degrees and were barred from most public offices because, with the exception of the post of sheriff of London, they entailed an oath requiring an affirmation of the "true faith of a Christian."

Neither Montefiore nor Rothschild and the other Jewish leaders were satisfied with these conditions. They fought for the elimination of the oath and for the right of Jews to hold public office.

The First Jew Enters Parliament

The son of Nathan Rothschild, Baron Lionel de Rothschild (1808–1879), was elected to Parliament four times in ten years, but resigned each time because the required oath of office was Christian in form. In 1858, the rules were finally changed so that Rothschild could take the oath on a Hebrew Bible as the faith of a Jew. He was the first Jewish member of Britain's House of Commons. Eventually a special oath was devised so that Jews could be sworn in to all public offices and hold professional positions.

When Prime Minister Benjamin Disraeli was negotiating for control of the Suez Canal, it was Lionel de Rothschild who provided him with the funds that made the purchase possible.

Benjamin Disraeli (1804–1881) was himself a symbol of the new position of the Jew in England. Although he had been baptized a Christian at an early age, he was proud to be descended from Spanish Jews who had fled from Spain in 1492. A brilliant statesman and trusted advisor to Queen Victoria, Disraeli also wrote novels and political essays. Many of his books deal with Jewish subjects. During his terms as Prime Minister (1867; 1874–1880) Britain gained control of the Suez Canal and solidified its control of India.

Coat of arms adopted by the Rothschild family in 1817.

Mayer Amschel Rothschild.

The Rothschild Family at Prayer, by Moritz Daniel Oppenheim.

Moses Montefiore / 1784–1885

Moses Montefiore

In 1838 Moses Montefiore was knighted by Queen Victoria, becoming the first Jew to attain this honor. Although active in public affairs, Sir Moses devoted much of his time and effort to the Board of Deputies of British Jews. As president of that body, he led the Jewish community's effort to secure the removal of the restrictions under which the Jews of England still suffered. One by one, during his long lifetime, the humiliating restrictions were abolished.

The Damascus Libel

In 1840, Sir Moses Montefiore learned that the Jews of Damascus in Syria had been falsely accused of murdering a monk. Jews there were being arrested and tortured, and Jewish children had been imprisoned to compel their parents to confess to a crime they had not committed. Since Syria was under Egyptian jurisdiction, Montefiore, with the backing of the British government, went to Egypt to press for the release of the prisoners and for an official acknowledgment of their innocence. He was accompanied by his wife, Judith, and by a committee he had organized, among whom was Adolphe Crémieux (1796–1880), a French Jew who had fought successfully for the civil rights of the Jews of France.

The incident in Damascus aroused indignation all over the world, and protest demonstrations took place in many countries, including the United States. In the end, the Egyptian government bowed to public pressure. The prisoners were released and their innocence was publicly proclaimed.

Sir Moses and the Tsar

In the vast, isolated land of Russia, the Jews still had no rights. While restrictions were being lifted throughout the rest of Europe, the situation of Russian Jewry was deteriorating. The Jews were still forced to live in the Pale of Settlement and were subjected to humiliating restraints. For centuries they had been artisans, innkeepers, and shopkeepers in the towns and villages of the Pale. Now the tsar wanted them to abandon their customary occupations and relocate to the far-off provinces of Astrakhan and the Caucasus region as farmers.

Moses Montefiore hoped to prevent this cruel decree from being put into effect. In 1846 he and his wife made the long journey to Russia, bearing with them a letter of introduction from Queen Victoria. They made another visit in 1872. Each time they were received courteously at the imperial court. The tsar permitted the Jews to remain in the Pale of Settlement, but nothing was done to alleviate the hardships under which they had to live.

British philanthropist Sir Moses Montefiore. He encouraged many of the early Jewish settlements in Palestine.

Soon after his return home, Montefiore was given the title of baronet by Queen Victoria, who desired to honor him for his courageous efforts on behalf of Jews everywhere.

Sir Moses and Palestine

Realizing that there was little he could do to better the position of his brethren in the lands of the tsar, Montefiore cast about for another solution.

Sir Moses dreamed of the return of the Jews to the Land of Israel. He visited Palestine six times, and each time brought assistance and support to the Jews there, helping them to build hospitals, schools, and synagogues. To attract settlers, he planted vineyards and olive groves, and opened an experimental agricultural school. On the outskirts of the Old City of Jerusalem, Montefiore built a group of homes that became the nucleus of what is now called the New City.

Sir Moses Montefiore lived to the prodigious age of 101. His 100th birthday, in 1884, was marked by elaborate celebrations and parades, for his name had come to be known far and wide as a symbol of charity, progress, and love of liberty.

Windmill in Yemin Moshe, a community named after Moses Montefiore. Much new building has taken place since the time of this photograph and the windmill is still there.

Sir Moses Montefiore speaking to Tsar Nicholas I in 1846 in St. Petersburg.

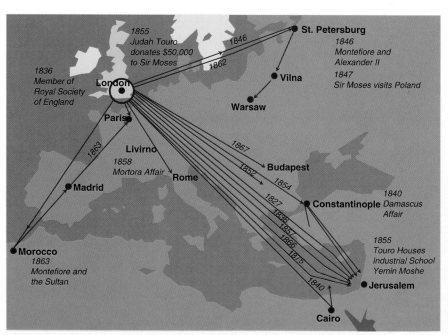

The travels of Moses Montefiore to protect the rights of the Jews. Note the seven trips to the Holy Land.

The Jews of Europe

JEWISH HIGHLIGHTS

The Renaissance 15th–17th century	Jews of Turkey 15th–16th century	Mystics and Kabbalah 15th–16th century	The Netherlands 15th–17th century	Italy 17th century

JEWISH EVENTS • PERSONALITIES • LITERATURE

The Renaissance	Jews of Turkey	Mystics and Kabbalah	The Netherlands	Italy
▷ Shtadlanim	▷ Solomon Ashkenazi	▷ Safed Kabbalah	▷ Amsterdam Dutch Jerusalem	▷ Moses Hayim Luzzatto *The Second Zohar* *The Way of the Righteous*
Joseph Suess Oppenheimer	▷ Doña Gracia Mendes	▷ Rabbi Isaac Luria (Ari) Kabbalah	Marranos	
Yosel of Rosheim	▷ Joseph Nasi Tiberias Silk production		Rabbi Jacob Sasportas	
▷ Ghettos Economic and social restrictions Religious intolerance		▷ Rabbi Joseph Caro *Shulhan Arukh*	Rabbi Manasseh Ben Israel	
▷ Jewish printers Soncino family		▷ False Messiahs David Reubeni Solomon Molcho Shabbatai Zevi	Baruch Spinoza	
▷ Abraham Usque				
▷ Moses de Leon Zohar				
▷ Simeon bar Yohai Lag Ba-Omer				

WORLD HISTORY

The Renaissance	Jews of Turkey	Mystics and Kabbalah	The Netherlands	Italy
▷ Reformation Charles V	▷ Ottoman Empire	▷ Charles V / Spain	▷ Protestant Reformation	▷ Italy
▷ Pope Paul IV	Sultan Suleiman	▷ Constantinople	▷ Dutch colonies	Tiberias
▷ Papal Bull Johann Gutenberg First printed Bible	Selim II		▷ Oliver Cromwell	
▷ Martin Luther	Venice		Rembrandt	
▷ Holy Roman Empire				

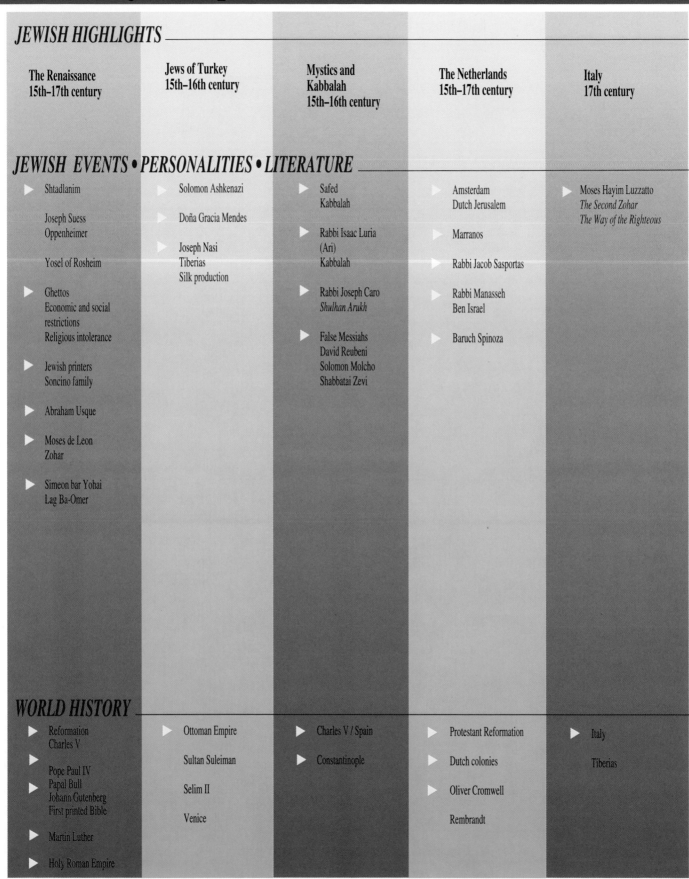

The Jews of Europe

JEWISH HIGHLIGHTS

Eastern Europe 16th–18th century	Pale of Settlement 17th–18th century	New Horizons 18th century	Changes in Germany 19th century	English Jews 19th century

JEWISH EVENTS • PERSONALITIES • LITERATURE

Eastern Europe	Pale of Settlement	New Horizons	Changes in Germany	English Jews
▶ Polish Jewry Warsaw Lublin Vilna Posen Cracow	▶ Council of Four Lands abolished	▶ Yiddish	▶ Reform Judaism Rabbi Abraham Geiger	▶ Rothschild Family
▶ Kahal	▶ Council of Lithuania dissolved	▶ Court Jews	▶ Orthodoxy Rabbi Raphael Samson Hirsch	▶ Moses Montefiore Damascus Libel Yemin Moshe
▶ Council of Four Lands	▶ Baal Shem Tov Tzaddikim Hasidim Besht	▶ Moses Mendelssohn German Bible	▶ Historical School Rabbi Zechariah Frankel	▶ Benjamin Disraeli
▶ Yiddish	▶ Gaon of Vilna Mitnagdim	▶ Wilhelm Dohm Edict of Tolerance	▶ Science of Judaism Rabbi Leopold Zunz Heinrich Graetz	
▶ Rabbi Moses Isserles *Shulhan Arukh*				
▶ Cossack Revolt 100,000 Jewish victims				

WORLD HISTORY

Eastern Europe	Pale of Settlement	New Horizons	Changes in Germany	English Jews
▶ King Casimir	▶ Poland loses independence	▶ Frederick the Great	▶ Germany	▶ Suez Canal
▶ King Sigismund	▶ Catherine the Great	▶ Edict of Tolerance Joseph II		▶ Queen Victoria
▶ Cossacks Bogdan Chmielnicki		▶ Napoleon French Revolution (1789) Napoleonic Code Rights of Man		

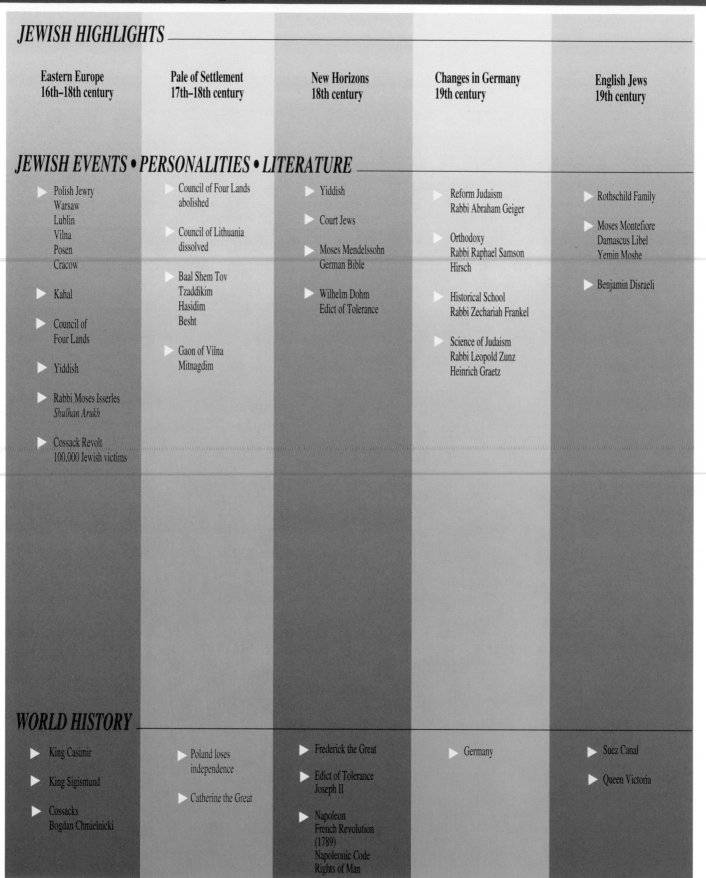

Looking for Refuge

The expulsion from Spain in 1492 had begun a long period of wandering for many thousands of Jews. Some found new homes in the cities of North Africa, Syria, and the Turkish Empire. Others found further oppression and hardship in other lands; and, all too often, another decree of expulsion.

Those exiles who went to Portugal found themselves betrayed by King Manuel. Thousands were forced to convert to Christianity. Pretending to adopt the new religion in order to save their lives, they remained secret Jews (Marranos), living under the threat of the Inquisition and in constant danger of discovery.

Marranos who were able to leave Portugal often sought refuge in free countries like Holland. Even after generations had passed, some still longed to return to their ancestral religion. Throughout the 16th and 17th centuries, small numbers of devoted secret Jews made their way to Brazil, the West Indies, Mexico, and other New World colonies.

The Colony of Recife

When the Dutch conquered the Portuguese colony of Recife in Brazil in 1630, the Marranos living there joyfully resumed the faith of their ancestors. They were able to join together in public worship and in observing the Sabbath, and openly to teach their children Torah.

To serve as their religious leader and teacher they invited Rabbi Isaac Aboab da Fonseca (1605–1693). Born to Marrano parents in Portugal, Aboab had escaped with his family to Holland and there had studied for the rabbinate. In 1642 he came to Recife from Amsterdam, becoming the first rabbi in the Western Hemisphere.

The freedom of the new Jewish community did not last long. In 1654 the Portuguese reconquered Recife and reintroduced the Inquisition. The Jews, who now were considered heretics, or traitors to the Christian faith, were forced once more to flee for their lives. Isaac Aboab and a few others returned to Amsterdam. Some of the refugees went to the Dutch Caribbean colonies of Surinam and Curaçao.

Isaac Aboab, the first rabbi in the Western Hemisphere. In 1642 he was called to the Dutch Jewish community of Recife, but he returned to Amsterdam when the Portuguese conquered the colony and brought in the Inquisition.

Artist's impression of Recife in the 1600s, the wall of the settlement and the church.

The First Jewish Settlers

First Jews in North America

Twenty-three of the exiles from Recife sailed first to the West Indies, and then, in a vessel named the *Saint Charles*, up the North American coast to the Dutch colony of New Amsterdam. Robbed on the way by pirates, the penniless group arrived in September of 1654 at the port that was later to be named New York.

Peter Stuyvesant

Peter Stuyvesant, the governor appointed by the Dutch West India Company, let the new arrivals know that they were not welcome. He "required them in a friendly way to depart," but allowed them to remain temporarily while he awaited instructions from Amsterdam. After some months, a letter arrived stating that because the Jews of Recife had fought for Holland, and because the Dutch West India Company had many Jewish shareholders, the newcomers were to be permitted to remain, "provided the poor among them shall not become a burden to the company or to the community, but be supported by their own nation."

Burgher Rights

These instructions did not find favor in the eyes of Stuyvesant and his council. Although the company had specified that the Jews were to be treated like everyone else, he denied them the right to stand guard with the colony's other residents, and instead required that they pay a special tax. This policy was abandoned when two Jewish colonists, Jacob Barsimson and Asser Levy, took legal action. Similarly, Abraham de Lucena, Salvador Dandrada, and other Jews filed legal petitions demanding the right to buy homes, to

The Mill Street Synagogue of the *Shearith Israel* Congregation of New York, erected in 1730. This chart for counting the *Omer* between Passover and *Shavuot* was used in the synagogue.

trade, and finally to enjoy full burgher rights.

Three years after they first landed, the Jews of New Amsterdam were granted citizenship. This did not mean that they enjoyed every civil right. They were not permitted to build a synagogue, being required to "exercise in all quietness their religion within their houses." They still had to petition the Dutch Council and later the British governor—for the British conquered the colony and renamed it New York in 1664—when they faced restrictions in trade or professions. Through their outspoken demands for justice and freedom, and their faithfulness to Jewish tradition, this small group of Jews proved themselves worthy ancestors of the American Jewish community.

Asser Levy

In 1657, Asser Levy became the first Jew in New Amsterdam, and therefore in North America, to enjoy the full rights of citizenship. He became the colony's first Jewish landowner when he purchased a plot of land on William Street which is now in the heart of the Wall Street financial district. He was also accorded the privilege of becoming one of its six licensed butchers.

The First Synagogue

In 1664, the British captured New Amsterdam and renamed it New York. Now Asser Levy expanded his business enterprises. In addition he bought a house on Mill Street to be used as a synagogue. Congregation Shearith Israel ("Remnant of Israel"), which had been meeting in private homes, now had its first official building.

Jews in the Colonies

The earliest Jewish settlers in North America were Sephardim, or, as they designated themselves, "of the Portuguese nation." The first synagogue in North America, Shearith Israel in New York, still follows the Spanish and Portuguese minhag, the Sephardic order of prayer. By 1750, however, half of the 300 Jewish residents of New York were Ashkenazim from Central or Eastern Europe.

During the 18th century, small numbers of Jews came to America from Europe, making their homes in Philadelphia, Charleston, Savannah, and other cities along the eastern seaboard.

Rhode Island, the colony founded by Roger Williams as an outpost of religious freedom, was a favorite destination. Among the prominent Jewish residents of Newport, its most important city, was

Interior of the beautiful Newport synagogue, first permanent synagogue in the New World. Named Yeshuat Israel, the congregation and its building were supported for many years by Judah Touro.

Aaron Lopez (1731–1782), son of an old Marrano family in Lisbon, who became a wealthy merchant-shipper in the New World. The Newport synagogue building, one of the earliest to be erected in America, is now a national shrine. It is often called the Touro synagogue in honor of Isaac Touro, its first spiritual leader.

The Chatham Square Cemetery in New York City is one of the oldest Jewish cemeteries in the United States. It was founded in 1656.

The Mill Street Synagogue of the Shearith Israel Congregation of New York, erected in 1730.

The Revolutionary War

There were about 3,000 Jews in the British colonies at the time of the American Revolution. Many of them fought for the patriotic cause. Francis Salvador (1747–1776), a Jewish planter born in England, was chosen a member of the provincial congress in South Carolina in 1774. Two years later, he gave his life in one of the Revolution's first battles.

Among the many other Jewish soldiers was Benjamin Nones (1757–1826), who came from France in order to participate in the battle for freedom and human rights which he felt the Revolution represented. He rose to the rank of major, and afterwards served the new country as a legislator.

Gershom Mendes Seixas

Supporters of the American cause were in danger of imprisonment when the British army occupied New York and Newport. Gershom Mendes Seixas (1745–1816), minister of Shearith Israel, was so outspoken a patriot that he had to flee the city when the British troops landed. Taking the Torah scrolls with him, he reestablished the congregation in Stratford, Connecticut, and then set up a new one, Mikveh Israel, in Philadelphia. In New York after the war, he was honored as a leading religious figure, took part in George Washington's presidential inauguration, and served as a trustee of Columbia College.

Isaac Touro, accompanied by many members of his congregation, fled from Newport when the British occupied it. Aaron Lopez, rather than collaborate with the British, left his wealth and holdings and settled in a small town in Massachusetts until the patriot forces were victorious.

Many volunteers came from across the ocean to join the Americans in their fight for freedom. Among them were Lafayette from France, Pulaski and Kosciusko from Poland, and Baron von Steuben and Baron Johann de Kalb from Germany. The latter, who died in action, commanded a unit of 400 men, so many of whom were Jews that it was sometimes called the Jewish regiment.

Most Canadian colonists remained loyal to England, but a few of them sympathized with the American rebels. David Salisbury Franks (1743–1793), a resident of Montreal, was arrested for making a slighting remark about a statue of King George. After he was released he left Canada and joined the American army.

Haym Salomon

Service beyond the call of duty was rendered by Haym Salomon (1740–1785), a Jewish broker who came to New York from Poland in 1772. Imprisoned for supporting the revolutionary cause, he managed to escape to Philadelphia. There he worked with Robert Morris, superintendent of finance, extending loans and arranging credit to pay for the costs of the war. Though in America only a few years, he was an ardent patriot, never hesitating to risk his own funds to bring about victory for the cause of right.

Aaron Lopez, distinguished citizen of Newport, Rhode Island. He came from a Marrano family in Portugal in 1752.

Washington and the Jews

Words of George Washington

When the new nation came into being, and George Washington became its first President, the Jews of Newport were one of the many groups to send a message of good wishes. They expressed their appreciation for "a Government which to bigotry gives no sanction, to persecution no assistance," and their thanks to God for "all the blessings of civil and religious liberty."

In answer, President Washington stated, "The citizens of the United States of America have a right to applaud themselves for having given to mankind examples of an enlarged and liberal policy. All possess alike liberty of conscience and immunities of citizenship." He continued with a clear statement of the position of the new nation on human liberty:

"It is now no more that toleration is spoken of, as if it was by the indulgence of one class of people, that another enjoyed the exercise of their inherent natural rights. For happily the Government of the United States, which gives to bigotry no sanction, to persecution no assistance, requires only that they who live under its protection should demean themselves as good Citizens, in giving it on all occasions their effectual support."

Freedom of Religion

The United States was the first country in the world to guarantee full freedom of religion. The First Amendment to the Constitution begins: "Congress shall make no law respecting the establishment of religion, or prohibiting the free exercise thereof." Although some states still had laws restricting the right of holding office to those of recognized Christian faith, all of these were soon challenged and revoked. Jews were able to take their place as active citizens of the new democracy.

Chicago's memorial to Haym Salomon, seen standing to the right of George Washington while Robert Morris stands on his left, both supporting him in his fight for freedom.

This painting by Ferris shows the forging of the Liberty Bell. It was cast by the Whitechapel Bell Foundry in England and cost £100. The inscription on the bell is from Leviticus, the third book of the Bible. It reads "Proclaim liberty throughout the land, to all its inhabitants." The Liberty Bell is now in Philadelphia

MOSES JUDAH
PVT PA MILITIA
REV WAR
SEPTEMBER 25 1822

Tombstone of Private Moses Judah, a soldier in the Revolutionary War. He served in the Pennsylvania Militia.

Men of Prominence

Ezra Stiles, a christian, was president of Yale College from 1778 to 1795, found much to praise in the Jewish citizens. Speaking of Aaron Lopez, he said, "His beneficence to his family, to his nation, and to all the world is without a parallel." Other Jews in early America also displayed the philanthropy and the desire to serve others that characterize the American Jewish community to this day.

Judah Touro, philanthropist of New Orleans, in his old age.

Mordecai Manuel Noah (1785–1851), writer, politician, and well-known public figure.

Judah Touro

One of the many civic-minded Jews was the wealthy New Orleans merchant Judah Touro (1775–1854), who willed his entire fortune to synagogues, schools, hospitals, and orphan homes in 18 cities. A patriotic soldier who was seriously wounded in the battle of New Orleans during the War of 1812, Touro gave the largest contribution, $10,000, for the building of the Bunker Hill Monument. A large portion of his estate went to build homes for the poor in Jerusalem, under the direction of Sir Moses Montefiore.

Mordecai Manuel Noah

A quite different public figure was Mordecai Manuel Noah (1785–1851), well known as a politician, playwright, and newspaper editor. For a short time he was American consul at Tunis, there learning about the poverty and persecution suffered by the Jews of North Africa. In a grand gesture, Noah rallied support and proclaimed the establishment of Ararat, a settlement on Grand Island in New York's Niagara River, as a "city of refuge" for the oppressed Jews of the world. Until the ancient homeland in Palestine was restored, he declared, the United States, as the world's premier free nation, would be the proper host for the persecuted of Israel.

Ezra Stiles, president of Yale.

The Jewish Commodore

The spirit of adventure and a sense of justice motivated Uriah Phillips Levy (1792–1862) throughout his life. At the age of 10 he ran off and enlisted as a cabin boy on a sailing ship. By 20 he had become a master seaman and was given the command of a U.S. warship, the *George Washington*. The sailors resented taking orders from so young a young commander and mutinied. They marooned him on a deserted island from which he was rescued by a British ship. When he refused to enlist in the British navy, he was put in irons, but at the first port he managed to escape.

Adventure and Bravado

When the United States and Britain went to war in 1812, Levy was assigned to the warship *Argus.* It sank or captured more than 20 British cargo vessels. Levy was put in command of one of the captured ships and ordered to sail it to Philadelphia. Once again, the spirit of adventure and bravado got the better of him. On the way he audaciously attacked a heavily-armed British warship. His ship was sunk and Levy once again became a British prisoner.

The Duel

After sitting out the rest of the war in an English prison, Levy was repatriated and commissioned a lieutenant in the U.S. Navy. When several of his fellow officers baited him by making anti-Semitic remarks, Levy refused to back down. He challenged one of them to a duel and killed him. Since dueling had been outlawed, Levy was court-martialed and dismissed from the navy, but later he was exonerated by a board of inquiry and returned to service. During the course of his career he was court-martialed five more times on various charges, but was always cleared.

Levy Challenges Naval Justice

Levy next challenged the use of corporal punishment aboard naval vessels. Sailors on U.S. ships were regularly flogged and starved even for minor infractions. Levy refused to use corporal punishment on ships he commanded. He went on to persuade Congress that something had

Uriah Phillips Levy (1792–1862) Fighting sailor and admirer of Thomas Jefferson. He helped abolish corporal punishment in the U. S. Navy.

to be done to stop this sadistic practice. In 1850, thanks to Levy's heroic efforts, Congress abolished corporal punishment in the navy.

Many ranking naval officers resented what Levy had done. In retaliation they had him court-martialed on trumped-up charges.

Once again Levy challenged the sentence. Acting as his own counsel, he put on a defense so impressive that the judges did not even leave the room to vote. He was acquitted and returned to active duty with the rank of captain. Two years later he was promoted to commodore, the highest rank in the U.S. Navy at that time.

Respect and Honor

Despite the insults and hardships, Uriah P. Levy loved America. A great admirer of Thomas Jefferson, he purchased his home at Monticello and restored it as a historical shrine. In 1943 the navy honored his memory by naming a new destroyer the U.S.S. *Levy.* In 1959 the Jewish chapel at the naval base in Norfolk, Virginia, was named the Commodore Levy Chapel.

Immigration and Westward Expansion

Encouraged by the promise of liberty and opportunity, great numbers of Europeans migrated to America during the 19th century. The Industrial Revolution was changing the way of life in the Old World, and many displaced workers and farmers sought new homes in the New World. The era of political reaction following the Napoleonic Wars and the failure of the revolutions of the 1840s in Central Europe led those who longed for freedom to turn their eyes across the Atlantic Ocean.

The Hand of Freedom

Millions of people in Europe saw the New World as the promised land of freedom. There had been revolutions in France and other countries, but the reactionary governments that gained power after Napoleon's defeat at Waterloo had no sympathy for the ideals of the French Revolution. They reinstated many of the old restrictive laws, and as a result, full equality and civil rights again became dreams.

As always, life was most difficult for Jews. Even in the 1820s and 1830s, but especially after the failed uprisings of 1848, Jews from Central Europe and the German states began flocking to America. At the time of the Revolution, there were about 3,000 Jews in the United States. By 1840 there were 40,000, the majority of them immigrants or the children of immigrants.

The newcomers became part of a growing country with open borders. When they arrived in America, they found well-established communities of fellow Jews in New York, Philadelphia, Baltimore, Richmond, Charleston, New Orleans, and many other cities. As early as the 1790s adventurous Jews had traveled alone into the interior to set up trading posts or start new farms in such areas as Natchez, Mississippi, and Montgomery, Alabama. John Law, a Jew from Montreal, was trading with Indians at Green Bay, Wisconsin, around the year 1800, and Samuel Solomon came to St. Louis in 1805.

The German Jews

Many of the new German immigrants, both Jewish and non-Jewish, settled in the Midwestern cities of Cleveland, Cincinnati, Milwaukee, and Detroit. All through the Midwest one could hear German spoken in the small Jewish communities. Synagogues were started in Cincinnati in 1824 and in Chicago in 1847.

Jewish immigrants worked at many different kinds of jobs. Their number included laborers, farmers, ranchers, watchmakers, tailors, doctors, lawyers, printers and editors, boatmen, and wagon drivers. A very substantial proportion were peddlers and storekeepers.

Julius Meyer (1851–1909) of Omaha. Nebraska, an Indian trader in the 1870s, with some of his Indian friends. Meyer spoke several Indian dialects.

Jewish Peddlers

Many of the Jewish immigrants who came to these shores became peddlers. With settlements spreading far and wide across the country, there was a need for men to travel from place to place, bring, needed goods to people on farms and in villages too small to support a store. Some peddlers plied their routes through the countryside on foot, carrying their goods in backpacks; others drove small wagons. The wares they offered ranged from needles and pins, combs and mirrors, ribbons and cloth, to pots and pans, knives, and books. Depending on the circumstances and the area they worked in, some returned home every weekend, others only every few weeks or months.

Though they usually received a warm welcome from their customers, especially because they were important sources of news, the Jewish peddlers led a hard life. Travel was difficult and dangerous. They were lonely and homesick. They might go many weeks without meeting a fellow Jew or another person who could speak their native language.

afternoon, "unwashed, unshaven, in a gentile inn," far from home and friends.

The peddlers were ambitious and hardworking. Many of them went on to open stores in new settlements, especially places located near roads or river landings. They saved their money and, as soon as possible, sent for their wives, parents, and siblings in the old country.

Once a few Jewish families had settled in the same area, a Jewish community would come into existence. Almost always it began by purchasing a cemetery and holding weekly prayer services. Before long a shohet would be hired to provide kosher meat, and a teacher engaged for the children. Larger groups would try to bring a rabbi or hazzan. With this done, the former peddlers came to feel at home in the new country.

Some Jewish storekeepers went on to become department store magnates. Among the many major stores founded or expanded by Jews were Filene's in Boston, Macy's in New York, Rich's in Atlanta, and Magnin's in San Francisco.

The Jewish Religion

One of the hardest things was not being able to keep kosher and to observe the Sabbath and other holidays. A letter written by one peddler says that he was about to start the Sabbath on Friday

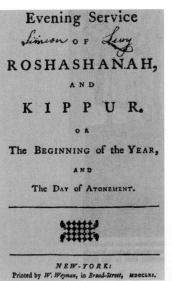

The first High Holiday prayer book published in America.

Macy's, one of the world's largest department stores, was founded by Lazarus Straus in partnership with R. H. Macy. Straus moved to New York City from Atlanta because of the Civil War.

Women of Valor

Rebecca Gratz

Jewish women in this country were active in the fields of education and good deeds. Lovely Rebecca Gratz (1781–1869), of a distinguished Philadelphia family, founded the first Jewish Sunday School in America, and worked for orphanages and other welfare institutions. It is thought that she was the inspiration for the virtuous heroine who bears her name in Sir Walter Scott's *Ivanhoe.*

Penina Moïse

Penina Moïse (1797–1880), an educator and writer, supervised the Jewish Sunday School in Charleston, South Carolina, and composed poems and hymns throughout her life, even though she became blind in middle age.

Penina Moïse was for many years the poet laureate of Charleston. She was born in 1797 to French-speaking parents who had escaped from a slave rebellion in the West Indies.

Young Penina studied by herself and was familiar with the Bible along with the writings of Homer and Shakespeare and authors of her own day. For many years she was the superintendent of the Sunday School of Congregation Beth Elohim in Charleston. Though she wrote poetry for newspapers and magazines, her favorite was writing hymns based on the psalms.

Penina and her brother Abraham were active in the group of members of Beth Elohim that wanted to modernize the service along lines similar to those advocated by the reformers in Germany. Among other things, they wanted to have choral singing and organ music to make the services attractive, and sermons in English to explain the Torah readings.

In 1841, Beth Elohim dedicated its new building. A hymn written by Penina Moïse was used at the service. Her long life was one of reading, writing, and teaching, activities which she continued, as much as possible, during her last 25 years, when she was blind and bedridden.

Emma Lazarus

The outstanding Jewish writer of this period was Emma Lazarus (1849–1887), whose early poetry on themes of nature and mythology won the praise of Ralph Waldo Emerson. The persecution of the Jews of Russia, and the steady stream of immigrants from Eastern Europe, made the young woman more aware of her people and faith. She studied Hebrew and Jewish history, gaining new pride and loyalty and a powerful theme for her later writings.

Songs of a Semite and *By the Waters of Babylon* are collections of poems by Lazarus expressing sympathy for her people's past and hope for the future. "Let but an Ezra rise anew," she wrote, "to lift the banner of the Jew!" Her best-known poem is "The New Colossus," inscribed on a plaque in the base of the Statue of Liberty in New York harbor.

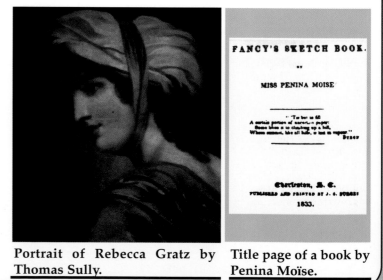

Portrait of Rebecca Gratz by Thomas Sully.

Title page of a book by Penina Moïse.

California, Here We Come!

In the year 1848 gold was discovered in California. Word spread swiftly across the country. "Gold, gold!" California was on everyone's tongue.

The Forty-niners

The Gold Rush began in 1849. There were many Jews among the Forty-niners, as those who joined the rush were called. Some hoped to find gold, others planned on becoming land developers, merchants, or professionals in the new towns springing up in California.

In the very first year of the Gold Rush, there were enough Jews in San Francisco to hold High Holiday services. Over the next few years, Jewish congregations were founded in many of the state's smaller towns.

Levi Strauss

Levi Strauss (1829–1902) was a German-born immigrant who arrived in New York in 1848. Two years later he caught the "gold fever" and sailed for San Francisco by way of Cape Horn, at the tip of South America. He arrived in California with a pack of needles, pins, string, sewing thread, and bolts of cloth. In no time, Strauss sold all of his stock except a few bolts of heavy canvas. He tried to sell the canvas to a miner for a tent, but the man said he needed a strong pair of pants much more. Strauss made all his canvas into pants. When these sold out, he ordered special denim cloth from France and dyed it blue.

Levi Strauss's name appeared on a red tag on every pair of pants he manufactured, and before long a new term for those pants was added to the English language: Levi's. Today, the Levi Strauss Co. is a multinational enterprise with factories in

Advertisement for denim work clothes produced by Levi Strauss & Co.

many countries. Strauss's descendants are active in Jewish affairs and have contributed to the support of Jewish institutions all over the world.

Pioneers and Civic Leaders

From the start, Jews helped to build up the new state of California. Some became fur traders, miners, grape growers, or cattle dealers. Adolf Sutro (1830–1898), the German-born engineer who built the great mine tunnel that carries his name in Nevada, served as mayor of San Francisco from 1895 to 1897.

Solomon Heydenfeldt and Henry A. Lyons were elected to the California Supreme Court. Other Jews were civic leaders in Los Angeles and other cities.

One Jew, Solomon Nunes Carvalho (1815–1897), a painter and photographer, accompanied the great explorer John C. Fremont on an expedition to map the land route to California in 1853. With him, he crossed the desert and climbed the Rocky Mountains, almost losing his life on the way. When Carvalho arrived in the city of Los Angeles, he sought out the local Jews and helped establish the Hebrew Benevolent Society there.

Workers in the Sutro tunnel.

Jews, the Civil War, the Union

The Civil War found most American Jews remaining loyal to the section of the country in which they lived. Jews were officers and fighting men on both sides.

In the years of controversy before the war, many Jews were active in the anti-slavery movement. Kansas Jews joined John Brown's army in the fight against slavery. Journalists like Moritz Pinner wrote articles in favor of abolition.

Moritz Pinner for the Union

Moritz edited the *Kansas Post,* a newspaper that tried to make Kansas a free state. This was a dangerous period, because there was a gang called "Border Ruffians," made up of people who wanted Kansas to be a slave state. They attacked those who opposed slavery.

Pinner was a delegate to the Republican Convention in 1860 which nominated Abraham Lincoln for the presidency. He later refused a government post that would have taken him to Honduras; he wanted to stay and fight for the Union.

Rabbis for the Union

Two outspoken rabbis, Sabato Morais (1832–1897) of Philadelphia and David Einhorn (1809–1879) of Baltimore, boldly preached against slavery despite strong opposition in their respective cities. The hostility against them was so intense that on one occasion, during the secession riots of 1861, Rabbi Einhorn had to flee Baltimore.

Soldiers for the Union

The surgeon general of the North was Jonathan Phineas Horowitz. The many Jewish officers in the Union army included several brigadier generals. One of them was Philip Joachimsen, who had helped to convict slave traders while serving as a U.S. attorney in New York.

Jewish Heroes

Edward Solomon, another general, led an Illinois regiment in which there were over 100 Jews. After the war he became governor of the Washington Territory. There were more than 6,000 Jewish soldiers in the Union army, many of them serving in units that were predominantly Jewish. From Pennsylvania came Cameron's Dragoons, commanded by Col. Max Friedman. Many Jewish soldiers died on the battlefield or in Confederate prison camps. Seven Congressional Medals of Honor were awarded to Jews in the Union army.

Michael M. Allen, of Philadelphia, served as unofficial chaplain of Cameron's Dragoons, a Pennsylvania cavalry regiment. The regiment was commanded by Col. Max Friedman.

August Bondi (1833–1907), abolitionist. After leaving Austria following the Revolution of 1848 , he, with Jacob Benjamin and Theodore Weiner, joined John Brown's anti-slavery army in Kansas.

Jews, the Civil War, the Confederacy

The Confederate Army

There were also thousands of Jewish soldiers on the Confederate side. The South's Secretary of War declared at one point that he could not give furloughs to Jewish soldiers for the High Holidays since there were at least 10,000 of them—more than could be spared from their posts.

The most important Jew serving the Confederacy was Judah Philip Benjamin of Louisiana (1811–1884). Elected to the U.S. Senate in 1852, Benjamin left Washington when Louisiana seceded from

Judah P. Benjamin (1811–1884), Confederate Secretary of War and Secretary of State. After the war he fled to England.

the Union. At various times he served as the Confederacy's Attorney General, Secretary of War, and Secretary of State.

Although he did not regard himself as a Jew, Benjamin was called an Israelite by his enemies on both sides of the conflict. A northerner described him as an "Israelite with Egyptian principles."

When the South began to lose the war, Benjamin's political enemies in the Confederacy placed the blame on his shoulders. After the war he escaped to England and became an attorney.

The President of the Confederate States of America, Jefferson Davis, on March 27, 1863, recommended a Day of Prayer. Rev. Michelbacher, of the German synagogue in Richmond, preached this sermon, to which he added a prayer for the Confederacy.

Captain Asher W. Garber.

Private Thomas Jefferson Goldman.

List of Confederate Jewish soldiers buried by Rev. George Jacobs.

General Robert E. Lee's battle-tested Army of Northern Virginia included many Jewish soldiers. Captain Asher W. Garber was an officer in the Virginia Light Artillery and Private Thomas Jefferson Goldman served in the 44th Georgia Infantry.

Isaac Leeser / 1806–1868

Isaac Leeser (1806–1868), the most activist American rabbi of his day, set about almost single-handed to try to remedy all the lacks in Jewish life and education. He published textbooks, and translations of the Bible and the prayerbook. In his Philadelphia congregation, Mikveh Israel, he delivered vigorous sermons in English, advocating intensified education and Jewish unity. In 1867, with the help of Sabato Morais, he established Maimonides College, an institution for formal Jewish studies, but it had few financial supporters and soon closed its doors.

Isaac Leeser (1806–1868), rabbi, teacher, translator, and organizer, did much to further Jewish education and raise the standard of Jewish communal life.

Isaac Leeser traveled to Albany, New York, to discuss American Jewry's problems and needs with Rabbi Isaac Mayer Wise. For many years afterwards, there were discussions between Wise and Leeser, both in person and in print. The two had different ideas about how to be a good Jew, but both wanted to unify American's Jews, and to strengthen their faith and knowledge.

It was not very difficult to bring Jews together when there was a crisis. Ten years after the Damascus libel of 1840, for instance, the United States and Switzerland were negotiating a treaty intended to open up each country to the citizens of the other for travel and business. The Swiss made it plain that American Jews would not be permitted in those parts of Switzerland that banned Jewish residents. If the United States accepted this, it would mean that it was not treating its Jewish citizens as worthy of the full protection of their government.

American Jewry protested vociferously, and so did many non-Jews, among them such distinguished political figures as Daniel Webster and Henry Clay.

The "Occident"

Isaac Leeser made his greatest contribution as editor of the *Occident*, a magazine that appeared monthly from 1843 to 1869. Its pages tell of the interests and problems of American Jews in those years, including items ranging from the arrival of a new Hebrew teacher in New York to protests against the kidnapping of an Italian Jewish boy, Edgar Mortara, by the Catholic church in 1858. At times of crisis, magazines like the *Occident*, David Einhorn's *Sinai*, and Isaac Mayer Wise's *Israelite* served to inform and in some measure to unite the Jews of America.

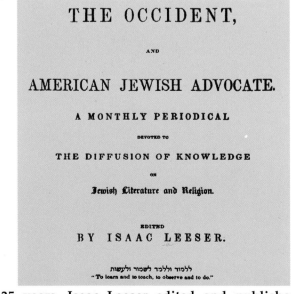

THE OCCIDENT,

AND

AMERICAN JEWISH ADVOCATE.

A MONTHLY PERIODICAL

DEVOTED TO

THE DIFFUSION OF KNOWLEDGE

ON

Jewish Literature and Religion.

EDITED

BY ISAAC LEESER.

ללמוד וללמד לשמור ולעשות
"To learn and to teach, to observe and to do."

For 25 years, Isaac Leeser edited and published the *Occident*, a leading Jewish periodical, which gave its readers essays, stories, poems, and news of Jewish communities all over the world.

Early Attempts at Reform

The free atmosphere and lack of central authority in pioneer America encouraged religious reform and innovation. In 1824, a group called the Reformed Society of Israelites broke away from Congregation Beth Elohim in Charleston. Led by Isaac Harby (1788–1828), a young writer, the Society issued its own prayerbook and for several years conducted services in English.

The Reform movement in the United States became stronger in the 1840s with the arrival of large numbers of Jews from Germany, including several rabbis who agreed with the ideas expressed by Abraham Geiger. While upholding the ethics and moral law of Judaism, they wished to adapt to modern times by abolishing rituals and ideals which they felt no longer had meaning.

Rabbi David Einhorn (1809–1879) came to Baltimore and Rabbi Samuel Hirsch (1815–1889) to Philadelphia with radical ideas. They no longer considered Judaism's ritual laws to be binding. They felt that the age-old hopes for the coming of the Messiah and the return to Zion had no meaning for American Jews. They dropped many Hebrew prayers, substituting German readings and hymns.

Other Reform rabbis, who had more moderate views and wished to preserve some of Judaism's ancient traditions, were Bernhard Felsenthal of Chicago (1822–1908) and Max Lilienthal of Cincinnati (1815–1882).

The Torah Ark of Congregation Beth Elohim, Charleston, South Carolina, is a replica of the one destroyed by fire in 1838. The original Ark was built in 1799.

Rabbi David Einhorn (1809–1879), radical Reform leader and outspoken abolitionist, served pulpits in Philadelphia and New York after leaving Baltimore at the time of pro-slavery riots.

MISCELLANEOUS WRITINGS

OF THE LATE

ISAAC HARBY, ESQ.

ARRANGED AND PUBLISHED BY HENRY L. PINCKNEY AND ABRAHAM MOISE, FOR THE BENEFIT OF HIS FAMILY.

TO WHICH IS PREFIXED,

A MEMOIR OF HIS LIFE,

BY ABRAHAM MOISE.

Charleston:
PRINTED BY JAMES S. BURGES,
NO. 44 QUEEN-STREET.
1829.

Title page of a collection of writings by Isaac Harby, published after his death by his associate in community and religious endeavors, Abraham Moïse.

Isaac Mayer Wise / 1819–1900

Father of Reform

The leading organizer of Reform Judaism in America was Isaac Mayer Wise (1819–1900). As rabbi of congregations in Albany, New York, and then in Cincinnati, he introduced English readings and sermons, instrumental music, Confirmation for both boys and girls, and the one-day observance of holidays instead of two. He founded and for years edited the weekly *Israelite,* advocating in its pages that American Jewry unite. He compiled a prayerbook, hoping to establish a minhag America, a uniform mode of observance and worship in which both traditional and Reform Jews could join.

Hebrew Union College

Calling together congregational leaders from 28 cities, Rabbi Wise, in 1873, founded the Union of American Hebrew Congregations. The next year he established and became the head of the Hebrew Union College in Cincinnati, America's first institution for higher Jewish education and the training of rabbis.

Wise was not able to induce American Jewry to adopt one pattern of belief and worship. The radical reformers of the eastern cities believed that he was unwilling to go far enough; they did not agree with his devotion to the use of Hebrew in the service and his insistence that the Sabbath be observed on Saturday instead of being transferred to the commonly accepted American day of rest, Sunday.

On the other hand, Orthodox or traditional Jews could not accept Wise's reforms in the service, his abolition of many rituals, and his denial of basic ideals like the return to Zion.

American Jewry, though it did not unite under his leadership, learned from Rabbi Wise how to organize and strengthen its religious life.

Title page of the first Reform prayerbook to appear in America. Prepared by a commission consisting of Rabbis Kalish, Wise, and Rothenheim, it was issued in English, German, and Hebrew.

Rabbi Isaac Mayer Wise

Very early photograph of the Hebrew Union College building in Cincinnati, Ohio.

The American Experience Begins

JEWISH HIGHLIGHTS

| **Jewish Refugees** 17th century | **First American Jews** 17th century | **Revolutionary War** 18th Century | **Men and Women of Prominence** (18th–19th century) | **Immigration** 19th century | **American Reform Movement** 19th century |

JEWISH EVENTS • PERSONALITIES • LITERATURE

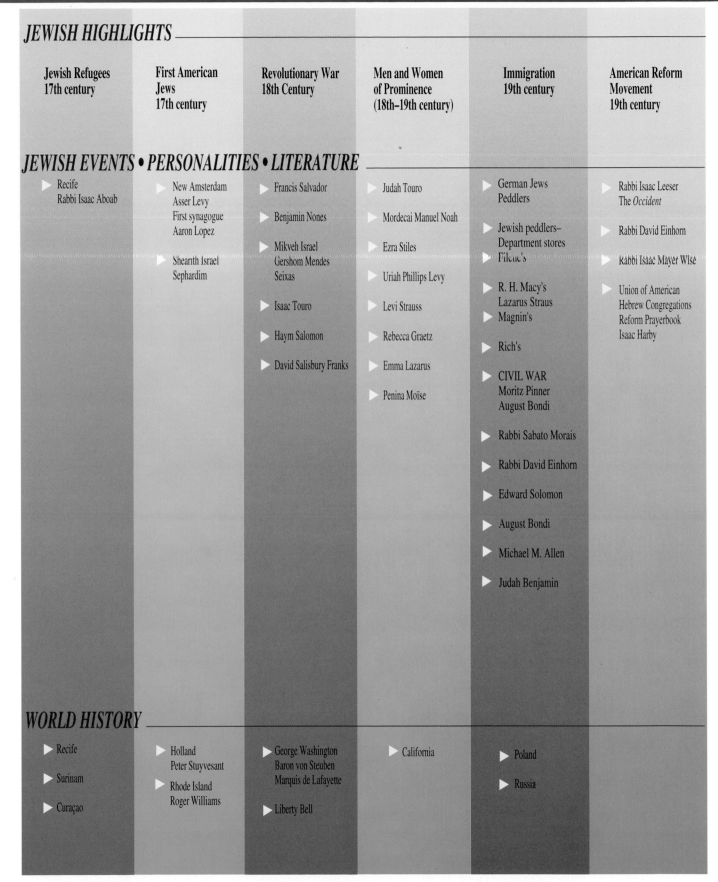

▷ Recife Rabbi Isaac Aboab	▷ New Amsterdam Asser Levy First synagogue Aaron Lopez	▷ Francis Salvador	▷ Judah Touro	▷ German Jews Peddlers	▷ Rabbi Isaac Leeser The *Occident*
	▷ Shearith Israel Sephardim	▷ Benjamin Nones	▷ Mordecai Manuel Noah	▷ Jewish peddlers– Department stores Filene's	▷ Rabbi David Einhorn
		▷ Mikveh Israel Gershom Mendes Seixas	▷ Ezra Stiles	▷ R. H. Macy's Lazarus Straus	▷ Rabbi Isaac Mayer Wise
		▷ Isaac Touro	▷ Uriah Phillips Levy	▷ Magnin's	▷ Union of American Hebrew Congregations Reform Prayerbook Isaac Harby
		▷ Haym Salomon	▷ Levi Strauss	▷ Rich's	
		▷ David Salisbury Franks	▷ Rebecca Graetz	▷ CIVIL WAR Moritz Pinner August Bondi	
			▷ Emma Lazarus	▷ Rabbi Sabato Morais	
			▷ Penina Moïse	▷ Rabbi David Einhorn	
				▷ Edward Solomon	
				▷ August Bondi	
				▷ Michael M. Allen	
				▷ Judah Benjamin	

WORLD HISTORY

▷ Recife	▷ Holland Peter Stuyvesant	▷ George Washington Baron von Steuben Marquis de Lafayette	▷ California	▷ Poland	
▷ Surinam	▷ Rhode Island Roger Williams	▷ Liberty Bell		▷ Russia	
▷ Curaçao					

Tsar Nicholas I and the Jews

Not even the intervention of so prominent a person as Sir Moses Montefiore could bring about an improvement in the situation of Russian Jewry. Tsar Nicholas I, who came to the throne of Russia in 1825, was bent on assimilating the diverse population of his empire into one vast Russian nation. During the reign of his brother, Alexander I (1777–1825), Napoleon's army had marched east, deep into the very heart of Russia. Russia had defended itself well and the French armies had retreated. But the new ideas of freedom and equality that had arisen in France had been carried by its soldiers into the lands of the tsar. Poland, which never had accepted Russia's rule gracefully, now chafed under its reins.

Tsar Alexander II (1818–1881)

Oath of a Jewish recruit from Stolin, sworn in the synagogue of Pinsk, 1829. This Jewish youth, under the 1827 statute of Tsar Nicholas I, was forced to serve in the Russian army. The document is printed in Hebrew with hand-written additions in Russian.

would be pressured to convert. Frequently they would be beaten and starved in an effort to persuade them to renounce their faith.

Governmental Pressures

To gain greater control over the minorities in his realm, Nicholas I instituted a double administrative policy. On the one hand he lifted some of the restrictions that had been imposed upon them, but at the same time he sought to divest them of their identities as separate nationality groups. He dealt a severe blow to the Jews of the Pale of Settlement when he ordered the Kahal, the time-honored instrument of Jewish communal self-government, to disband.

The tsar wanted the Jews to give up their Yiddish language, their religion, and their traditions. He also wanted a large and powerful army, and to realize this aim he instituted a draft of young men at the age of 18, for a term of 25 years. Jews, however, were drafted at the age of 12 and had to serve for 31 years. Recruiters would come and take Jewish boys from their homes by force. Once they were in the army, they

Crown Schools

As another means of hastening the disappearance of Russian Jewry as a distinct group, Tsar Nicholas I set up special schools in the Pale of Settlement. In these crown schools, as they were called, Jewish children were to learn Russian and be given an education that would wean them away from their traditional way of life and toward conversion to Christianity.

Despite the pressures brought upon them by the tsarist government, the Jews of Russia remained loyal to their heritage. The community was hard-pressed. Many were forced to leave the villages of the Pale and move to cities where they had no way to earn a living. When the tsar realized that his Jewish policy was not bringing about conversions, he invoked sterner restrictions.

Alexander II, a Liberal Ruler

Nicholas I died in 1855 and was succeeded by his son, Alexander II, a man of liberal leanings. In 1861, Alexander abolished serfdom, making it possible for peasants to buy land and establish farms. The Jews of the Pale of Settlement hoped that soon their lot, too, would be improved.

Their hopes were realized in great measure, for Alexander II abolished the draft of Jewish boys.

Alexander wanted to keep pace with developments in Western Europe by furthering the growth of Russia's factories and industrial centers. He permitted Jews to move from the Pale to the large cities and encouraged them to go into manufacturing, learn trades, become merchants, and take professional training at the universities.

Many educated Jews believed that a secular education was compatible with Jewish culture. Judah Leib Gordon (1831–1892), an important poet and journalist, coined the motto "Be a man outside, but a Jew in your own home."

No longer did all Jews have to live in the Pale of Settlement. Some became respected and successful merchants and manufacturers; others practiced law and medicine in the large cities. Still others became skilled workers in the new industrial centers.

Alexander II Assassinated

Russia was a hotbed of revolutionary movements. Despite the reforms, many Jewish youngsters joined the revolutionary parties. In 1881 Tsar Alexander II was assassinated. The assailant was caught and implicated his fellow plotters, one of whom was a Jewish girl named Gessia Helfman. Government officials used this incident to incite pogroms against the

Title page of the first prayer book *Tifilot Yisrael* ever translated into Russian. The *siddur* was translated by Rabbi Joseph Hurwitz in 1869. It was published in Warsaw, the capital of the Polish provinces of the Russian Empire.

Jews. Over the next two years thousands of Jews were murdered, and innumerable businesses and homes looted and destroyed. To make matters worse, the reforms instituted by Alexander were rescinded by his successor, and the government issued the May Laws, which restricted Jewish residence and professional rights.

The pogroms of 1881–82 in Russia and Ukraine were decisive in establishing Zionism as a major movement. The outbreak of violence on such a broad scale, and with government collusion, made many Jews feel that they could never lead a normal life in Russia. While some decided to emigrate to the United States, others concluded that the only viable solution was Eretz Yisrael, the Land of Israel.

After the Pogrom by Maurice Minkowski (1881–1930). The pogroms claimed thousands of Jewish victims.

The Haskalah

The Haskalah ("Enlightenment") was a movement in Judaism that introduced modern ideas and religious approaches and advocated mastery of secular knowledge. Its adherents often pursued secular professions and abandoned practices that differentiated them from their non-Jewish neighbors—wearing modern clothing, trimming their beards, and speaking Russian or German instead of Yiddish. Although opposed by many Orthodox rabbis and by Hasidim, the Haskalah made rapid progress, initially in Germany and Western Europe, and later in Russia, especially among members of the Jewish middle class.

The new ideas of enlightenment that first arose in the West found their way into the Pale of Settlement as early as the reign of Nicholas I, arousing interest in secular learning. This trend was furthered by the newly-established crown schools, which taught history, Russian, and science in addition to religious subjects.

Judah Leib Gordon

Hebrew Reborn

In Western Europe, the Haskalah had lured many Jews away from their heritage—but not so in the East. There it took the direction, not of assimilation, but of a more intense cultivation of the Hebrew language and modern Hebrew literature along with secular knowledge. Thus began the rebirth of Hebrew as a living language. Hebrew and Yiddish writers applied their talents to immortalize the folkways and customs of the Jews of the Pale, their ideals and their daily lives. In their works, both prose and poetry, they described the negative as well as the positive aspects of life in Russia, thereby stimulating their readers to social and intellectual development.

Among the great exponents of Russian Haskalah were several authors whose works left an indelible mark in the annals of modern Hebrew literature and culture: Abraham Mapu (1808–1867), pioneer Hebrew novelist famed for *Ahavat Zion*, a biblical romance written in a classical Hebrew style; Judah Leib Gordon (1831–1892), greatest of the 19th-century Hebrew poets, who fought valiantly against what he considered primitive customs, but remained loyal to Jewish tradition; and Yitzhak Ber Levinsohn (1788–1860), erudite author of works demonstrating the complete harmony of Torah and the scientific spirit.

Yitzhak Ber Levinsohn

The Development of Yiddish Literature

Mendele Mokher Sefarim

Many authors wrote in Yiddish, the everyday language of the Jewish people of Russia and Poland. One of the best-loved Yiddish writers was Sholem Yaakov Abramovich (1836–1917), who used the pen-name Mendele Mokher Seforim ("Mendele the Bookseller"). He started his career as a Hebrew author, and, in fact, is also counted as one of the founders of modern Hebrew prose. It is, however, as a Yiddish writer that he gained special fame. He painted a vivid picture of life in the towns of the Pale, and his books were read with great enthusiasm. The writings of Mendele and others revealed Yiddish for the first time as an expressive language, capable of reflecting the thought and character of the Jews of Eastern Europe.

Sholem Aleichem and family.

Sholem Aleichem

Among the other great luminaries of Yiddish literature was Sholem Aleichem (pen-name of Shalom Rabinowitz, 1859–1916). He created the character of Tevye der Milchiger ("Tevye the Milkman"), a light-hearted pauper who drives his rickety wagon in search of a living, but whose thoughts reach up to God. The story of Tevye has been retold as *Fiddler on the Roof*, one of the most successful musicals ever performed. *Fiddler on the Roof* has been staged in many languages and its message has universal appeal.

Sholem Aleichem went to the United States for the first time in 1906 and again upon the outbreak of World War I. The sketches he wrote in his last years give insight into the immigrant generation on American soil.

Isaac Leib Peretz

Isaac Leib Peretz (1852–1915) was one of the founders and giants of modern Yiddish literature. He was a prosperous lawyer, but because of governmental restrictions was forced to find another job. Eventually, Peretz was placed in charge of the Jewish cemeteries. This position was a blessing in disguise, since it provided him with the opportunity to concentrate on writing stories, plays, and poems both in Yiddish and in Hebrew.

With simplicity and power, Peretz's prolific pen produced a stream of stories about the common people. He felt for their misery, and discovered in their lives the virtues of love, faith, and heroism. His Hasidic stories reflect his religious background and position the Rebbe as the ideal for the messianic future.

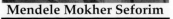

Mendele Mokher Seforim

Persecutions and Pogroms

Arrests and Accusations

Alexander II was succeeded by his son Alexander III. Determined to establish his rule securely at all costs, the new tsar was coldly indifferent to the well-being of his people.

Like the rulers of the Middle Ages, he looked for a defenseless minority group that could be blamed for the country's troubles. Naturally, the choice fell on the Jews. Alexander accused them of fomenting revolt and of having been involved in the assassination of his father. He persecuted anyone suspected of inciting rebellion. Many were arrested and shot; others were sentenced to long prison terms in the freezing wastelands of Siberia.

Pogroms Spur Emigration

The tsar had a special punishment in store for his chosen scapegoat. Government officials and agents stirred up the Russian people with anti-Semitic speeches, inciting them to attack the Jewish community. Jews were brutally beaten and many lost their lives.

The years 1881–82 were marked by terrible pogroms that shocked and saddened Jews the world over. In two years, thousands of Jews were murdered. Innumerable Jewish businesses and homes were looted and destroyed.

Anti-Jewish legislative measures accompanied the pogroms. Alexander II's reforms were rescinded. The May Laws in 1882 prohibited Jews from acquiring rural property and expelled them from Moscow. Official quotas were estab-lished for Jewish students in secondary schools and universities.

Conditions deteriorated rapidly. By the mid-1880s, fully one-third of Russian Jewry depended upon relief provided by Jewish agencies. The first response to this dire situation was emigration. About 3 million Jews left Eastern Europe between 1881 and 1914. Of these, 2 million settled in the United States. Many others went to Canada, Argentina, and Britain. In addition, a hardy but idealistic few began resettling the ancient homeland of Palestine.

The pogroms and the May Laws gave a powerful impetus to the development of a Zionist sensibility. Many Russian Jews began to realize that they would never truly be safe and secure as a people until they had a home of their own. These ideas first found expression in the Bilu movement.

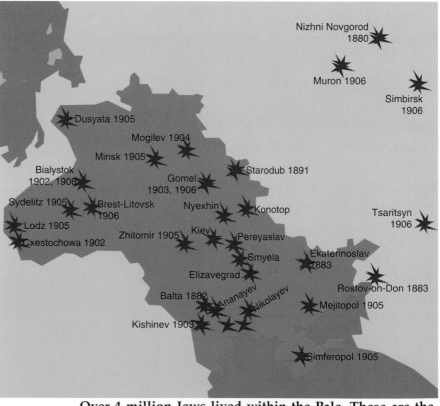

Over 4 million Jews lived within the Pale. These are the cities where pogroms and anti-Semitic violence occurred during the period of 1871–1906.

The Bilu Movement

After the pogroms of 1881–82, 17 young Russian Jewish students settled in Palestine. These young people, known as Bilu'im, were deeply committed to the Zionist ideal. They labored long, hard hours in the fields under the blazing sun—and they suffered nights of cold, fear, and danger in the new farm settlements.

The Bilu'im took their name from the initials of a four-word passage in the Bible, *Beit Yaakov lekhu venelkhah*, "House of Jacob, let us arise and go" (Isaiah 2:5). They interpreted these words as encouragement to rise up from their diaspora homes and go to Israel to rebuild the Jewish homeland.

Hovevei Zion

In 1881 Leon Pinsker, a physician, excited Russian Jewry with a pamphlet entitled *Auto-Emancipation*. It caused a great stir, particularly among students and young people. Pinsker maintained that no one could really emancipate the Jews except the Jews themselves. And the only way in which the Jews could secure their freedom and self-respect, he declared, was by returning to their ancient homeland. Pinsker's call gave rise to a society which took the name Hovevei Zion, "Lovers of Zion."

The Hovevei Zion and the Bilu'im founded the first agricultural settlements in the Land of Israel, Rishon le-Zion ("First in Zion") and Petah Tikvah ("Gate of Hope"). Nes Ziyyonah, Zikhron Yaakov, and several others soon followed.

Title page of the original statutes of the Bilu organization. The Hebrew motto means, "The little one shall become a thousand, and the small one a strong nation" (Isaiah 60:22).

A Jewish farm family in Rishon le-Zion reaps the grape harvest. Note the leaf-covered watchtower. During the harvest season, armed Jewish watchmen protected the crops from Arab raiders. The leafy hut on stilts is a sukkah. Ancient Jewish farmers, also stood guard to protect their crops from raiders and built sukkot to shade themselves from the hot sun.

The Bilu Pioneers

The pioneers who went to Palestine set themselves a mighty task, but their idealism and comradeship carried them through the arduous beginnings. They found a barren land—dry, rocky, and sandy, with many swampy areas. They saw that the desert would have to be irrigated before vegetables and trees could be planted. Most of the colonists were students and townspeople. What they lacked in knowledge of farming they made up in enthusiasm.

The Jews of Europe followed the progress of the new settlements with keen interest. Wealthy men like Baron Edmond de Rothschild (1845–1934), the French financier and philanthropist, generously contributed much-needed money to buy land and tools.

The settlers worked by day and stood guard at night with their guns, ready to defend themselves against Arab marauders. Their orange groves and olive trees attested to their labors, as did the towns of Rishon le-Zion and Petah Tikvah, which are still the pride of Israel.

The Dreyfus Affair / 1884–1899

French Jewry

The situation of French Jewry in the late 19th century resembled that of German Jewry. Although full civil rights had been extended to them by law, French Jews often found themselves face-to-face with prejudice when they sought to enter certain professions. The old picture of the Jew as a convenient scapegoat could not be wiped out by the enactment of liberal legislation. It was easier to pass laws proclaiming freedom and tolerance than to educate people to abide by their spirit.

Captain Alfred Dreyfus

In October of 1894, Captain Alfred Dreyfus (1859–1935), a Jewish officer on the French general staff, was charged with espionage and arrested. Accused of giving military secrets to Germany, Dreyfus was tried, convicted of high treason, and imprisoned on Devil's Island. To the end, he insisted that he was innocent. When he was stripped of his military rank and honor, he cried, "Long live France! Long live the army!"

Emile Zola

Many people believed that Dreyfus was innocent—framed by anti-Jewish officers who had used forged documents to convict him. Among those who championed the captain's cause was Emile Zola, the great novelist, whose passionate crusade on behalf of Dreyfus was heralded in an essay entitled "J'Accuse," condemning the French government as unjust, intolerant, and corrupt.

The trial of Captain Dreyfus

Dreyfus Is Pardoned

In time it was found that the real culprit was one Major Ferdinand Esterhazy, who had sold information to the Germans. In 1899 Dreyfus was recalled from Devil's Island and granted a pardon.

Freedom-loving people in many lands had taken part in the fight to prove Dreyfus innocent. His fate had become a

Photograph of part of a letter Dreyfus sent to the chief rabbi of France from prison, the day after he was found guilty.

test case in a much larger struggle then taking place in Europe between those who clung to old prejudices and those who demanded civil rights and equality for all. In 1906 the French government finally admitted that Dreyfus was innocent of all charges and reinstated him in the army.

Theodor Herzl:
The Journalist at the Trial

Among the reporters at the Dreyfus trial in 1894 was Theodor Herzl (1860–1904), a young newspaperman from Vienna. The miscarriage of justice and the degrading treatment to which Dreyfus was subjected made a deep impression on Herzl. Up to that time he had led a fully assimilated life, but when he saw what

Caricature of the four army officers involved in the Dreyfus trial.

harm anti-Semitic hatred could do even in a civilized country like France, he felt himself united in a bond of shared suffering with Dreyfus, the French Jew, and with all of his fellow Jews.

The degradation of Captain Dreyfus

Theodor Herzl

"The Jewish State"

Influenced by the patriotic and nationalist ideas that were so strong in the 19th century, Theodor Herzl conceived a daring solution for the problems the Jews faced in their quest for equal rights. If they established a state of their own, he reasoned, they would once again be a nation like the other nations of the world. No one would be able to victimize or mistreat them. In 1896 Herzl explained his ideas in a book entitled *The Jewish State.*

Herzl soon realized that there was only one possible site for the Jewish state he imagined: Palestine. In 1902, he set forth his vision of the return to Zion in a novel, *Altneuland* ("Old-New Land"). He and his associates, who called themselves Zionists, founded a periodical, *Die Welt* ("The World"), through which to publicize their program.

The Zionist Movement

In 1897 Herzl convened the First Zionist Congress in Basel, Switzerland, inviting Jewish representatives from all over the world who shared his vision. It was at this Congress that the Zionist movement was officially founded and its basic platform proclaimed—the establishment of a legally secure Jewish homeland in Palestine. Herzl became the first president of the World Zionist Organization.

Theodor Herzl dedicated his whole life and energy to the realization of this ideal. Since Palestine was then part of the Turkish Empire, he met with the sultan to obtain permission for Jews to resettle the Holy Land. When the sultan refused, Herzl despairingly approached officials in Egypt and England to see whether he could obtain some territory in East Africa as an alternative site for a Jewish homeland. This idea was soon dropped because of bitter opposition in Zionist circles.

Herzl inflamed the Jews of Europe with the Zionist idea and gave Zionism its basic organizational and political structure. His diplomatic efforts on its behalf won it international standing and recognition. Although he laid the essential groundwork, Theodor Herzl did not live to see even the beginnings of the realization of his plans. He died in 1904 at the age of 44, leaving his associates to continue the work he had begun.

The Gate of Hope

Herzl's most enthusiastic followers did not live in Austria, Germany, or France, but in Russia, where tsar and nobles ruled with a heavy hand, and Jews lived under very oppressive conditions. Herzl opened a gate of hope for many Russian Jewish young people, who looked to Palestine for a life of dignity and freedom.

The land for the first settlements in Palestine was purchased by Keren Kayemet Le-'Yisrael (Jewish National Fund), established in 1901 as the land-purchasing agency of the Zionist movement.

The Jewish National Fund depended on small sums of money collected from Jews throughout the world. The blue-and-white JNF box found a place in millions of Jewish homes.

A Gate of Hope

Zionism After Herzl

After Theodor Herzl's death, David Wolffsohn (1856–1914), one of his close co-workers, took over the leadership of the Zionist Organization. These were stormy days. New and terrible pogroms were taking place in Russia, and many thousands of Jews fled. Most of them made the long journey across the Atlantic and found new homes in the United States. Others went to the countries of Western Europe or to England. Only a few were permitted to enter Palestine. Yet Jewish immigration to the Holy Land continued steadily and a number of new settlements were founded.

The First Aliyah

The Hebrew word *aliyah* (lit. "going up") refers to the ascent to the reader's desk of a person who is called upon to recite blessings during the reading of the Torah. Ever since the time of Ezra, it has also designated the return of Jews to the Land of Israel, both in groups and individually. Each of the five great waves of immigration to Israel in modern times is called an aliyah.

The First Aliyah began in 1880 and continued until 1905. The first *olim* ("ascenders," a noun derived from *aliyah*) were the Bilu'im. Their numbers were reinforced by settlers stimulated by Herzl's writings and the establishment of the World Zionist Organization.

The men and women of the First Aliyah faced an enormous task. They literally had to make the desert bloom again. They began by draining the land's malaria-laden swamps and irrigating its parched, sandy soil. Then they proceeded to plant vineyards and fields. The agricultural settlements they founded, living and working together for the common good, were forerunners of the kibbutzim of later decades.

The Heritage of Enlightenment

The settlers of the First Aliyah brought with them the heritage of the Haskalah. Many of them had studied science, literature, and modern languages at Russia's universities. They began to create new literary works and, most important, made Hebrew—so long used only for prayer and study—come alive again as a spoken, everyday language.

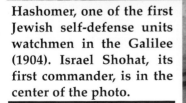

Hashomer, one of the first Jewish self-defense units watchmen in the Galilee (1904). Israel Shohat, its first commander, is in the center of the photo.

In 1909 Tel Aviv was nothing more than a series of sand dunes. This rare old photo shows the allocation of plots of land to the first residents of Tel Aviv.

232

The Revival of Hebrew

As settlers from many different places arrived in Palestine, the need for a common language became apparent. Some settlers advocated that it be Yiddish or even German, but these tongues were both of European origin, and were unfamiliar to Sephardim and Jews from the Muslim countries. Hebrew was the obvious choice; although not yet suited to modern uses, it was the one language known to most Jews, and had been the language of the Jewish homeland before the exile.

Eliezer Ben-Yehudah (1858-1922), the father of spoken Hebrew.

allowed only Hebrew to be spoken in his home, and his family and friends followed his example. He coined new words for tools and ideas that were unknown to ancient Hebrew. Some years before the outbreak of World War I, he embarked on the monumental task of compiling an unabridged dictionary of the Hebrew language which included the new expressions he had created.

The Haskalah, despite the opposition of some religious leaders, had already introduced the use of Hebrew for secular purposes. The two most ardent champions of the Hebrew revival were Eliezer Ben-Yehudah (1858–1922) and Asher Ginzberg (1856–1927), who called himself Ahad Ha-Am ("One of the People").

Eliezer Ben-Yehudah

Eliezer Ben-Yehudah, considered the father of modern Hebrew, was a talented linguist and educator who foresaw the creative role that Hebrew could play in the everyday life of the new Jewish homeland. Once he arrived in Palestine in 1881, Ben-Yehudah

Ahad Ha-Am

Ahad Ha-Am was the leading essayist in modern Hebrew. He fashioned it into an instrument of precise and articulate expression. Ahad Ha-Am was not a Zionist, and believed that most Jews would continue to live in the diaspora even if a Jewish state was established. Nonetheless, he argued that the Land of Israel must be the spiritual and cultural center of the entire Jewish people. His writings inspired a whole generation of creative Hebrew writers, chief among whom was his close disciple, the poet of the Hebrew national renaissance, Hayim Nahman Bialik (1873–1934).

Hayim Nahman Bialik (1873–1934), the greatest Hebrew poet of modern times. Bialik's first poem was about his longing for Shivat Zion, the Return to Israel. Bialik supported himself as a businessman, teacher, and publisher.
In Israel today, Bialik is considered the national poet, just as Shakespeare is in English-speaking countries.

Israeli poster promoting the study of Hebrew

The Second Aliyah / 1905–1914

The Second Aliyah extended from 1905 until the outbreak of World War I in 1914. This wave of immigration marked the development of a new type of agricultural settlement in Palestine, the kibbutz or cooperative. The members of a kibbutz not only worked and lived together, but actually owned everything jointly. The kibbutz supplied their food, clothing, and other necessities, paying for these goods with the proceeds from the sale of its agricultural products.

A Keren Kayemet poster in Hebrew, Polish, and Yiddish inviting settlers to settle in the valley of Jezreel, in Palestine.

The Jewish National Fund

The land for the settlements was provided by the Keren Kayemet Le-Yisrael, or Jewish National Fund, which was established in 1907 as the land-purchasing agency of the Zionist movement. The JNF was and still is supported by contributions from Jews the world over.

The Histadrut

The pioneers in Palestine organized into a strong federation of labor unions known as the Histadrut Ha-Ovdim ("Federation of Workers"). Eventually the Histadrut evolved into a powerful organization which included all the Jewish working people in the country.

Mounted Shomrim on patrol

Members of the Second Aliyah opposed the practice of hiring Arab laborers to do their field work.
Women stood shoulder to shoulder with the men and shared the back-breaking work in the kibbutzim.

America Beckons

Throughout its history, one country in particular opened its doors to the poor and wronged of all nations and creeds. Indeed, at the very gateway to this land stood a statue, the symbol of liberty, on which were engraved words written by Emma Lazarus (1849–1887), a compassionate and gifted Jewish poet.

Give me your tired, your poor,
Your huddled masses yearning to
breathe free,
The wretched refuse of your teeming
shore,
Send these, the homeless, tempest-tost,
to me.
I lift my lamp beside the golden door!

Polish Jews asking advice about emigrating to the United States at the information desk of the Hebrew Immigrant Aid Society in Warsaw.

In the latter part of the 19th century and the beginning of the 20th, hundreds of thousands of Russian Jews left their homes and sailed to America. Most of them had to make the long journey under difficult conditions, crowded together in the steerage—the most cramped and uncomfortable part of a passenger ship. But they were glad to leave Russia for the land of promise across the Atlantic.

In 1905 a revolution took place in Russia. It was brutally crushed. As in 1881–82, there were bloody pogroms against the Jewish communities. Jews in Europe and America held out a helping hand to the refugees who poured out of Russia. Jewish philanthropists donated generous sums of money, and organizations were formed to aid the immigrants in establishing new homes. Some of them settled in Western Europe or in South America, but most went to the United States.

Front page of the HIAS journal, the *Jewish Immigrant*. The lady is opening the gates of America to the wandering Jew.

The Statue of Liberty was a golden door and beacon of hope and freedom for all immigrants.

Jews in the American Community

About a quarter of a million Jews lived in America in the year 1880. In the next fifty years, two and a half million more came to these shores.

The great majority of this vast influx of immigrants came from Eastern Europe, from lands, including Poland and Lithuania, which were now under Russian rule.

The May Laws

Jews suffered harsh oppression under the government of the tsars. The assassination in 1881 of Tsar Alexander II, who had attempted some reforms, brought on a rapid worsening of their condition. Government-inspired pogroms were followed by the May laws of 1882, which expelled the Jews from many towns and many professions.

The Great Exodus

As hopes for living a good life or improving the lot of their children faded for the Jews of Eastern Europe, a great exodus began. Without funds and with few skills for living in the industrialized Western world, hundreds of thousands crossed the western borders of their homelands, seeking new lands and new opportunities.

Some went to France, Germany, and other West European countries; some to England and to South Africa. A small idealistic group went to Palestine, although they knew that Turkish oppression and the hardships of an undeveloped land awaited them. Baron Maurice de Hirsch, the great philanthropist, aided the emigration from Russia, setting up the Jewish Colonization Association to aid resettlement, particularly in Argentina. The Alliance Israélite Universelle in France, and later the Hilfsverein der Deutschen Juden in Germany, furnished some help. The British Mansion House Committee helped those who arrived in England.

The great majority of those fleeing Old World persecution had no other wish than to go to the land of opportunity, the free country of America. After miserable voyages, usually in the crowded steerage or cheap compartment of the steamships that carried them, these hopeful refugees arrived in the "Golden Land."

Baron Maurice de Hirsch.

Mauricia, Jewish farm colony in Argentina founded by the Jewish Colonization Association of Baron de Hirsch for East European Jews who wished to settle there.

The Love of Learning

Some Jewish immigrants became farmers, encouraged by the Jewish Agricultural Society and the National Farm School, but they were few. For the most part, the newcomers wished to live in cities, in communities where there were many fellow Jews, and where there would be synagogues to attend and religious schools for their children. The shul and the heder, which they had loved in the old country, were transplanted to the new one.

The Jews of Eastern Europe brought with them their love of learning. They managed to find the few dollars necessary to pay the melamed who taught their children Hebrew, Humash, and prayers. They wished in this new country to fashion the life of faith and piety they had known in their small towns in Europe.

Even those who no longer strictly observed Jewish law, and those who devoted themselves to Haskalah or to secularist political movements, had the Jewish love of learning and the printed word. Jewish immigrants published and read more periodicals than any other immigrant group, before or since. They read Yiddish newspapers and Hebrew magazines, and flocked to the Yiddish theater and to public lectures and discussions.

After a day of hard work, many of the adults went to night school to learn English and to qualify to become American citizens. They sacrificed to send their children to high school and, if possible, to college, so that they could do more in life than their parents had been able to do. The ideal profession they wished for their children was one that combined learning and service, such as medicine, law, or teaching.

Helping Each Other

Poor as most of them were, the immigrant Jews never forgot their responsibility to one other. They set up free loan societies, charities, and organizations for fellowship and mutual help. Many belonged to landsmanshaftn—societies made up of immigrants from the same European town.

The old tradition of charity and good deeds was continued in the New World. As poor as an immigrant might be, no home was too crowded to take in a cousin or other relative who had just arrived from the old country.

Jews who were already established in the United States also helped the newcomers. Organizations like B'nai B'rith and the American Jewish Committee, supported largely by German Jews whose parents or grandparents had come to America a few decades earlier, fought anti-Semitism and protected the rights of new immigrants.

Poverty, crowded slum conditions, and unfamiliarity with the lifestyle of the New World were all handicaps for the immigrant. To make the younger people feel at home in America, educational and vocational courses and group social activities were sponsored by the Hebrew Immigrant Aid Society, the National Council of Jewish Women, the Educational Alliance in New York, and the YMHA's and settlement houses.

The Educational Alliance in New York, 1895

The Second Generation

The Jewish Tradition Weakens

The second generation, the children of the immigrants, were able to find better jobs and often to enter professions. In the free atmosphere of America, many of them left the old way of life. They were unwilling to be different from their neighbors, or to lose jobs refusing to work on the Sabbath. Many felt that the religion of their parents was not suited to modern America.

Even the secular culture so dear to some of their parents was often not important to them. They did not attend the Yiddish theater and lecture hall, or read the Yiddish newspapers and magazines of their parents. Their language was English, and they wanted above all to be like other Americans. Some were ashamed of their parents because of their foreign accents or old-fashioned ways.

The Reform Temples

The Reform temples of the late 19th century and the early 20th were not places where the children of East European immigrants could feel at home. Many temples held their Sabbath services on Sunday. Often their members disliked the foreign accents and mannerisms of their East European brethren, and preferred the society of their own kind.

Not respecting their parents' ways, and not welcomed in the Reform temples, young people were all too often growing up detached from Jewish tradition and from the Jewish community.

Jews of all ages reading in the Aguilar Free Library, New York, 1895

Temple Emanuel of New York as it appeared in 1868 at the corner of Fifth Avenue and 43rd Street; it is now located at Fifth Avenue and 65th Street.

Some American boys went to heder, studying Torah the way it had been studied in Europe, for many hours each week.

The First World War / 1914

The Shot Heard Round the World

In 1914 the shot heard round the world sparked off the First World War, in which the Central Powers (Germany, Austria-Hungary, and Turkey) and the Allies (France, Russia, England, and Italy) were pitted against each other in Europe, Africa, and the Middle East.

In each belligerent country Jews fought side by side with their fellow citizens. Many Jewish soldiers died on both sides. When the war began there were more than 500,000 Jews in Germany. More than 100,000 served in the armed forces; 35,000 were decorated for bravery and 12,000 were killed in action.

Most of the major battles of the war were fought in France and Belgium, the western front, and in Poland and Russia, the eastern front. The eastern front stretched along the borders of Russia and through the Pale of Settlement. The war brought great suffering to the Jews in these territories. Most of the able-bodied men served in the Russian army. Many lost their homes. Others were deported because the Russians suspected them of disloyalty. Many Russian Jews were sent deeper into the vast eastern areas of the tsarist empire.

In 1917 the Russian people revolted. The tsar was deposed and executed. The following year, torn by confusion and bloodshed, Russia signed a separate peace treaty with the Central Powers. Civil war broke out in western Russia, with supporters of the new Communist regime fighting an opposition ranging from moderate socialists to advocates of restoring the tsarist monarchy.

Jewish self-defense unit in Odessa, April 1918. This unit was very well-equipped compared to most, as its members had uniforms and even a machine gun.

Jewish soldiers and officers of the Austro-Hungarian army at prayer. Painting by Joseph Ehrenfreund.

The Balfour Declaration / 1917

Chaim Weizmann

One of England's most brilliant chemists, Dr. Chaim Weizmann (1874–1952), was also a leader of the World Zionist Organization. Weizmann, who was born in Russia, settled in England in 1903, where he taught chemistry at the University of Manchester. During World War I, England had to cope with a serious shortage of acetone, a material required for the manufacture of explosives. Weizmann discovered a new formula for acetone, thus making an invaluable contribution to the Allied war effort.

When government officials asked Weizmann to name a price for his discovery, he refused to accept any payment, but asked that Britain allow unrestricted Jewish immigration into Palestine once the war was won. The British agreed, for they knew that the Jewish settlers, having no bonds with Turkey, could be relied upon to help England.

The Balfour Declaration

On November 2, 1917, Arthur James Balfour, the British Foreign Secretary, sent a letter to Lord Walter Rothschild asking him to inform the Zionist Organization of the British government's favorable attitude toward the proposed Jewish national home in Palestine. This letter, which is now known as the Balfour Declaration, brought rejoicing to Zionists the world over.

The Balfour Declaration

The Jewish Legion

In addition to the Jewish soldiers already serving in the British armed forces, all-Jewish fighting units were organized to fight under the blue-and-white Zionist flag. The first of these was the Zion Mule Corps, which served in the Gallipoli campaign in 1915. Its successor, the Jewish Legion, fought under General Edmund Allenby in the campaign to liberate Palestine from the Turks. One of the members of the Jewish Legion was a young immigrant from Russia, David Ben-Gurion, who later became the first Prime Minister of the State of Israel. Another was Vladimir Jabotinsky (1880–1940), the founder of Revisionist Zionism. It was largely thanks to his advocacy that the British agreed to form all-Jewish fighting units.

Vladimir Jabotinsky (1880–1940) in the uniform of the Jewish Legion, which he founded in World War I. Jabotinsky was imprisoned by the British for organizing the Haganah. Later, he founded the Zionist Revisionist movement and the Irgun Zvai Leumi.

After World War I

World War I interrupted the flood of immigration which had increased the number of Jews in the United States to nearly 4 million. Immigrants who had entered the country during the past 33 years made up most of the Jewish population. They had learned how to live in the new land and had established themselves as citizens. Their children were growing up as Americans.

Following the war, when the flow of immigrants resumed, nationalist feelings in the United States were aroused, and resentment against foreigners grew. In 1924 Congress passed the Johnson Act, a restrictive immigration law that established a quota system favoring the Germanic countries and England, and severely limiting immigration from the countries of Southern and Eastern Europe.

The Johnson Act reduced Jewish immigration to several thousand a year. After 1924, with the rate of immigration from Europe curtailed, the problem of preserving Jewish identity in America assumed new forms. The problem was not how to integrate the newcomers into America, but how to raise the native-born American

The new land for some was as poverty stricken as the old. This basement heder, somewhere on Hester Street in the ghetto of New York, was photographed by Jacob Riis.

Jewish citizen to a higher level of Jewish knowledge and awareness.

American Jewry had established its own institutions and was beginning to develop its own leaders and teachers, while the great Jewish communities of Europe faced a period of darkness and destruction.

ALBERT EINSTEIN

Albert Einstein, mathematician and Jew, fled Germany in 1933 and found refuge in the United States. Six years later he sent President Franklin Roosevelt a letter informing him that atomic research in Germany created the possibility that the enemy was making a new kind of superbomb. Roosevelt took the warning seriously and set up a committee of scientists to develop the atomic bomb. Many Jewish refugee scientists worked on the Manhattan Project. The atomic bomb shortened the war with Japan and saved thousands of American lives. The bomb ushered in the Atomic Age and has been both a blessing and a plague to humanity.

Painting depicting the stream of numbed immigrants and their back-breaking labor in the sweatshops. Albert Einstein, in front, with the white hair, was one of them.

The Palestine Mandate

After the war, the newly formed League of Nations gave Germany's colonies and many former Turkish territories in trusteeship to England and France to be guided and controlled until such time as they would be able to govern themselves. Palestine became a British mandate, and the Balfour Declaration was incorporated into the charter by which it was to be governed. This meant that the League endorsed the principle that Palestine was to become the Jewish homeland. Under the mandate, Hebrew became one of Palestine's three official languages (the other two were English and Arabic).

The Arabs

Many of Palestine's Arab inhabitants opposed the Balfour Declaration and Jewish immigration. Wealthy Arab landowners feared that Jews from Europe would bring in a standard of living much higher than that of the Arab peasants who tilled the soil of Palestine with the same primitive tools as their ancestors centuries earlier, causing them to become discontented with their lot. Arabs marauders were incited to raid Jewish settlements in order to force the Jews to abandon them. But the Jews fought back. They worked their land by day and guarded it at night with their guns.

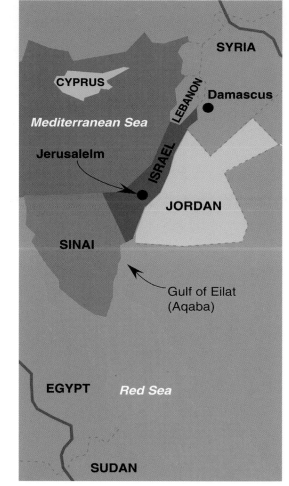

The British government in 1922 divided the promised Jewish homeland by cutting off three-quarters of the land area of Palestine. A new Arab state was created, called Transjordan. In 1946 Transjordan became independent. It is now called Jordan.

The Third Aliyah

The early years of the British Mandate, 1919 to 1923, marked the period of the Third Aliyah. This wave of immigration consisted mainly of Jews from Poland and Russia.

Lawrence of Arabia (right) arranged a meeting between Emir Feisal (center) and Chaim Weizmann (left). Weizmann traveled by boat and camel to discuss the Palestinian situation with the emir. The two leaders developed a friendly respect for each other's view. They issued a statement agreeing to the recognition of Zionist aims in Palestine if the Arabs were given independence in Syria and Iraq. The territories, which were then ruled by the French and the British, were not given independence and the Jewish-Arab alliance collapsed.

The Jewish Awakening

JEWISH HIGHLIGHTS

The Tsars
19th century

Alexander II
19th century

Haskalah Movement
19th century

Persecution
19th century

The Jewish State
19th-20th century

JEWISH EVENTS • PERSONALITIES • LITERATURE

The Tsars	Alexander II	Haskalah Movement	Persecution	The Jewish State
▷ Kahal abolished	▷ Abolished draft	▷ Hebrew reborn	▷ Pogroms (1881–1884)	▷ Dreyfus convicted Emile Zola
▷ Crown schools	▷ May Laws	▷ Haskalah Abraham Mapu	▷ May laws	▷ Theodor Herzl
▷ Jewish boys drafted	▷ Pogroms / 1881	Judah Leib Gordon	▷ Expulsion from Moscow	▷ First Zionist Congress 1897
	Bilu movement	Yitzhak Ber Levinsohn	▷ School quotas	▷ First Alyah Tel Aviv founded 1909
		▷ Yiddish literature	▷ 3 million Jews emigrate	
		Mendele Mokher Seforim	▷ Bilu movement	▷ Revival of Hebrew Eliezer Ben-Yehudah Ahad Ha-Am Hayim Nahman Bialik
		Sholem Aleichem	▷ Leon Pinsker Lovers of Zion	
		I. L. Peretz	▷ Rishon Le-Zion Petah Tikvah	▷ Keven Kayemet Jewish National Fund
			▷ Zikhron Yaakov	

WORLD HISTORY

The Tsars	Alexander II	Haskalah Movement	Persecution	The Jewish State
▷ Tsar Nicholas I	▷ Tsar Alexander II Tsar Liberator Assassination	▷ Russia	▷ Alexander III	▷ Sultan of Turkey
▷ Alexander I		▷ Poland		▷ France
				▷ Major Esterhazy

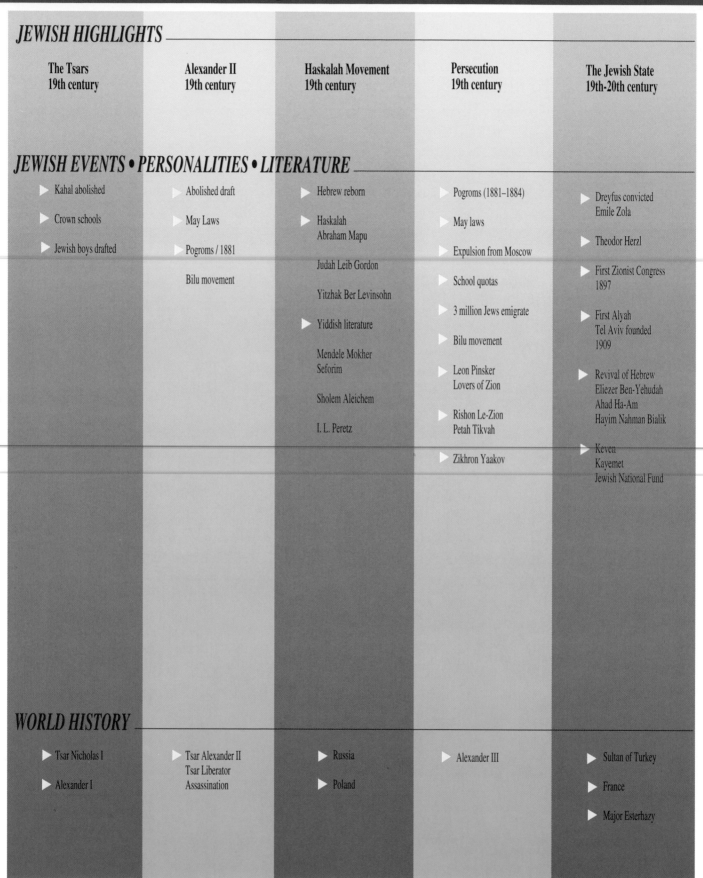

The Jewish Awakening

JEWISH HIGHLIGHTS

Second Aliyah	Jews in America 20th century	Jewish Organizations 20th century	World War I 1914

JEWISH EVENTS • PERSONALITIES • LITERATURE • HOLIDAYS

▷ Jewish National Fund	▷ Baron Maurice de Hirsch Jewish Colonization Association	▷ B'nai B'rith	▷ Civil War in Russia
▷ Histadruth	▷ Alliance Israelite Universelle	▷ American Jewish Committee	▷ Chaim Weizmann
		▷ Hebrew Immigration Society	▷ Balfour Declaration
		▷ Landsmannschaft	▷ Vladimir Jabotinsky Jewish Legion David Ben-Gurion
		▷ Reform temples	▷ Mandate restrictions
		▷ Johnson Act 1924	▷ Third Aliyah
		▷ Sweatshops Unions Samuel Gompers	

WORLD HISTORY

▷ Basle Switzweland	▷ Tsar Nicholas I	▷ Tsar Liberator Assassination	▷ World War I
	▷ Alexander I		▷ Allenby defeats Turks
			▷ Amir Feisal

244

Life in the New World

For most of the immigrants, the fulfillment of America's promise was long delayed. The majority of them landed in New York, and great numbers found homes there and in the other large cities of the east. They lived in crowded tenements in neighborhoods like the Lower East Side of New York. Unlike the ghettos of Europe, Jews congregated in these neighborhoods for social and economic reasons, not because of legal restrictions, and those who eventually gained some measure of success were able to move to better areas.

Not knowing English, the immigrants worked at low-paying jobs and were often exploited. The great new industry in the cities was the manufacture of clothing. Many of the newcomers became workers in the garment industry, sewing or tailoring or pressing. Often they worked for 12 or more hours a day, six days a week. In addition, they brought piecework home for the whole family, including the children, to work on till late at night. Even with everyone working, the family's income was very meager.

Samuel Gompers (1850-1924), a British-born Jew who started as a cigar-maker in New York, became founder and president for 38 years of the American Federation of Labor.

Poor conditions at work and at home often led to shortened lives. Tuberculosis claimed many exhausted workers. More dramatically, unsafe conditions led to injuries and to fires which took many lives. When the Triangle Shirtwaist factory in New York burned in 1911, 156 workers were killed, nearly all of them Jewish women. The newcomers were willing to submit to these conditions because of their great need to make a living for themselves and their children.

Driven by a desire to improve working conditions, Jews played a major part in the growth of trade unions in the United States. Samuel Gompers (1850–1924), the founder of the American Federation of Labor, was an immigrant from England. In the early years of the 20th century, East European Jews built up the International Ladies' Garment Workers Union, which fought for shorter hours, safe conditions, and steady pay. By cooperating with the manufacturers when possible, the unions ultimately benefitted them as well.

A black-bordered circular in three languages (English, Yiddish, Italian) calling upon the people of New York to pay their last respects to the victims of the Triangle Fire. 156 workers, mostly Jews, were killed.

Jewish tradition was observed even amidst the poverty of the ghetto. This poor Jew is preparing for the Sabbath in his cellar home.

The Jewish Theological Seminary

Sabato Morais (1823–1897) and a group of like-minded associates founded the Jewish Theological Seminary of America in 1886 in New York. They hoped that the rabbis ordained there, all of whom were to be English-speaking college graduates, would be able to keep Jewish youth loyal to their heritage. The movement that came into being with the founding of the Seminary is known as Conservative Judaism.

Alexander Kohut (1842–1894), Benjamin Szold (1829–1902), and Marcus Jastrow (1829–1903) were among the scholars who helped fashion this new religious denomination. From the start the Conservatives differed with the Reform movement, upholding loyalty to Torah and Talmud, observance of the Sabbath and dietary laws, Hebrew as the language of prayer, and the preservation of hopes for the return to Zion.

Solomon Schechter

From England's Cambridge University in 1902 came Dr. Solomon Schechter (1847–1915) to head the Seminary. Schechter was a dynamic teacher whose great learning combined East European devotion with modern scholarly discipline. He had become famous for his discovery of the Cairo Genizah, a storehouse of discarded ancient manuscripts that shed much light on Jewish history.

Under Schechter's leadership, the Seminary became a first-rank scholarly institution with an unsurpassed library. The Conservative movement, as Schechter and his associates saw it, was a continuation of the Historical School of Judaism founded by Zechariah Frankel. In the Conservative view, Judaism, like all other human institutions, has developed through the ages, not by sudden reforms but in response to the will and needs of its faithful adherents.

Early photograph of the Jewish Theological Seminary of America in New York.

Solomon Schechter (1847-1915), scholar of Eastern Europe, Germany, and England, called from Cambridge University to head the Jewish Theological Seminary of America in 1902. He gathered the great faculty and library of the Seminary, and gave form to the Conservative movement.

The People of the Book

The Jews are the "people of the book," but they are also the people of the magazines, newspapers, and periodicals. Wherever Jews have set roots, even temporarily, some enterprising intellectuals always found reason to publish a newspaper or magazine.

The Yiddish-speaking masses in the major U.S. cities, not yet fluent in English, created a cultural life of their own which helped them to adjust to their new and difficult environment. Hundreds of newspapers, magazines, and periodicals in Yiddish, Hebrew, German, Ladino, Russian, Polish, Hungarian, and other languages appeared to offer guidance, news, entertainment, and advice for a generation struggling to accommodate itself to a new world. In particular the Yiddish press served these ends.

The Jewish Press in the 1900s

In the early 1900s the Jewish press in the United States included over 200 periodicals, 147 in English, 27 in Yiddish, and 11 in Hebrew. The 5 daily Yiddish newspapers had a combined circulation of over 300,000 copies. There were 69 weeklies which provided news of Jewish life throughout the world and furnished forums for discussion.

With the modernization of the Jewish people, there was a flowering of Yiddish literature in Europe and in England, Canada, France, Argentina, and the United States. Besides being a spoken tongue, Yiddish now became the language of books, newspapers, theatrical productions, and political activism. It became the first and also the second language of two-thirds of the Jewish people.

The Jewish Daily Forward

In its heyday, the *Jewish Daily Forward* (*Yiddish Forvets*) was the most widely read Yiddish newspaper in the United States. Its 11 regional editions reached as far as Chicago and had a peak circulation of 200,000.

Abraham Cahan (1860–1951) edited the *Forward* from 1903 to 1951, combining a commitment to good journalism with a belief in the Jewish labor movement. The *Forward* published stories, serialized novels, gave English lessons, and kept the immigrants in touch with local and world events. Its most famous feature was the Bintel Brief, a "Dear Abby"–style advice column which counseled readers on their domestic, personal, and business problems.

The front page of the first issue of the *Jewish Daily Forward*, Wednesday, September 8, 1897. At that time the price of a newspaper was one cent.

The front page of the first Jewish daily in the United States, April 6, 1883.

Front page of the English edition of the *Foward* of July 5, 1996. Inflation has raised the price of the newpaper from one cent to one dollar.

As the pace of immigration fell, the *Forward*'s readership dwindled. By 1970 it had fallen to 44,000. The Yiddish edition of the *Forward* ceased daily publication in 1983 and became a weekly. In 1990 a weekly English edition of the *Forward* made its debut. In 1995 a Russian edition was introduced.

Abraham Cahan, the editor of the *Jewish Daily Foward.*

The Boston Blat

In 1913 a Boston printer named Joseph J. Shore felt the call to provide a newspaper that would serve the Jewish communities of New England. His weekly paper, the *Boston Blat,* was mostly in Yiddish, but because he wisely saw the need to serve a wider audience, it included columns in Hebrew and English.

Undercapitalized, the *Boston Blat* folded its pages after six years of struggle. This typical startup and failure was common among the early newspapers. The renaissance of Hebrew, the Holocaust, and other social changes sent Yiddish into decline.

Yiddish Today

As the search for ethnic identity grows, interest in Yiddish continues to increase. Yiddish courses are becoming common on college campuses. The Yivo Institute for Jewish Research and the Workmen's Circle have published Yiddish textbooks for beginners. The National Yiddish Book Center is building a $5 million complex in Amherst, Massachusetts, and is cataloguing thousands of Yiddish books.

In the Hasidic community, Yiddish is an everyday, living, working, studying, singing tool. Children study their lessons in Yiddish, mothers sing Yiddish lullabies, merchants do business and advertise in Yiddish, and Hasidic comedians (*badchanim*) tell jokes in Yiddish.

Joseph J. Shore, printer and publisher of the *Boston Blat.* He was also an accomplished artist and woodcarver. Shore often carved the large-size Hebrew type for *Boston Blat*'s headlines.

The *Boston Blat,* August 1, 1913. Price, 2 cents. The *Boston Blat—Boston Jewish News* was edited by Joseph J. Shore.

Jewish Public Servants

By the year 1900 there were a million Jews in America. Many, mostly descendants of immigrants who had arrived in the first part of the 19th century, had attained prosperity and status. Among them were well-known public servants and philanthropists, whose activities and charities benefited many others besides their own people.

Oscar Straus (1850–1926) was appointed envoy to Turkey by Grover Cleveland and three Presidents after him, and served in the cabinet of Theodore Roosevelt as Secretary of Commerce and Labor. His brothers Nathan (1848–1931) and Isidor Straus (1845–1912), owners of Macy's in New York, were known for their good deeds. Isidor, at one time a Congressman, was president of the Educational Alliance. Nathan brought about the compulsory pasteurization of milk in New York, and gave generously for health clinics in Palestine in response to an appeal from Henrietta Szold (1860–1945), the founder of Hadassah.

Julius Rosenwald (1862–1932), of Sears Roebuck, gave tremendous sums for many philanthropic causes, including the higher education of blacks. Others who supported learning through their activity and contributions were Judge Mayer Sulzberger (1843–1923) of the Court of Common Pleas in Philadelphia, who was one of the founders of the Jewish Theological Seminary, and his cousin Cyrus L. Sulzberger, president of the Jewish Agricultural Society.

Louis Marshall (1856–1929), outstanding attorney and civic leader, founded the American Jewish Committee and worked for Jewish minority rights at the Versailles Conference after World War I. Though not a Zionist, he supported the building of Palestine as a Jewish refuge. Jacob H. Schiff (1847–1920) worked with him on many projects and helped persuade the U.S. government to censure Russia for its mistreatment of Jews. Schiff was perhaps the outstanding patron of learning of the time, giving funds to institutions ranging from Harvard and Barnard to the Jewish Theological Seminary and the Haifa Technion.

David Sarnoff (1891–1971) began as a messenger boy and wireless operator. He rose to become head of RCA. He was active on behalf of Jewish causes.

Louis Dembitz Brandeis (1856-1941), justice of the Supreme Court and Zionist leader. A champion of liberal causes, he became interested in Judaism and Zionism when he met Jewish garment workers during settlement of a strike in 1910. He said that following Jewish ideals made one a better American.

Jacob H. Schiff (1847–1920), outstanding Jewish philanthropist, gave support to universities, hospitals, and cultural activities both Jewish and general, helping religious institutions of all groups. His firm would not lend money to tsarist Russia because of its persecution of the Jews.

Orthodox Jewry

The leading rabbis and congregations at the turn of the century, as well as the leading philanthropists, were mostly in the Reform wing of Judaism. Rabbis Kaufmann Kohler (1843–1926), Emil Hirsch (1851–1923), David Philipson (1862–1949), and Henry Berkowitz (1857–1924) were among the leaders of Jewish religious life. Conservative and Orthodox rabbis and congregations were not as yet well-organized.

Yeshiva University in New York, an Orthodox institution which includes high schools, undergraduate colleges for men and women, graduate and medical schools, and a rabbinical seminary.

The great majority of Jewish immigrants from 1881 on were Orthodox in background. They attempted to set up the same type of communities as had served them in their former homes. Each congregation, following Jewish tradition and the customs of its members, felt it could stand by itself without looking toward a central authority.

A group of Orthodox Jews in New York City made an attempt to attain unity under the leadership of Rabbi Jacob Joseph (1848–1902), whom they brought from Vilna in Lithuania to be the city's chief rabbi. He proved unable to bring order to New York's teeming Jewish community because most of its Orthodox leaders refused to accept his authority. In Chicago a similar attempt failed.

Umbrella organizations met with more success. In 1898, the Union of Orthodox Jewish Congregations was founded, thanks to the efforts of Rabbi H. Pereira Mendes (1852–1937) of the Shearith Israel Congregation in New York. A group of Orthodox rabbis joined together to form the Agudas Harabonim in 1902. One of their aims was to aid academies of learning, yeshivot, both in America and abroad.

Yeshiva University

The outstanding yeshiva in the New World was founded in 1896. Named for a great European scholar, Rabbi Isaac Elchanan, this New York institution began as a rabbinical seminary for students who had already steeped themselves in Jewish learning in European academies. Over the years it expanded into a complete university. Under the presidency of Rabbi Bernard Dov Revel (1885–1940) and his successor, Dr. Samuel Belkin (1911–1976) it grew to include a high school, an undergraduate college, and a variety of graduate and professional schools, including the Albert Einstein Medical School, the Benjamin Cardozo Law School, Stern College for Women, the Sy Sims School of Business, and the Wurzweiler School of Social Work. Under Belkin's successor, Rabbi Norman Lamm (b. 1927), Yeshiva continued to grow. In the 1990s it had 5,200 undergraduate and graduate students, an additional 1,000 students at the affiliates, and an annual operating budget of $350 million.

Dr. Norman Lamm, 1996

Anti-Semitism

In the democratic climate of America, Jews found themselves accepted, as they had never been elsewhere, as first-class citizens and productive members of society. Still, anti-Semitism all too often made itself felt even on these shores. In the early part of the 19th century, several states did not grant full legal rights to Jews. Later on, the Know-Nothing party, populist agitators of various stripes, and the Ku Klux Klan aroused feelings against foreigners and minority groups, primarily Catholics and Jews.

Polite Anti-Semitism

"Polite" anti-Semitism, which meant the exclusion of Jews from high society and the refusal to sell them homes in certain areas, was always known to exist. In a famous case in 1877, a hotel in Saratoga, New York, refused to accept Joseph Seligman (1819–1880), a prominent Jewish banker who had been a friend of Presidents Lincoln and Grant, as a paying guest, informing him bluntly that "no Israelite shall be permitted to stop in the hotel." Public opinion was outraged by this incident, but it was not until several decades later that restrictive practices of this kind were outlawed.

More seriously, the great influx of Jewish immigrants and the growth of European anti-Semitism triggered anti-Jewish sentiments among many Americans around the turn of the century. Hatred aroused knows no rhyme or reason. At one and the same time Jews were accused of running the government and of seeking to overthrow it; of being wretchedly poor and fabulously rich; of sticking clannishly to themselves and of trying to break into society. In September 1928, the medieval blood-libel accusation came to life for a brief moment when state troopers in Massena, New York, searching for a missing child who turned out to have been lost in the woods, questioned the local rabbi about reports that Jews offered human sacrifices on Yom Kippur.

The problems Jews experienced in the United States, however troubling, did not compare, either in frequency or in seriousness, with the persecutions and pogroms to which they were subjected in Europe and the Near East. Moreover, the Jews of America stood up for their rights.

Equality for All

From the very beginning, American Jews demanded that they be treated the same as everyone else. In the 19th century they successfully fought against restrictive voting laws. They lobbied the government to take action at the time of the blood-libel of Damascus in 1840. They protested to President Millard P. Fillmore about the restrictions imposed on Jews by Switzerland. They similarly protested, with the support of Protestant leaders, at the time of the Mortara case. And in 1859 they established the Board of Delegates of American Israelites to defend Jewish rights. In 1913 they founded the Anti-Defamation League of B'nai B'rith to combat anti-Semitic libels and protect the civil rights of Jews and other minorities.

The Dreyfus Affair in 1894 aroused widespread concern among all who loved justice, Jews and non-Jews alike. The Kishinev pogrom of 1903 and the wave of pogroms in 1905 were followed by mass demonstrations and protests throughout the civilized world. Congress passed a unanimous resolution expressing American horror at the incidents. Oscar Straus and Jacob Schiff headed a committee which raised $1 million to help the survivors.

The American Jewish Committee

Because of the need for a national organization to safeguard Jewish rights, the American Jewish Committee came into being in 1906. Louis Marshall, the Sulzbergers, Judge Julian Mack, and Rabbi Judah Magnes (1877–1948) were among the founders of this body, whose objectives were "to prevent the infraction of the civil and religious rights of the Jews in any part of the world; to render all lawful assistance; to secure for Jews equality of economic, social and educational opportunity; and to afford relief from calamities affecting Jews, wherever they may occur."

The AJC encouraged the organization of the 1.5 million Jews of New York City into a Kehillah, or communal organization, which was to regulate Jewish law, settle disputes, protect civil rights, and further education. The Kehillah came into being in 1908 and continued in existence for ten years, under the chairmanship of Rabbi Magnes, who later became president of the Hebrew University of Jerusalem. Like most other attempts at Jewish unity, the Kehillah soon came to an end, but its legacy included the New York Bureau of Jewish Education, a model agency imitated in many other cities.

The AJC was active in a long campaign to prevent discrimination by Russia against Jews. Though it spoke for American Jewry, it was initially strongly anti-Zionist, reflecting the Reform ideology of most of its founders.

Commentary
February 1997

On the Future of Conservatism
A Symposium

Robert L. Bartley • Peter L. Berger • Walter Berns • William F. Buckley, Jr.
Midge Decter • David Frum • Francis Fukuyama • Mark Helprin
Gertrude Himmelfarb • William Kristol • Michael Novak • Norman Podhoretz
Irwin M. Stelzer • George Weigel • Ruth R. Wisse

The cover page of *Commentary Magazine*, dated May 1996. *Commentary* is one of the leading journals of political thought, published by the American Jewish Committee.

Julian Mack

American Jewish Committee delegation in 1911. *From left to right:* Louis Marshall, Harry Friedenwald, Judge Mayer Sulzberger, Harry Cutler, Oscar S. Straus, Judge Leon Sanders, Henry N. Goldfogle, Samuel Dorf, Leon Kaminsky.

American Zionism

Many Americans, Christians as well as Jews, looked forward to the prophetic return of Jews to the Land of Israel. In 1852, Warder Cresson of Philadelphia converted to Judaism and, bearing the new name of Michael Boaz Israel, tried to establish a Jewish colony near Jerusalem. Clorinda S. Minor of Philadelphia led a Christian group to a settlement called Mount Hope near the site where Tel Aviv was later built.

Emma Lazarus looked forward to a revival of the Jewish national spirit and a rebuilt homeland. Immigrants from Eastern Europe brought the Hovevei Zion movement to the United States, setting up chapters in New York, Boston, and other cities in the 1880s.

Only a token delegation from America attended the First Zionist Congress, convened by Theodor Herzl in Basel in 1897. Yet the Zionist movement in the United States was steadily growing. In 1898 nearly 100 small Zionist clubs united into the Federation of American Zionists, which in 1917 became the Zionist Organization of America.

The rank-and-file members of America's Zionist movement were largely of East European origin, but the leaders included some outstanding Reform rabbis, among them Bernhard Felsenthal (1822–1908), Gustav Gottheil (1827–1903), and Maximilian Heller (1860–1924), who opposed the Reform doctrine that Jews must remain dispersed throughout the world in order to fulfill the "mission of Israel." True fulfillment would come, they felt, when a Jewish model state was allowed to flourish in Palestine.

The Zionist Federation's first secretary was Stephen S. Wise (1874–1949), a Reform rabbi already known for his fiery oratory.

Left to right: Rabbi Stephen S. Wise, Rabbi Israel Goldstein, Louis Lipsky

During World War II he was to become American Jewry's outstanding spokesman to the conscience of the world.

Many American Jews opposed Zionism, arguing that loyalty to America required them to forsake all interest in a Jewish national homeland. The strongest statement of the compatibility of Zionism with loyalty to America came from Louis Dembitz Brandeis (1856–1941), who in 1916 was appointed to the Supreme Court of the United States. "The ideals of the 20th century," he said, "have been Jewish ideals for 20 centuries. To be good Americans, we must be better Jews, and to be better Jews we must become Zionists."

Among the other leading figures in early American Zionism were Henrietta Szold (1860–1945) and Louis Lipsky (1876–1963). Szold, a rabbi's daughter, scholar, and editor of the Jewish Publication Society, founded Hadassah, the women's Zionist organization, in 1912. Lipsky founded America's first English-language Zionist periodical, the *Maccabean,* and was its editor for many years.

The Peace Conference / 1919

After World War I, the victorious nations were anxious to establish a lasting peace and better conditions in the postwar world. The face of Europe had changed. Germany and Austria had lost their empires and become republics. Russia had become a Communist dictatorship. France, although a victor in the great conflict, was exhausted, ravaged by the many bloody battles fought on her soil.

The Peace of Versailles

At the great peace conference at Versailles in 1919, many countries that had been part of the Russian, German, or Austrian empire before the war gained their independence. Poland, Finland, Estonia, Latvia, and Lithuania became independent countries, as did Hungary and Czechoslovakia. Germany lost its African colonies, and in the Middle East, Palestine and Iraq, formerly part of the Ottoman Empire, became British mandates, while Syria became a French mandate.

President Woodrow Wilson was instrumental in creating the League of Nations, an international organization which was to be responsible for maintaining peace in the world. The League supervised the administration of the mandates, including Palestine.

Attending the Versailles Peace Conference, along with the representatives of both the conquered and the conquering lands, were delegates from the many nations that were about to win independence or to gain mandatory status. Also present were Jewish delegations from many countries. American Jewry was represented by Louis Marshall and Judge Mack, among others. Marshall succeeded in uniting all the Jewish delegations to speak with one voice on behalf of the rights not only of Jews but of all minority groups.

The League of Nations

Guarantees of minority rights were included in the treaties negotiated at the Versailles Peace Conference and in the constitutions of the new states that came into existence after the war. The League of Nations was the guardian of the rights of minority groups, but in the years that followed was unable to enforce them, for it had no concrete powers.

At the peace conference Woodrow Wilson exercised a dominating influence. In this painting by William Orpen, he is sitting third from the left. Wilson's Fourteen Points were a summary of America's mission—the extension of self-government and democracy to the whole world.

The Jews of Poland

After World War I, the newly established state of Poland had a Jewish community of 3.3 million, the largest and one of the oldest in Europe and the second-largest in the world. Since Jews were regarded as members of a distinct nationality protected by the minority guarantees laid down at Versailles, Polish Jewry was organized as a Kehillah, with autonomy on the local level. The Kehillah organization owned all communal property, such as synagogues, cemeteries, and hospitals, and ran the community's educational, religious, and social-cultural institutions. The members of the ruling council of the Kehillah were elected by the Jews of each town by direct, secret ballot.

A typical heder in the city of Vilna, part of Poland until World War II, now part of Lithuania.

The Educational System

The greatest achievement of Polish Jewry was its educational system, maintained at its own cost. The different ideological and religious movements all had their own schools. Of the total Jewish school-age population of 425,000, some 340,000 attended these schools. The Jewish community also maintained teacher-training schools, rabbinical academies, trade schools, and other cultural institutions, such as museums, libraries, and adult study courses.

In secular higher education, Jewish students were greatly handicapped because of prejudice against them. As many as half of the Polish Jews who attended universities had to do so in other countries.

Jewish Cultural Life

The cultural life of Polish Jewry, both religious and secular, flourished. There was a large output of books, magazines, newspapers, and other publications. Institutions of higher Jewish learning, such as the famous yeshivot of Lublin and Mir, the Yivo Institute for Jewish Research (in Vilna), and the Institute for the Science of Judaism (in Warsaw), produced well-trained graduates who later spread Jewish knowledge throughout the world.

The Jews of Poland observed Sabbaths and holidays in an atmosphere that glowed with joy and piety. Communal life abounded with a variety of political, social, philanthropic, and mutual aid organizations and institutions which helped Polish Jews cope with the many complex problems that called for action.

Jews also contributed their full measure to the general culture of Poland in science, art, literature, and music.

The Jewish community of Poland functioned under tremendous hardships of financial limitations and governmental discrimination, which drove large many into poverty and emigration. The anti-Semitism of the government and the populace at large produced economic boycotts and outbreaks of violence against Jews. Nevertheless, the Jews of Poland fought for survival with the aid of American Jewry.

Jewish War Victims

Some of the founders of the Joint Distribution Committee. Seated at the left is Felix M. Warburg, philanthropist and first JDC chairman.

The Jews of Western Europe did not regard themselves as minorities, for they had achieved complete emancipation. But the Jews in the many newly-created countries of Central and Eastern Europe were in need of protection. Despite the minority rights guarantees, they were still victims of discrimination. The only country to fully recognize their rights was the new Republic of Czechoslovakia. For several years (1918–24), Jews were granted national autonomy in Lithuania.

The territories of the Ukraine and eastern Poland had been ravaged by heavy fighting during World War I. After the war they remained a battleground, first between the Communist government of Russia and its opponents, then between Russia and Poland. In all of these conflicts, the Jews of the region suffered grievously. Tens of thousands were killed in bloody massacres; the survivors faced the problems of poverty, disease, and homelessness.

The Joint Distribution Committee

The Jews of the United States, aware of the desperate plight of their brethren across the sea, were anxious to help. Although many American Jews were poor, they contributed vast sums of money—in 1917 alone, more than $10 million. To further the relief effort, American Jewry's charitable and relief organizations consolidated into one vast body, the American Jewish Joint Distribution Committee, generally known as the JDC or the Joint. Its aim was to bring quick, effective assistance to the Jews of Russia and Poland. In addition to providing food, clothing, tools, and medicine, it would, whenever possible, help them to emigrate to other countries.

The American Jewish Congress

During World War I American Jewry was concerned about the status of the Jews of Eastern Europe. In 1918 it set up the American Jewish Congress to protect their rights. Judge Julian W. Mack was chosen president. Harry Friedenwald and Henrietta Szold, ardent Zionists, were among the vice-presidents.

The American Jewish Congress sent a delegation to the postwar peace conferences to demand recognition of Jewish rights and fulfillment of the Balfour Declaration. At the San Remo Conference it successfully lobbied for Britain to be given the Palestine mandate, with the purpose of bringing about a Jewish state.

Country	Number of Jews
Germany	250,00
England	150,000
France	50,000
Belgium, Holland, Spain, etc.	50,000
Poland, Russia, Rumania, Hungary, etc.	2,400,000
	2,900,000

Table showing the origins of Jewish immigrants to the United States up to 1922.

Jews of The Soviet Russia

Despite the huge emigration from Russia in the preceding few decades, about 2.5 million Jews remained in the Soviet Union when the war ended. They were faced with a completely new situation. On the one hand, anti-Semitism was officially outlawed. On the other, Jews were required to give up their religion and culture to become part of the new Communist order. Some Russian Jews were able to adjust to the new life, but many found it impossible to abandon their traditional way of life, language, and religion.

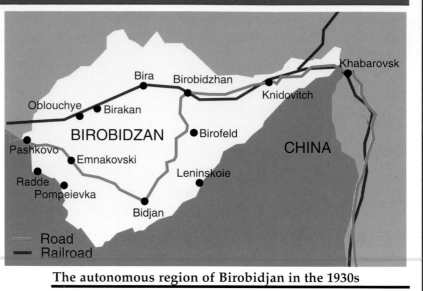

The autonomous region of Birobidjan in the 1930s

Birobidjan

The Soviet government decided to settle the Yiddish-speaking Jews in Birobidjan, a remote area in southeastern Siberia near the Manchurian border, where they could engage in farming. But life in Birobidjan turned out to be very disappointing for those who accepted the offer and settled there.

The Communist Way

The Jews of the Soviet Union hoped that they would be given all the rights of citizenship, including the freedom to preserve their religious and cultural heritage. The Communists, however, were determined to forge a new Russia with only one way of living—the Communist way. And so once again the Jews of Russia found themselves outside the accepted order. Zionists and religious leaders were declared enemies of the regime and arrested. Many Jews who had fought in the Russian Revolution came to view the new system with bitterness and disappointment. Yet for several decades many Soviet Jews continued to hope that life would improve under the new order. Their final disillusionment was not to come until after another world war even more terrible than the first.

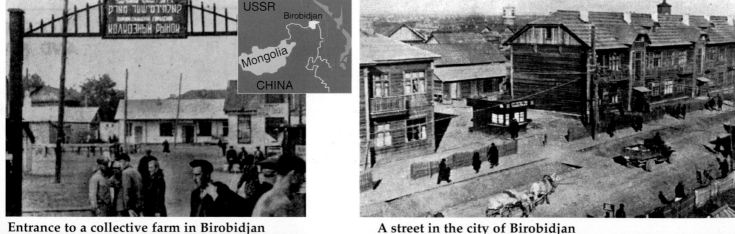

Entrance to a collective farm in Birobidjan

A street in the city of Birobidjan

Jewish Problems and Sucesses

JEWISH HIGHLIGHTS

People of the Book The Jewish Press	Jewish Institutions and People	American Zionism	Peace Conference 1919	Eastern Europe 19th century

JEWISH EVENTS • PERSONALITIES • LITERATURE

People of the Book / The Jewish Press	Jewish Institutions and People	American Zionism	Peace Conference 1919	Eastern Europe 19th century
▶ *Jewish Daily Forward* Abraham Cahan	▶ American Federation of Labor Samuel Gompers	▶ First Zionist Congress Bernard Felsenthol Gustav Gotthel	▶ Peace of Versailles Louis Marshall	▶ Poland Kehillah Educational system Yeshiva of Lublin Yeshiva of Mir
▶ The *Boston Blat* Joseph J. Shore	▶ Jewish Theological Seminary Solomon Schechter	▶ Rabbi Stephen S. Wise	▶ American Jewish Joint Distribution Committee	▶ Russian Jewish cultural life Birobidjan
	▶ Jewish personalities Louis Dembitz Brandeis Julius Rosenwald Oscar Strauss Jacob H. Schiff David Sarnoff Jacob Joseph	▶ Henrietta Szold Hadassah	American Jewish Congress	▶ Jewish war victims
	▶ Yeshiva Universiy Rabbi Norman Lamm Rabbi H. Pereira Mendes	▶ Louis Lipsky The *Maccabean*	▶ Jewish leaders Cyrus Adler Meir Berlin Leo Jung	▶ Joint Distribution Committee
	▶ Anti-Semitism Joseph Seligman Blood-libel of Damascus			▶ American Jewish Committee
	▶ American Jewish Committee Julian Mack			

WORLD HISTORY

▶ Boston ▶ New York	▶ USA	▶ Basel	▶ League of Nations Woodrow Wilson	▶ Poland ▶ Russia

The Jews In Pre-Nazi Germany

After World War I, Germany became a republic. Many Jews played an important role in its political life. The most prominent of them was Walther Rathenau (1867–1922), one of the great statesmen of his time. As Minister of Reconstruction, and later Minister of Foreign Affairs, Rathenau made every effort to improve relations between Germany and France. But reactionary German forces opposed Rathenau, and he was assassinated in 1922.

Members of the German general staff and Adolf Hitler.

The Weimar Republic

Germany's postwar government was known as the Weimar Republic. In the early 1920s Jews became prominent in the arts, sciences, education, banking, and business. For a time it seemed as if the forces of progress would triumph. The Weimar Republic struggled valiantly to solve its problems but was hampered by nationalist military organizations. Their members, yearning for the "good old days," were unable to accept the fact that Germany had been defeated in the war.

Fascism in Italy

In Italy, too, many dreamed of a powerful military regime. In 1922 the Fascist Party, headed by Benito Mussolini, who called himself Il Duce ("The Leader"), seized power. The Fascists were extreme nationalists. Everyone who did not agree with them was conveniently silenced—by imprisonment; many opponents were tortured and put to death.

Hitler and "Mein Kampf"

The German General Staff was not destroyed by the war. It just changed its name. In a short time, even though the postwar treaties forbade such weapons, German officers had made arrangements to manufacture tanks, aircraft, and even poison gas.

By 1919, all of Europe was in a deep economic depression. Millions of unemployed Germans were looking for work. This was fertile ground for the evil genius of Adolf Hitler.

Hitler had been a corporal in World War I and won an Iron Cross for bravery. After the war, he became the leader of a small political organization, the Nazi Party. In 1923, he attempted to overthrow the German government. Tried and convicted, Hitler spent nine months in jail, where he wrote the book *Mein Kampf* ("My Struggle").

No one should have been surprised by the political program Hitler adopted when he came to power, for it was detailed in *Mein Kampf*. But no one took him seriously, and few bothered to read his book.

Anti-Jewish poster issued by the Minister of Propaganda, Berlin, in 1940, with the slogan "Behind the enemy, the Jew" and in French from 1942, with the slogan "And behind the Jew."

Adolf Hitler and Nazism

A new kind of fascism now developed in Germany. In addition to the militarists, there were many other groups that disliked the Weimar government. Many were bitter about Germany's defeat in the war and its loss of territories and prestige. These groups, which fought the democratic builders of the new Germany, eventually found a leader in Adolf Hitler.

Hitler promised the disappointed groups a different, powerful Germany—a Germany that would conquer the world and become an empire such as it had been under the Kaiser; indeed, he promised to make Germany even greater than it had been before.

The Nazis expounded the notion that the German people were a "master race," superior to all others. They and the other "Nordic" peoples, so the Nazis declared, were the master race of mankind which would lead and dominate the world and wipe out all inferior peoples.

Hitler's ideas were not taken seriously in other countries. Even many Germans laughed at them. Nevertheless, Hitler succeeded in winning more and more followers who were blindly devoted to their leader and his ideas.

The Nazi Rise to Power

Throughout the 1920s, the Nazis slowly gained in strength. But it was not until the late 1920s, which saw the combination of a decaying economic order and financial backing from some wealthy industrialists, that the party gained significant popular support. Hitler received funds from Fritz Thiessen of the German steel trust, Emil Kidorf of the German coal industry, and other wealthy businessmen.

In the Reichstag elections of 1928, the Nazis won about 800,000 votes and 12 seats. By 1930, the Nazis had gained over 6 million votes and 107 seats. In 1932, the Nazis received almost 14 million votes, 120 seats, and became Germany's largest political party.

Stormtroopers

Following the example of Mussolini in Italy, the Nazi Party set up a quasi-military unit called the SA, or stormtroopers, to terrorize its opponents and disrupt their political activities. Dressed in military uniforms, trained like soldiers, the stormtroopers marched through the streets, shouting, singing, and breaking up orderly meetings of democratic groups. They started fights and made trouble. In addition to the SA, an elite group called the SS was organized to protect party leaders and maintain discipline among the members.

DER DEUTSCHE STUDENT

KÄMPFT FÜR FÜHRER UND VOLK
IN DER MANNSCHAFT DES NSD-STUDENTENBUNDES

Racist attitudes in Germany developed from the idea that the Aryan-Nordic race was superior to all other races. To the Nazis, the Teuton stood for goodness, strength, courage, and beauty. Although the Aryan myth existed prior to the Nazis, they turned it into a reality which was readily applied to society.

Hitler Assumes Power

The Great Depression of the 1930s caused great suffering throughout the Western world. Many Germans were unemployed and desperate. During the years of the Depression, Hitler's following increased rapidly.

The Nazis in Power

In 1933, Adolf Hitler came into power, marking the end of the Weimar Republic. The Nazis took over the country. All democratic organizations were systematically dissolved. Germany was in the hands of uniformed men, the SA and the SS. The people were forced to spend their time in military parades and demonstrations to show their loyalty to Hitler—their Fuehrer, or "Leader."

The German people adored the tramp of massed men, the music of military bands, the waving of banners and the conquering songs of thousands. Hitler catered to this feeling, and in a short time, the Germans were ready for a war of conquest.

Behind this masquerade of zeal and devotion the Nazis conducted a reign of terror. Aided by the police, Hitler's stormtroopers made thousands of arrests. No man or woman who had a different point of view or refused to support the new Nazi regime was safe.

Germany: Land of Fear

Germany became a land of fear. People whispered stories of a new kind of prison—the

Adolf Hitler

Nazi stormtroopers gathering Jewish books for destruction.

concentration camp. In Hitler's first years of power, the Nazi concentration camps were filled mostly with political opponents. But from the very beginning Hitler declared war on the Jews. He used them as a scapegoat, inciting latent anti-Semitic prejudices. Cruelties against Jews were encouraged, and one humiliating restriction after another was imposed upon them.

Hitler's main ambition was to forge a Germany that would follow him blindly into a great, victorious war. All obstacles hindering the unity and mindless obedience of such a Germany had to be removed. The German people became afraid to speak freely, even to think. German history was shamelessly rewritten in accordance with the new Nazi viewpoint. Many respected educators and scientists were removed from their posts and replaced by loyal Nazis. The new replacements did as they were told, and helped fashion a Germany that would follow Hitler to war.

More and more Jews were subjected to restrictions. Jewish lawyers, physicians, teachers, scientists, journalists, and actors lost their jobs. Jewish places of business were boycotted by Hitler's party troops and stormed by angry mobs. Jews were insulted publicly and physically attacked.

The 1936 Summer Olympics

In the spring of 1936, Hitler with no opposition, carried out the military occupation of the demilitarized Rhineland. In the summer of that year Berlin was the host city to the Olympic Games. The foreign visitors were impressed with the friendliness of the Germans and enjoyed the red carpet hospitality of the Third Reich.

Behind the Scenes

Everything was open to the visitors except the torture chambers of the stormtroopers and the misery of the concentration camps. The Hollywood facade was wonderful. But behind the scenes, the Nazis refused to allow Jewish athletes to compete for Germany. Gretel Bergmann, a high jumper, and Bruno Lampert, a long jumper, were purposely left off the German team.

The Olympic Games

The opening ceremony at Olympic Stadium in Berlin was reviewed by Hitler, and cheers greeted the teams that dipped their colors and saluted Nazi-style. All other athletes were acknowledged only with silence from the crowd.

The American Controversy

The anti-Semitic and anti-black policies of Adolf Hitler had created a controversy in the United States. Avery Brundage, head of the American Olympic Committee, had urged that the United States should participate in the Berlin games. Judge Jeremiah T. Mahoney, a Catholic and president of the Amateur Athletic Union, argued for a boycott by which no American team would be sent to represent the United States.

Brundage claimed that the boycott plan was a Jewish-Communist conspiracy. He was able to defeat the resolution calling for a boycott. Mahoney resigned as AAU president, and Brundage succeeded him becoming the head of both the AAU and the AOC.

The American Track Team

The American track team included 10 black athletes. The German newspapers called them "the black auxiliary," and printed stories which degraded them. Cornelius Johnson, a black athlete, achieved a record leap in the high jump. Hitler had personally congratulated the first two track and field winners, but he deliberately snubbed Johnson by leaving his box in the stadium.

The blacks on the American track and field team won eight gold medals, three silver medals, and two bronze medals outscoring every national track and field team. Jesse Owens, grandson of slaves, won four gold medals.

Another political incident took place when two American Jewish runners, Marty Glickman and Sam Stoller, were dropped from the 400-meter relay team by coach Dean Cromwell.

The 1936 Berlin games will always be remembered as the "Nazi Olympics." Stormtroopers swastikas, anti-black and anti-Semitic propaganda destroyed what should have been the non-political competition of the Olympics.

Jesse Owens shatters records, showing what "non-Aryan" athletes can do.

Kristallnacht / 1938

In 1935 the German Reichstag passed the so-called Nuremberg Laws, which deprived Germany's Jews of citizenship and officially demoted them to an inferior status. During the next several years, Jewish businesses, homes, and property were expropriated.

On November 9, 1938, the Nazis staged a nationwide terror action that became known as Kristallnacht ("Crystal Night") because of the many broken windows.

Hundreds of synagogues in Germany and Austria were set afire, and about 10,000 Jewish businesses were destroyed and looted. Fifty Jews were murdered by organized mobs of blood-thirsty Nazis.

The excuse for this outrage was the assassination of a German diplomat, Ernst vom Rath, by Herschel Grynszpan, son of Jewish refugees.

Grynszpan, in Paris, had received a letter from his sister in which she stated that the Grynszpan family, together with all Polish Jews living in Germany, had been arrested and deported. Seeking revenge for the suffering of his family. Grynszpan, who was 17 years old, bought a gun, went to the German embassy, and shot Vom Rath.

By 1939 Jews had been completely eliminated from the economic, cultural, and governmental life of Germany and Austria.

Herschel Grynszpan

Beginning in 1939, the passports of all Jews were marked with the letter "J". Also, the name Israel was added to the names of all Jewish males, and Sarah to all Jewish females.

Kristallnacht was an anti-Jewish pogrom on November 9-10, 1938. Jewish property, businesses, and synagogues were attacked and burned by Nazi mobs.

The Voyage of the Doomed

In a speech delivered on January 30, 1939, Adolf Hitler declared, "If a World War breaks out, the Jewish race in Europe will be eliminated." Thousands of frightened Jews fled from Germany to seek refuge in other countries. Thousands more would have done so but could not, because it was difficult to find a country that would allow them in.

Outside Germany, few people cared about what was happening there, and many felt that Hitler and his Nazis were a temporary phenomenon that would disappear. An anti-German boycott was organized in a few places, but it had little effect.

The countries of Europe and the Americas admitted only a small number of Jews. The immigration process was often controlled by anti-Semitic officials. Some officials would only cooperate if given a bribe.

The voyage of the *St. Louis* illustrates the indifference of the Western nations.

The St. Louis

On May 13, 1939, the passenger ship *St. Louis* left Hamburg with 930 German Jewish refugees aboard, all carrying landing certificates for Cuba. When the ship arrived in Havana, the Cuban government would not allow them to land. For nine days the *St. Louis* circled off Havana and Florida. On June 5, Cuba said the refugees could go ashore if they posted a $500,000 bond within 24 hours, but it was impossible to accumulate so large a sum in so short a time.

The United States, too, refused to admit the passengers. On June 6, the ship headed back to Europe. On June 11, the captain threatened to beach it on the English coast in order to delay its return to Germany. The British allowed 280 "enemy aliens" to enter.

On June 17, the *St. Louis* docked in the Belgian port of Antwerp and the Jews were allowed to land. Within 12 months the German blitzkrieg had overrun Europe and they were sent to the concentration camps where they ultimately were murdered.

Not just the passengers on the *St. Louis* but millions of Jews could have been saved from the Nazis, but the U.S. State Department chose to ignore the signs of their impending doom.

Shipload of Jews pleading for entrance to any country that would accept them.

Where Did the German Jews Go?

Some Jews were able to escape from Nazi Germany. Among the refugees were prominent bankers and merchants, writers and scientists.

Some went to European countries, others to the United States, where the first German Jews had settled in the mid-19th century. Many German Jews who had formerly ignored or opposed Zionism now emigrated to Palestine.

The Fourth Aliyah / 1924–1928

The Fourth Aliyah was of a different social background: It brought shopkeepers and artisans, mostly from Poland, where economic restrictions were being applied. The majority of the new arrivals settled in the cities of Tel Aviv, Haifa, and Jerusalem.

During the years 1924 to 1929, some 50,000 Jews came on aliyah to Israel. At the end of this period, the Jewish population of Israel was about 170,000.

The Fifth Aliyah / 1929–1939

The Land of Israel beckoned as a refuge. Although German Jews had often been ambivalent about Zionism, many of them now turned to the land of their ancestors. As a result the Fifth Aliyah, which extended from 1929 to 1939, was made up mostly of settlers from Germany and adjoining areas. The olim included students expelled from school by the Nazis, musicians, actors, artists, and writers whose work had been condemned as decadent, professionals unable to find work because of anti-Semitic restrictions, and manufacturers and businessmen no longer permitted to function in Germany. The skills, experience, and capital they brought had a major impact on the development of the Palestinian economy.

The Hebrew University was founded on Mount Scopus in Jerusalem in 1925. The first books for the library were brought on a donkey.

Many German Jews, however, hesitated to leave their homeland, the land where their ancestors had lived for hundreds of years. Like many other Germans, they still believed that Hitler's regime would soon come to an end.

June 7, 1936 edition of the *Palestine Post* detailing the beginning of the widespread terror and destruction which Arab uprisings were to inflict upon Jewish settlements during the next three years.

Henrietta Szold

One of the most important American Zionist activists was Henrietta Szold (1860–1945). In 1912, she founded Hadassah, an organization of American Zionist women. Over the years since, Hadassah has devoted itself to establishing hospitals and health and welfare services in Israel. These are open to everyone in the country, Jews, Arabs, Muslims, and Christians alike. The Hadassah Hospital and Medical Center in Jerusalem is widely regarded as the finest and most up-to-date medical facility in the entire Middle East.

Youth Aliyah

During the years preceding World War II, Henrietta Szold also organized Youth Aliyah to rescue as many children and adolescents as possible from Nazi Germany. Once the youngsters arrived in Palestine, Youth Aliyah placed them in homes and helped them to obtain schooling and vocational training. All this was done with the help of funds raised in America and other free countries. Youth Aliyah saved thousands of children. Their parents, naturally enough, found it difficult to part with them. Many fathers and mothers did not succeed in leaving Germany, but they were glad that at least their children would be safe.

The Growth of the Yishuv

The Jewish community of Palestine in the years before the State of Israel was founded was known as the Yishuv. Throughout the 1920s and 1930s it steadily grew larger and more diversified.

New industrial centers and kibbutzim were founded. Tel Aviv, founded in 1909 as a garden suburb of Jaffa, became a beautiful modern city. Stockade-and-tower settlements, designed with an eye to defense against Arab marauders, sprang up throughout the land, especially in the undeveloped Negev area.

The Hebrew University

On the outskirts of the Old City of Jerusalem, in the area where Moses Montefiore had once built model houses, a new Jerusalem was coming into existence. In 1925 the Hebrew University was founded on Mount Scopus. Its first lecture was given by the great physicist Albert Einstein (1879–1955), and its first chancellor was Judah Magnes (1877–1948), a prominent American Reform rabbi. Under his leadership, scientists, scholars, and educators from all over the world now pursued their work in Jerusalem.

Today the Hebrew University has two main campuses, the original one on Mount Scopus and a new one at Givat Ram. Its facilities include medical and professional schools, an agricultural institute, and Israel's National and University Library, with over 2 million books.

Henrietta Szold (1860-1945), humanitarian and Zionist leader. After a distinguished career as educator and editor, she founded Hadassah and settled in Jerusalem, where she supervised Hadassah's social services and headed Youth Aliyah.

The Arab Situation

The progress the Jewish settlers were making was viewed with great anxiety by rich Arab landowners and many Muslim leaders. Arab propagandists stirred up hatred against the Jews, and anti-Jewish riots broke out repeatedly.

In 1936 the Grand Mufti of Jerusalem, religious head of Palestine's Muslim populace, helped to stir up a major Arab revolt. When the British tried to arrest him, he escaped to Lebanon and then to Germany. There he publicly endorsed Hitler's anti-Jewish program and spent the World War II years broadcasting Nazi propaganda to Muslims around the world.

As Jewish immigration increased, due to persecution in Europe, and Arab hostility intensified, the situation in Palestine became more and more difficult. In 1939 a British commission of inquiry proposed that the country should be divided into two parts, one Jewish, the other Arab. The Arabs rejected the proposed partition and stepped up their anti-Jewish activities. But the Yishuv kept right on growing.

was from Germany, Austria, and Czechoslovakia. As the Nazi terror spread, Jews came to Palestine from Poland, Rumania, Bulgaria, and Yugoslavia. A few even managed to leave Russia, despite the danger of being arrested or killed by Communist border guards.

The people of the Yishuv learned to live together and to know one other. To a great extent this was made possible by the fact that they had a common language—Hebrew. The language of the Bible had been transformed into a modern tongue. It was used by poets and writers, scientists, farmers and workers, cab drivers, and housewives doing their shopping. Newspapers were published in Hebrew, unions recruited members in Hebrew, and the Va'ad Leumi, the Yishuv's governing body, conducted its affairs in Hebrew.

In the land which had been the scene of biblical history, a new Jewish community was building a new life using the language of the Bible in everyday speech for the first time in 2,000 years.

New Immigrants

The population of the Yishuv was made up of Jews from many lands and many walks of life. It included Jews from Iraq, Yemen, and North Africa who were very similar in culture to their Arab neighbors. There were many from Eastern Europe, and a few from the United States. In the 1930s, with Hitler in power, most of the new immigration

A 1948 Histadrut poster issued after the War of Independence features the theme of physical labor and vigilance.

A stockade-and-tower settlement established during the 1930s. Despite British disapproval, the settlements were set up under cover of night. Walls provided protection against attacking Arabs.

The Evian Conference / 1938

In May 1938, officials of 32 nations met at Evian-les-Bains, in France, to find a way of dealing with the flow of refugees from Nazi Germany. The United States was represented by Myron C. Taylor, former chairman of the U.S. Steel Corporation. With the exception of the Netherlands and Denmark, every country made clear its unwillingness to accept significant numbers of refugees.

Australia, with vast, unpopulated areas, announced: "As we have no real racial problem, we are not desirous of importing one."

New Zealand refused to lift its immigration restrictions.

Britain declared that its colonial empire "contained no territory suitable to the large-scale settlement of Jewish refugees."

Canada only wanted immigrants with farming experience and would take no one else.

France, whose population already included 200,000 refugees and 3 million aliens, stressed that it had reached its saturation point.

Nicaragua, Honduras, Costa Rica, and Panama issued a joint statement that they could accept no "traders or intellectuals."

Argentina, with a population one-tenth that of the United States, reported that it had welcomed almost as many refugees as the United States and hence could not be counted on for large-scale immigration.

And the United States, the nation at whose initiative the conference had convened, what would it offer? The answer was soon forthcoming. The United States, with its tradition of asylum, its vast land mass, and its unlimited resources, agreed, for the first time, to accept its full, legal quota of 27,370 immigrants annually from Germany and Austria—a totally inadequate figure in light of the huge number of Jews desperately seeking someplace to go. That was the major American concession made at Evian.

Some historians feel that the Evian Conference taught the Nazis that the world, for all its moralistic posturing, was unwilling to do much about the persecution of Jews in Germany. Noting that Evian spelled backwards is naive, they say that the Jewish delegates were naive to ever have expected help from the assembled nations.

FOREIGN-BORN POPULATION IN THE UNITED STATES IN 1920

Immigrant quotas for each country were fixed in such a way as to keep the proportion of foreign-born Americans the same as it was in 1920. In practice it proved superfluous, since in the thirties immigration dropped to an average of just over 10,000 a year.

The British White Paper / 1939

With the growth of the Yishuv, Arab resistance increased. The English, unwilling to antagonize the Arabs, could not deal with this friction between Arabs and Jews. The Jews secretly organized their own defense groups of men and women of the Yishuv, farmers and workers, city and country folk. These citizens trained to defend themselves against Arab terrorists who preyed upon isolated settlements. This group of defenders took the name of Haganah ("defense").

The White Paper

The British White Paper of 1939 declared that in 10 years Palestine would be partitioned, and in the meantime Jewish immigration would be severely restricted. This document was a complete and utter disavowal of the Balfour Declaration and of Great Britain's international obligations under the Mandate. The British appeasement of the Arabs was motivated by fear that the Arabs would support Germany, and threaten England's hold on the Middle East, if war broke out in Europe.

In 1939 the British government invited Iraq, Jordan, and Egypt, the Palestinian Arabs, the Jewish Agency, and Jews in Britain and America to send representatives to London to discuss the political future of Palestine. The Arabs refused to meet with the Jews, and two separate sets of meetings were held.

Prime Minister Neville Chamberlain presides over the Jewish representatives at the abortive London Conference of February 1939. Shortly after the conference the British government published its White Paper, freezing Jewish immigration to Palestine. The participants included Nahum Goldmann, Chaim Weizmann, David Ben-Gurion, and Moshe Sharett, each of whom became an important figure in the State of Israel.

The Desperate Search for Refuge

The publication of the White Paper of 1939 brought consternation to Jews everywhere. What would happen now to the Jews in the lands under Nazi domination? Where would they go? Restrictions on immigration were increasing in every country; even the gates of America were closing, for so many Jews had emigrated there that the German, Polish, Czech, and Austrian quotas were now filled.

The Jews of Europe went wherever they could. However, it became increasingly difficult to find a place of refuge. Some fled to South America, to Africa, and even to war-torn Shanghai. But even so, only a few could manage to escape at this late date. President Franklin D. Roosevelt had called an international conference at Evianles-Bains, France, in 1938 to discuss ways and means of saving European Jewry. The conference was a dismal failure. The results of other endeavors were equally meager.

Secret message from a British spy warning of the activities of two "underground" ships, the *Colorado* and the *Atratti*. In 1939, these two ships, crammed with desperate Polish-Jewish refugees escaping Hitler's Holocaust, were intercepted by British warships and turned back. There is evidence that some of the spies were Jewish traitors who sold out to the British.

Aliyah Bet

In these dark days a desperate new kind of aliyah was started. Operating illegally and in secret, it was called Aliyah Bet—Immigration Wave B. Agents of the Haganah, the Yishuv's underground defense force, secretly began transporting refugees from Europe to Palestine. Some of their ships were intercepted by the British, but many others got through, Their human cargo would be landed on deserted beaches, late at night, and quickly spirited away to hiding places on the kibbutzim.

A boatload of "illegal" immigrants landing in Palestine under cover of darkness

The Western Democracies

The Western democracies feared another conflict on the scale of World War I and did everything possible to appease Hitler. His appetite for aggression was endless. After swallowing up Austria and Czechoslovakia without having to strike a blow, he attacked Poland in September 1939. The Poles fought back; Britain and France, aware that appeasement did not work, declared war on Germany.

The three leaders of the war against the Nazis with their advisors. *From left to right,* Winston Churchill of England, Franklin Delano Roosevelt of the United States, and Stalin of Russia.

The Second World War Begins

On April 9, 1940 the Germans attacked and overran Norway and Denmark. Soon after, Holland, Belgium, Luxembourg and France were attacked. None of the armies could withstand the fast-moving German armor and their deadly air strikes.

By June 22, France sued for peace and 330,000 British and French troops were evacuated from the beaches of Dunkirk to England.

Millions of Jews were now under German control. Hitler felt that he was now in a position to solve the "Jewish Question." As Hitler saw it, the Jewish Question was simply the fact that Jews existed. He and his criminal cohorts devised a "Final Solution" as a way to eliminate the Jews. In all countries under Nazi control, Jews were rounded up, confined to ghettos, or shipped to concentration camps.

The Blitzkrieg

At first, Hitler had everything his own way, and his armed forces was victorious on every front. By 1941 his troops had conquered most of Europe: Norway, Denmark, Holland, Belgium, France, Yugoslavia, and Greece. Britain stood alone and was hard-pressed, despite Lend-Lease aid from the United States. Then Hitler attacked the Soviet Union. His winning streak continued for a while, but by 1943, with both the Soviet Union and the United States allied against him, the tide finally turned.

The German commander's first announcement: "The German soldiers have come to free the population from Communist bondage. The Jews must wear armbands with a Star of David, they must not leave their quarters; they must carry out their required work and yield their radios."

The Master Race

The Final Solution

Germany's victories brought millions of Jews under Nazi control. The Final Solution was now put into effect to kill all of Europe's Jews. The details of the program were worked out by a group of Nazi officials at the Wannsee Conference in January 1942.

In every occupied country, Jews would be rounded up, confined to ghettos, then shipped to concentration camps. Most would be killed outright. Some would be used as slave laborers until they were too worn out, from starvation and harsh treatment, to be useful. Among the most notorious of the death camps were Chelmo, Sobibor, Treblinka, and Auschwitz. The treatment of the inmates was almost beyond rational description. By the end of the war, somewhere between 3 million and 4 million Jewish inmates had been gassed and their bodies incinerated. Overall about 6 million Jews were killed. Many thousands of non-Jews, opponents of the Nazis, were also killed in the camps.

After the war Eli Wiesel, Primo Levi, and other survivors wrote gripping accounts of their terrible experiences in the camps. In addition, the Nazis kept methodical records of what they were doing, and some of the more sadistic took photographs as "souvenirs."

SS Colonel Adolf Otto Eichmann was chief of operations in the scheme to exterminate all of European Jewry. At the end of the war, he escaped to Argentina, but in 1960 was kidnapped by the Israelis. Eichmann was tried before the Jerusalem District Court and was sentenced to death by hanging. Eichmann was the only criminal ever put to death in Israel. His body was cremated and his ashes were scattered over the Mediterranean.

Jewish men, women, and children being loaded onto cattle cars for shipment to the death camps.

A heap of concentration camp victims.

Anne Frank

Growing up in Frankfurt, Germany, Anne Frank (1929–1945) dreamed about writing a novel and a book of poems. Sadly, Anne's dream was shattered by the rise of Nazism. In 1933, the Frank family fled to Amsterdam to escape the Nazi regime. When the Germans occupied Holland in 1940, the Franks once again found themselves under the thumb of Hitler.

Into Hiding

Two years later in 1942, the Germans began deporting Holland's Jews, supposedly to work in labor camps. The Frank family and four other people went into hiding in the attic of a building owned by Anne Frank's father. War and conflict bring out the best and the worst in people. The hidden Jews were kept alive by friendly Gentiles who put their own lives in danger to bring them food and other necessities. However, an act of betrayal resulted in their discovery by the German police. All eight people in the attic were caught and sent to Bergen-Belsen, where Anne and six of the others died; only her father survived.

The Diary

During her time in hiding, Anne retained her equilibrium by writing short stories, beginning a novel, and keeping a diary. Anne's diary describes the constant fear of being discovered, the petty irritations and discomforts of being confined and living at close quarters with others, and the hopes and dreams of an adolescent filled with the spirit of life. In her diary she wrote, "I hear the approaching thunder which will destroy us. I can feel the sufferings of millions, and yet, if I look into the heavens, I think that it will all come right and that this cruelty will end, and peace and tranquility will return."

After the war, Anne's diary was discovered and published. It received instant acclaim and has been translated into many languages, dramatized on Broadway, and made into a film. The house in Amsterdam where the Frank family hid is now a museum.

Anne Frank's voice became the voice of six million vanished Jewish souls.

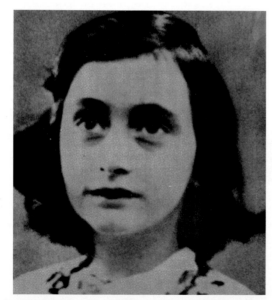

Anne Frank, the author of the "single most compelling personal account of the Holocaust"

The Anne Frank house in Amsterdam is now a museum.

The Dutch Church cooperated and issued baptismal certificates to Jews. Many Jews were saved because of these certificates.

Auschwitz

Auschwitz, the largest extermination complex, was located at a railroad junction in southern Poland. It consisted of three camps.

Auschwitz I was a labor camp and administration center. Within this camp were armament plants belonging to Siemens and Krupp.

Auschwitz II had a special extermination area called Birkenau where at least 1 million Jews were murdered. Its four gas chambers, using Zyklon-B, exterminated over 12,000 victims each day.

Auschwitz III had a huge I. G. Farben plant in which Jewish slaves labored to manufacture synthetic rubber from coal. The life expectancy of a Jewish worker in the rubber plant was three months; those in the coal mines that supplied the plant lasted 30 days.

The process of mass extermination was carried out with the full knowledge and cooperation of many business executives. They benefited by taking over Jewish-run

The Nazi death camp of Auschwitz. Thousands of Jews were gassed, shot, and burned to death there.

factories and businesses. They also benefited from the labor of the slaves who worked in their factories. I. G. Farben also earned a handsome profit by manufacturing Zyklon-B, the gas used in the extermination chambers.

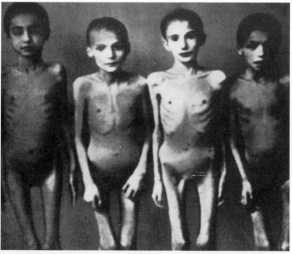

Josef Mengele was physician of the Auschwitz camp, where he conducted cruel medical experiments on Jewish inmates. After the war, Mengele was traced to Argentina, but he escaped. These are some of Mengele's victims.

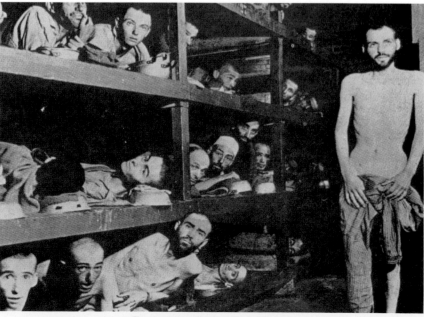

Concentration camp photo.

Gas Chambers and Ovens

Camps like Auschwitz, with their mass-production death machinery, were a product of German efficiency. Originally the Nazis had begun killing Jews by means of starvation and firing squads. By the winter of 1941, 1.5 million Jews had been eliminated, but the killing methods were too slow and inefficient. After a number of experiments, the system used at Auschwitz was devised.

Lined up at the railway station for shipment to a concentration camp.

The victims were assembled and packed in special sealed trains. On arriving in the camps they were forced into undressing rooms where they were shaved by barbers and stripped of their possessions. They were then packed into chambers and gassed. This highly efficient killing process could kill 2,000 Jews in the space of five minutes.

The Nazis mobilized Jewish slaves called Sonderkommandos to "process" the bodies. They removed gold fillings from teeth, shaved off the hair, then piled the bodies into crematoria where they were burned. In the meantime the clothing, hair, and other possessions were packed and sent to Germany for use in the war effort. Even the ashes of the victims were used— as fertilizer for German farms.

To minimize the possibility of a revolt in the camp, the Sonderkommandos were periodically exterminated and replaced with fresh slaves. Many of them, driven mad by their macabre duties and the fate of their fellow Jews, willingly joined the victims in the gas chambers rather than continue to do the bidding of the Nazis.

A German indoctrinating new troops on the fastest way to murder a Jew. Note his handiwork at the bottom of the pit.

Sonderkommandos at an extermination camp rushing to perform their duties. They too ended up in gas chambers and in mass graves.

American Jews Speak Up

In September 1941 the Germans began deporting Jews from elsewhere in Europe to concentration camps in Poland. The World Jewish Congress brought this to the attention of the Allied authorities in London and Washington.

The Morgenthau Diaries

In his diaries, Secretary of the Treasury Henry Morgenthau Jr. (1891–1967), a Jewish member of President Roosevelt's cabinet, accused State Department officials of suppressing information about the atrocities.

Anti-Nazi demonstration in New York City on May 10, 1933.

According to some historians, hundreds of thousands of Jewish lives could have been saved if the White House and the State Department had not sabotaged efforts on their behalf. It has been suggested that President Roosevelt was aware of the deportations but deliberately refused to interfere.

The Morgenthau diaries record, "On December 17, 1943, the State Department received a cable from London. . . . the British Foreign Office was concerned with the difficulty of resettling considerable numbers of Jews should they be released. For this reason we are reluctant to approve financial arrangements. The financial arrangements would have permitted the World Jewish Congress to spend 100 million Rumanian leis for the release of thousands of Jewish children in France and Rumania."

While the politicians debated, millions of Jews were being gassed and incinerated into piles of ashes.

The Extermination Plot

On August 8, 1942 Gerhard Regner, the representative of the World Jewish Congress in Geneva, sent a telegram to the State Department detailing the mass murder of Jews taking place in Nazi-occupied Europe. The information came from the Allied underground, German deserters, and a report by SS Officer Kurt Gerstein, who had served in three extermination camps.

Sumner Welles, the Deputy Secretary of State, did not disclose the contents of the telegram to President Roosevelt. By the winter of 1942, information of Nazi atrocities had become public knowledge and the Allies could no longer ignore the facts. On December 17, 1942 they issued a statement condemning the mass exterminations.

Pope Pius XII, the head of the Roman Catholic Church, refused even to condemn the atrocities, explaining that the reports were exaggerated for propaganda purposes. To this day, the Vatican has not fully explained or dealt with the pope's failure to take action.

Why Auschwitz Was Not Bombed

Although the Allies knew about Auschwitz, they made no attempt to interfere with the killings. The Jewish Agency pressed the Allies to bomb the gas chambers and the railroad tracks leading to the camp. All such requests were turned down with the excuse that the operation would endanger the lives of the pilots and had no clear military purpose.

British Prime Minister Winston Churchill, who advocated the bombing, wrote to Anthony Eden, his Foreign Secretary, "There is no doubt that this is the most horrible crime ever committed in the history of the world."

The Allies certainly had the capability of bombing Auschwitz. This was demonstrated in August of 1944, when American aircraft attacked the synthetic rubber plant there. In addition, American planes based in Italy regularly bombed synthetic oil factories less than 5 miles from the gas chambers.

Why the Allies failed to bomb Auschwitz has never been fully explained. Had they done so, it is possible that many lives might have been saved.

The Brand Mission

In 1944 Adolf Eichmann, the Nazi official in charge of exterminating the Jews of Hungary, approached Joel Brand, a member of the Hungarian Zionist underground, and offered a deal. The German government would trade 100,000 Hungarian Jews for 10,000 trucks. Eichmann promised that the trucks would be used only on the eastern front against the Russians. Brand passed on this strange offer, but nothing came of it because the trucks would have helped the German war effort, and there was no way of knowing whether Eichmann could be trusted.

Meanwhile, on July 2, 1944, Allied planes bombed Budapest, the capital of Hungary. On July 7, fearing further raids, Admiral Horthy, the dictator of Hungary, halted all deportations of Jews. In the preceding three months, over 450,000 had been murdered.

On September 13, 1944, American airplanes bombed the industrial complex near Auschwitz. Several bombs were dropped by mistake on the camp itself, killing 15 SS men and scores of prisoners and workers.

The Warsaw Ghetto

The Judenrat

When the Germans captured Warsaw in 1939, there were 400,000 Jews living there. The Nazis confined them to a ghetto about 1 mile square and set up a Judenrat, headed by Adam Czerniakow (1880–1942), to govern the ghetto and carry out their orders.

The Judenrat members faced many very difficult moral decisions. They wanted to be able to help their fellow Jews but often had to do terrible things, such as selecting people for deportation. By forcing the Judenrat members to do this, and thereby making them unwilling accomplices to the Final Solution, the Nazis were purposely trying to degrade them. While the existence of the Judenrat seemed to give the Jews some control over their destiny, in reality it had no power to do anything except enforce Nazi orders. Refusal to carry out orders resulted in severe punishment.

To the extent possible, the Judenrat tried to alleviate conditions in the ghetto. It maintained order and established hospitals, kitchens, schools, and recreation facilities. Clandestine religious services were also held, as were lectures and musical recitations. The ghetto residents also put out underground publications in Yiddish, Hebrew, and Polish with information on German activities and how to sabotage factories. In 1942, deportations to Treblinka began on a mass scale. Three days later Adam Czerniakow committed suicide rather than cooperate with the deportations.

The Ghetto Uprising

In the next few months the great majority of the ghetto's residents were deported and killed. On April 18, 1943 the underground

Dr. Janusz Korczak, a physician, writer and educator, headed a children's orphanage in the Warsaw Ghetto. On August 12, 1942, he accompanied the children to the gas chambers, although he himself did not have to go.

Fifty Jewish combat groups—a thousand men and women armed with 80 rifles, three light machine guns, a few hundred revolvers, and 1,000 hand grenades—put up a desperate fight against 2,000 members of the occupying forces under SS General Stroop, who had been ordered to destroy the Warsaw Ghetto.

learned that the Germans intended to wipe out the 50,000 remaining Jews. Everyone took shelter in carefully designed bunkers, and the 1,000 members of the ghetto's fighting organization, armed with homemade bombs and a few guns, prepared for the hopeless battle. Every man, woman, and child in the ghetto became a warrior.

On Passover morning, April 19, 1943, a heavily armed SS brigade moved into the ghetto. The surprised Nazi troops came under fire and suffered many losses in dead and wounded. To avoid street fighting, the Germans used artillery and flame-throwers.

It took four weeks of heavy fighting to obliterate the ghetto. When all the buildings were destroyed, the SS moved in with poison gas to kill the Jews who remained alive in hidden bunkers. A few survivors escaped through the sewers to other parts of Warsaw.

The Yishuv Fights

The Jewish Brigade

During World War II the men and women of the Yishuv gave valiant aid to Britain in the fight against Nazi tyranny. At the outset, David Ben-Gurion, the head of the Jewish Agency, spoke for all the Jews of Palestine: "We will fight the war as if there were no White Paper," he said, "and we will fight the White Paper as if there were no war."

Very few Palestinian Arabs fought in the war, but many Jewish settlers volunteered to serve in the British Army. The Nazis, anxious for a foothold in the Middle East, flooded the area with agents and propaganda. They found many sympathizers among extreme Arab nationalists who hated the British and opposed Jewish immigration to Palestine.

Eventually, the British permitted the Palestinian Jewish soldiers to organize their own Jewish Brigade and fight under their own blue-and-white flag, emblazoned with the Star of David.

Behind Enemy Lines

Volunteers from the Haganah carried out dangerous assignments behind enemy lines. Several were dropped by parachute into Nazi-occupied territory to make contact with the local resistance movements.

The Jewish fighters from Palestine who were parachuted behind enemy lines were part of the British intelligence service. They performed many missions for the Allies, as well as special missions for the Jewish people. Returning to their native lands using false names and false passports, they tried to organize ways to help Jews escape from the Nazi death camps. Many of them were captured and executed as spies.

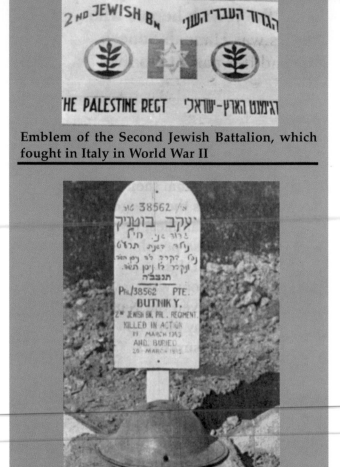

Emblem of the Second Jewish Battalion, which fought in Italy in World War II

Private Yaakov Butnik of the Second Jewish Battalion was killed in action in Italy on March 19, 1945.

Six volunteers who were about to parachute into occupied Europe to help their fellow Jews. Most of them were captured and executed by the Nazis.

Hannah Senesh

One of the Jewish heroes who operated in secret against the Nazis was Hannah Senesh (1921–1944). She had left her parents and a comfortable home in Budapest to live the life of a pioneer in Palestine. She was parachuted into Yugoslavia, where she contacted the resistance and aided their underground operations. After this mission was accomplished she made her way to Hungary to bring help to the Jews. There she was captured and put to death by the Nazis. Hannah Senesh had a strong, dedicated spirit. Before she died she wrote a poem, "Blessed Is the Match," in which she compared herself to a fiery match, which kindles a flame and is itself consumed in performing this task.

Enzo Sereni

Another hero was Enzo Sereni (1905–1944), an Italian Jew whose father had been a physician to the royal family of Italy. After going to Palestine as a pioneer, Sereni worked for the Haganah for years. While on a secret mission in German-occupied Italy, he was captured and killed.

Enzo Sereni (*second from right*), **with Italian fellow officers, in 1926.**

Hannah Senesh wrote this short letter before she parachuted into Yugoslavia.

The passport of Hannah Senesh

Leo Baeck—Hero of the Concentration Camps

There was another kind of heroism during this trying time—the quiet heroism displayed by Jews in the German concentration camps. Many of these martyrs preserved a spirit of hope and compassion despite bestial treatment by the Nazis.

Leo Baeck

Rabbi Leo Baeck (1873–1956), a brilliant preacher and a leader of liberal Judaism, was the spiritual leader of the Berlin Jewish community. When the Nazis came to power, Dr. Baeck, an old man of great courage and dignity, devoted himself entirely to the welfare of the Jewish community. He had many opportunities to leave Germany, but chose to remain there, ministering to his people and serving as head of the Reichsvertretung, the council which represented German Jewry before the Nazi government.

Rabbi Leo Baeck

Theresienstadt

In 1943, Baeck was sent to the concentration camp of Theresienstadt. Despite the intolerable conditions, he conducted religious services, gave classes and lectures, and did everything possible to keep up the morale of his fellow inmates. The Nazis assigned the elderly Baeck the most degrading forms of physical labor but were unable to break his spirit.

Baeck survived the war and settled in London, where he became chairman of the World Union for Progressive Judaism.

Jews loaded onto trucks and on their way to the extermination chambers.

Joop Westerweel, a non-Jewish school principal in Holland, helped Jewish children escape over the Pyrenees into Spain. He was caught and executed by the Gestapo.

Righteous Gentiles

Thousands of heroic men and women who were not Jewish put themselves in mortal danger to save the lives of Jews fleeing the Nazi Holocaust. Some saved just one person or one family, others were able to help thousands. Whatever the number of their beneficiaries, these courageous people—the Righteous Among the Nations—did what they did because they believed it was right. Some of them were pious Christians who believed in a religion of love; others were simply decent human beings who rose above the horror. The files of the Yad Vashem Memorial in Israel are filled with their stories. Many of these heroes have been publicly honored in the years since the war.

Raoul Wallenberg

One of the most outstanding Righteous Gentiles was Raoul Wallenberg (1912–1947?), First Secretary of the Swedish embassy in Budapest.

The moment he arrived in Budapest, Wallenberg applied to the Hungarian government for a quantity of *Schutzbriefen*, safe-conduct passes stipulating that the bearer was protected by the Swedish embassy. The Hungarians agreed to give him 1,500, but he obtained an increase to 15,000 by bribing the officials.

In November of 1944, the Nazis began rounding up the Jews of Hungary and sending them to the death camps. Wallenberg boarded the trains and distributed safe-conduct passes to the outstretched hands, then told everyone with a pass to walk over to a caravan of cars marked with the Swedish colors. Repeatedly confronting the Nazis this way, Wallenberg saved thousands of Jewish lives.

After the Russians captured Budapest, they arrested Wallenberg, and he was never heard from again. According to some reports, he died in a Soviet prison camp.

Raoul Wallenberg

Raoul Wallenberg distributed Swedish passes like this one, with which he is believed to have saved at least 30,000 Jews.

The Danes hit upon the idea of wearing skullcaps as a symbol of resistance and a token of unity with the Jewish people.

Holocaust Punishment

The death of Hitler and the German surrender (May 8, 1945) arrived too late for 12 million human beings, 6 million of whom were Jews. One-third of the entire Jewish people had been destroyed; barely 30 percent of the Jews of Europe remained alive.

The International Military Tribunal

Of the thousands who had perpetrated war crimes and the Holocaust, only a small fraction were brought to justice. In 1945, an International Military Tribunal was set up to prosecute Nazi war criminals. Meeting in Nuremberg, the tribunal tried a number of Nazi leaders: 12 were sentenced to death, and 3 were given life imprisonment. Hitler and Himmler had committed suicide just before the war ended, and Goering, who was sentenced to death by the tribunal, cheated the hangman by taking poison.

A session of the International Military Tribunal, Nuremberg, 1945–1946. In the dock are: (1) Hermann Goering, (2) Rudolf Hess, (3) Joachim von Ribbentrop, (4) Wilhelm Keitel, (5) Ernst Kaltenbrunner, (6) Alfred Rosenberg, (7) Hans Frank (8), Wilhelm Frick, (9) Julius Streicher, (10) Walther Funk, (11) Hjalmar Schacht, (12) Karl Doenitz, (13) Erich Raeder, (14) Baldur von Schirach, (15) Fritz Sauckel, (16) Alfred Jodl (17), Franz von Papen, (18) Arthur Seyss-Inquart, (19) Albert Speer, (20) Konstantine von Neurath, (21) Hans Fritzsche.

A few dozen minor war criminals were also tried by the Allies or by the Russians, but most were never caught or brought to trial, and an uncertain number escaped from Germany to South America or the Middle East, or even to the United States. Some former war criminals were protected by the American government, either working for the CIA in the Cold War struggle against Communism or, like Dr. Werner von Braun, helping to develop the space program.

Switzerland and the Holocaust

Switzerland was "neutral" during World War II. Many Jews anticipating problems, deposited their assets in Swiss banks. High-ranking Nazis also hid jewels, cash and gold, which they stole from their Jewish victims in numbered bank accounts.

Until 1997, the Swiss officially denied the existence of these Jewish and Nazi assets. However, under pressure of the World Jewish Congress, the Swiss have reluctantly opened their accounts and have agreed to return hundreds of millions of deposited and looted Jewish assets to Holocaust survivors.

The WJC also has documentary evidence regarding Nazi gold transfers and Jewish assets in other "neutral" countries such as Sweden, Turkey, Spain and Portugal.

As a consequence, the French government has appointed a committee to identify property stolen from French Jews. Over 2000 works of art in French museums have been identified as stolen from the Jews.

Foundations of the Holocaust

JEWISH HIGHLIGHTS

The Beginning of Nazism 20th century	Looking for Refuge	Britain and Arabs	Searching for Refuge	Failure of the West

JEWISH EVENTS • PERSONALITIES • LITERATURE • HOLIDAYS

▶ Assassination of Walther Rathenau 1922	▶ Fourth Aliyah / 1923	▶ Grand Mufti	▶ British White Paper / 1939	▶ Surrender at Munich 1938 Neville Chamberlain Daladier
▶ Nazi Master Race	▶ Illegal aliyah *St. Louis*	▶ Yishuv Stockade and Tower Settlements Vaad Leumi	▶ National Origins Act	▶ World War II / 1940
▶ Hitler comes to power / 1933 Concentration camps Stormtroopers Nuremberg Laws *Mein Kampf*	▶ American Zionists Rabbi Abba Hillel Silver Felix Frankfurter Brandeis	▶ Hebrew language	▶ Immigration Quotas	▶ France surrenders
		▶ Evian Conference / 1938	▶ Aliyah Bet / 1939 Underground Railroad	▶ Final Solution
▶ Kristellnacht Herschl Grynszpan	▶ Henrietta Szold Hadassah Youth Aliyah			▶ Wannsee Conference 1941
				▶ Death camps
▶ Olympic Games Blacks and Jews				▶ Anne Frank
				▶ Auschwitz
				▶ Gas Chambers

WORLD HISTORY

▶ Death of the Weimar Republic	▶ Palestine	▶ Palestine	▶ France	▶ Germany
▶ Italian Fascism	▶ America	▶ England	▶ Myron C. Taylor	▶ France
Il Duce				▶ England

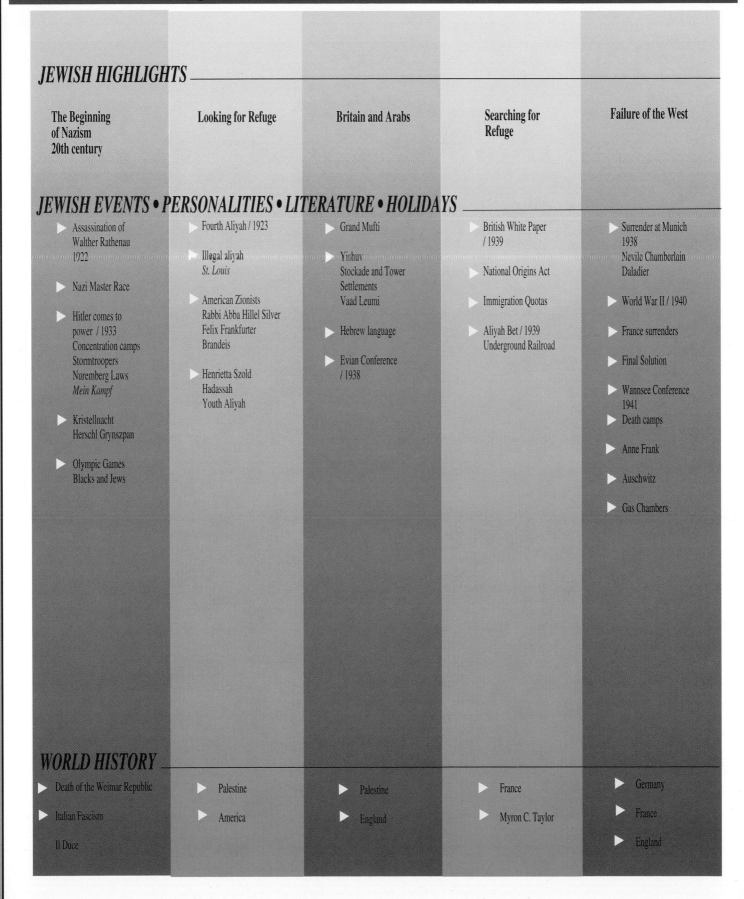

The Holocaust

JEWISH HIGHLIGHTS

American Jewish Response 1940–1943	Warsaw Ghetto 1943	The Yishuv Fights 1941–1945	Heroes of the Spirit	Holocaust Punishment 6 Million Jews Killed

JEWISH EVENTS • PERSONALITIES • LITERATURE

American Jewish Response 1940–1943	Warsaw Ghetto 1943	The Yishuv Fights 1941–1945	Heroes of the Spirit	Holocaust Punishment 6 Million Jews Killed
Henry Morgenthau	Judenrat Adam Czerniakow	Jewish Brigade	Leo Baeck	Hitler commits Suicide
State Department turns deaf ear	Jewish combat groups	Haganah	Raoul Wallenberg *Shutzbrief*	Nuremberg Trials Hermann Goering
Extermination plot Gerhard Regner	Nazis destroy Warsaw Ghetto	Hannah Szenesh	Joop Westerweel	Goering commits suicide
Sumner Wells	Janusz Korczak	Enzo Sereni		War criminals recruited by American industry
Pope Pius XII				
Auschwitz deliberately not bombed				
World Jewish Congress				

WORLD HISTORY

American Jewish Response	Warsaw Ghetto	The Yishuv Fights	Heroes of the Spirit	Holocaust Punishment
Vatican	Poland	Italy	Holland	International Military Tribunal Nuremberg
Poland		Palestine	Sweden	
Geneva				
I. G. Farben				
Dutch underground				

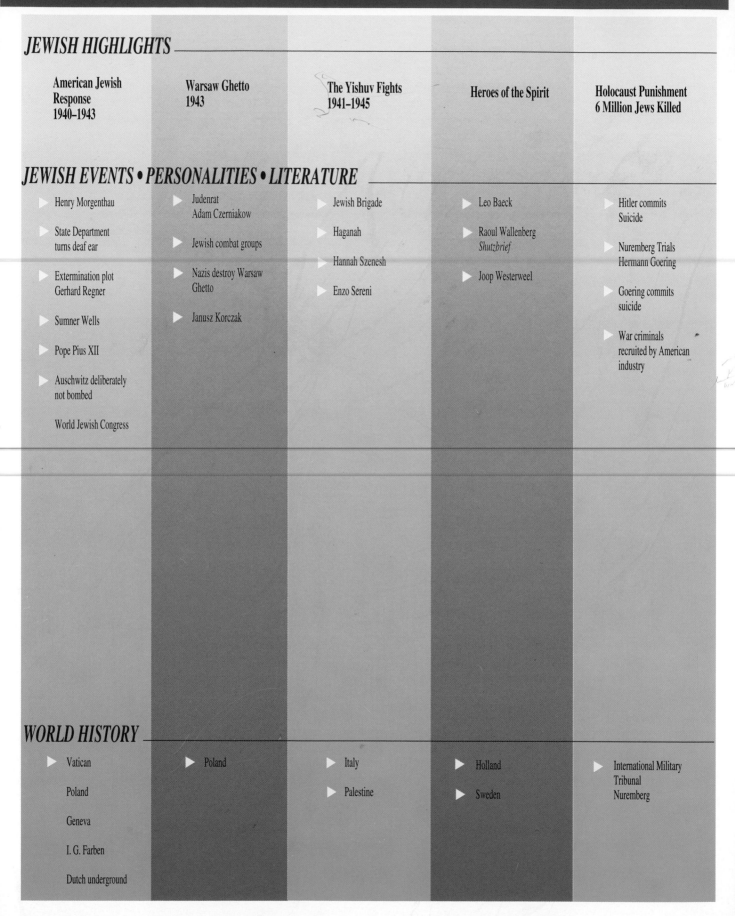

Displaced Persons

In the liberated concentration camps, there were hundreds of thousands of displaced persons (DPs), former prisoners or slave laborers who had nothing to return to and no place to go. The war and the Nazis had uprooted them and destroyed their lives.

The problem of the Jewish displaced persons was particularly acute. Most of the few Jews who had managed to survive no longer had homes or families. Many of them wanted to go to Palestine.

Illegal Immigration

Unfortunately, the British White Paper of 1939 was still in effect, a pitiless barrier to further Jewish immigration to Palestine.

The Haganah, which had aided illegal immigration during the war in spite of the White Paper, again went into action. "Underground railroads" were again organized. The survivors of Hitler's death camps waiting in detention centers had cause for new hope.

Again, the Haganah took on the perilous task of landing illegal immigrants in secret, under cover of night. Often the passengers, young and old, many of them scarred by years of camp life, had to wade through a stormy surf or row in small boats to elude the British guards.

The Irgun Zvai Leumi, a Palestinian underground movement founded in 1937 by members of the Betar youth organization and the Zionist Revisionist movement,

Refugees at a detention camp strain at the barbed wire that keeps them from freedom and their homeland.

was also very active in the "illegal" immigration of Jewish displaced persons.

The Internment Camps

The British showed little sympathy for the plight of the Jews. Their main concern was to maintain good relations with the Arab nations and avoid trouble in the Middle East. They used their military forces to prevent Jewish immigration and succeeded in intercepting most of the ships. The passengers were arrested and sent to internment camps especially set up for them on the island of Cyprus. There, once again behind barbed wire and watched by armed guards, they awaited the moment when they would be able to ascend to the homeland.

The S.S. "Exodus"

In 1947 the British policy became even more harsh. In order to set an example, they sent back to Germany the S.S. *Exodus*, a Haganah boat crammed full of illegal immigrants, men, women and children who had survived the Nazi death camps. These refugees had risked their lives to come to Palestine. Now they were sent back to Germany, where there was no room for them except in DP (displaced persons) camps where, for all they knew, they might languish forever without home or hope.

The fate of the *Exodus* stirred the Jews of Palestine to open revolt. Haganah and Irgun units destroyed British radar stations, bridges, and other military installations, and attacked British patrols. Arms were manufactured in secret factories and smuggled in from abroad.

The Palestine Problem

As the situation deteriorated, the British closed-door policy became a matter of world concern. Britain being unable to solve the Palestine problem, the United Nations took up the question. In 1947 it sent a Committee of Inquiry to Palestine. The committee returned with a proposal to partition Palestine into two states—one Arab and one Jewish.

Illegal immigrants preparing to land on the coast of Palestine. The immigrants were transferred into small boats and under cover of darkness landed on the shores of the Promised Land.

The *Exodus*, a Haganah ship, carried 4,500 Jewish refugees to Palestine from the camps in Europe at the end of World War II. The British, still holding the mandate over Palestine, refused to allow the ship to dock and returned it to Hamburg, Germany. This brutal act helped swing world opinion against Britain and toward the creation of a Jewish state.

The Zionist Spokesmen

Before World War I, there were about 20,000 active Zionists in the United States. Most of them were affiliated with the Federation of American Zionists, which in 1917 was renamed the Zionist Organization of America. Associated with the ZOA were Hadassah, the women's Zionist organization; the Sons of Zion, a fraternal order; and Young Judaea, a youth group. There were also American branches of the Socialist Zionist Party (Poale Zion) and the Orthodox Mizrachi Party.

The ZOA and its affiliates was largest in size and put forth major spokesmen who fought for the formation of a Jewish state. The dynamic oratory of Louis Lipsky, Stephen S. Wise, and Abba Hillel Silver moved thousands of Jews at national Zionist conventions and helped persuade the general American public to support the Zionist cause.

By 1930 the number of active Zionists in the United States rose to 150,000. The growth of the Nazi movement in Europe aroused many American Jews. By 1940 there were 400,000 enrolled Zionists, and at the highest point, following World War II, there may have been twice that many.

America Speaks

In 1943 the American Jewish Conference made it clear that most American Jews favored statehood. During the United Nations deliberations on the partition of Palestine in 1947, American Jewry spoke out almost unanimously for this cause. The UN's decision to establish separate Jewish and Arab states in the mandated territory of Palestine was hailed with joy by American and world Jewry.

Rabbi Meir Berlin (*left*), American president of the Mizrachi World Organization, talking with Jewish Agency leader David Ben-Gurion

American public opinion, a series of resolutions passed by Congress, and the favorable attitude of President Truman all carried weight in persuading the nations of the world to vote for a Jewish state.

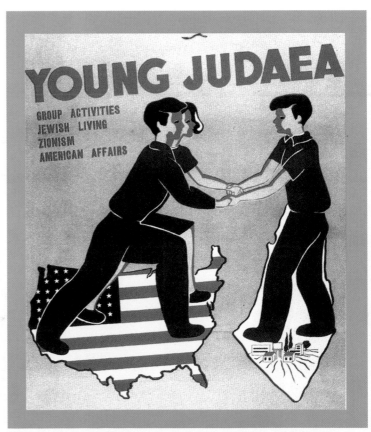

Poster of the American Zionist youth movement.

The State of Israel Is Born / 1948

Despite Arab protests, the United Nations passed a resolution in favor of partition on November 29, 1947. Jews everywhere rejoiced. Although the plan gave the Jews of the Yishuv only part of Palestine, the Jewish state of which generations had dreamed had become a reality. In Palestine Jews danced in the streets.

On May 14, 1948, the British gave up their mandate and left Palestine. The Jews at once set up a provisional government headed by David Ben-Gurion, and proclaimed the establishment of the State of Israel.

The emblem of Israel tells us a lot about the history and ideals of the Jewish people. The Temple menorah reminds us of the glory of the city of Jerusalem and also its sad destruction. The olive tree branches are symbols of peace. They tell the world that Israel wishes to live in peace with its neighbors.

Arabs had the advantage of superior numbers and weapons.

The Israelis fought valiantly, holding out against ferocious attacks by Arab artillery, armored cars, and aircraft. On isolated kibbutzim in the Galilee and the Negev, settlers defended themselves with rifles, mortars, and homemade Molotov cocktails. Although the Arabs appeared to have the upper hand when the war began, the tide soon turned. They were defeated on every front.

In January 1949, after months of fighting and thousands of casualties on both sides, a truce was declared. Twenty months after the first attack, the severely beaten Arab governments agreed to end the war.

Israel's stunning victory came at great human cost. More than 4,000 of its bravest soldiers and 3,000 civilians lost their lives defending the homeland.

The yearning of so many Jews, during the 2,000 years of exile, was now realized. Israel was reborn! The Jews now had a homeland of their own.

War of Independence

The Arabs bitterly opposed the Partition Plan and refused to accept the United Nations vote. On May 15, 1948, the day the State of Israel came into existence, the armies of Lebanon, Syria, Saudi Arabia, Jordan, Iraq, and Egypt jointly attacked, vowing to drive the Jews into the sea. The British, before leaving the country, did all they could to help the Arab invaders. The

A banner headline announces the birth of the new state. Although the State of Israel was proclaimed on Friday afternoon, May 14, 1948, the paper is dated Sunday, May 16, because the *Palestine Post* in Israel was not printed on the Jewish Sabbath.

The Haganah

During the First and Second Aliyot, there were many Arab attacks against Jewish settlements in Eretz Yisrael. Hundreds of Jews were murdered and much property was destroyed. In response the Jews "rose up" and established Hashomer ("The Watchman"). This tiny defense force had only 100 members. But each of them was a deadly marksman, an expert horseman, and fluent in Arabic.

The Haganah Is Founded

In 1920, Hashomer was disbanded and a much larger defense force called Haganah ("The Defense") was established. Haganah members, both male and female, took responsibility for defending Jewish towns and settlements.

When Arab riots swept the country in 1929, Haganah volunteers saved the Jewish communities of Jerusalem, Tel Aviv, and Haifa from destruction. After 1929 Haganah began a period of expansion and improved training. Modern arms were smuggled into Palestine in barrels of cement and agricultural machinery crates. By 1939, the Haganah had 25,000 members armed with smuggled rifles, machine guns, and homemade grenades manufactured in secret factories.

After World War II, the British continued their pro-Arab policy of restricting Jewish immigration into Eretz Yisrael. The Haganah countered by destroying British radar stations, bridges, and other military establishments. Haganah's main activity during the period of 1945–1948 was the organization of illegal immigration into Palestine. Tens of thousands of so-called "illegal immigrants" were smuggled into the country.

On May 31, 1948 the Haganah officially became Tzahal, the regular army of Israel.

A Haganah member stands guard at a defense perimeter.

This photo was taken at Kibbutz Hanita in 1938. *Left to right:* Moshe Dayan, Yitzhak Sadeh, and Yigal Allon. Each of these young men became a high-ranking officer in the Haganah as well as an important political leader.

The First Years of the New State

In January 1949 an armistice was declared. The State of Israel held elections and formed its first government. Dr. Chaim Weizmann, the revered Zionist leader, became its first President and David Ben-Gurion its first Prime Minister. In May 1949, Israel was admitted to the United Nations.

To many who witnessed the birth of Israel it seemed like a miracle. After pain and hopelessness, after the deaths of 6 million martyred Jews, the day of liberation had dawned for the survivors.

The State of Israel had many problems. It was a small country, and most of the holy places of Jewish tradition were in Arab territory. Hebron, with the cave of Machpelah and the graves of the Patriarchs, was outside Israel. Even the Old City of Jerusalem, and the Western Wall area, where once the Temple stood, were not in Israeli territory.

Exodus and Absorption

To compound Israel's difficulties, the Arab states remained hostile after the armistice, so defense was a major concern. In addition, there were vast numbers of newcomers to be absorbed—DPs from Europe and from British internment camps, as well as hundreds of thousands of refugees from Arab countries where Jews were no longer welcome. All of them had to be provided with food, medical care, a place to sleep, classes in Hebrew; ultimately, they needed jobs and homes as well.

Israel was an energetic young country. Its cities and villages were growing. Jews from many walks of life, many cultures, and many different nations eagerly began learning to live together. Many of them were devoted to Orthodox traditions and teachings. Others had no religious affiliations but were dedicated to building and developing the homeland. The doors of the new land were open to any Jew who wished to come and live there.

Almost immediately after the establishment of the State of Israel a campaign was organized to rescue the Jews of Yemen, Iraq, and Iran from persecution. They were evacuated by plane and brought safely to Israel. This courageous project was known as Operation Magic Carpet.

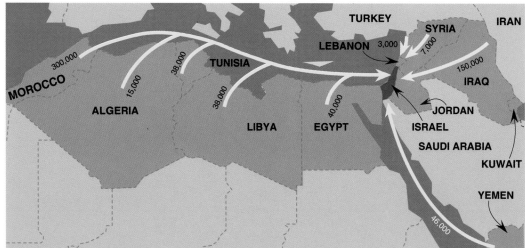

IMMIGRATION (Aliyah) FROM ARAB COUNTRIES

Israeli independence had a tremendous effect on Jewish communities in Arab lands. Most of the Arab countries instituted severe restrictions on their Jewish citizens. The hostile governments deprived them of their properties, their homes, and their businesses. These repressive measures initiated a huge exodus of Jews. Most of them arrived penniless, with only the clothes on their backs. In 1949, Operation Magic Carpet evacuated 50,000 Jews from Yemen.

The Suez Campaign / 1956

The War of Independence in 1948 was followed by a short period of quiet. For Israel it was the best of times; for eight years there was no large-scale shooting war. For Israel it was also the worst of times. For eight years there was a series of threats and terrorist attacks against the infant state.

In 1956, President Gamal Abdel Nasser of Egypt closed the Suez Canal to Israeli shipping and ships trading with Israel. The Arabs applied pressure against Israel on all sides, slowly choking its economy. Israel needed to keep its shipping lanes open, for they were its lifeline to the outside world, but diplomatic efforts failed to make the Egyptians relent.

On October 29, 1956, Israel attacked Egypt, operating in coordination with France and Britain, which hoped to regain control of the Suez Canal. In an eight-day campaign, the Israeli forces, under the command of General Moshe Dayan (1915–1981), captured the Gaza Strip and the entire Sinai Peninsula.

At this point the United States and the Soviet Union stepped in, forcing the British and French to withdraw from the Canal. Israel withdrew from Sinai, but only after a

Israeli soldiers shout in triumph as they reach the Suez Canal.

United Nations peacekeeping force was stationed along the Egypt-Israel border. As part of the settlement the United Nations guaranteed that Israeli shipping would have complete access to the Suez Canal.

Israel was now in a position to develop trading links with the Asian and African countries. It also now had an open port, Eilat, for importing oil from the Persian Gulf.

Israeli armored column waiting its turn to cross the Suez Canal.

Eichmann the Butcher

Jews have long memories, and sometimes many years pass before a wrong against them is avenged. After World War II many of the monsters who murdered Jews during the Holocaust escaped. Some found a safe haven in Arab countries. Many escaped to South America, where they lived under new identities. In many instances they were protected by anti-Semitic government officials.

Israel organized a special group of secret Nazi hunters whose job it was to find and expose these criminals.

In 1941, Adolf Eichmann had become head of the Department of Jewish Affairs at Nazi headquarters in Berlin. Eichmann organized the deportation of Jews to the death camps and was responsible for stealing their property. He had personally supervised the effort to destroy Hungarian Jewry.

After the war Eichmann was captured by the Allies, but in 1950 he managed to escape to Argentina. Friendly officials fur-

Eichmann on trial in Israel.

nished him with false identity papers, and he lived there till 1960, when he was discovered by the Israeli Nazi hunters. Eichmann was kidnapped and secretly flown to Israel. After a long trial he was found guilty and sentenced to death. His body was cremated, just as he had cremated 6 million Jews, and his ashes were scattered over the Mediterranean Sea.

His was the first and only execution ever carried out by the State of Israel.

The Yad Vashem Memorial: Ohel Yizkor - Hall of Remembrance. The walls are built of large, unhewn black lava rocks. On the mosaic floor are inscribed the names of the 21 largest concentration camps, and near the wall in the west burns a light.

The Six-Day War / 1967

June 1967 will be forever remembered as one of the most fateful periods in the history of Israel. For six fantastic days, the Middle East crossroads was torn by gunfire and screaming rockets. Then all was still. On the seventh day, when the smoke had cleared, the map of the world had been altered.

The tension was terrific on Sunday, June 4. Tel Aviv and Cairo buzzed with rumors. Tiny Israel, hemmed in by foes, listened to bulletins coming over the radio station Kol Yisrael: Syria had joined Egypt and Jordan in a military alliance. President Nasser of Egypt had proclaimed that Israel would be driven into the sea. Ahmed Shukairy, head of the Palestine Liberation Organization, arriving in Amman, stated: "When we take Israel, the surviving Jews will be helped to return to their native lands." Then he added: "But I think that none will survive."

The cities of Israel were empty of men—those 18 to 49 had left for the army. Yet spirits were high in this country of 2.5 million people, the size of Massachusetts, all included in one telephone book. Surrounded by 110 million Arab enemies, Israelis dug foxholes and trenches and marked time. And there was evening and there was morning . . . Monday, June 5.

A decade had passed, during which the Arabs had plotted revenge. In the spring of 1967, bolstered by a huge supply of Russian armaments, Nasser felt the time had come for action. He forced the 3,400-man UN force to withdraw from its buffer position in the Sinai and then blockaded

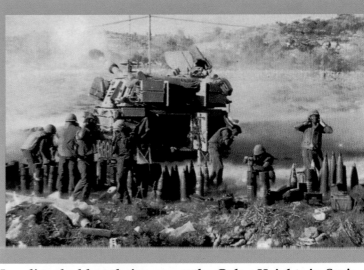

Israeli tanks blast their way up the Golan Heights in Syria.

the Strait of Tiran, shutting off Israeli shipping from the East. This was an act of war.

Israel Strikes

On June 5, 1967 Israeli planes made a pre-emptive strike against Egyptian, Jordanian, and Syrian air bases. Swooping out of the skies, the Israelis destroyed 450 enemy planes. With lightning speed, Israeli armored columns smashed through the Egyptian army in the Sinai, not stopping until they reached the Suez Canal.

Before the war began, Israel had promised King Hussein of Jordan that no harm would come to his country if he stayed out of the fighting. Hussein ignored the peace overture and attacked Jerusalem. Israel counterattacked, and within a few days had defeated the Jordanians. Israeli forces were now in control of the West Bank (Judea and Samaria), and had captured the Old City of Jerusalem. The Temple Mount was under Jewish rule for the first time in almost 2,000 years.

Jerusalem Liberated / 1967

By Thursday, Egypt and Jordan had been defeated. The Old City of Jerusalem, liberated at great sacrifice by the unbelievable bravery of paratroops under Colonel "Motke" Gur, was in Jewish hands.

Hardened soldiers, who had wrestled with death in the fight to free the city, rushed to the Western Wall. There they found an outlet for their emotions. Some kissed the ancient stones. Others wept for friends who had fallen in Jerusalem's streets.

Soldiers cheered as they saw the blue-and-white flag raised above the wall. Then—a hush as the blast of a shofar pierced the air. Chief Chaplain Shlomo Goren, among the first to enter the Old City, had lifted the ram's horn to his lips for the historic call. Rabbi Goren offered a Yizkor prayer for the dead, and then somebody raised his voice in the Israeli national anthem, Hatikvah, and at once the sound swelled in a thousand throats.

Now, only Syria remained on the field of battle. The entire Israeli air force—some 400 planes—flew non-stop raids against deeply-dug Syrian gun emplacements on the heights above the Sea of Galilee. The morning sun on Shabbat revealed Syrians running toward Damascus on roads littered with equipment and clothing. Israel's ground forces then conducted a mopping-up operation. At 6:30 p.m. a ceasefire was put into effect. Thus, by June 10, after only six days, victorious Israeli troops had defeated the combined Arab armies. Israel had control of the entire Sinai Peninsula, the Golan Heights, the West Bank, and the Old City of Jerusalem. Meantime President Lyndon Johnson and Premier Alexei Kosygin, using the famous hot line, had assured each other that both superpowers wished only peace in the Middle East, and the UN Security Council had met in New York to hammer out a ceasefire resolution.

The capitals of the world breathed a sigh of relief. The tinderbox had not exploded. What might have spread into a global conflict had been confined, and the flames of war were snuffed out. The Israeli Chief of Staff, Major General Yitzhak Rabin (1922–1995) solemnly declared: "All this has been done by us alone, with what we have, without anybody else." Said Moshe Dayan: "We have returned to our holiest of places, never to depart again."

A few days later, on a sunlit day, these two great leaders joined Prime Minister Levi Eshkol (1895–1965) in a visit to the Kotel Ma'aravi (Western Wall), the last remnant of the Second Temple.

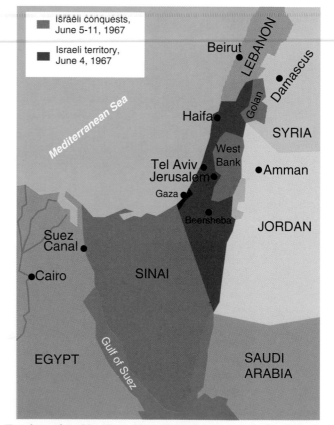

During the Six-Day War, Israel captured the Sinai, the Gaza Strip, the Golan Heights, and Judea and Samaria (West Bank).

Each one, following an old Jewish tradition, had written a prayer to place in a crevice in the wall. "What did you write?" curious reporters inquired. "Shema Yisrael," said Eshkol. "May peace be upon all Israel," said Dayan. "This is the Lord's doing; it is marvelous in our eyes," said Rabin, quoting Tehillim, the Book of Psalms.

A week after the war ended, on Shavuot, 200,000 Jews prayed at the Western Wall. Their tearful joy at the return of the sacred city expressed itself in prayer and in song.

The 28th of the month of Iyar, the day the city was liberated, is now celebrated in Israel as Jerusalem Day (Yom Yerushalayim). Israelis rejoice at the unification of the holy city, but sadly mourn the brave soldiers who fell in battle.

Rabbi Shlomo Goren, Chief Chaplain of the Israel Defense Forces, prays at the liberated Western Wall.

Entering the Old City of Jerusalem, *from left to right:* Chief of Staff Gen. Uzi Narkiss, Defense Minister Moshe Dayan, Gen. Yitzhak Rabin, commander of the Central Sector.

MOSHE DAYAN (1915–1981)
Israeli general and statesman: Moshe Dayan was born in Kibbutz Degania and at an early age was taken to live in Nahalal, the first moshav. As a teenager he joined the Haganah. During the Arab terrorist attacks in 1936, Dayan served in an elite commando force headed by Orde Wingate, a Bible-reading British officer who supported Zionism even though he was a Christian.

During Israel's War of Independence, Dayan held the rank of lieutenant colonel and commanded various fronts. He became a major general in 1953 and led the Israeli army during the Sinai Campaign in 1956.

In 1957 Dayan left the army to enter politics. Just before the Six-Day War in June 1967, Dayan was appointed Minister of Defense. After the great Israeli victory, Dayan administered the area occupied by the Israeli army on the West Bank of the Jordan River.

The Yom Kippur War / 1973

Almost daily between 1968 and 1973, marauding Arab terrorists sneaked across Israel's borders to attack innocent people. Tel Aviv was shelled. A school bus was blown up in Eilat injuring 28 children. Arab leaders encouraged their people to hate the Jewish state. Russia encouraged the Arabs and sent them billions of dollars worth of arms.

At the 1972 Olympics, Arabs murdered 11 Israeli athletes. In reprisal, Israel hit terrorist bases in Syria and Lebanon. Tensions in the Middle East rose steadily and ominously.

On October 6, 1973—the holy day of Yom Kippur—the Arabs attacked Israel on two fronts at once. Syria attacked Israel's northern Golan front, and Egypt attacked across the Suez Canal into the Sinai.

Since Yom Kippur is the most sacred day of the Jewish year, most soldiers were in the synagogues with their families. The Arab sneak attack succeeded and caught Israel off guard.

By the time Israel's troops could assemble to defend their land, the invading Arab armies had broken through the Israeli lines to both the north and the south. Massive Egyptian and Syrian armies penetrated Israel's defenses, the Egyptians pushing into Sinai and the Syrians moving into the Golan Heights.

An Arab poster depicts Israel as a snake. An Arab knife is severing its head from its body.

By the third day, Israel recovered fast and started to take the offensive. With prayerbooks in one hand and machine guns in the other, Israeli soldiers left the synagogues and went straight to the battlefield. In nine days the Israeli army pushed back all the invaders. The Egyptian army was surrounded in the Sinai and Israeli troops threatened Cairo, Egypt's capital. The Syrians were also forced back, and Israel was poised to attack Damascus, Syria's capital.

Once it had become clear that Israel was winning, the Egyptians urged their Soviet backers to force an end to the fighting.

Russia and America Act

Meanwhile, a dangerous confrontation was brewing between the United States and Russia. The Soviet Union had been resupplying the Arabs. The losses suffered by the Israelis made resupply by America a vital necessity. At first the United States hesitated, but when it learned that the Russians were resupplying Egypt and Syria by means of the largest airlift in history, American planes began flying tons of equipment to Israel.

The Israeli participants in the 1972 Summer Olympics in Munich, Germany, prepare to board an El Al flight home, taking with them the bodies of 11 comrades who were brutally massacred by Arab terrorists.

Kissinger's Shuttle Diplomacy

Henry Kissinger (b. 1923) had come to America as a refugee from Hitler's Germany while still a boy. As Secretary of State in the administration of President Richard Nixon, he reasoned that the war was ending in a draw: the Arabs had fought well enough to recover their "honor," but now knew that even with the advantages of more manpower, better equipment, and complete surprise, they could not defeat Israel. In the agreement that Kissinger worked out with the Russians, Israel was to refrain from completely destroying the Arab armies, and direct talks were to begin between Israel and Egypt aimed at a "just and durable peace" in the region.

The Ceasefire

By the time the ceasefire took effect, Israel had managed to trap over 20,000 men, Egypt's elite Third Army. An Egyptian defeat on such a scale was unacceptable to the Russian patrons of the Arabs, and would also have upset the battlefield stalemate Kissinger wanted in order to force the start of peace negotiations.

On October 24 the Russians sent President Nixon a message in which they threatened to take matters into their own hands if America did not force Israel to withdraw from its advanced positions west of Suez, thereby freeing the trapped Third Army. The United States could not allow Russia to intervene directly in the Middle East. Nixon ordered American nuclear forces around the globe to be put on alert. For a few hours a much more destructive type of war seemed to menace the world, but a compromise was reached. Instead of Russian or American troops, a neutral UN force was sent to patrol the ceasefire lines. Israel allowed food and water to reach the Third Army but kept it trapped.

More than 11,000 Arabs died in the Yom Kippur War, but so did over 2,500 Israelis. Israel emerged victorious on the battlefield, but at a bloody price.

After the ceasefire, all Israel mourned the nation's loss of its soldiers. Prime Minister Golda Meir (1898–1979) said: "For the people of Israel, each human life is precious. Our dead soldiers are the sons of all of us. The pain we feel is felt by all of us."

As a result of the surprise attack, Golda Meir was forced to resign. Many voters had lost confidence in her. Yitzhak Rabin, of the Labor Party, became the new Prime Minister.

Secretary of State Henry Kissinger (*right*) talks to Abba Eban (*left*) and Yigal Allon (*center*) during his shuttle diplomacy which led to a settlement between Israel and Egypt in 1979.

Golda Meir / 1898–1979

Women played an important role in the creation of the State of Israel. They were members of the First Aliyah and of every other wave of settlers. Young and old women were in the thick of the fighting during each of Israel's wars.

Golda Meir was one of Israel's outstanding heroines. She was born in Kiev, Russia, where her father was a carpenter. There Golda Meir witnessed the violent pogroms against the Jews. Later in life she said that her childhood memories of the pogroms influenced her to become a Zionist.

When Golda was eight years old, her family moved to the United States and settled in Milwaukee, where she became a schoolteacher. In 1921 she and her husband, Morris Meyerson, moved to Palestine, where they joined a kibbutz. As a symbol of their dedication to the Jewish homeland, they changed their name from Meyerson to Meir, which means "giver of light."

Golda Meir became active in politics and was elected to head the Histadrut, Israel's central labor union. In 1948, before the War of Independence, she disguised herself as an Arab and secretly visited Emir Abdullah of Jordan in an effort to persuade him to keep his country out of the war. In 1949 Golda Meir became a member of the Knesset and Minister of Labor. She also served as Israel's first ambassador to the Soviet Union.

Golda Meir

Golda Meir's organizational abilities propelled her onto the international political stage, first as Foreign Minister and in 1969 as the first female Prime Minister of Israel. After serving as Israel's leader during the Yom Kippur War, she submitted her resignation. In 1974, because of ill health, she retired from all of her political posts. When she died on December 8, 1978, people all over the world mourned this great and courageous woman.

President and Mrs. Richard Nixon of the United States with Prime Minister Golda Meir of Israel at the White House in 1972.

Rescue at Entebbe / 1976

Wars are fought on many different levels. There are battlefields where soldiers, tanks, and airplanes shoot at each other. But there is also war by terrorism directed against innocent civilians. Bombs are planted in department stores, civilians are shot or stabbed on the street, explosives are planted in automobiles.

On June 27, 1976 an Air France plane carrying 300 people was hijacked by terrorists. The plane, with its 300 passengers, was forced to land at Entebbe, the capital of the African nation of Uganda. The hijackers demanded that Israel release terrorists serving time in Israeli prisons in exchange for the passengers. This hijacking took place with the cooperation of the Ugandan government, headed by Idi Amin. He was known as the butcher of Uganda because of his savage cruelty. All non-Jewish prisoners were released, but more than 100 Jews were kept and threatened with death.

The Israel Defense Forces set up a plan called Operation Yonatan, named for its leader, Col. Yonatan (Yoni) Netanyahu. At a very young age Yoni Netanyahu had distinguished himself as an officer with the

Lieutenant Colonel
Yonatan Netanyahu.

paratroopers. In 1967 he fought in the Six-Day War and was wounded. In 1973 he fought bravely in the Yom Kippur War. Now Yoni was entrusted with the job of freeing the Jewish prisoners in Entebbe.

Under cover of darkness, transport planes carried 100 highly trained Israeli commandos to Entebbe, more than 2,500 miles from Israel. The unmarked planes flew an indirect course to avoid detection.

The Israeli troops silently deplaned and in a short fight quickly eliminated the Ugandan troops and the terrorists. Within 90 minutes the hostages were on the plane and on the way back to safety.

There was one tragic death. Col. Yoni Netanyahu, the leader of the raiding party, was killed. His death was mourned by Jews all over the world. Several months later Idi Amin, the butcher of Uganda, was overthrown. He found refuge in Saudi Arabia.

In 1996, Yoni's brother, Benjamin Netanyahu, defeated Shimon Peres and became Prime Minister of Israel.

The C-130 Hercules transport plane in which the Israel commando forces were flown to Entebbe.

The Israel–Egypt Peace Treaty / 1979

In May 1977, Israeli voters elected a new government. The Likud, headed by Menachem Begin (1913–1992), became the largest party in the Knesset.

Menachem Begin wanted peace for Israel, and he hoped that he and President Anwar Sadat of Egypt might reach an agreement. In November 1977, for the first time ever, an Arab leader, President Sadat, visited Jerusalem. Sadat addressed the Knesset on his wish for peace.

In 1979 Begin and Sadat met at Camp David in the United States. There, with the assistance of President Jimmy Carter, they hammered out their many differences. On March 26, 1979, they signed a peace treaty in Washington, D.C.

The other Arab states bitterly opposed the Camp David Agreement. They swore to take revenge on Sadat for having negotiated with the Jewish state. In October 1981, he was killed by an assassin's bullet and was succeeded by Hosni Mubarak.

Hosni Mubarak
Hosni Mubarak, the new President of Egypt, soon became the target of Islamic extremists, partly because he maintained diplomatic relations with Israel. His corrupt government offered little hope of a better life for the poor Egyptian people.

Despite severe repression and countless death sentences, Muslim fundamentalists have waged an ongoing war of terror against the Mubarak regime, targeting government officials and Coptic Christians. On June 15, 1991, Hosni Mubarak escaped an assassination attempt in Ethiopia.

The Two Faces
The President of Egypt has been the most vocal defendant of the Palestinians. He has organized anti-Israel conferences and accused the Israelis of human rights violations. President Mubarak has urged the Arabs to resist Israel with violence.

Left to right: Begin, Carter, and Sadat after the peace treaty was signed in Washington on March 26, 1979.

Hosni Mubarak

Mission to Iraq / 1981

Ever since the beginning of the conflict with Israel, the Arab countries have been able to obtain the most up-to-date weaponry—short of nuclear arms. In 1980 the Israeli government grew very anxious over reports that Iraq was developing nuclear, chemical, and biological weapons. Israel was especially concerned about the nuclear production facilities in Osirak, 10 miles from Baghdad.

On June 7, 1981 Israeli aircraft flew about 600 miles through enemy air space and bombed the Iraqi nuclear facility. The plant was destroyed and all the aircraft returned safely.

The whole world condemned Israel, but secretly most of Iraq's neighbors applauded the raid, since an Iraq armed with nuclear bombs would have been a threat to the whole region. The full benefit of the raid on Osirak was seen during the 1991 Persian Gulf War. Iraq used biological weapons against U.S. troops, and might have used nuclear weapons if they had been available, but fortunately, thanks to Israel, it had none.

President Saddam Hussein of Iraq launched an ambitious program to modernize his arsenal of offensive weapons. He built chemical, gas, and biological weapons and used them against the Kurds and Iranians. In addition, he began building a nuclear weapons facility at Osirak. In 1981 an Israeli air attack destroyed the half-built reactor.

Peace for Galilee / 1982

Lebanon is a pipeline terminus for oil coming from Saudi Arabia and Iraq. Before 1970, it was a very prosperous and modern country with a highly skilled and educated work force. Its capital, Beirut, was the banking, commercial, and resort center of the Middle East.

Things began to change in 1970 when the Palestine Liberation Organization, now headed by Yasir Arafat, was expelled from Jordan and set up a base in Lebanon. Israeli settlements along the Lebanese border came under frequent rocket and artillery attack. The residents of border towns in Galilee had to live in shelters because of the PLO bombardments.

Israel—Lebanon

In 1975, a brutal civil war broke out between Lebanon's Christians and Muslims. After many battles and thousands of casualties, the Syrians moved in and restored order. They became the power behind a new Lebanese government. The Syrians allowed the PLO to continue its attacks on northern Israel, which became more and more intense.

Finally, on July 6, 1982, The Israeli army launched Operation Peace for Galilee. Under the command of General Ariel Sharon, Israeli troops pushed into Lebanon and captured Beirut. Many of the PLO terrorists and their Syrian allies were killed or captured. A large amount of guns, tanks, and missiles was also taken.

Most of Lebanon's Christians were happy to see the Israelis. They had been robbed and beaten by the PLO and the Syrian troops. Now, thanks to the Israelis, they once again had some security. Prime Minister Menachem Begin hoped that the PLO threat would be ended once and for all. But Operation Peace for Galilee caused much controversy. Many foreign governments objected, and thousands of Israelis protested as well.

Israel Withdraws

In 1983 the Israeli troops were withdrawn and Begin resigned. A small contingent of Israeli troops and Christian Lebanese militia maintained a small security zone on the frontier to prevent terrorist infiltration into Israel. Despite the troops there are still enemy incursions and rocket attacks on the towns of northern Israel.

General Ariel Sharon commanded Operation Peace for Galilee.

Menachem Begin headed the Betar movement in Poland before he was 20 years old. Because of his Zionist activities, the Russians sentenced him to a Siberian labor camp. In 1942 he immigrated to Palestine, where he organized the armed Jewish underground struggle against the British. He evaded the police by disguising himself as a bearded rabbi. Begin founded the Herut (Freedom) Party and in 1977 became Prime Minister.

Israel and the Gulf War / 1991

In July 1990 President Saddam Hussein of Iraq threatened to use force against any Arab country that continued to pump oil above its OPEC quota. The price of a barrel of oil had fallen from $20 to $13. Each dollar dropped meant a $1 billion loss for Iraq. The Iraqi threat was especially aimed at the adjoining kingdom of Kuwait.

On August 2, 1990, 100,000 Iraqi troops invaded Kuwait and quickly took control of the country. Six hundred oil wells were set afire. Torture, killings, mass arrests, and looting of anything of value continued without a stop. The whole world condemned the invasion except King Hussein of Jordan and the PLO.   On August 7, 1990 President George Bush set in motion Operation Desert Storm under the command of General Norman Schwarzkopf. A huge airlift of soldiers, arms, and ammunition began flowing into staging areas in Saudi Arabia. Egypt, Saudi Arabia, and most of the countries of Western Europe joined the coalition against Iraq.

Israel, however, was not part of the coalition because the Arab members did not want to be seen fighting side-by-side with Israel against their Arab brothers. President Bush extracted a promise from Prime Minister Yitzhak Shamir not to take military action against Iraq even if Israel was attacked.

Scud Missiles Hit Israel

On the first night of the war, eight Iraqi Scud missiles hit Israel, two in Haifa, two in Tel Aviv, and four in unpopulated areas. As the missiles fell, Arabs in the West Bank watched from their rooftops and cheered.

Saddam Hussein fired a total of 86 Scud missiles, 40 at Israel and 46 at Saudi Arabia. Some were intercepted by U.S. Patriot missiles. In Israel 250 people were wounded. In and around Tel Aviv about 9,000 apartments were damaged. The most lethal Scud attack was on a U.S. barracks in Saudi Arabia; 28 Americans were killed.

Iraq's defeat in the Gulf War had important consequences for Israel. The PLO lost the financial backing of Saudi Arabia and Kuwait because it had supported Saddam Hussein. Weakened by its loss of funding, the PLO was for the first time willing to begin peace negotiations with Israel.

General Norman Schwarzkopf explains the aims and objectives of Operation Desert Storm.

The Peace Agreement / 1993

The Middle East Peace Conference convened in Madrid, Spain, in 1991. While further meetings were taking place in Washington in 1992, a tiny group of PLO and Israeli delegates met secretly in Norway. Their discussions continued for 15 months. On September 13, 1993, Prime Minister Yitzhak Rabin of Israel and Yasir Arafat, head of the PLO, signed a peace agreement in Washington.

Some of the terms were:

1. The PLO would have jurisdiction over the city of Jericho and the Gaza Strip.

2. The PLO would have jurisdiction over police, fire, health, water, and education.

3. Israel would have jurisdiction over borders, roads, and the protection of Jewish settlements in the PLO enclaves.

4. A phased Israeli troop withdrawal would begin on December 13, 1993. Within nine months Israel would withdraw from all West Bank cities. Soon after that it would transfer all remaining land except the Jewish settlements to the Palestinian National Authority.

5. The final status of the territories would be settled at the end of five years.

On September 3, 1993, the Israeli Knesset, which has 120 members, approved the peace agreement by a vote of 61 to 50. Although all Israelis yearn for peace, many did not trust Arafat and the PLO, and felt that Israel was giving up too much too soon. Victory came, as expected, from the 44 members of Rabin's own party, 12 votes from the leftist Meretz party, and 5 votes from the Israeli Arab Knesset members. Without the Arab votes the agreement would not have been ratified.

Prime Minister Yitzhak Rabin, and Yasir Arafat in Washington. President Bill Clinton negotiated a handshake between these two enemies.

Qalqilya

As part of the agreement, Israel agreed to withdraw the IDF from six major Arab cities in Judea and Samaria: Qalqilya, Ramallah, Jenin, Bethlehem,Tulkarm, and Hebron. Israel has kept its part of the agreement, and has withdrawn from all cities. As part of its agreement, there is a small detachment of Israeli troops to protect the 450 Jews who live in Hebron.

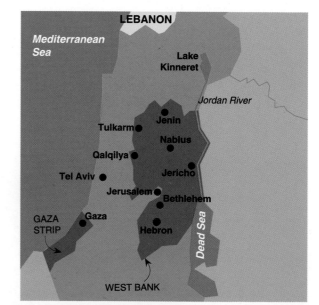

The Oslo accords stipulated that Israeli troops would withdraw from all West Bank cities. Israeli troops have not been withdrawn from Hebron because of the danger from the hostile Arab population.

Reasons for the Agreement

On September 13, 1993, Prime Minister Yitzhak Rabin and Yasir Arafat signed a peace agreement in which Israel and the PLO recognized each other's right to exist. The negotiations for this historic agreement took place in Norway over a period of 15 months. After so many years of warfare the two combatants decided, each for its own reasons, that it was time to call a halt and seek an accommodation.

The Palestinian Reasons

1. Hamas, the extremist party, was getting stronger and gaining more and more recruits. The influence of the PLO was slowly being eroded. In time its ability to command the loyalty of the Palestinians would disappear. Its prestige would be restored if it gained control of part of the occupied territories.

2. The PLO government in exile was bankrupt. During the Gulf War, the PLO had sided with Iraq against Kuwait and Saudi Arabia. At the end of the war the two kingdoms cut off their financial support for the PLO. As a result, the destitute PLO had not paid its employees and military personnel for many months. Without financial support, it would have to close its offices and disband its guerilla troops.

3. During the Cold War the Russians had supported the PLO politically in the United Nations. They had also supplied it with weapons and money. Now that the Soviet Union had broken up and the Cold War had ended, Russia lost interest in the Middle East and the PLO. As a matter of fact, several of the states of the former Soviet Union were having their own problems with Muslim extremists.

The Israeli Reasons

The Israelis also had some special reasons for seeking a peaceful, though imperfect, solution to the Palestinian problem.

1. Israel had been at war for 45 years since 1948, and many Israelis were psychologically and physically tired. Three generations of Israelis, grandparents, parents, and children, had tasted the bitterness of war, and a majority of them were ready for some sort of compromise.

2. Hamas, the extreme wing of the Arab liberation movement, was gaining strength. Its terrorists were totally dedicated to the destruction of Israel. The security situation within Israel would worsen if Hamas gained control of the Arab masses.

3. Hundreds of thousands of Russian immigrants had come to Israel. Many of them were highly educated and skilled professionals. Israeli economists believed that peace with the neighboring Arab countries would provide a beneficial dividend. Israel would be transformed into a high-technology center for the entire Middle East and thus be able to provide work for the immigrants.

Israeli and Palestinian policemen on joint patrol.

History of Hebron

The ancient city of Hebron is located 19 miles south of Jerusalem, in the Judean Mountains. It is the site of the Cave of Machpelah, revered by Jews as the burial place of the Patriarchs and Matriarchs. Muslims venerate it as Al Haram Al-Ibrahami, the Tomb of Abraham.

Hebron was destroyed by the Romans in the 1st century C.E., and the Byzantines built a Christian church on the site of the Cave of Machpelah. After the Arab invasion in the 8th century, Caliph Omar, the Muslim ruler, allowed Hebron's Jewish inhabitants to build a synagogue near the cave. The Muslim conquerors converted the Christian church at the cave into a mosque.

They built a wall at the entrance of the cave, in which they put a small window through which Jews could pray. A decree prohibiting Jews and Christians from entering the holy shrine remained in effect until 1967, when Israeli troops captured Hebron during the Six-Day War.

The Destruction of the Jewish Community

In 1929, the Jews of Hebron were attacked by an Arab mob. In the riot, during which the British police refused to intervene, 69 Jewish men, women, and children were murdered. The Jewish community of Hebron was totally destroyed.

The Arab rioters in 1929 demolished or burned all of Hebron's synagogues. This Jewish survivor managed to salvage a Torah scroll from the ruins of a synagogue.

The Cave of Machpelah

As result of the Six-Day War, Hebron came under Israeli rule. In 1972, Jewish settlers established the community of Kiryat Arba half-mile from the Cave of Machpelah.

Seven years later, in 1979, Rabbanit Miriam Levinger led a group of women and children into Hebron, where they re-occupied the old Hadassah Hospital in the Jewish quarter, which had been destroyed in 1929. By 1994, the Jewish community of Hebron numbered more than 400.

Baruch Goldstein

On February 24, 1944, Dr. Baruch Goldstein, a resident of Kiryat Arba, entered the Cave of Machpelah and killed 29 Arabs. He himself was beaten to death. In contrast, to the massacre in 1929, this incident was the act of one deranged individual. In the aftermath, the Israeli government apologized for the murders, and has paid compensation to the families of the victims. Nevertheless, Goldstein's grave has become shrine to many Jews.

Hebron Today

The Palestinians insist that the Jewish settlers must be removed from Hebron, so that it becomes an entirely Arab city. The Jewish inhabitants say that they have the right to live anywhere that they wish. Benjamin Netanyahu and Yaser Arafat have concluded an agreement whereby the Jews of Hebron can continue to live there.

Israel and Jordan / 1994

When Israel became independent in May 1948, Jordan's Arab Legion joined in the attack on it and occupied East Jerusalem, Judea, and Samaria. Jordan gave citizenship to thousands of Arab refugees from Israel. After the Six-Day War in 1967, Jordan lost control of Jerusalem, Judea, and Samaria to Israel, but its population still included a huge number of Palestinians. In September 1970—known in the PLO's annals as Black September—Yasir Arafat and his guerilla fighters tried to overthrow Hussein's government. Syria planned to invade Jordan at the same time, but was prevented by the threat of Israeli intervention. Thanks to Israel's support, the Arab Legion crushed the Palestinian revolt. The PLO, expelled from Jordan, found a new base of operations in Lebanon.

On October 26, 1994, Prime Minister Yitzhak Rabin and Prime Minister Abdul Salam Majali of Jordan signed a peace agreement. The two countries are cooperating in the development of water resources, transportation, postal service, and telecommunications, and have agreed to alleviate the human problems caused by the Middle East conflict. Israel and Jordan have exchanged ambassadors. King Hussein reacted positively to the election of Prime Minister Benjamin Netanyahu in 1996, in part because of concern that a PLO state on the West Bank would be as much of a danger to Jordan as to Israel.

King Hussein has shown his skill as a survivor on the Arab political map. The King is now mending his fences with the PLO and Yasir Arafat. In September 1996 he made an appearance with Arafat and voiced his support for the political ambitions of the PLO.

King Hussein

March 13, 1997
A Jordanian soldier opened fire and killed seven girls from an orthodox Jewish high school, and wounded eight. In a gesture of consolation, King Hussein visited the bereaved families and offered his heartfelt apologies and condolences.

Signing the peace treaty between Israel and Jordan. President Clinton (*front row, center*) and Secretary of State Warren Christopher (*rear row, second from left*) participated in and signed the agreement.

Syria and Israel

Peace Talks Between Israel and Syria

Since 1991 Syria and Israel have been holding peace talks, in which Damascus has demanded full Israeli withdrawal from the Golan Heights. Israel has called for normalized relations, open borders, and diplomatic recognition. Prime Minister Rabin indicated a willingness to withdraw from the Golan in stages over a period of eight years, but Syria demanded immediate full withdrawal or nothing. On July 12, 1995, the Israeli-Syrian peace talks in Washington were terminated, and the delegates returned home.

The Grapes of Wrath

In April 1996, Hezbollah, a Palestinian guerilla organization backed by Iran and Syria, fired hundreds of Katyusha rockets into northern Israel from its bases in Lebanon, forcing the evacuation of thousands of Israelis. Israel retaliated with a massive air and artillery bombardment called Grapes of Wrath. Unfortunately, thousands of Lebanese civilians were affected by the fighting and fled northward.

Warren Christopher

American Secretary of State Warren Christopher made a series of more than 20 diplomatic trips between Damascus and Jerusalem. After numerous meetings President Assad agreed to a ceasefire. The terms of the agreement localized the hostilities into the Israel-held strip in southern Lebanon. On May 30, 1996 the day of the Israeli election, Hezbollah once again attacked, wounding four Israeli soldiers.

Unsettled conditions, with periodic outbreaks of fighting, continue on Israel's northern border.

Many observers feel that Syria is not really interested in making peace.

Archeologist have identified several ancient synagogues on the Golan Heights. Five have been partially excavated. The best-preserved synagogue in the Golan is near the capital Katzrin. An Aramaic inscription was found in the building: "Uzi made this square." The building was partly destroyed in the 7th century C.E., <u>and in the 13th century it became a mosque.</u>

In recent decades, the Israelis have rediscovered its great wine-making tradition. The Golan Heights cooperative is located near Katzrin, the capital of the Golan. It produces quality wines under 3 labels: Yarden, Gamla, and Golan. <u>All of Golan's wines are kosher, since only Jews are involved in all stages of production.</u>

Jerusalem and the Arabs

One of the most important issues in the Arab-Israeli dispute is the control of Jerusalem.

This holy city has always played a central religious and political role in Jewish life. King David recognized its importance and made it the capital of ancient Israel. King Solomon made Jerusalem the religious center of Judaism by erecting the Holy Temple there. According to rabbinic tradition, Jerusalem is the center of God's spiritual world.

During the 2,000 years of exile, Jews never lost their love for the holy city. As they were led into Babylonian captivity in 586 B.C.E., they tearfully sang:

If I forget thee, Jerusalem,
May my right hand lose its cunning,
May my tongue cleave to its palate.

There are many references to Jerusalem in the daily, Sabbath, and holiday prayers. Worshippers in the synagogue always face toward Jerusalem.

In every generation there has been a Jewish presence in Jerusalem. Jews continued to worship at the ancient Western Wall. Because of the tears of exile, the Wall was often called the Wailing Wall.

As part of the 1949 armistice agreement, the United Nations split Jerusalem into two parts, the New City to be controlled by Israel, the Old City and its holy shrines, by Jordan. The agreement stated that Jews would have free access to worship at the Western Wall and the shrines in the Old City.

In spite of the agreement, the Jordanians did not allow Jews to worship at the Western Wall. To further aggravate the situation, they vandalized the Jewish cemetery on the Mount of Olives and destroyed many of the Old City's historic synagogues.

In 1967, during the Six-Day War, Israel captured the Old City and reunited Jerusalem.

Jerusalem is sacred to three religions: Judaism, Christianity, and Islam. The Israeli government guarantees all religions freedom of access to their holy places and shrines. Everyone is free to worship God in complete freedom.

The Muslim View of Jerusalem

The two holiest cities of Islam are Mecca and Medina. Mecca is where Muhammad, the founder of Islam, was born. Medina is where he preached and developed the Muslim religion. Jerusalem is also considered a holy city by Muslims, although its role in the earliest years of Islam was comparatively minor.

Muslims believe that Muhammad, in a dream, was transported up to heaven from the Temple Mount in Jerusalem. In the 7th century, several decades after the Muslim conquest of Jerusalem, Caliph Abd Malik ibn Marwan built the Mosque of Omar on the site where Muhammad's dream was said to have occurred—the exact spot

The Old City of Jerusalem is divided into four sections or quarters: Jewish, Arab, Christian, and Armenian. The Christian quarter contains many churches, schools, and important historical and religious sites.

where the First and Second Temples had stood some 1,600 years earlier.

Jerusalem and the Palestinian Authority

The Palestinians insist that East Jerusalem must be the capital of the state they hope to establish on the West Bank. Israel maintains that Jerusalem is and will always be Israel's capital—to quote Yitzhak Rabin, "Jerusalem is the ancient and eternal capital of the Jewish people."

Because of these seemingly irreconcilable positions, the peace treaty with the PLO refers to Jerusalem in deliberately vague language. Israeli and Arab diplomats hope to solve the questions pertaining to the holy city before the treaty goes into full effect.

Jerusalem and the United States

Despite the bonds of friendship between Israel and the United States, the U.S. government continues to locate its embassy in Tel Aviv. The State Department refuses to recognize Jerusalem as the capital of Israel. In addition, it maintains a separate American consulate in East Jerusalem for the convenience of Palestinians.

The U.S. Senate has passed a resolution which requires the the State Department to move the American embassy to Jerusalem, but no steps in this direction have been taken.

The golden dome of the Mosque of Omar in Jerusalem is a highly visible landmark. It was built by Caliph Abd Malik ibn Marwan in 691 C.E.

POPULATION MAP OF THE LARGEST CITIES IN ISRAEL

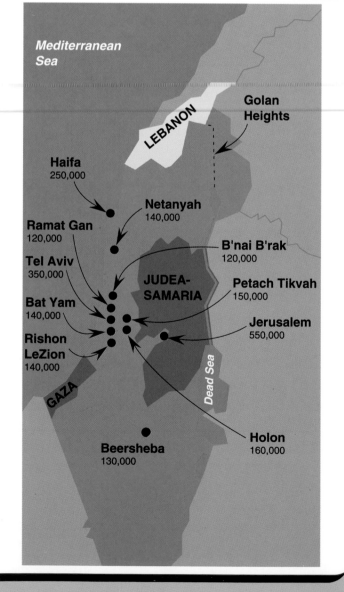

Mediterranean Sea

Golan Heights

LEBANON

Haifa
250,000

Netanyah
140,000

Ramat Gan
120,000

B'nai B'rak
120,000

Tel Aviv
350,000

JUDEA-SAMARIA

Petach Tikvah
150,000

Bat Yam
140,000

Jerusalem
550,000

Rishon LeZion
140,000

GAZA

Dead Sea

Holon
160,000

Beersheba
130,000

The Knesset building in Jerusalem. The Knesset is the legislative body of the State of Israel. Its 120 members are elected by a secret ballot.

The Assassination of Yitzhak Rabin / 1995

Saturday night, November 4, 1995, was one of the most fateful times in the history of modern Israel. On that darkest of nights, Yitzhak Rabin, Israeli's Prime Minister and one of its great military heroes, was assassinated.

That evening 100,000 Israelis had assembled in Tel Aviv to participate in a political rally. Rabin delivered a speech and joined in singing the "Song of Peace." After the rally Rabin and Shimon Peres began to walk to their cars.

Lurking in the dark shadows of the night, a young assassin named Yigal Amir was waiting. As Rabin approached his limousine, Amir quietly stepped out of the shadows and from about a yard away pumped three bullets point blank into the Prime Minister.

Rabin was rushed to a nearby hospital, where he died on the operating table. The shocked nation went into mourning, and the spot where Rabin was shot became a shrine filled with memorial candles, flowers, and posters.

Rabin's funeral was attended by President Bill Clinton, former Presidents

YITZHAK RABIN (1922–1995) served his country both as a soldier and as a diplomat. Born in Jerusalem, he graduated from the Kadoori agricultural school. In 1940, he enlisted in the Palmach and participated in numerous underground actions against the British Mandate. In 1946, he was arrested by the British and imprisoned for six months. During the War of Independence, Rabin commanded the Harel Brigade, which was active in the battle for Jerusalem. Appointed Chief of Staff in 1964, he led Israel's forces to victory in the Six-Day War of 1967. After serving as Israel's ambassador to the United States, Rabin became Prime Minister in 1974–77 and was reelected in 1992. On November 4, 1995, he was assassinated by Yigal Amir.

Bush, Carter, and Ford, and the leaders of many other countries, including President Mubarak of Egypt and King Hussein of Jordan. Rabin was succeeded as Prime Minister by Shimon Peres, who vowed to continue his policies.

Among the foreign dignitaries paying their last respects to Yitzhak Rabin were *(from left to right)* President Bill Clinton, former Presidents Jimmy Carter, and George Bush, Queen Beatrice of the Netherlands, Mrs. Peres and Prime Minister Shimon Peres, Queen Nur and King Hussein of Jordan.

The Election of 1996

On June 2, 1996 Benjamin Netanyahu (b. 1949), of the Likud Party, defeated Shimon Peres and became Israel's new Prime Minister. His victory was in large part due to public disquiet about the way the peace agreement with the PLO was proceeding. While Israel had been carrying out all of its commitments, the PLO was not. It had not modified its covenant to eliminate language calling for the destruction of the Jewish state. Even worse, terrorist attacks had become increasingly more frequent and brutal. While Israelis desperately wanted peace, a majority of voters agreed with Netanyahu that it was necessary to proceed cautiously and slowly, and with more concern for security than Peres had shown.

SHIMON PERES

Shimon Peres had a varied and distinguished political career. At the age of 24 he became the manpower chief of the Haganah. After the formation of the State of Israel he was appointed Director General of the Defense Ministry. In 1981 he became Deputy Defense Minister under Prime Minister David Ben-Gurion and then under Levi Eshkol, and was responsible for setting up Israel's nuclear capabilities. In 1977 he ran against Menachem Begin and lost. In 1988 he ran against Yitzhak Shamir, and also lost.

As Foreign Minister in Yitzhak Rabin's cabinet, Peres conducted peace talks with the PLO which ushered in the Oslo accords for Palestinian self-rule. Prime Minister Rabin and Peres shared the Nobel Prize for their peace efforts.

In 1995, after the assassination of Rabin, Peres became Prime Minister.

The following year he ran against Benjamin Netanyahu but was defeated.

Benjamin Netanyahu

Netanyahu was the first sabra Prime Minister of Israel. Although born in Israel, he lived for several years in the United States and earned degrees in business and architecture from the Massachusetts Institute of Technology. In 1967 he returned to Israel to serve in the army. As an officer in an elite commando unit, he played an important part in the team that rescued hostages from a hijacked Belgian plane in 1972. He served as Israel's United Nations ambassador in the 1980s and was also Deputy Foreign Minister.

Benjamin Netanyahu addresses the U.S. Congress. In the background is Vice President Al Gore. Newt Gingrich, House Majority Leader, congratulates him.

Israeli Politics / 1971–1996

1971
Menachem Begin of the Likud came to power, however, because Likud controlled only 43 of the 120 Knesset votes, it was forced to share power with the Labor Party.

November 1977
President Anwar Sadat of Egypt came to Israel and in September 1978 signed a peace treaty called the Camp David Accords in which the Sinai was returned to Egypt. For their efforts, Begin and Sadat were awarded a Nobel Peace Prize.

1983
Menachem Begin, resigned as Prime Minister and was succeeded by Yitzhak Shamir. Once again a unity government of Likud and Labor was formed. For the first two years Shimon Peres was Prime Minister.

1988
A general election and a new coalition government was formed by Likud and Labor. Yitzhak Shamir remained as the Prime Minister.

May 1989
Prime Minister Shamir called for Arab elections in Gaza and the West Bank. The elected representatives would negotiate a solution to the Arab-Israeli conflict.

January 1992
The first secret meeting between the PLO and Israel took place in Norway. Yossi Beilin, a member of the Knesset and an aide to Shimon Peres, Israel's Foreign Ministe,r was the Israeli delegate.

August 1993
The secret Norway meetings initiated talks on Palestenian self-rule.

September 13, 1993
Prime Minister Rabin of Israel and Chairman Yasir Arafat of the PLO signed a peace agreement in Washington.

October 13, 1993
The Israelis and the PLO met in Tabis, Egypt, and arranged the transfer of authority. Israeli withdrawal from Gaza and Jericho was to be completed by April 1994.

November 6, 1993
The transfer of authority was postponed because of the differences between the PLO's and Israel's interpretations of the peace plan.

December 12, 1993
Prime Minister Rabin and Yasir Arafat decided to postpone the implementation of the Peace Treaty. The murder of numerous Jewish settlers by Arab terrorists had turned the Israeli electorate against the treaty.

December 14, 1993
United Nations adopted a resolution that endorsed the peace treaty between Israel and the PLO.

February 24, 1994
Dr. Baruch Goldstein, a resident of Kiryat Arba, a Jewish settlement on the outskirts of Hebron, entered the Cave of Machpelah and killed 29 Arabs, and was then himself killed. Hebron has had a long history of violence between Jews and Arabs. In 1929

Arabs murdered 69 Jewish civilians. Seven years later, in 1936, the entire Jewish community was destroyed.

May 4, 1994

Premier Yitzhak Rabin of Israel, and PLO Chairman Yasir Arafat signed a self-rule peace accord in Cairo.

November 4, 1995

Yitzhak Rabin was assassinated by Yigal Amir. Shimon Peres assumed the post of Prime Minister.

June 2, 1996

Benjamin Netanyahu narrowly wins a hard-fought victory over Shimon Peres. The upset victory of Netanyahu proved that the Israeli public was aware that the Labor Party had disregarded many of its promises. The vote indicated that a majority of Israeli Jews wanted Israel to remain a Jewish country, a Jewish state with Jewish values, and wished to maintain its Jewish identity.

July 8, 1996

Prime Minister Benjamin Netanyahu visited the United States and had a high-level meeting with President Bill Clinton. The subject was terrorism in the Middle East and the future of the peace accord in Israel.

The Americans were very concerned about the terrorist threat to the political stability of Saudi Arabia, the largest supplier of oil to the free world.

Benjamin Netanyahu indicated that his primary goal was the security of Israel. In addition, he stated in absolute terms that Jerusalem would remain the capital of Israel and would not be divided. He also stated that he was against the creation of a PLO state. In his words, "There is no Palestine."

September 26, 1996

The opening of an ancient tunnel in Jerusalem ignited three days of rioting by the Palestinians.

June 13, 1997

After months of deliberation, the Israeli Parliament, in an 87 to 14 vote agreed to carry out the Israeli–Palestinian Peace Agreement of the previous Rabin government.

Israel has notified the Palestinian Authority that it is prepared to carry out the first of three withdraws as stipulated in the Oslo Agreement. The first withdrawal from nine percent of the West Bank has angered the Palestinians who have demanded a thirty percent slice of the West Bank.

February 4, 1997

At 7:30 in the evening, two Israeli helicopters ferrying 73 soldiers, collided in mid-air over the Northern Galilee, killing every one on board. The helicopters were en route to the Israeli security zone, in Southern Galilee. This accident was the worst military disaster in IDF history.

February 27, 1997

The Israeli Cabinet approved the development of a new Jewish neighborhood in East Jerusalem. When completed, the new neighborhood will contain 6500 apartments and is being built on Jewish owned land in Bar Homa.

The Struggle of Modern Israel

JEWISH HIGHLIGHTS

Displaced Persons	Zionist Spokesman	State of Israel 1948	Six Day War	Yom Kippur War 1976

JEWISH EVENTS • PERSONALITIES • LITERATURE

Displaced Persons	Zionist Spokesman	State of Israel 1948	Six Day War	Yom Kippur War 1976
▷ Haganah	▷ Rabbi Meir Berlin	▷ End of Mandate	▷ Jerusalem liberated	▷ Israeli Olympic athletes mudered
▷ Irgun Zvai Leumi	▷ Abba Hillel Silver	▷ Arabs attack Israel	▷ Yitzhak Rabin Chief of Staff	▷ Kissinger's shuttle diplomacy
▷ Internment camps		▷ Haganah repels attack	▷ Jerusalem Day	▷ Golda Meir resigns
▷ S.S. *Exodus*		▷ Chaim Weizmann President of Israel		▷ Yitzhak Rabin New Prime Minister
		▷ Ben-Gurion Prime Miniser		▷ Golda Meir dies 1978
		▷ Jewish refugees Suez Campaign		▷ Rescue at Entebbe Jonathan Netanyahu dies

WORLD HISTORY

Displaced Persons	Zionist Spokesman	State of Israel 1948	Six Day War	Yom Kippur War 1976
	▷ United States	▷ England	▷ Israel	▷ American Nuclear Alert
		▷ France		
		▷ Suez Canal		
		▷ Egypt		

The Struggle of Modern Israel

JEWISH HIGHLIGHTS

Israel–Egypt Peace Treaty 1979	Peace for Galilee	Peace Agreement 1993	Yitzhak Rabin	Benjamin Netanyahu

JEWISH EVENTS • PERSONALITIES • LITERATURE

Israel–Egypt Peace Treaty 1979	Peace for Galilee	Peace Agreement 1993	Yitzhak Rabin	Benjamin Netanyahu
▷ Menachem Begin Premier of Israel	▷ General Ariel Sharon	▷ Rabin and Arafat sign peace agreement	▷ Yitzhak Rabin assassinated	▷ Netanyahu meets President Clinton
▷ Sadat comes to Jerusalem Sadat murdered 1981	▷ Begin resigns	▷ Knesset approves peace agreement	▷ Yigal Amir	▷ Anatole Sharansky
▷ Mission to Iraq	▷ Scud missiles attack Israel / 1990	▷ Israelis evacuate six Arab towns	▷ Shimon Peres becomes Premier	▷ Russian Jews continue to arrive
	▷ Patriot missiles protect Israel	▷ Israelis remain in Hebron	▷ Election 1996	▷ Islamic guerrillas attack Israel and America
		▷ Israel and Jordan sign peace treaty	▷ Benjamin Netanyahu defeats Peres	
		▷ Syria and Israel agree not to agree		

WORLD HISTORY

Israel–Egypt Peace Treaty 1979	Peace for Galilee	Peace Agreement 1993	Yitzhak Rabin	Benjamin Netanyahu
▷ Iraq	▷ Gulf War	▷ Syria		▷ United States
▷ Egypt				▷ Russia

Judaism in America

In the early years of the 20th century, many American Jewish young people, the children of immigrants, began to give up elements of their Jewish identity and lifestyle in order to become "like other Americans." This attitude accounts, in part, for the growth of modern denominations of Judaism more attuned to the New World environment.

Assimilation was, and is, widespread, because of the virtually total acceptance accorded minorities in the United States. By the second half of the century, however, many began to realize that America was made up of many diverse groups, all of them of immigrant origin, and that each group, by preserving the best of its own heritage, might add variety and richness to American life—differences, in other words, were respected and respectable.

Rebirth of Identity

As a result, there was a rebirth of Jewish identity and commitment among a substantial minority of American Jews. This was reflected in the 1960s and afterward in the havurah movement on many college campuses, in the baal teshuvah movement that has brought many young people back to Orthodoxy, and in the energetic response to Christian missionary activities.

Though Jews in present-day America are few in number, amounting to less than 3 percent of the population, Judaism is regarded as one of the nation's three great faiths—a key component of its Judeo-Christian heritage. Jewish and Hebraic studies are an important part of the curriculum of many major colleges and universities. In addition, the American Jewish community supports a network of yeshivot and other religious schools.

The Jews of America enjoy freedom, good fortune, and the respect of their neighbors. Organized into Orthodox (1,200), Conservative (800), Reform (853), and Reconstructionist (87) congregations, American Jews regularly unite for purposes of education, social action, and help to the needy. By learning and practicing the Jewish tradition, and by living according to Jewish ideals of justice, they are writing a glorious chapter in the history of their people.

Jews in American Society

After World War II, when the terrible details of the Holocaust were made known, anti-Semitism became a fringe or underground activity. There was a dramatic improvement in publicly expressed attitudes about Jews and Judaism. Quotas restricting the number of Jews in universities, professional schools, and certain jobs largely ceased, although the existence of affirmative action programs on behalf of other minorities has raised concerns in this area. Overall, young people growing up in America today find it hard to believe that their parents and grandparents met prejudice and had to fight discrimination.

The American Jewish Congress, the American Jewish Committee, the Anti-Defamation League of B'nai B'rith, and the Jewish Labor Committee all worked to fight anti-Semitism and to protect the rights of fellow Jews. They lent their support, as well, to the cause of civil rights for all minorities.

Jews play a prominent role in American art, literature, and general culture. They have long contributed to science and medicine, and are active in education, industry, and government.

American Jewry Unites to Give

Throughout the 20th century, American Jewry donated great sums for the relief and rescue of suffering coreligionists. No other group has ever given so much or organized itself in the same manner for voluntary taxation to help needy brethren.

In 1925 the Keren Hayesod, or Foundation Fund, and the Jewish National Fund joined forces and became the United Palestine Appeal. When war broke out in 1939, and the need for rescuing the Jews of Europe became desperate, the Joint Distribution Committee combined its efforts with the UPA. Thus was formed the United Jewish Appeal. The UJA has remained active ever since, helping Jews in every country of the world.

Jewish Philanthropy

In almost every American city, the UJA, the Joint Defense Appeal, and local causes (such as hospitals, Jewish centers, homes for the aged, educational institutions) combined their efforts so that there was one major fund drive for the entire community each year. Generally the umbrella agency conducting the drive is known as a Jewish Federation.

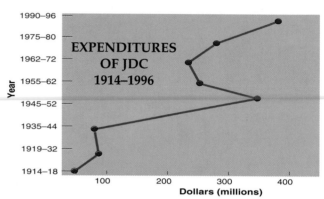

The Joint Distribution Committee has been the most remarkable and far-reaching of all private philanthropies, feeding, rescuing, training, and resettling persecuted Jews all over the world. The amount given by Jews of the democratic countries for JDC activities has increased as the need has grown greater.

Photo taken at the 92nd Street Y in New York, largest and most famous community center in the world and a member agency of New York's Federation of Jewish Philanthropies. The Federation aids Jewish education, hospitals, and other Jewish activities.

In giving to welfare and charity funds, the Jews of America have set an example for all other groups. In the first 20 years after World War II, Jews donated $1.5 billion to the UJA. This generosity is not exclusive to Jewish causes, for Jews have been among the largest supporters of welfare, educational, and cultural projects of all kinds.

American Jews and Israel

Since the State of Israel became a reality in 1948, American Jews have felt a close kinship with the Jews of that land. They show their interest through membership in organizations like Hadassah, through contributions to the United Jewish Appeal, which helps new residents and educates them for citizenship, and by purchasing Israel Bonds and other investments for industrial development.

Defenders of Freedom

Wherever Jews have settled and planted roots, they have participated in the defense of their adopted countries. Even in countries which openly discriminated against them, Jews joined the armed forces and heroically fought for their ungrateful adopted homeland.

There were Jewish soldiers and sailors in the armies of the tsars, the Polish kings, the rulers of Austria–Hungary and pre-Holocaust Germany.

Patriots and Soldiers

In the building of America Asser Levy and his fellow Jews fought for the right to stand guard and protect New Amsterdam against Indian attacks. Although there were only 2,000 Jews in the colonies, they were prominent among the patriots who fought and sacrificed their lives during the Revolutionary War. Francis Salvador, of South Carolina, was one of the first casualties. Haym Salomon is said to have suspended Yom Kippur services to appeal for funds for George Washington's impoverished army in Valley Forge.

Commodores John Ordoneaux and Uriah P. Levy distinguished themselves in battles against the superior British navy in the War of 1812. Abraham Wolfe was killed at the Alamo, during the Texas war of independence. Surgeon General David de Leon acquired the nickname of "the fighting doctor" for his heroic exploits during the Mexican-American War.

The Civil War

Sadly, the Civil War found Jews killing each other on the battlefield. Among the Confederates, there were Judah P. Benjamin, the Secretary of State, and a heroic soldier named Max Frouenthal. His legendary bravery became a symbol of courage for the Confederate armies.

Close to 10,000 Jews served in the Union army, and seven were awarded the Congressional Medal of Honor. 5,000 Jews saw service during the Spanish-American War, and many won medals for courage under fire.

World Wars I and II

During World War I more than 250,000 Jewish men were in the armed services. The majority were in the infantry; 12,000 were wounded or gassed, and 3,500 were killed in action. More than 9,000 Jews were commissioned officers, and seven won Congressional Medals of Honor.

Leopold Karpeles, awarded the Congressional Medal of Honor for bravery in the Battle of the Wilderness, as color-sergeant of the 57th Massachusetts Infantry.

CONGRESSIONAL MEDAL OF HONOR WINNERS

The following American Jews won the Congressional Medal of Honor for valorous deeds and extraordinary bravery in the defense of the United States.

Benjamin Levy	Civil War
Abraham Cohen	*
David Obranski	*
Leopold Karpeles	*
Isaac Gans	*
Abraham Grunwalt	*
Charles Gardner	Indian Wars
David Goodman	*
Jacob Trautman	*
Louis C. Mosher	*
Samuel Gross	Mexican War
William Zion	Peking, China
William Sawelson	World War I
Sydney Gumpertz	*
Benjamin Kaufman	*
Philip C. Katz	*
Samuel Sampler	*
Eduardo V. M. Izac	*
Matt Urban	World War II
Raymond Zussman	*
Samuel G. Fuqua	*
Isadore S. Jachman	*
Jack H. Jacobs	Vietnam

Sydney G. Gumpertz, captain in the 23rd Infantry Division, fought in the Argonne. On September 28, 1918, he single-handedly silenced several enemy machine-gun nests. For his gallantry under fire, he was awarded the Congressional Medal of Honor.

650,000 Jewish men and women served in World War II, and 50,000 received medals and citations for bravery. Lt. Raymond Zussman, a lieutenant in the tank corps, received a Medal of Honor. Zussman's single-handed heroics resulted in the capture of more than 100 Germans and the liberation of a whole town. Sadly, Zussman lost his young life on a battlefield in France. His father had fought in the Russo-Japanese War, and his brother, Abraham, was killed in World War I.

The National Museum of American Jewish Military History in Washington documents and educates the public concerning the courage, heroism and sacrifices made by Jewish Americans who served in the armed forces.

America Honors Its Outstanding Jewish Personalities

The poetess Emma Lazarus wrote, "Give me your tired, your poor, your huddled masses." And millions of Jews, yearning for freedom and opportunity, heeded her words and streamed into the United States. America was good to them, and fulfilled its promise. Through hard work and a desire for education, the immigrants succeeded and built a place for themselves and their children in the land of opportunity.

In turn, the immigrants rewarded America with their patriotism, their genius, and their creativity. The United States post office has recognized and honored some of these outstanding individuals by dedicating postage stamps for their contributions to America.

Walter Lippmann (1889–1974) Journalist and author

Touro Synagogue
First permanent synagogue in the New World. Located in Rhode Island, it is named after its first rabbi, Isaac Touro.

Bret Harte (1836–1902) Author.

Benny Goodman (1909–1986) Musician and band leader.

Charles Steinmetz (1865–1923) Electrical engineer and inventor.

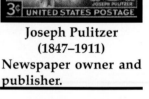

Joseph Pulitzer (1847–1911) Newspaper owner and publisher.

Four Chaplains
During World War II Rabbi Alexander Goode and three Christian military chaplains gave their life-vests to wounded soldiers when their transport, the *Devonshire*, was torpedoed.

Al Jolson (1886–1950) Star of stage, screen, and radio.

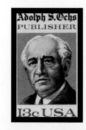

Adoph Ochs (1858–1935) Publisher and owner of the *New York Times*.

Bernard Revel (1885–1950) Orthodox rabbi and president of Yeshiva University

Fanny Brice (1891–1951) Singer and comedienne.

George Gershwin (1898–1937) Composer of operas and musical comedies and film scores.

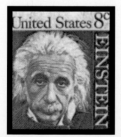

Albert Einstein (1878–1955) Physicist. Developed theory of relativity.

Haym Salomon (1740–1785) Revolutionary War patriot.

Samuel Gompers (1850–1924) Labor leader and first president of the American Federation of Labor

Jewish Nobel Prize Winners

Alfred Nobel, a Swedish industrialist, established the Nobel Prize. The prestigious annual awards are given to individuals from all over the world who have made special contributions to humankind.

The following is a list of the Jewish winners. Jews have been awarded more than 100 Nobel prizes. Jews are less than 1% of the world's population, yet they have made up more than 15% of all recipients.

NOBEL PRIZES, awarded annually to men and women who have "rendered the greatest service to mankind." Since the inception of the prize in 1899, it has been awarded lo the following Jews or people of Jewish descent:

World Peace
1911 Alfred Fried
1911 Tobias M. C. Asser
1968 René Cassin
1978 Manachem Begin
1986 Elie Wiesel
1994 Shimon Peres
1994 Yitzhak Rabin
1995 Joseph Rotblat

Literature
1910 Paul J. L. Heyse
1927 Henri Bergson
1958 Boris Pasternak
1966 Shmuel Yosef Agnon
1966 Nelly Sachs
1976 Saul Bellow
1978 Isaac Bashevis Singer
1981 Elias Canetti
1987 Joseph Brodsky
1991 Nadine Gordimer

Physiology or Medicine
1908 Eliė Metchnikoff
1908 Paul Ehrlich
1914 Robert Bárány
1922 Otto Meyerhof
1930 Karl Landsteiner
1931 Otto Warburg
1936 Otto Loewi
1944 Joseph Erlanger
1944 Herbert S. Gasser
1945 Ernst B. Chain
1946 Hermann J. Muller
1950 Tadeus Reichstein
1952 Selman A. Waksman
1953 Hans Krebs
1953 Fritz A. Lipmann
1958 Joshua Lederberg
1959 Arthur Kornberg

1964 Konrad Bloch
1965 François Jacob
1965 Andre Lwoff
1967 George Wald
1968 Marshall W. Nirenberg
1969 Salvador Luria
1970 Julius Axelrod
1970 Sir Bernard Katz
1972 Gerald M. Edelman
1975 David Baltimore
1975 Howard Temim
1976 Baruch S. Blumberg
1977 Rosalyn S. Yalow
1978 David Nathans
1980 Baruj Benacerrof
1984 Cesar Milstein
1985 Joseph Goldstein
1986 Rita Levi-Montalcini
1986 Stanley Cohen
1989 Harold Varmus
1992 Edwin Krebs

Chemistry
1905 Adolph Von Baeyer
1906 Henri Moissan
1910 Otto Wallach
1915 Richard Willstaetter
1918 Fritz Haber
1943 George de Hevesy
1961 Melvin Calvin
1962 Max F. Perutz
1972 William H. Stein
1977 Andrew Schally
1978 Daniel Mathias
1979 Herbert Brown
1980 Paul Berg
1980 Walter Gilbert
1982 Aaron Klug
1989 Sidney Altman

Physics
1907 Albert A. Michelson
1908 Gabriel Lippmann
1921 Albert Einstein
1922 Niels Bohr
1925 James Franck
1925 Gustav Hertz
1943 Otto Stern
1944 Isidor Isaac Rabi
1952 Felix Bloch
1954 Max Born
1958 Igor Tamm
1959 Emilio Segrè
1960 Donald A. Glaser
1961 Robert Hofstadter
1962 Lev D. Landau
1965 Richard P. Feynman
1965 Julian Schwinger
1969 Murray Gell-Mann
1971 Dennis Gabor
1973 Brian D. Josephson
1975 Benjamin R. Mottleson
1976 Burton Richter
1978 Peter Kaitea
1978 Arno A. Pensias
1979 Sheldon Glashow
1990 Jerome Friedman
1995 Martin Perl
1995 Frederick Reines

Economics
1970 Paul A. Samuelson
1971 Simon Kuznets
1972 Kenneth J. Arrow
1975 Leonid Kantorovich
1980 Lawrence R. Klein
1987 Robert Solow
1990 Harry A. Markowitz
1990 Merton H. Mille
1992 Gary Becker

Lubavitch in the Twentieth Century

After the death of the Besht in 1760, Dov Ber, the Maggid (preacher) of Mezerich (1710–1772), became the second leader of Hasidism. One of his disciples, Shneur Zalman of Lyady (1745–1813), established his own movement. His book, the *Tanya*, became the foundation of Lubavitch Hasidism. Based on his teachings, this movement is also known as Habad Hasidism, an acronym made up of the first letters of three Hebrew concepts central to its doctrines, *hokhmah* (wisdom), *binah* (understanding), and *da'at* (knowledge).

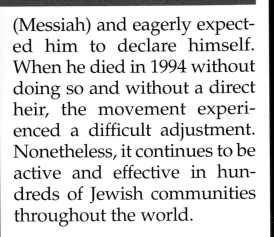

Rabbi Menachem Mendel Schneerson, 1902–1994

(Messiah) and eagerly expected him to declare himself. When he died in 1994 without doing so and without a direct heir, the movement experienced a difficult adjustment. Nonetheless, it continues to be active and effective in hundreds of Jewish communities throughout the world.

Under the dynamic leadership of Rabbi Joseph Isaac Schneerson (1880–1950), a brilliant administrator with an outstanding talent for communal and civic activities, Habad Hasidism resisted the Soviet government's efforts to stamp out religion. Arriving in the United States in 1940, he steadily built up the Habad movement in this country, establishing yeshivot, a publishing empire, schools for Jewish youth, and an outreach program.

In 1950 Rabbi Menachem Mendel Schneerson (1902–1994) became the seventh Lubavitch Rebbe. He continued the work of Rabbi Joseph Isaac, creating a huge outreach program with mitzvah tanks and Lubavitch centers in hundreds of cities in the United States and all over the world, especially in Russia and Poland. In addition to its synagogues, university Habad houses, yeshivot, schools, and outreach programs, Lubavitch was also involved in rehabilitation and drug outreach programs.

Many Lubavitch adherents believed Rabbi Schneerson to be the Moshiach

Lubavitch mitzvah tanks travel throughout the country and invite Jews to put on tefillin, light Sabbath candles, reciting blessings over the lulav and etrog, and light Hanukah candles.

Lubavitch representatives use a variety of vehicles to service outlying Jewish communities. The representatives from Minneapolis use a chartered plane for a trip to LaCrosse, Wisconsin.

WORLD JEWRY: The Jews of Mexico

Overall, the world Jewish population at the end of the 20th century amounted to about 14 million. The largest Jewish communities were in Israel (5 million), the United States and Canada (6 million), and Russia (800,000). There were another 1.7 million Jews in Europe—half a million in France, many of them immigrants from North Africa, and about 350,000 in Great Britain. The Jewish community of South Africa, though much smaller, was well organized and had many ties with Israel. In Latin America, where about 500,000 Jews resided, the largest community was in Argentina. Lacking adequate religious leadership, the Jews of South America looked to the United States and Israel to provide them with rabbis and teachers.

There have been Jews in Mexico since 1521, when Hernando Cortez and his tiny army, which included a number of Marranos, destroyed the mighty Aztec empire and founded the colony of Nueva España (New Spain). The Inquisition soon extended its reach to the New World, but despite persecution Jews managed to survive and to engage in trade and commerce. Some even held government posts.

In 1821, Mexico gained its independence from Spain. Years of chaos and dictatorship followed. During the presidency of Benito Juarez a civil war broke out, and in 1862 Archduke Maxmillian of Hapsburg, supported by Napoleon III of France, became emperor of Mexico. Maximillian's personal physician was Samuel Bosch, a Jew from Austria, and during his reign Jewish immigration to Mexico increased.

Hernando Cortez (1485–1547) conquered the Aztec civilization of Mexico by 1521. In addition to this, set up colonies as far north as California.

The country's Jewish populace continued to grow and prosper after Juarez overthrew Maxmillian in 1867. The brutal pogroms in post–World War I Eastern Europe induced many more Jews to see Mexico as a safe haven. Numbers of them settled in Mexico City, where they prospered despite the growing anti-Semitism and the imposition of a quota on Jewish immigration. The pace of immigration picked up after World War II.

Most of the country's Jews are concentrated in Mexico City, where the many educational and religious institutions reflect their ethnic and religious diversity. There are Ashkenazi, Sephardi, German, Hungarian, and Syrian synagogues as well a great variety of cultural institutions. Mexican Jews sponsor many cultural and artistic activities.

WORLD JEWRY: The Jews of France

Jews first made their appearance in France sometime in the 4th century. Although in the rest of Europe their presence was restricted, in France the Jews were active as merchants and as doctors.

In 1096, members of the First Crusade attacked and killed Jews, and local bishops and rulers were powerless to protect them. The 11th and 12th centuries are called the Golden Age of France. Scholars such as Rashi, Rabbenu Gershom, and the tosafists established schools and produced a treasure house of important literature. Unfortunately, anti-Semitism in the form of forced conversions, blood-libels, and well-poisonings, plagued the Jewish communities and often led to murder, expulsion and book-burnings.

In 1306 King Philip IV banished more than 100,000 Jews and seized their business assets and properties.

Ten years later they were readmitted and once again active Jewish communities sprang to life in many French cities. However, in 1394 Charles VI once again expelled the Jews, and for 200 years they were almost non-existent in France.

Following the expulsion from Spain in 1492, Marranos began to arrive and because of their skills and business connections were welcomed with open arms. In 1648, the Chmielnicki massacres in Ukraine sent a wave of Jews into Alsace–Lorraine. By 1800 there were about 40,000 Jews living there, and by decree they were freely allowed to practice their Judaism.

French Anti-Semitism

Even though French Jews had complete civil rights they often found their upward mobility curtailed by prejudice. In 1894 Captain Alfred Dreyfus, a Jew, was convicted on a charge of espionage. Finally in 1906, he was declared innocent and reinstated. The Dreyfus Affair brought anti-Jewish discrimination in France to the surface and provoked bitter debates.

During World War II the Vichy regime cooperated with the Nazis and deported 80,000 Jews to death camps. French President François Mitterand declared July 16, the anniversary of the arrest of Jews in 1942, as a yearly "national day" for the commemoration of the anti-Semitic persecutions by the Vichy government.

Relations with Israel

The Jews of France have strong personal ties with Israel. The peace negotiations between Israel and the PLO were unpopular, especially among North African Jews and Israeli representatives were publicly attacked.

France as of 1996

France is home to the fourth-largest Jewish community in the world. It is the home of 600,000 Jews, 200 synagogues, 100 day schools, 200 afternoon schools, and more than 500 Jewish organizations. These groups are a rainbow of communal, social, professional, and religious organizations.

Over the years the French Jewish community has included many prominent personalities. Among them are Nobel Prize winners Henri Bergson, and René Cassin. André Citroën founded the automobile company that bears his name. Three Jews, Léon Blum, René Meyer, and Pierre Mendes-France served as Premier. Numerous other Jews have achieved prominence in government service, in the arts, and in commerce and industry. Jewish tradition in France is strong. However, intermarriage is making inroads into the Jewish community.

WORLD JEWRY: The Jews of Canada

The earliest records of Jews in Canada date back to the 18th century, when England and France fought for mastery of the northern part of the New World. Among the officers on the staff of Britain's General Amherst during the French and Indian War were three Jews: Aaron Hart (1724–1800), Emmanuel D. Cordova, and Isaac Miramer.

In 1750, after Canada became an English possession, a number of Jews settled in Montreal. Some of them were fur traders, others were veterans of the British army that had defeated the French. Montreal's first synagogue, Shearith Israel, was established in 1776. Most of the members were of Sephardic ancestry and followed the Sephardic rite.

In 1807 Ezekiel Hart (1767–1843), a son of Aaron Hart, was elected to the legislature of Lower Canada (now the province of Ontario). He refused to be sworn in on a Christian Bible, and instead took the oath on a Hebrew Bible with his head covered. This raised a storm of protest and he was expelled from the legislative chambers.

Years of agitation followed, and in 1832 a bill was passed extending the same political rights to Jews as to Christians. Since that time Jews have won seats in all of the provincial legislatures and in the Federal Parliament, have served as mayors of Toronto, Vancouver, and other cities, and have been judges in courts at all levels. In 1970 Boris Laskin became the first Jewish member of Canada's Supreme Court.

Jews were also very active in Canada's commercial life. Jewish merchants set up general stores in small railroad towns and were also active in the fishing industry, telegraph communications, and the fur trade. Jews participated in the gold rush in British Columbia in 1858. This led to the erection of a synagogue in Victoria in 1862.

Many Jewish refugees came to Canada during and after World War II. Substantial numbers of French-speaking Jews from North Africa settled in French-speaking Quebec in the 1950s and 1960s.

Canada has the fifth-largest Jewish population in the world. The Canadian Jewish community, 350,000 strong, has developed a dynamic educational system comprising 100 schools attended by 20,000 students. There are yeshivot, teachers' seminaries, and a great variety of cultural, religious, and Zionist organizations. The majority of the country's Jews reside in Montreal, Toronto, and Winnipeg, and are active in all phases of communal life.

Jews have made great contributions to Canada's economic, political, communal, and artistic life. Among the more well known Canadian Jews are the novelist Mordecai Richler (b. 1931), Rabbi Reuven Bulka, and philanthropist-communal leader Charles and Samuel Bronfman.

Samuel Bronfman,
Canadian industrialist and philanthropist.

WORLD JEWRY: The Jews of Russia

Since the beginning, the lives of Russian Jews have been difficult and permeated with anti-Semitism. Each of the governing regimes, from the tsars to the Communists, have imposed restrictions on economic opportunities and on Jewish cultural and religious expression.

Leon Trotsky (Lev Davidovich, 1879–1940) was exiled to Siberia in 1898 for revolutionary activities, but in 1902 he escaped to England. During the October Revolution in 1917 he returned and played an important part in the Communist uprising. Leon Trotsky organized the Red Army. In 1929 he was exiled by Stalin and went to Mexico, where he was murdered by the Russian secret police. To the very end he was antagonistic to Judaism. Leon Trotsky, seated in the center, is shown with a group of army officers, some of whom were Jews.

During the black years of the Stalin era, from 1919 to 1953, Soviet Jewry was decimated, first by the Nazis and then by the Communist regime. Over half of Russia's enormous Jewish community, which at one time totaled over 5 million, was murdered in the

Joseph Stalin (1879–1953) ruthlessly eliminated all of his political rivals after the death of Lenin. The police state he created murdered more than 20 million Russians.

Holocaust. At the end of World War II, Stalin launched a campaign to destroy Jewish cultural and religious identity. Tens of thousands of Jewish intellectuals and professionals were murdered, and hundreds of thousands were exiled to Siberia in a wave of terror.

Stalin's death brought some relief, but official anti-Semitism still limited Jewish economic, cultural, and religious life. The establishment of the State of Israel in 1948, awakened a spirit of hope and the struggle for the right to immigrate. Jewish refuseniks led by Anatole Sharansky challenged the regime by organizing hunger strikes and secret groups for the teaching of Judaism.

Golda Meir, Israel's first ambassador to the USSR, mobbed by Moscow Jews outside the synagogue, Rosh Hashanah, 1948.

By the end of the 1970s, the USSR was in an economic crisis and the political infrastructure was in a state of collapse. When Mikhail Gorbachev became Premier, in 1985, he set in motion the policy of perestroika (reorganization) and removed all emigration barriers. Gorbachev's policy of glasnost (openness) officially permitted cultural, religious, and political activities and unloosened a flood of Jewish emigration to Israel, America, and other countries.

Boris Yeltsin

The reelection in 1995 of President Boris Yeltsin was much better than a loss could have been. Yeltsin's opponents conducted a campaign filled with smears and open anti-Semitism and a loss could have had a catastrophic affect on Russian Jewry. As of 1997, Jews, despite the bureaucracy, were free to emigrate to Israel and anywhere else they pleased.

Internally, the Russian Jewish community is making progress. Individual groups are pooling their resources under an umbrella organization called the Russian Jewish Congress. Their aim is threefold: fund-raising, fighting anti-Semitism and Jewish education.

Russian and Israeli authorities have established transit schools called Ma'ariv schools to facilitate those intending to make aliyah. These schools, much like an American day school, provide a secular program as well as a Hebrew language and Judaic studies curriculum.

Jewish culture and religion are being introduced and spread by Orthodox, Lubavitch, Conservative, Reconstructionist, and Reform groups. They have organized a rainbow of synagogues and managed to attract thousands of worshippers.

Jewish sports clubs—a part of the Maccabee movement—attract 50,000 youngsters with a variety of programs. In addition to sports, the youngsters are exposed to Jewish music, culture, and religious activities.

For more than 70 years Russia was a Jewish cultural desert. Now, through the committed efforts of world Jewry, the Russian Jewish community, which some believe numbers about 1.5 million, is slowly making progress and struggling to regain its former stature.

Boris Yeltsin

The United Jewish Appeal has established a youth program called Naaleh, ("we will go up"). It sends thousands of Jewish teenagers from Russia to Israel, to complete high school and prepare for college. This experience has encouraged many of them to settle in Israel.

The Joint Distribution Committee has throughout the years shipped matzot to Russia for Passover. With the help of the JDC, local committees in the former Soviet Union are producing their own. This matzah factory in Kiev provides for the needs of Jews in Ukraine, Belarus, and Moldova.

WORLD JEWRY: *The Jews of Israel*

On May 14, 1948, the fifth day of the Hebrew month of Iyar, in the year 5708, according to the Jewish calendar, Israel gained its independence. On this great day, David Ben-Gurion announced, as if an answer to the familiar Hebrew prayer, that the new state would be open for *Kibbutz Galuyot*, the Ingathering of the Exiles.

In the years that followed, hundreds of thousands of Jews of different cultures, different languages, different worlds, streamed into the Jewish homeland. Never before in the history of the world had so many people from so many different lands descended so quickly upon so small an area.

Today Israel's population is close to 5 million Jews, and the diversity of its people makes the country almost like a miniature United Nations.

In addition to its Jewish citizens, Israel also has more than a million non-Jewish citizens, mainly Muslims, but also including Christian Arabs and Druze. Under Israel's democratic system, all citizens have full political and civil rights.

Ashkenazim

About half of Israel's Jews are the children and grandchildren of German and Eastern European Jews. They are called Ashkenazim, from the Hebrew word *Ashkenaz,* the name for the area that is now northern France and Germany. Most of the Zionist settlers who built up Palestine were from Eastern Europe. Many other Ashkenazim found freedom and security in Israel after the bitter sickness of the Nazi Holocaust in Eastern Europe.

Many Ashkenazim especially the Hasidim, speak Yiddish, a language which combines Hebrew and German words. Yiddish developed during the years of Jewish exile in European countries.

The Sephardim

Sephardim and Oriental Jews make up the other half of Israel's Jewish population. Sephardim are descendants of the Jews expelled from Spain in 1492 by King Ferdinand and Queen Isabella. These Jews scattered to many countries, but since they were originally from Spain they were called Sephardim, which in Hebrew means "Spaniards." Many Sephardim speak Ladino, a language which combines Hebrew and Spanish words, just as Yiddish combines Hebrew and German. Ladino developed during the years when Jews lived in Spanish-speaking countries.

Newly arrived Russian Jewish immigrants to Israel. More than 500,000 Russians have found new homes in Israel. As the political situation in Russia deteriorates, many new arriving families are welcomed.

Oriental Jews

Many of Israel's Jews are immigrants from Oriental countries like Iraq, Yemen, Kurdistan, Persia, Afghanistan, Morocco, Libya, Tunisia, and Algeria. The special expertise of the craftsmen from these countries is renowned , and the souvenir shops of Israel are filled with jewelry and metal sculptures that capture the spirit of the Orient in their delicacy and precision.

Sometimes Oriental Jews are called Sephardic Jews, although in actuality their backgrounds differ, since unlike the Sephardim they are not descended from ancestors who once lived in Spain and Portugal.

The Sabras

The Ashkenazic, Sephardic, and Oriental Jews of Israel are not separated by geographical barriers the way their ancestors once were. They live side by side in Israel. Their children play together in the same kindergarten classes and attend the same high schools; they grow up together in the same neighborhoods and youth groups, and serve together in Israel's army regiments. They all speak modern Hebrew in the same Sephardic pronunciation.

As the distinctions between the groups blur, Jews born in Israel no longer identify strongly as Ashkenazic, Sephardic, or Oriental; instead, they are sabras, native-born Israelis with their own Israeli culture—an amalgam of all three immigrant groups, plus a touch of something uniquely Israeli.

The term *sabra* is a nickname for Jews born in Israel. The sabra is a desert fruit that grows on cactus; it is hard and prickly on the outside but soft and juicy on the inside.

Ethiopian immigrants on an Israeli air force plane from Addis Ababa to Israel during Operation Solomon.

The thorny sabra plant and its sweet and juicy fruits. Native Israelis are called sabras because they are thorny on the outside, but friendly when you get to know them.

WORLD JEWRY: The Jews of Latin America

The history of Latin American Jewry began in 1492, when Christopher Columbus arrived in the West Indies with several Marrano seamen in his crews. In the next few decades, due to the excesses of the Inquisition, many New Christians from Portugal and Spain made new homes for themselves in Brazil, Mexico, and Peru.

The arrival of the Inquisition in the New World meant that the Marranos once again had to lead double lives. Despite the difficulty and danger, many of them remained faithful to their Jewish identity and secretly kept up Jewish traditions and customs, including holiday observances and the dietary laws. Thousands of New Christians were punished and many burned at the stake for their adherence to the Jewish faith.

During Latin America's wars of independence from Spain between 1808 and 1826, freedom of religion was introduced. In 1816 Argentina, Mexico, Peru, and Uruguay abolished the last symbol of Spanish oppression—the Inquisition.

Due to the more favorable conditions, Jewish immigration to Latin America increased, spurred especially by the severe oppression in Russia and Eastern Europe. Most of the newcomers settled in Brazil and Argentina.

Baron Maurice de Hirsch

Immigration to Argentina was encouraged by Baron Maurice de Hirsch, who in 1891 purchased more than 500,000 acres of land there and donated $10 million, a huge sum in those days, to set up the Jewish Colonization Association (ICA). The ICA funded a number of agricultural colonies in Argentina, and by 1925 there were 30,000 Jews engaged in farming and cattle ranching. Colonization attempts were also made in Bolivia, Mexico, Ecuador, and Uruguay, but these initiatives failed.

The Jewish farmers in Argentina encountered many difficulties, and today most of the country's Jews are concentrated in the big cities, especially the capital, Buenos Aires.

Between 1901 and 1914, as conditions in Eastern Europe deteriorated, immigration to Argentina reached a high of more than 100,000 new arrivals. The rise of Nazism in the 1930s, when the need for a safe haven was greatest, tragically witnessed a decrease in Jewish immigration, for the Argentine government instituted a series of restrictive immigration laws. Despite this, some Jews managed, both legally and illegally, to settle in Argentina, and others found their way to Brazil, Panama, Chile, Bolivia, and Ecuador. Today there are 500,000 Jews living in Latin America. Most of the Jewish communities in Latin America enjoy middle-class status and stable economic conditions. They are active in manufacturing, communications and in the professions.

Anti-Semitism has always been a serious problem in Argentina, sometimes from Nazi sympathizers, other times from radical leftists. On March 17, 1992 a massive terrorist bomb destroyed the Israeli embassy in Buenos Aires.

Jewish delegations from all over the world flew to Buenos Aires to offer their support to the survivors. The seven-story headquarter of the Jewish Mutual Aid was reduced to rubble. One hundred people were killed and more than 200 were wounded.

Index

N

PHOTO CREDITS
While every effort has been made to trace and acknowledge all copyright holders, we would like to apologize for any ommissions.

BEZALAL MUSEUM, Jerusalem, Israel; BRITISH MUSEUM, London, England; INSTITUTE OF ARCHEOLOGY, Tel Aviv, Israel; ISRAEL GOVERNMENT PRESS OFFICE, Jerusalem Israel; ISRAEL MUSEUM, Jerusalem, Israel; METROPOLITAN MUSEUM OF ART, New York City;. MUSEUM del PRADO, Madrid, Spain; MUSEO NATIONALE, Naples, Italy; NATIONAL MUSEUM, Damascus, Syria; NATIONAL MUSEUM OF TEHERAN, Teheran, Iran; NEW CARLSBERG GALLERY, Copenhagen, Denmark; ORIENTAL MUSEUM, Chicago, Illinois; PALAIS de LOUVRE, Paris, France; ROCKFELLER ARCHEOLOGICAL MUSEUM, Jerusalem, Israel; ROYAL CHAPEL, Granada, Spain; STAATLICHE MUSEEN, Berlin, Germany; YIVO INSTITUTE for JEWISH RESEARCH, New York City; AMERICAN JEWISH HISTORICAL SOCIETY, Waltham, Mass.; NATIONAL MUSEUM of AMERICAN JEWISH MILITARY HISTORY, Washington, DC; UNITED STATES HOLOCAUST MEMORIAL MUSEUM, Washington, DC; JACK HAZUT, Special Photographer